Transformation of Egypt Through Revolution: Issue Analysis from the Fall of Mubarak (2011) to the Rise of El-Sisi (2014)

Dr. Yassin El-Ayouty

ISBN-13: 978-1517273446
ISBN-10: 1517273447

DEDICATION

To the women and men who changed the face of Egypt throught bravery, courage and self interest. Not once, but twice: January 25th, 2011 and June 30th, 2013. They started with "IRHAL" (LEAVE) addressed to Mubarak and ended with TAHIYA MISR (Long Live Egypt!).

CONTENTS

Transformation of Egypt Through Revolution: Issue Analysis from the Fall of Mubarak (2011) to the Rise of El-Sisi (2014)

PREFACE

Listening to Egyptians

My blog "Tahrir Forever" was created to report regularly on the New Egypt as seen through the Egyptian press in Arabic. In 2011, four years ago, I returned from Tahrir Square, Cairo, where I spent 20 days in April listening, lecturing, and communicating with all strata of Egyptian society. I was enthralled by the post-Mubarak Egypt, home for one quarter of the Arab people numbering more than 300 million.

I went for dinner at the home of an Egyptian judge. His 6 year old daughter, Lojeen, came to give me a gift. It was an Egyptian flag!! I asked the people on the streets of Cairo about how they felt after Mubarak's removal. Their nearly uniform answer was, "No more fear."

I left my hotel (the Ramses Hilton, at the edge of Tahrir) to cross a side street at a little cafe for the rank and file. The shoe-shine person came to serve me and began to talk politics. I realized that people have found their voice in a re-birth of freedom.

I was interviewed by two young women, one from the Egyptian magazine "October"; the other from the Kuwaiti newspaper "Al-Rai" (The Opinion). Their questions were mostly about how we can retrieve the billions of dollars allegedly siphoned off by Mubarak and his regime to be deposited in banks abroad.

The hotel restaurant at breakfast was nearly empty, so the restaurant help would surround me to praise the January 25 Revolution, although tourism has nearly, for now, evaporated. These impressions and the desire to support democracy propelled me to create "Tahrir Forever," the blog that has now been compiled in this book.

Dr. Yassin El-Ayouty

ACKNOWLEDGMENTS

This work would not have seen the light of day if not for the dedicated assistance of Vittoria Fariello, Esq., and Wil Carter, who joined forces with Raymond Chan, a very inspired Webmaster. Throughout the issuance of the blog postings, Grace Lasser El-Ayouty, my spouse, and our son, Joseph El-Ayouty, never failed to move this work forward.

1 INTRODUCTION

Under Construction: Egypt

News from the Egyptian Street and Media Translated without Comment from Arabic into English as a Public Service
****

A secular state is presently under construction in Egypt. It is a return to a historical status of the pre-Nasser Egypt. In the new Egypt, following the January 25 Revolution, religion and the state do not mix. In Tahir, the Egyptian flag of the 1919 revolution against British occupation - a crescent embracing the cross, symbolizing Muslim/Coptic unity - was again raised at Tahrir. At a meeting between Dr. Abdullah Al-Husseini, Egypt's Minister for Religious Affairs, and the Russian Ambassador, Al-Husseini stated that Egypt is a secular state with religious traditions. These traditions, the Egyptian Minster added, do not mix religion with the state.

At this transitional period from Mubarak's Egypt to a newly-reconstructed Egypt, the Supreme Council for Armed Forces issued its Internet message No.45. In it, it warned against Facebook messages with no attribution spreading false rumors aiming at inflaming sectarian strife. Among the false rumors which the Supreme Council's message is refuting is that some of the January 25 youth are being detained. In this regard, the Council stressed that the Armed Forces of Egypt, a conscripted army, is the security shield of the Revolution.

Under the leadership of Dr. Abdel-Aziz Higazy, Minister for National Dialogue, and a former Prime Minister of Egypt, 51 national leaders, including some of the January 25 youth, began their work in Cairo. In a statement to the press, Dr. Higazy defined 5 axes to that dialogue. These are democracy; human rights; development of human and social resources; development of economic and financial resources; and culture, inter-faith dialogue, and public information. The aim is to hold these national dialogue sessions to all governorates of Egypt and to translate these findings into national policies.

In his first public statement, Dr. Muhammed Morsi, leader of the new party called "Liberty and Justice," with 90% membership of the Muslim Brotherhood, declared that this new party, which is presently under construction, would be ready to join a future coalition government in Egypt.

An unprecedented meeting took place between the Rector of Al-Azhar, the main religious institution for Islamic learning (established more than 1000 years ago), Imam Dr. Ahmed-El-Tayieb, and the General Guide of the Muslim Brotherhood on May 3. Following that meeting, Dr. El-Tayieb stressed that Al-Azhar aims at unifying the message of Islam to its people and to the world. He went on to say that Al-Azhar aims at propagating moderation and tolerance, and the elimination of extremist fatwas (religious pronouncements).

The news of the slaying of Osama Bin Laden in Pakistan at the hands of the U.S. Special Forces on May 1, were greeted as the most important event in anti-terror activities throughout the world since 9/11. The main comments on that event was that Bin Laden's rise to notoriety was the direct consequence of dictatorship in the Arab/Muslim region. But after a decade has passed since 9/11, a new type of youth arose in that region leading to the revolutions in Tunisia, Egypt, Libya, Yemen and elsewhere. The new generation, using social information technology had as a global objective, not terror a la Al-Qaeda, but the Rule of Law and states based on democratic principles. The popularity of Bin Laden had drastically waned even before his demise.

Mubarak and Sons on Trial

News from the Egyptian Street and Media Translated without Comment from Arabic into English As a Public Service
****

Why are Mubarak and sons on trial in Egypt? The immediate reason for the detention and criminal investigations of the three most visible symbols of the collapsed Mubarak regime is the theft of public resources. In my co-authored book (with Kevin Ford and Mark Davies with a contribution by Vincent Green) Law Enforcement and Government Ethics (Praeger, 2000), corruption was simply defined as the conversion of public funds and other resources into private funds and resources.

In 1983, while I was on an assignment to write an article for Forbes magazine on the Egyptian economy, I interviewed Ambassador Frank Wisner, the then U.S. Ambassador to Egypt. I posed the following question to the Ambassador, "What is the future of U.S. aid to Egypt (then under Mubarak)?" His short but enlightened answer was, "Egypt has plenty of resources. Egypt does not need aid. It needs trade."

With the January 25 Revolution toppling the 32-year long Mubarak dictatorship, the first set of charges levelled by Egypt's Prosecutor General is: "How did you, Mr. Mubarak, on your salary as Egypt's President, amass billions of dollars deposited abroad?" This is the central charge on which the former President and his two sons, Gamal and Alaa, are being subjected to detention pending investigation before trial.

No other issue has galvanized all of Egypt as seeing the law being applied for the massive corruption engaged in by the ousted regime, including several members of the various

Mubarak cabinets. And anti-corruption measures have also included the abuse of power, police brutality, and the peddling of influence through bribes.

The ecstasy generated by the sight of the formerly high and mighty, wearing prison garb and sitting at the Tora massive detention camp south of Cairo, for their misdeeds is palpable. In an upper Egypt city of Souhag, nearly halfway between Cairo and Aswan, a popular political figure declared recently, "These investigations and prospective trials have filled our hearts with joy. They like medals which are now worn by every Egyptian. Jail is the logical abode for Mubarak."

During my recent visit to Egypt (April 2 to April 22), I delivered a lecture in Arabic before the Egyptian Council for Foreign Affairs, an NGO which I represent before the U.N., New York City. Most of the questions addressed to me following that lecture were focused on how to undo the great harm done to Egypt for 32 years by the Mubarak regime. The audience were in a hurry to know, "How can we get our money back?"

That interest, which accurately reflects the spirit of the millions in Tahrir Square and beyond was reflected in headlines of seven daily newspapers of mass circulation in the Arab world. One of them, Al-Akhbar (The News) headlined in its edition of April 15: "Yassin El-Ayouty of Fordham University School of Law Asserts that Recovery of the People's Stolen Funds Is Not Impossible." So was the tenor of other news media.

In Al-Ahram newspaper of May 12, that 135-year old newspaper, declared on its front page: "Investigating the Former Minister of Interior Next Week for Illegal Profiteering." It is therefore expected that the Egyptian media will give prominence to what the New York Times reported, also on May 12, on President Obama's "own impatience" with the fact that "many of these countries remained mired in corruption." For there is a definite link between corruption and the upheavals now taking place in the Arab world.

Egyptian Folklore in Aid of the Revolution

Since time immemorial, folklore has been a powerful popular
instrument. It draws its force from the shared experiences of its
public. This has proven its strength in aiding the Egyptian
Revolution of January 25. Egyptian poetry, chants, jokes, songs,
anthems and slogans were all on display at Tahrir Square, Cairo
for all the world to see. That folklore was and shall always be a
powerful tool in moving people, especially in this case, the
Egyptians from bandage to liberty, from silence to participation,
from submission to sovereignty.

So this Friday's blog is dedicated to the beautiful noises
which made for the grand symphony of "we are now free!!" It is
a global message which resonates across all cultures, religions,
borders, affiliations, governmental systems and even
international animosities. It is the Esperanto [presumed
international language] of the Arab Spring and beyond.

Samples:
- IRHAL - in Arabic "BEGONE" - Chanted in unison
  telling Mubarak and his motley crowd: after 32-years
  of dictatorship, the game is up. Go!!
- "AL-SHAAB YUREED ISSQAT AL-NIZAM" - In
  Arabic: "The people want the fall of the regime." As
  it did on February 11.
- "YA TAYYAR YA TAYYAR: MENEEN GIBT
  SABATASHER MILLIAR?" Since Mubarak was a
  pilot, yet allegedly amassed $17 Billion, the chant is:
  "Pilot, Pilot: How did you get $17 Billion?"
- "Come Back, Mubarak: We were only kidding!"
  Mocking Mubarak after his fall by asking him to
  return because the public was only kidding.
- "Come Back, Mubarak: How are we going to rename
  670,000 establishments bearing your name?" Too
  much to change all those signs!!
- "Please Return: The loaf of bread is now getting

bigger, threatening my plan to lose weight!!" During Mubarak's time, and as a result of corruption and cronyism, the loaf of bread, a main part of Egyptian diet was getting smaller and smaller.

- "Mubarak, Please, Come Back. I am now talking freely and I am not accustomed to that."
- "Please Return!! I am afraid that Egypt will forge ahead to become a modern nation."

But one of the best pieces of poetry which emerged was that by Mohja Kahf entitled, "My People Are Rising." Here is the first part:

My people are rising my people are rising,
with olive branches and song, they are waking;
the earth underneath their marching is shaking;
my people are rising! They are not crouched;
they are not stooping;
they are not hungry for bread alone;
we don't want your bread they say, we are hungry for more.

Above everything else, the Revolution taught the Egyptians the love of country, of the flag, of their civilization, of their diversity, and of their national anthem which begins by: "Biladi, Biladi, Fidak Dammi:" "My Country, My Country, for Thee I Sacrifice!! And their slogan has become: "Love Egypt!!" There is an Arab proverb that says: "Love of Country is a part of faith."

A Unique Revolutionary Flag

Wednesday, May 25, 2011

On that flag, the Crescent embraces the Cross. No stars. It is the flag hoisted by the Egyptian Revolution against British occupation in 1919, after World War I. That revolution, led by Saad Zaghloul, was inspired by De Valaira, the leader of the Irish revolt against the British at that time. So the Irish inspired the Egyptians, and Ghandi of India, who led the Indian Congress

Party in its pacific struggle against the British, gave Egypt the name of his party, the Congress Party modified in 1919 to the "Delegation", or the "Congress" or the "Wafd" party. An imponderable revolutionary borrowing between oppressed nations: Irish, Indians, Egyptians. They all succeeded against foreign occupation and exploitation.

The time space between 1919 and 2011 is more than 92 years. Following the pattern of Tunisia, Egypt with its 90 million people convulsed on January 25, 2011. The Arab Spring was in full swing, this time revolting against internal dictatorships and corruption. A new Middle East was being born, and in Egypt, the old flag of the Egyptian revolution of 1919 was resurrected in Tahrir Square: the Crescent was again embracing the Cross.

That symbolism had a message, not only for Egypt, but also for the whole world: Islam is diversity; and down with Al-Qaeda and terrorism which caused 9/11 and other world calamities!! The New Renaissance embraces all faiths and the principle in the Quran is: "There is no compulsion in religion. The right direction is henceforth distinct from error." (Sura II/verse 256). Enough is enough!!

With the overthrow of 60 years of military dictatorship, which produced an unintended product, militant Islam, cosmopolitan Egypt is being resurrected. Not only does the Crescent embraces the Cross. Old historic Jewish temples are being refurbished. New churches are being built. Al-Azhar, that citadel of Islam as a moderate system of beliefs of all Islamic sects for more than 1000 years (built by Shiites) in Cairo, is reassuming its historic independence and interfaith role. The secular State is asserting itself.

Yet the remnants of the defunct Mubarak regime are still at work. Attacks on Coptic churches in Cairo and Alexandria have taken place. Muslims and Copts in Imbaba (an underdeveloped section of Cairo) have resulted in nine fatalities and 119 persons injured (May 12).

Responses of the New Egypt came very swiftly:

- The Women's Rights Coaltion, made up of 21 organizations condemned all attempts to tear at the Egyptian fabric made up of Muslim/Coptic unity;
- Egypt's Mufti, Dr. Aly Gomaa declared at a press conference that a sectarian struggle in Egypt could put the country back 500 years;
- Al-Azhar's Grand Imam, Dr. Al-Tayib, and Pope Shenouda III, the Pope of Alexandria, stressed the historic amity between the Church and the Mosque since the 8th century;
- The Supreme Council of Armed Forces declared that those who are trying to foment sectarian discord would be prosecuted to the maximum extent of the law.
- The Coordinating Committee of the Revolution devoted Friday, May 20 for a "million person" demonstration in Tahrir for "the protection of National Unity."
- The flight of the Holy Family to Egypt was recalled and celebrated. And the initiative of Al-Azhar, called "The Family's Home" became a national program.

After all, Egypt is the Greek name for the "Land of the Copts."

2 JUNE 2011

The Sound of Music in Aid of the Revolution

Friday, June 10, 2011

The Egyptian Revolution lives on by its resort to music and films. Since the age of the Pyramid builders, nearly 5000 years ago, Egypt integrated music, dance and festivals into its faith which evolved into monotheism

Not surprisingly, modern Egypt was the first in the Arab world to use the arts of music, song and story-telling to produce its films in the early 1930s, which have been the rage of the Arabic-speaking world. Its opera theater was inaugurated in 1869 in the heart of Cairo by the opera "Aida" to celebrate the opening of the Suez Canal. This great opera was written by Verdi in celebration of that event which made Egypt the world's cross-roads and bridgeway.

The names of Egypt's singers, like Umm Kalthoum, Muhammad Abdel-Wahab and Abdel-Haleem Hafez continue to be house-hold names from the Atlantic to the Gulf. Its historic film stars from Youssef Wahbi, to Anwar Wagdi, to the lovely Laila Murad, that great Egyptian woman singer of the Jewish faith (one of her great songs are eternalized in the film, "Ghazl El-Banat - the Girls Romance") continue to please, inspire and liberate the imagination. The great song entitled "Don't Lie," in which a lover expresses his devastation at discovering that his girl friend was cheating on him made its woman singer, Nagat Al-Sagheerah, the heart throb of all Arabs.

Then came a long period of dearth: the dearth of military dictatorships which stunted the vibrancy of Egyptian society as represented by song, dance, music and performing arts for half a century. And with dictatorship came a weird interpretation of Islam which depicted those arts as profane. The descent of Egypt into darkness during the period preceding the Egyptian Revolution of January 25, 2011 proved that a great society deserves great art - the Key to Life (Ankh) inspired by the Pharaos. The image of the Ankh is that of constant rebirth. It is a key-like cross as a symbol of enduring life and generative energy. The Revolution of January was not only led by youth; it infused Egypt with youthfulness through returning it to its true cultural heritage. It is back to the future.

Now all Arab singing stars are converging on the Cairo International Stadium from June 21 to June 24 to celebrate Egypt's return to its artistic life. That four day - all Arab event is entitled, "For You - Egypt." A huge song and music fest led by Nancy Agram, Assy Al-Hibary, Hussein-Al-Gismy, Saber Al-Rubaie, and Shereen Abdel-Wahab to cite only a few from among 25 great singers covering the length and breadth of the Arab World. They are all volunteering their great talent, with the proceeds going to charities and the families of those nearly 900 martyrs who dared to stand up to the Mubarak goons to say "No to Fear! Yes to Democracy!" Out with the goons; in with the music and songs for the heart of the Arab lands.

A historic events like this one is under the sponsorship of the Egyptian Ministry of Tourism, Egyptair, the Ministry of Social Interdependency, and the Cairo International Stadium

Authority. Commenting on that huge artistic event, Egypt's Minister of Culture, Dr. Emad Abu-Ghazy said: "Culture is not at war with religion. Our concern is the development of the re-discovered citizenship which accepts the other, within secularism, democracy and political participation."

The sound of music is shrinking the sound of religious lunacy which helped produce Osama Bin Laden, 9/11, the invasions of Afghanistan and Iraq, and the likes of Terry Jones (the Quran burner).

At the Cairo new opera theater (the original building of the Opera theater was consumed by fire in 1973), an event was held in honor of a great opera figure, Ziad Bakeer, who was martyred during the January 25 Revolution. Two thousand mourners participated as the singer Aly Al-Haggar sang, and the Cairo Opera Company performed a new ballet entitled "The Revolt of the People" choreographed by Arminia Kamel with music by the young composer Kareem Abdel-Wahab.

Art is a true-revolutionary weapon of mass re-construction!!

No More Fear - Almost

Friday, June 17, 2011

The news were electrifying. It was February 11, 2011, evening, when the big TV screen in Tahrir Square, in Cairo, came alive with the thundering news that Hosni Mubarak has relinquished his post as President. The dark night of military dictatorships which descended upon Egypt since 1952 was suddenly over. The youth revolution which began on January 25, returned Egypt to its historic role of guiding the Arab world towards the promised land of democracy, dignity and equal opportunity.

Yes, the Arab Spring began in Tunisia, but Egypt, with its demographic weight of a population of 90 million (25% of the entire Arab population) gave its unlimited oxygen. On that evening of February 11, Tahrir, and with it all Arabs beyond its boundary, went wild with joy. A foreign correspondent, in Tahrir, shouted this question to a young Egyptian woman, "What do you say now?" Her answer is seared in my mind: "NO MORE FEAR!!"

The legacy of oppressive fear which began with Nasser in July 1952 and ended nearly 60 years later began to dissipate. The phantom of fear, both real and imagined proved to be no match for the millions shouting all over Egypt, "Go/IRHAL!!"

The success of the masses in ending the 60-year military coup brought to my mind the last scene in a novel which was published for me in Cairo in 1948. It is entitled, **"Charlatan in the Village" (Dajjal Fi Qariah)**. In it, the Charlatan's aide runs to him at night to urge him to leave the village that night because the villagers had discovered that they were the victims of a huge swindle. Upon hearing that, and fearful for his life, the Charlatan snatches from the hands of his aide the bag in which his ill-gotten loot was placed. Then he flees under the cover of darkness for fear of his victims' wrath. His last words to his hapless aide whom he leaves behind to face his fate, "I do not care about them. I was their shelter and refuge... Those ingrates!!"

Every Arab dictator perceives himself as the great savior, not the wicked oppressor. Like the Charlatan in my novel, revolt against his wicked ways is an unforgivable treason. In the hands of those dictators, fear of the unknown is their great barrier against regime change. The army, the police, the intelligence personnel (which in Egypt numbered 1.2 millions, more than the number in Egypt's armed forces), the Republican Guard, the one-party system, the media and corruption are all in the service of the perpetual degradation of human freedoms. The people's voice in these fear regimes, became an inaudible whimper that can only be heard in the dungeons of torture.

Now fear is largely gone. During the first session of the Giza Criminal Court, south of Cairo, three of the symbols of the defunct Mubarak regime sat in mid-June in the defendeants' enclosure to hear the people's thunder. They were Amr Asal, the former Commissioner for Industrial Development, Ahmed Izz (the former monopolizer of the steel industry) who was a stalwart in the now dissolved Democratic National Party, and in absentia, Rasheed Muhammad Rasheed, the former Minister of Commerce and Industry. The charge: wasting and stealing public funds.

In a full-throated voice, devoid of any trace of fear, the Public Prosecutor, Counselor Abdel-Lateef Al-Sharnoubi told the 3-panel Court, "I stand before you today to accuse these defendants of destroying Egypt, of emptying its treasury and of causing perverse poverty among millions of Egyptians."

If fear from dictatorship is gone, yet fear of chaos which usually ensues after a prolonged period of oppression. The diehards of the Mubarak regime are still lurking in the alleys. Tourists are afraid to return, though they are beginning to trickle back. Coptic-Muslim relationships are still being repaired. Border security is on the mind of policy-markers. But, as the Berlin wall fell, so did the fear wall in Egypt and beyond.

The Glorious (Al-Azhar) Document

Friday, June 24, 2011

Al-Azhar, (in Arabic: The Glorious) the oldest and most venerable Islamic institution in the world of Islam, has just issued a historic document. Established more than one thousand years ago by the Fatimide Dynasty (Shii) in Cairo, it is the center of Islamic learning, both Sunni and Shii, that exerts moderation on the Muslim faith. It has branches all over Egypt and the entire Arab world from Sudan to Gaza to other far-flung areas. It is not only a great focus for Islam as a moderating force; it has also played a key role in guiding Egypt's quest for both modernity in times of peace, and nationalistic fervor in times of war.

You can tell an Azhari graduate male by his white turban (my late father wore one which he bequeathed to me). Female students usually wear a simple scarf over their hair. Traditionally, Al-Azhar enjoyed full independence from the Egyptian Government until internal dictatorship, beginning with Nasser in July 1952 and ending with Mubarak's ouster in February 2011, destroyed that Al-Azhar status. The institution's Imam Al-Akbar (the highest Imam) became an appointed functionary, instead of an elected authority and pre-eminent scholar chosen democratically by his peers. Thus began the decline of Al-Azhar in both prestige, and the advent of militant Islam in a hopeless attempt to fill that huge void. The void was then filled with ridiculous fatwas (religious opinions) and militant movements which fed on both ignorance and unemployment.

Then came the Egyptian Revolution of January 25, 2011 and the departure of Mubarak's reign of terror. With that, Al-Azhar revived. And on June 20, 2011, Al-Azhar's Rector, Imam Dr. Ahmed Al-Tayyeb (who speaks fluent French), promulgated a historic document (Al-Azhar Document) signaling the return of that institution to its independence from the Executive, and to its pre-eminence in Islamic thought, Islamic jurisprudence, and Islamic centrism. Another fatal blow to Al-Qaeda and all its franchise units everywhere. Real Islam is suddenly ascendant; extremism is now in flight with its places of refuge shrinking.

Approved by a very broad consensus by the leaders of the entire spectrum of political, academic, religious, social and economic groupings, including the Muslim Brotherhood, the Document calls for a secular Egypt. It declares Al-Azhar's abhorrence of a New Egypt based on religion. Though it recognized Islamic Law (Sharia), as moderately interpreted, a primary source of legislation, yet it fully guarantees to Coptic Egyptians their full right to resort to the Church's rulings in personal status matters (marriage, divorce, inheritance, worship, entails, and such).

Elucidated by a prominent member of the Consortium of Islamic Research (an arm of Al-Azhar), by the name of Dr. Abdel-Mottee Bayoumi, a co-drafter of that Document, said,

"We now have the bases for a modern State based on the Constitution, and free from the concept of a state based on faith." He went on to say, "The New Egypt shall be democratic, whose new Constitution (to be drafted in 2012) will guarantee separation of powers and the Rule of Law, especially equality of all before the law."

The Grand Imam, Dr. Al-Yayyeb, pointed out at a press conference held at Al-Azhar, that the Document guarantees free elections, diversity, the peaceful transfer of power periodically from one elected President to another, transparency and accountability, the fight against corruption, and the freedom of information.

The full rights of women and children are also declared in that document, and the recognition of all religious beliefs (including Christianity and Judaism), and the right to full citizenship are integral components of Al-Azhar Document.

The Al-Azhar Rector also highlighted the Document's condemnation of groups arrogating for themselves the authority to signal someone as an apostate or a traitor to Islam. It regarded such usurpation of the power to exclusiveness as anti-Islamic and as leading to sectarian conflict, religious apartheid, and a derogation of the power and capacity of the community represented by Parliament to pursue the development goals of Egypt in its newly-found renaissance.

The Document also equated between Muslims, Christians and Jews in their right to freely pursue their efforts in building up the New Egypt. It also emphasized Egypt's commitment to the observance of all its international treaties and obligations.

The Al-Azhar Document called for the re-establishment by the New Egypt of its harmonious relationships with all its sister States in the Arab, African and Islamic geographic spheres. It stressed the need for respecting the right of the Palestinians to an independent and sovereign State.

The Document highlighted that Egypt's renaissance is a vital factor in regional stability, that the Arab Revolution is anchored in the quest for dignity, development and equality, and that the new Constitution shall be the framework for the march of post-Mubarak Egypt toward a future of equal opportunity for all.

Welcome Back, Al-Azhar (The Glorious) to your historic roles in the national and international arenas of moderation in Islam, belief in inter-faith, nullification of crazy fatwas, and delegitimation of Al-Qaeda and terrorism!!!

3 JULY 2011

Stoking the Fires of the Arab Spring

Friday, July 1, 2011

"The Violation of the Rule of Law as Motivation of the Arab Uprisings"

Delivered at the meeting of the World Justice Forum, held in Barcelona, Spain in June 2011 by Ambassador Dr. El Sayed A. Shalaby Executive Director, Egyptian Council for Foreign Affairs, Cairo, Egypt.

Historical analysis of the political systems in the Arab region during the last decade will reveal a prevalence of the violations of law, human rights, abuses of power and consequent corruption. This paper will focus on manifestations of the violations of the rule of law, and their role in motivating the recent uprisings in the Arab region.

Disregard for the rule of law has been commonplace within the Arab world. The violations and corruption became structural in many Arab States, with numerous individuals consistently abusing their positions for personal gain, thereby depleting state resources.

Part of this injustice involved the consistent undermining of the authority and independence of the judicial system by the authoritarian regimes of the Arab world. One common aspect of this was the incomplete implementation of the law, with examples including violations of traffic laws, import-export laws, and building regulations, as well as prevalence of smuggling and black market operations. The judicial branch has been further weakened by the fact that court rulings are seldom enacted,. Additionally, the decaying rule of law and government authority was accentuated by several official bodies, such as through the insertion of loopholes into laws, thus providing impunity for violators. Furthermore, the governing elite have often built personal fiefdoms upon government institutions and assets, in order to increase the elites' private wealth and secure their hold on power.

Human rights violations have also been rife in Arab States, further driving the recent popular uprisings. Prevalent examples of this have included the unlawful detention and release of people from prison, the use of torture, and widespread 'disappearances'. Moreover, the security sector has often been authorized to violate human rights in the name of maintaining stability and law and order. In practice, this has usually involved crushing the government's opponents and silencing opposition parties. Indeed, laws relating to the freedom of speech in the Arab world have often restricted this freedom instead of protecting it. These human rights abuses are key issues which must be addressed by new governments in the Arab region.

The judicial system's independence has been threatened both by legal limitations on the judicial system's power and independence, and by the permeation of the more generally unlawful and corrupt conditions of the Arab States. The reduced independence of the judicial system rendered it unable to counterbalance the veritable fusion of the executive and legislative bodies in many Arab States. Additionally, in the Arab region the authority of the military justice systems has often been extended to civilian matters, thus reaching beyond their rightful jurisdiction. In addition to the violation of the rule of law, we can not also neglect major factors of the uprisings namely economic and social deprivations of a large sector of society in the form of better education, jobs and climbing of the social ladder.

It is obvious that the political corruption and the flagrant violations of the rule of law in the Arab region were among the main reasons that helped to motivate the Arab uprisings and revolutions. Those uprisings were successfull in some cases, such as Egypt and Tunisia, where the popular movement was strong enough to overthrow the regime's corruption symbols. However, other similar popular uprisings in the region are still at status quo, as is clearly seen in the Arab countries of Yemen, Libya, Syria and Bahrain. Since the blatant disrespect of the rule of law was one of the main factors behind the overthrow of the Arab regimes, it is expected that the new regimes will avoid any violations of the rule of law and build a strong democratic governing system that is based on respect of the law and human rights. This is the main challenge facing the post-revolutionary Arab countries.

Between Faith and Fiction

Friday, July 8, 2011

The general wisdom, when teaching law, is that law tends to codify trends and custom of societies which have proceeded such codification by, say, 10 years or more. The lesson therefore is that law follows what people have practiced prior to its enactment.

But in the Egypt which is emerging from the debris of 60 years of military dictatorship of Nasser/Sadat/Mubarak, is applying the above adage in reverse. The traditional maxim of custom precedes the law has now been re-invented in Egypt to say the law precedes society's reconstruction. The three generations of military/security/dictatorship, swept aside by the January 25, 2011 Revolution, the first to be engineered by everyone and no one at Tahrir Square, confronted the new Egypt with a vacuum - a void.

The void was a gaping hole confronting 90 million Egyptians: No independent political parties; no visible leadership symbols after the so-called Democratic National Party, Mubarak's political instrument, was destroyed; no legitimate Parliament; no free media; no social or economic fairness; no independent judiciary. The only structure which was left standing after the January 25 hurricane was that of the Muslim Brotherhood, banned form political or civic participation by Nasser since 1954. And the Brotherhood, also known as "the Banned" (Al-Mahzourah) represented various shades of Islamic faith, a spectrum which included both extremism and liberalism without modernity. And the new Egypt was bent on secularism in the aftermath of a Revolution during the first phases of which the Brothers played no part.

The ethos of the new Egypt is: "faith is for God; homeland is for all." It is an ethos that separates faith from the fiction propagated by the likes of Bin Laden that Islam is the propeller of a forever war against non-Muslims. That was the criminal fiction behind 9/11 and behind the on-going confrontation between Al-Qaeda and global co-existence within diversity which is a pivot of the Muslims' faith.

That historic separation between faith and fiction brought about an interim administration of the military and technocrats to fill the void facing post-Mubarak Egypt. The interim period is expected to end toward the end of 2011 with a new constitution and legal order in place - law is galloping ahead of Egyptian society to save the Revolution from the vagaries of a slide-back into the unknown.

How does that separation between faith and mischievous fiction operates in the environment of the new Egypt where Friday of July 8 declared: "The Revolution Above All," (Al-Thawrah Awwallan)?

Retreat by the Muslim Brotherhood and Salafi newly-minted parties from the slogan of "The Constitution First" to espouse at Tahrir the basic demands of the January 25 Revolution for elections, both Parliamentary (Sept.) and presidential (Nov.) followed by a constituent constitutional assembly followed by a plebiscite for constitutional ratification. Waiting for that last step would have prolonged the void;

More than 26 political parties, guided in part by the spirit and content of the Glorious (Al-Azhar) Document (see this blog of June 26) calling for a separation between the State and religion, reached a historic consensus on what they call "the Guide for a Democratic Coalition."

The cooperation of both the Muslim Brotherhood, now split between a political party and a faith sector, and the Salafis with no less than 3 political parities, was a primary objective of the youth who, through social media, collapsed the Mubarak regime and are now bent upon prosecuting its symbols.

The Freedom and Justice Party, made up of a sector of the Muslim Brotherhood, has raised the secular flag as a banner around which the new Egypt is coalescing.

The Friday of July 8, called "Revolution Above All" Friday in which all political parties participated had, beside the goal of unity of all political shades, a message for the Supreme Military Council: "Speed up the trials of Mubarak and his family and his henchmen." It is a thunderous call for equality before the law, even as the new laws are being drafted.

Separation between "faith and fiction" has also required the formulation of a new law on the construction of places of worship. Mubarak has used the sectarian conflict between Muslim and Copt resulting from an unspoken prohibition of new churches construction as a means of prolonging his security and dictatorship State. The new law was approved as a draft by the Sharaf Cabinet before submitting it to the new Parliament later this year. Its central features are "no security clearance before construction" and no fake mosques in apartment buildings and cellars, none on arable land, none with a Nile or Nile canals front, and none in antiquities areas.

The hilarious Salafi fiction of the mindless fatwa describing "tourism" as a "anti-Islamic" has been mercilessly interred. Said the Minister of Tourism, Mounir Fakhry Abdel-Noor, a Copt; "Before the Revolution, Egypt earned $13 billion annually from tourism. We shall push this figure now to reach $25 billion. Every Egyptian who loves this country should participate in building a democratic, just and fair State"

The Egyptian Revolution: A Work In Progress?

Friday, July 15, 2011

Tahrir is alive again. Its historic revolution has not yet run its course. The armed forces rule; the Government of Issam Sharaf manages as best as it can; the trials of Mubarak, his sons and his stalwarts have not yet begun; and those, young and old, who brought Mubarak down, feel that their basic demands remain unfulfilled. The Revolution is not yet a work of progress, but a work in progress.

Impatience is everywhere. The Deputy Prime Minister, Dr. Yehia El-Gamal, a friend of this blogger and a colleague at Cairo University School of Law has resigned; the populace now want Prime Minister Sharaf be replaced; nearly 700 of the top Egyptian police leadership are pushed into retirement, with 17 of them stigmatized by the killing of hundreds of protesters in January/February; and the Tahrir revolutionaries are not yet mollified.

Some voices reach me to bemoan what they call "the dictatorship of anarchy" and the young at Tahrir and at other similar places in Alexandria and Suez are described as the multitudes of "No." The doom sayers are worried that, as they put it to me on the phone from Cairo, "Egypt is on its way toward destruction." Very dire predictions which are not backed by the events on the ground.

For after 60 years of stifling dictatorships which began with Nasser in 1952, and ended with Mubarak in 2011 after recasting Egypt into a security State, Egypt has vaulted over the high fence of oppression into the green meadows of popular sovereignty. Some demands are basic, others are not so basic. But the public somehow knows that there is no going back to the prior age of darkness.

The Minister of Interior, Mr. Mansour Issa, has declared on July 13 that his Ministry will no longer intervene in political matters, but will focus on criminal justice and maintenance of public order. The Supreme Military Council, the interim collective presidency, announced that elections for the two houses of Parliament will take place in either October or November this year. The Coalition of revolutionary organizations has abandoned the call for sacking Prime Minister Sharaf to allow for continuity which will produce a new cabinet. It is expected that the Governor of the Central Bank of Egypt (equivalent to the U.S. Federal Reserve), Farouk Al-Okda, shall be the new Finance Minister. Others, including prominent Copts, like George Ishaak, are slated to join the new Cabinet.

Stability begets prosperity. The Revolution returned to the Egyptians their dignity, but delayed their economic recovery. Tourism has been badly hit; unemployment remains high; public institutions remain in quasi paralysis. Yet public spiritedness is back in full. Threats to the freedom of navigation in the Suez Canal were short lived; calls for civil disobedience in Alexandria and Suez were abandoned; and the Cairo Stock Exchange witnessed an unexpected euphoria.

So what brought the pendulum of the Egyptian Revolution to its natural center, after the dire proclamations that the mother of all Arab revolutions was in danger of a slide back to anarchy? The Supreme Military Council and the Prime Minister held extensive dialogues with the Revolutionary Coalition; the

Supreme Judicial Council declared that the trials of the symbols of the Mubarak regime will be aired on radio and TV in real time; the armed forces stressed that they and the people are together bound in unity; new police forces were back in the streets; generous monthly pensions, reaching up to $500 per family of victims of the Revolution began flowing; and popular committees were formed to protect public institutions from counter-revolutionary attacks. The work in progress is turning into a work of progress.

A Constitutional Republic on the Nile is rising.

A New Meaning For Fridays

Friday, July 22, 2011

Religious tradition allocates one day per week for worship, reflection and rest. Friday for Muslims; Saturday for Jews; and Sunday for Christians. But with the Arab Spring and Summer, Friday in Egypt as well as in several other Arab countries has acquired a new meaning. Worship, yes; reflection, maybe; rest, has been now replaced by the word "revolution." And each Friday has not only a revolutionary connotation, but also a name indicative of the progression of the revolutionary mood, demands and aspiration.

To illustrate, at Tahrir Square, which has become the pulsing revolutionary heart of Egypt and which is being emulated in other Arab lands, Friday of July 15 was named: "Last Warning Friday," or "Final Ultimatum Friday." But ultimatum to whom and for what?

The fear for the future of the Egyptian Revolution is palpable. In op-ed articles in the Egyptian press, the most used phrase is "beware of the theft of the Revolution." Arabic language newspapers which are published outside Egypt frequently headlines "The Egyptian Revolution is in Danger." The continuous sit-ins and demonstrations in Tahrir Square and elsewhere in Egypt have paralyzed more than traffic in Cairo, Alexandria and Suez. They have paralyzed the swearing-in of a new Cabinet, headed again by Prime Minister Issam Sharaf, because of unending popular demand for a Cabinet whose members had nothing to do with the collapsed Mubarak regime.

Superficially, the scene appears chaotic. But a close examination, the phenomenon is confirming in the Egyptian public mind that sovereignty belongs to the people, and that the present role of the Supreme Military Council, headed by Defense Minister General Tantawi is transitional, leading to a parliamentary democracy, where a secular state is firm, though gradually, in place.

Through "Final Ultimatum Friday," the demonstrators demands produced a Cabinet of technocrats. Beyond that, 34 parties and political movements issued what they called "The Tahrir Manifesto." That document called for: ending the political polemics which have tended to fragment the broad revolutionary movement; speedy and public trials of the "symbols" of the Mubarak regime, including Mubarak, his wife and sons; muscular powers for the Sharaf Cabinet; trial of security personnel implicated in the death of nearly 900 demonstrators and in injuring thousands; return of public funds spirited outside of Egypt; abolishing trials of civilians before military tribunals; and the abrogation of laws prohibiting public demonstrations. Twenty-five persons suspected of attacking the Tahrir demonstrators in Feb. 2 and 3 in what is known as "the Camel Battle" are being tried by the Egyptian criminal justice system. They include the former Presidents of the two chambers of Parliament.

The Prime Minister, in the spirit of the new openness of the Egyptian political environment, one day before the swearing in of his new Cabinet before General Tantawi on July 21, used his Facebook page to complain of unnamed quarters which he said are working hard to impede the progress of Egypt towards stability and productivity. He stressed that: "The most important thing I care for now is for the public to develop public trust in the fact that every decision I took or shall take has only one objective: to benefit Egypt."

In consequence of that steady march toward stable governance, demonstrators in cities all over Egypt, including Zagazi, the provincial capital of Sharkia where I have originally hailed from, have marched peacefully. No police was on hand except for guarding critical installations. The public has been policing itself. "Selmia, Selmia" (Peaceful, Peaceful).

The ripple effects on the march of Egypt towards democracy have been in evidence: the laws governing the composition of the two parliamentary chambers and the practice of political rights have been promulgated; dates for the one-day elections of 504 members of the House of Representatives and of 390 members of the Senate will be announced in September; the minimum age for candidates has been reduced to 25 years, a nod for the youth who brought about the Tahrir dramatic changes; election dates will be spread over 30 days covering all of Egypt as divided in 3 huge electoral zones constituting 120 districts.

A new magazine from Cairo's Al-Ahram newspaper establishment has just made its debut. Its title is "Democracy"; its editor is a woman journalist, Dr. Hala Mustapha who wrote its lead editorial under the title of "The Elections and the Constitution." Among the articles of that maiden issue is one written by another woman journalist, Dr. Mona Abu-Sinnah, under the tantalizing title of "Democracy and the Terrorism of Demagoguery."

Within the framework of this emerging democracy, a new organization has been established in Cairo under the name of "The Arab/African Working Group for Democratic Action," whose Executive Director is a young articulate Judge, Aly Mokhtar. I could not turn down the invitation to becoming its President, though residing for the most time in the USA.

Here we again quote from the poem by Mohja Kahf entitled "My People are Rising." "I see their faces changing under fresh fresh tears, mine and theirs... some spigot in my chest just opened that has been stopped up for forty-eight years..."

Now, every Arab dictator wishes that he could expunge Fridays from the weekly calendar!!

Mubarak Behind Bars

Friday, July 29, 2011

Why is Mubarak behind bars? The revolutionaries in Egypt who, through peaceful means, have, with the Armed Forces acquiescence, toppled him from power on February 11, have unanimously demanded it. It was not a desire for retribution; it was a desire to firm up the principle that in the new Egypt, nobody was above the law.

Muhammad Hosni Mubarak has ruled Egypt for 32 years. During that nearly one-third of a century of dictatorial rule, that President has thoroughly converted Egypt into a fully-fledged Security State.

What is a Security State? It is a State where the ruler denies his people the right to freedoms of speech, assembly and conscience (defined as the moral sense of right and wrong). How does such a dictator do that? Well, through a large body of enforcers (police, secret service and informants) whose number, under Mubarak, was greater than the number of the entire Egyptian armed forces.

The security state of Mr. Mubarak spread fear, showed favors for those who cooperated with it, watched what people did or did not do, and acted above the law by denying the Egyptian people the right to due process and equality before the law.

Mubarak's trial and in public has been a primary demand by his aggrieved people whom he took for granted for nearly 32 years of his unrelenting dictatorship. The trial's delays were a cause for Tahrir becoming again and again full of thousands of protesters.

His poor health proved to be no excuse for transferring him from his hospital in Sharm El-Sheikh by the Red Sea to a Cairo prison and a Cairo court. The pleadings of his lawyer about unfitness to stand trial were to no avail. Finally the newly-restructured Cabinet of Issam Sharaf, supported by the Supreme Military Council, declared that Mubarak, in early August, would be in the dock in Cairo to stand a televised trial, the first of its kinds for a former head of state in the Arab world.

Mubarak's example will surly send shock waves in the entire Middle East. It will scare every Arab dictator, president or monarch in the vast Arab world. The banners have already been raised in Yemen and Syria proclaiming one chilling warning, "Who Is Next?"

The Mubarak case has been joined to the cases of his two sons, Alaa and Gamal, and of his former Interior Minister, El-Adly and other symbols of the former Security State. The charges cover the main areas of abuse of authority, theft of public funds, give-aways of national resources, killing of demonstrators, fomenting sectarian violence, and other forms of repression.

Mubarak's journey from absolute power to absolute humiliation has been both dramatic and historic. Its lessons will not be forgotten anytime soon.

4 AUGUST 2011

Selmia, Selmia: The Lethal Weapon of "Peaceful, Peaceful"

Friday, August 5, 2011

When the January 25, 2011 Revolution broke out in Egypt, its demands were rather modest. Its central demand was for jobs and the elimination of emergency laws. The crowds came out seeking dignity. But they were met with the brutal force of the Mubarak security forces which turned their cries of "Selmia, Selmia" into cries of death and pain. More than 850 were killed in various parts of that beautiful country. Thousands more were injured. The more people were felled by bullets, the more thousands, came out to form a human avalanche which numbered nearly 8 million. Only then were the demands upon Mubarak of "IRHAL" - Leave, and "The People Want the Regime to Fall."

The Egyptian armed forces, numbering in all its branches including reservists a million kept their powder dry. The false accusations by the Mubarak media that the throngs were foreign agents who were bent up on chaos and who were destabilizing Egypt sounded very hollow. The armed forces, being made up of conscripted soldiers, represented a true spectrum of the people in Tahrir and elsewhere.

Thus the banners of the "Selmia" throngs were raised proclaiming that "the people and the army are one." The slogans reflected the reality. The tanks went to Tahrir to give credence to those slogans. Flowers were offered to tank crews; children were helped by soldiers atop of those tanks; and tanks, when it rained, which is an infrequent event in Egypt, sheltered the demonstrators from getting wet. And the Supreme Council of the Armed Forces quietly told Mubarak "go away."

So when February 11 came about, there was nowhere for the 83 year old dictator to go but out. The shout of a young Egyptian woman, issuing from Tahrir, upon hearing the news, summed up the feelings of ecstasy of the millions: "No More Fear!! (Mafeesh Khofe Tani!!)."

The wall of fear which came down crashing in Egypt, the most populous Arab nation, was a signal to the whole region, indeed to the whole world, that non-violence has become the weapon of mass reconstruction for the millions of Arab masses everywhere.

In its methods of non-violence, "Selmia, Selmia" was a true vindication of the principles articulated by the scholar Gene Sharp of the Albert Einstein Institution in Boston in his "**From Dictatorship to Democracy - A Conceptual Framework for Liberation**." That 76-page booklet was translated into 30 languages including Arabic. The throngs in Tahrir and in the rest of the Arab world had read it.

Al-Azhar (The Glorious) As a Lighthouse to the Ship of the New Egypt

Friday, August 19, 2011

On August 17, Al-Azhar (The Glorious), a more than a thousand year citadel in the heart of Cairo of Islamic faith, and guidance to all Arab and Muslims issued a historic document. The document enunciated by Al-Azhar Rector, Dr. Ahmed El-Tayeb is billed: **"Al-Azhar Document on Egypt's Future."** It is the product of a unique consensus among leaders of various fields of faith, politics, laws, art, literature, history, society, psychology, and other areas of academe.

Out of the turbulence of the Revolution of January 25, 211 which swept aside the military rule of 60 years, emerged a consensual document of guidelines for constitutional formulation. All aspirants to the presidency of Egypt, all leaders of all parties and of various fields of thought, all opinion-makers of various stripes sat at El-Tayeb rectangular table to say, "yes" to those guidelines.

Al-Azhar document whose text was made public at a press conference at Al-Azhar on August 17 took into account those inimitable Egyptian perspectives anchored in Islamic jurisprudence; Al-Azhar's history of struggle for freedom and independence; the civilizational depth which merges physical sciences with social sciences and the arts; the political perspectives whereby future decision -makers of Egypt are nurtured; and the linkage between knowledge, renaissance, and cultural resurgence in the Arab homeland and the Islamic world.

The names of great lights of Al-Azhar, especially in the modern era were cited bringing them back from beyond the grave to historic life, such as: Sheikh Al-Islam Hassan El-Attar; his disciple Sheikh Rifaa El-Tahtawi; Sheikh Muhammad Abdo, the great modern reformer, Sheikh Al-Maraghy, together with other Al-Azhar leaders of reform such as Muhammad Abdullah Diraz, Mustapha Abdel-Razik, and last but not least, the venerable Sheikh Shaltout.

The Al-Azhar document frames the principles which will guide the drafters of Egypt's new constitution within eleven such principles. These, in summary, are:

First: Egypt as a State is based upon a constitutional democracy with separation of powers, of which the legislative power is to be exercised by the people's representatives. Islam, in its legislation, civilization, and history does not recognize a "religiously-based" State. The overall arching principles of Islamic law (Sharia) are the primary source of legislation, providing that the adherents of other religions are guaranteed, in their personal status cases, resort to their own religious laws.

Second: Democratic rule is based on free and direct elections, which encapsulate the modern formulation of the application of the Islamic precepts of Shura (consultation). Such rule guarantees diversity, the peaceful transfer of powers, a well-defined exercise of authority whose custodians are accountable to the people's representatives with a view to the provision of public service, subject only to the rule of law. Corruption is punishable under the law, and transparency and the freedom and transmission of information are to be applied.

Third: Commitment to basic rights and freedoms with regard to both thought and opinion, including full respect of the rights of the individual, of women and children, and of the principle of diversity. Citizenship is the primary basis from which emanates obligations to society.

Fourth: Full respect to the view of the other, which implicates the necessity of avoidance of declaring others to be apostates, traitors, or the abuse of religion for the purposes of sowing divisiveness and hatred among the citizens. Sectarian conflict and racist advocacy are criminally injurious to the homeland.

Fifth: Commitment to international covenants (treaties) and decisions (declarations), and to civilizational norms and accomplishments in human (friendly) relationships which accord with the Islamic and Arab traditions of tolerance and with the long experience of the Egyptian people throughout its historical periods which produced luminous examples of peaceful co-existence and the striving towards humanity's benefits as a whole.

Sixth: Full attention to the dignity of the Egyptian nation and its national pride, and to an assured protection of places of worship of all faiths, and of the freedom of expression and artistic and literary expression.

Seventh: Education, scientific research, and the embarking upon the age of knowledge (information) are to be regarded the locomotive of Egypt's civilizational progress, including the eradication of illiteracy.

Eighth: Implementation of the ladder (jurisprudence) of priorities with regard to the achievement of development, social justice, confrontation of oppression (hegemony) and of corruption, elimination of unemployment, all within the recognition of veritable and serious health care as a duty of the State towards all citizens.

Ninth: The establishment of Egypt's solid relationships with its sister Arab States, as well as States within its Islamic, African and other international spheres, along with support of Palestinian rights, of safe-guarding the independence of Egypt's decision-making (will), and of the re-establishment of Egypt's traditional and historical leadership role as the basis of cooperation for the universal good, and of environmental protection and just peace among nations.

Tenth: Enhancement of the independence of the instituitoin of Al-Azhar, and the resurrection of the "Commission of Great Ulemas (Islamic Scholars)" endowed with responsibility for the appointment through elections of the Rector of Al-Azhar.

Eleventh: Recognition of Al-Azhar "Al-Shareef" as the source and focus of responsibility to which reference should be made in all matters of Islam, its disciplines, its traditions, and its jurisdictional interpretation (ijtihad) and modern thought patterns. This is without the elimination of the right of all to the voicing of opinions on the basis of recognizable and acceptable scientific parameters.

From the above, we could see that the Glorious (Al-Azhar) is back, as a beacon, a lighthouse guiding the ship of the Egyptian State towards a safe harbor.

Said General Sami Anan, Deputy Chairman of the Egyptian Supreme Council of the Armed Forces, in line with the above: **"The secularity of the State is a matter of national security which is non-negotiable."**

From a House Cleaner to a Cook for the Masses

Thursday, August 25, 2011

Ghalia Mahmoud, a poor house cleaner, has become on Egyptian TV a celebrated cook for the masses. The 33-year old gal from "Old Cairo" had cleaned house for the sister of a TV producer at Channel 25 (named in honor of January 25 when Egypt began its uprising which toppled Mubarak on February 11.

Picture this: Egyptian masses live mostly on falafel and beans and over-sweetened tea. Manhattan pushcart vendors sell a falafel pita sandwich for $3 (equivalent of 18 Egyptian pounds). This huge underclass had been victimized by the corruption of the Mubarak regime which split 90 million Egyptians in two classes: a thin veneer of the mega-rich and a gigantic poor class. A middle class of dwindling proportions in between. The underclass people have been living on an average of $200 a month.

In came the revolution of the masses. And with that came Ghalia Mahmoud whose father had died when she was too young to remember when. So Ghalia had to go to work with 8 of her siblings to help the family survive in a land of plenty whose riches were the reserve of the high and mighty.

But in Tahrir Square, the masses (the millions) who shouted to Mubarak IRHAL (Leave) stood as one to reclaim dignity, democracy and development (the new 3Ds of the Arab Spring). And with the army siding with the people, the 83-year old dictator relinquished his 32-years of one man rule and was then put on trial publicly.

The discovery of Ghalia Mahmoud was made by the man who launched the TV channel "Twenty-Five," Muhammad Jawhar. Ramadan, the month of fasting for Muslims was approaching (no food or drink from dawn to sunset), and Jawhar had inspiration for how could poor families cope with soaring food prices. His inspiration came from Ghalia Mahmoud. Before he put her on TV, he asked her to prepare a simple meal to feed a hungry family of 8 but would cost no higher than $4. For Ghalia, that was a test which she had no problem passing with flying colors.

With Ghalia came her pleasing personality, her simple ways, her motherly explanation to urban ladies on TV in how to make their families survive on the little they have. She stood in her simple kitchen, with pots without handles on a simple stove which she lights with matches, and prepares delicious meals made from vegetables sold on open carts lining up the streets of Old Cairo.

In no time, Ghalia Mahmoud became a huge hit all over Egypt and became known as "the Cook of the 25th January Revolution." Her long practice in feeding her family of 15 on a monthly budget of $200 paid off. With a captivating smile, Ghalia talks directly to all of Egypt, if not the entire Arab world, saying, "You, women, are smart and you can cook anything, if you just try."

When she cooks for her TV audiences, her measuring cups are made of plastic. Her table is laden with all kinds of Egyptian vegetables: eggplant, tomatoes, cucumber, lettuce, scallions ... etc. Her stuffed vine leaves, stuffed zucchini, and stuffed cabbage, with cucumber and cheese on the side, are tantalizingly inviting. As for meat, that expensive item, it is only reserved for a weekly meal on Friday -the Muslim Sabbath.

Ghalia also describes recipes for Copts (Egyptian Christians) for food during the season of lent. In this regard, she comments: "In poor Egyptian neighborhoods, there is no Muslim/Christian divide. That divide was of Mubarak's making."

How about Ghalia's hopes for the New Egypt. "I have lots of hope for Egypt after Mubarak. Egypt will be vastly different." Then she picks up a telephone donated to her by the TV station to answer an incoming call. The call is from a group of young and rich Egyptian girls, calling "the Revolutionary Cook" from their car to ask her "How do you make your delicious lentil soup?"

She also gets calls from children who tell her "Auntie Ghalia , we love you." One of them put up on a page on the Internet calling for **"Ghalia Mahmoud for President!!"**

5 SEPTEMBER 2011

Libya: What Does the Egyptian Street Say About the "The Tyrant's Family"

Tuesday, September 6, 2011

Headlining about Gaddafi "The End of a Tyrant," the Egyptian media dissects the roles and fortunes (or misfortunes) of his eight sons and two daughters.

Son #1: The oldest "Muhammad" was born to the Qaddafis by his first wife. He became a businessman, in fact one of the most important as he owned the biggest communications network in Libya; owned 40% of the soft drinks industry with a Coca Cola exclusive concession; headed the Libyan Olympic Committee, and presided over the Libyan Commission for postal and telecommunications services.

Son #2: "Saif Al-Islam" who prior to the February 17 Revolution, which did away with Gaddafi's 42 year of dictatorship, was being groomed to succeed his maniacal father. He was largely the face of Libya to the West. An engineer by training with supposedly a Ph.D from the London School of Economics; spoke good English (a good entree to the Western mind), he had called for reform through his "Gaddafi World Charitable Organization." Since 2000, Saif, in spite of the fact that he occupied no formal position in the governmental structure, played a huge role in both internal and external Libyan affairs. He is credited with "settling the Lockerbie tragedy"; warned of civil war in Libya after the uprising, and has been issued an arrest warrant by the International Criminal Court.

Son #3: "Al-Saidi" 36 years old; famous (or infamous) for his incendiary temper; a drug user; had several brushes with the law in Europe, especially in Italy. Al-Saidi, who has fled with his brother, Son #4 (Hanibal) with their mother and several children to Algeria, is said to have an engineering degree. He is a soccer player and had his own special forces.

Son #4: "Hanibal", husband of a Lebanese fashion model, Elaine Skaf, with whom he fathered two sons. Nicknamed "the Trouble Maker," Hanibal was arrested with his wife in Geneva for beating up their maid. That criminal complaint against them resulted in their arrest by the Swiss police, thus precipitating a diplomatic confrontation between Gaddafi's Libya and Switzerland whose national airline (Swissair) was temporarily denied landing rights in Libyan airports. With Gaddafi threatening to withdraw all Libyan deposits in Swiss banks, the Swiss suspended their legal action against Hanibal and Elaine. Yet in 2009, while the couple were at the Claridge Hotel in London, the London police was called to investigate the screams coming out from Hanibal's suite. Elaine was found to be badly disfigured but she refused to press charges against "the Trouble Maker."

Son #5: "Al-Motassin" was his father's National Security Advisor. In that capacity, and in competition with his younger brother, Son #6 Khamis, he demanded $1.2 Billion to establish a military security unit of his own. The Serbian Ambassador to Tripoli had once characterized him as "possessing no acute intelligence," which may explain why his siblings maneuvered in his absence abroad to gut out his extensive commercial and personal holdings between the years 2001-2005.

Son #6: "Khamis" established and led the fearsome "Division No. 32" whose personnel were thoroughly trained in modern warfare in the Russian Federation. Khamis' role, in that regard, was akin to that of the Presidential Guard in Syria or the Islamic Republican Guard in Iran, namely, the protection of the Gaddafi regime. Khamis spearheaded the brutal suppression of the Revolution which began on March 17, in Benghazi and ended up with NATO's help, vanquishing the Gaddafi army, his mercenaries, his snipers and his informers.

Son #7: "Saif Al-Arab" The least known among his brothers; was killed, together with 3 Gaddafi grandsons on April 30 in a NATO raid on his house which was suspected of harboring, at that time, Gaddafi himself.

Daughter Aisha: Child #8, A daughter of 34 years of age, and the one who mediates the family disputes. A lawyer by training, she was involved with defending Saddam Hussein after the collapse of that Iraqi brutal regime in 2003. Her father, whose entire honor guard was made up of young Libyan women, gave every girl in that corps the name of "Aisha" followed by a number. Examples: Aisha #1, Aisha #2 and so on. A Libyan University gave her an honorary doctorate as a consolation prize for not being able to complete her graduate study in international law in Paris. News have been confirmed of her flight, together with her children and other members of her family to Algeria after the rebels' conquest of Tripoli in late August.

Hana: Child #9, an adopted daughter who was reported to have been killed in a US aerial bombardment of Tripoli in 1986. Those bombarded premises were declared by Gaddafi a historic site form which he called for the routing of the rebels when the revolution began in Benghazi in March.

Milad: Child #10, a boy who was born to a brother of Gaddafi, then later adopted by uncle Muammar.

From that list, only #1 Gaddafi and his son, Saif Al-Islam are named on the arrest warrant issued by the International Criminal Court in the Hague.

Though news were broadcast worldwide on September 6 regarding a long convoy of cars moving south from Libya to Niger, under Niger army protection, no credible information has yet come out as to whether Gaddafi himself was in that country.

The Guns of the Egyptian Army Remain Silent

Friday, September 9, 2011

In the Egyptian Revolution of January 25, 2011, the guns of the Egyptian army were not turned on the demonstrators. And Mubarak, a dictator for 32 years, fell from power. Why were the guns of the largest Arab army did not mow down the Tahrir Square revolutionaries? After all, Mubarak, like his predecessors, Nasser and Sadat, were members of that nearly one million man strong army establishment.

When we pose the question of why did Egypt's armed forces, by its silence on January 25 and beyond, did not turn on that historic rebellion? The answer lies in the history, background, and make-up of those armed forces sitting on their tanks by the banks of the Nile.

The Egyptian army is a nationalist army. In 1805, an Albanian tobacconist, by the name of Muhammad Aly, became the Ottoman Sultan's Viceroy in Egypt. The Ottoman Empire was in decline. Rebellions against it raged from the Balkans to the north, to the Sudan to the south, to Arabia to the East. Fires, fires everywhere against the far-flung Empire, the locus of the then-Caliphate, with no effective fire brigades. Muhammad Aly, once Napoleon had withdrawn in 1803 his troops from Egypt, an important province of the Ottomans, saw his chance to pry Egypt loose from the dying Empire. His tool was the establishment of the mightiest army in the Empire. Two-hundred thousand man strong, with a navy whose ships were built from the famous cedars of Lebanon. His trainers were French. His recruits were Egyptian peasants.

Those peasant soldiers of the great Muhammad Aly, who also industrialized Egypt (and whose sons built later the first girls school in the Muslim world in the 1860's), knew no geographical or sectarian affiliation. They only knew that they were Egyptians. Cohesiveness came not from the province or the faith in which they were born. It came from the flag and the national territory over which it was raised. Thus, as one, they fought first for the Sultan in the Sudan, in Arabia and in the Balkans, then, for Egypt, against the Sultan, and helped make Egypt a hereditary monarchy, with autonomy, then independence from the Ottomans.

That army, born in Egyptian nationalism, then fought the British occupation which began in 1882 and ended in 1954. Its sense of onness with the people was first manifested in those late 1880s in the rebellion led by Ahmed Orabi, a native of my village in the Province of Sharkia (the Oriental). Orabi was exiled to the Seychelles in the Indian Ocean, but the spirit of nationalism in that army never waned. It, together with the police engaged the British forces in the Suez Canal in the early 1950s in non-conventional warfare. Later came several wars with Israel over the question of Palestine, which ended with the Egyptian army crossing into Sinai in October 1973. That October/Ramadan/or Yom Kippur War during the Sadat presidency led to two results, a peace treaty with Israel in 1979, and a huge boost to the reputation of the Egyptian army in the eyes of the

Egyptian public.

So when the January 25 Revolution for freedom from dictatorship erupted, the Egyptian army whose conscripts could see their brothers, sisters, cousins, uncles and aunts in Tahrir Square, sat smiling on top of their tanks over which children played.

No wonder that the revolutionaries of Tahrir Square, finding that the vacuum left by the collapse of the Mubarak regime was leading to chaos, had no problem calling in their national army to govern in an interim capacity. Simultaneously a civilian government was set up under Dr. Essam Sharaf, as Prime Minister until Egypt could pull itself together through both parliamentary and presidential elections in late 2011. Now, with Mubarak and his sons being tried before a civilian criminal court in Cairo, the Chairman of the Supreme Council of the Armed Forces, Field Marshal Muhammad Tantawi is expected to testify, together with his Deputy General Sami Anan, before that court which will determine Mubarak's guilt or innocence.

So when the question is asked, "Who owns the Egyptian Revolution?", the response from Tahrir is: the people of Egypt, from whom that proud army sprang.

A Journey in the mind of the Salafis in Egypt

Sunday, September 18, 2011

The word "Salafi" in Arabic means a Muslim who harks back more than 1400 years ago to the way he or she thinks Islam was practised in Arabia at the time of the Prophet Muhammad. "Salaf" means "ancestor." The Salafi movement in Egypt and elsewhere encompasses those who believe that progress and justice lie in what they deem the purity of the Muslim faith during its first three centuries.

As an ideology, the Salafis especially in Egypt, a traditionally cosmopolitan country of a Muslim majority and a Coptic (Christian) indigenous minority, has nothing to do with Al-Qaeda. In its genesis, Salafism is inward oriented towards Islamic worship in mosques, and fear from secularity. That anti-secularism lies at the root of their problem both at the time of dictatorship in Egypt (from 1952 to 2011, the year when

Mubarak was pushed out of power on February 11) and now in the New Egypt born in Tahrir Square on January 25, 2011. So what is the problem or problems faced by the Salafis or raised by them?

During Mubarak's reign, they were brutally suppressed. Here we should remember that Mubarak on October 6, 1981, was, as Vice President of Egypt, seated next to President Sadat during the military parade from which a band of soldiers, Islamic terrorists, rushed toward the stand and assassinated the Egyptian President. Their suppression thereafter was brutal, forcing them to go below the radar of Mubarak's security State.

Then came the Revolution of January 25in which both the Muslim Brotherhood and the Salafis, two distinct and at times antagonistic groups, had no leadership role. The Supreme Council of Egypt's Armed Forces was invited by the representatives of the Revolution to step into the void left by Mubarak; an interim civilian government was formed to transition the 90 million population country to democracy through parliamentary elections (now scheduled for this November); and Al-Azhar (the Glorious), the most important seat of Islamic learning, declared in Cairo on August 17 that:

Islam, in its legislation, civilization, and history does not recognize a "religiously-based" State. The overall arching principles of Islamic law (Sharia) are the primary source of legislation, providing that the adherents of other religions are guaranteed, in their personal status cases, resort to their own religious laws.

So in the New Egypt, the principle of "faith and politics do not mix" has been established, and the separation of powers had been affirmed. The Al-Qaeda in Afghanistan, Yemen, and elsewhere has no place in Egypt. And the flags which were raised in Tahrir did not proclaim "Islam is the solution." They proclaimed "Democracy is the solution."

Have I just said, "democracy?" Yes!! Now there are 38 political parties and movements to compete in the parliamentary elections. Amongst those, there are 4 Salafi parties, and one party which was formed by former members of the Muslim Brotherhood. Then came a "red line" announcement by the Supreme Council of the Armed Forces: **"The secularity of Egypt is non-negotiable."**

Note here that the Turkish model of governance is being replicated in Egypt. These proclamations from Tahrir, from Al-Azhar, and from the

Armed Forces, declare loudly and clearly that Egypt shall not become Iran II, a theocracy. And the Copts, though still worried about the Salafi and other Islamic influences, are beginning to see in the New Egypt the face of traditional Egypt which raised during its revolution against the British occupation its real flag of inclusiveness which shows the Crescent embracing the Cross.

The Salafi parties are "Al-Fadhilah" (Virtue); "Al-Noor" (Light); "Salamah and Tanmiyah" (Security and Development); and "Islah and Tanmiyah" (Reform and Development). Now that the Salafis have resurfaced after the Revolution toppled their tormentor Mubarak, they want primarily to preserve in the new Egyptian Constitution which shall be drafted in 2012 by a constituent assembly, Article II of the present Constitution.

That Article provides that no bill shall be legislated into law if it contravenes Islamic Law (Sharia) principles. The fact of the matter is that Sharia, whose two primary sources are the Quran and the Sunna (Muhammad's utterances and conduct) has, over 1432 years evolved. Its evolution has been through ijtihad (interpretation). The result has been summed up in Al-Azhar's Declaration of August 17 as follows:

Democratic rule is based on free and direct elections, which encapsulate the modern formulation of the application of the Islamic precepts of Shura (consultation).

The Salafi concern for the future role of Islam in a democratic Egypt is being alleviated. In the mosque, Muslims pray and sermonize; in the Church, the Copts do the same; and in Parliament, the people's representatives legislate for a secular New Egypt.

In the newly-born Egypt, faith is not separated from life; it is separated from the politics of inclusiveness of Muslims, Copts, and all other beliefs.

Towards Deomocracy By Baby Steps

Friday, September 23, 2011

Those who say that Egypt has never experienced democracy should revisit its history. The Egyptian Constitution of 1923, promulgated during the monarchy was a model Basic Law. It guaranteed popular elections based on a multiparty system, freedom of expression, and the right to assemble peacefully. That was 88 years ago.

So what happened? In came Colonel Nasser with his Coup d'Etat in 1952. Creeping military rule was now in motion. The difference between a coup and a revolution is that a coup is undertaken by a junta; a revolution is undertaken by the masses. Dictator Nasser found in the Constitution an obstacle to his rule. In 1954, he directed his goons (baltagiahs) to attack an iconic institution, the Council of State, and its then Chairman, the great jurist El-Sanhouri. El-Sanhouri was beaten up by the Nasser mob to the ignorant cries of "Down with the Constitution!!" A dark age has descended on Egypt, and was to continue till the dawn of the Revolution of January 25, 2011.

A body politic, like that of Egypt of today, is beginning to learn again how to walk in the flowery park of a constitutional system. The call for a constitutional change was in fact uttered in 2009, during the Mubarak dictatorship. It was courageously uttered by Dr. Muhammad El-Baradie, the former head of the International Atomic Energy Agency. El-Baradie, a Nobel Laureate, is today running for the post of President later this year.

But the crippling effects of the non-practice of democracy are a temporary restraint. Baby steps toward democracy are usually transformed into forward leaps. Hardly any training is required. Practicing democracy is an on-the-job training. The innate desire for freedom kicks in, and all that is needed is choosing the candidate, finding the way to a polling station, being in the proper voting district, proving your identity, being safe as you vote, and, BINGO, you have become a voter!!

This formula applies neatly to Egypt's present baby steps towards a democratic and secular State: Some of these steps or manifestations thereof are produced hereunder as a guide post for this historic march:

Selection of university presidents and college deans by elections held by their peers, not by appointment by the country's President upon recommendations by the security apparatus of that President;

Broad criticism of Prime Minister Dr. Essam Sharaf for his recent statements to Turkish media that "the Camp David Agreements of 1978 which led to the Egypt/Israel Peace Treaty signed in Washington, D.C. in March 1979 is not a sacred document which is immune from amendment."

Egypt has a long history for respect of treaties.

The euphoria of the masses at seeing their former tormentors (Mubarak, his sons, and members of his cabal) standing trial. The notion of equality before the law is seeping in.

The Youth Coalition, namely the young millions in Tahrir who lost 850 victims to the guns and tear gas of the Mubarak security regime, and for whom the guns of the military remained silent thus forcing Mubarak out of power, that Revolutionary Youth Coalition will field as many as 200 candidates in the Parliamentary elections. Why? "To counter organized Islamic groups."

Ahmed Ezz, the steel tycoon and monopolist, who was the Secretary of the now defunct National Democratic Party, was sentenced to 10 years in jail for unfair monopolistic practices. During the Mubarak regime, Ezz was feared to the point that, prior to the Revolution which brought him to the halls of justice in Egypt, used to change the law on his own to suit his own monopolistic and corrupt devices.

Egypt now laughs at a statement made by Omar Soliman during his few days of tenure as VP of Egypt during the waning days of the Mubarak dynasty. The TV interview by Christiane Amanpour with Soliman featured Soliman's response to her question regarding Egypt's readiness for a transition to democracy. His emphatic answer was: "The Egyptians do not possess the culture of democracy!!" So in his popular column in Al-Ahram newspaper, entitled "The Reconstruction of the State," Atef El-Ghamry says: *"The Mubarak regime has robbed Egypt of 30 years. For it ran the country with the logic of a business corportation to which the regime grew accustomed, namely profit for the management (i.e. the Dictator and his cronies)."*

Now there is a clearly announced schedule for parliamentary elections in November, followed by presidential elections in December, followed by drafting a new constitution which will be submitted to a popular plebiscite in 2012.

Are these "baby steps" towards a secular and democratic Egypt? Maybe that baby has a sudden spurt of growth. Go!! Go!! Go!!

6 OCTOBER 2011

The Tahrir Refrain

Sunday, October 2, 2011

"Hold Up Your Head High - You Are an Egyptian!!" It is the joyful cry of retrieved dignity and national pride. The flags of Egypt were held high, some emblazoned with the inscription "I Love Egypt." After 60 years of dictatorship, of which the last 32 years were under Mubarak, Egypt woke up to a new dawn of liberty. The long search for reviving democracy has begun.

How do these feelings of "don't step on Egypt's dignity" manifest themselves in this 8-month old revolution, internally and externally?

Internally, 38 political parties were created. The spectrum stretches from the liberal secular to the parties which sprang from the Muslim Brotherhood and the Salafis. They were all licensed except for groups which espoused archaic precepts of Islam.

How about the now-dissolved National Democratic Party, the Mubarak party, whose imposing Headquarters overlooking the Nile with a sign reading "We Are for You," was torched by the Tahrir demonstrators at the start of the Revolution in January, 2011? Its members were suspected of coming back to the halls of Parliament through the elections of November 2011 as "independents." The new elections law allowed for one-third of the seats to be allocated to non-party affiliated independents; Two-thirds for voting on party lists.

The fear and suspicion of that group were palpable. Thus the Supreme Military Council, the interim Government of Egypt, pending the full return to civilian rule, had to be pressured through the Tahrir demonstrators to amend that offending article (Article 5). The military gave in to the national will.

The right to peacefully assemble and demonstrate has become enshrined by both law and practice of the new Egypt. Tahrir has proved this principle of civil rights. That right cannot possibly be abridged by a fatwa (a religious decree), as in the case of Saleh of Yemen, declaring that it was sinful to protest against the State. That impossibility comes not only from Egypt's legislated laws; but also from Islamic jurisprudence under which an unjust ruler should be toppled by his subjects, when circumstances permit.

Thus the Friday of September 30 called "the Friday of Retrieval of the Revolution," meaning demonstrations to pressure the Egyptian military to amend the Elections Law, as noted above, and to end the so-called Emergency Laws was both possible and productive regarding the Elections Law. Now proportional representation on the basis of voting for party lists is the means to become an Egyptian legislator once the November elections are held.

But again **"Hold Up Your Head High - You Are an Egyptian"** was at work externally. The calls from abroad for elections supervisors from outside Egypt were rebuffed. "Observers," yes; "supervisors," no. After all, Egypt, since 1923, has been in the business of democratic elections - a tradition which was aborted by the onslaught of military dictatorship which began with Nasser, in 1952, and ended with Mubarak, in 2011. Egypt would thus accept observers, for example, from the Carter Foundation.

Within the same trajectory of pride in the new Egypt, the conditions which are now attached by the US Senate Appropriations Committee to U.S. aid to Egypt are objected to beforehand. This objection applies to both economic as well as military aid.

That objection was announced by Egypt's new Minister for Foreign Affairs, Muhammad Kamel Amr, after meetings with US officials in Washington D.C. The conditionality applied, among other things, to increasing border security in Sinai, and to having the Egyptian army commit to observing Egypt's obligations under the 1979 Egyptian-Israeli peace treaty. The new Egypt, while not expressing its present objections as rejection of U.S. aid, said in effect, through its Foreign Minister, "Before the Revolution, no conditions were placed on that aid. So why now?"

The issue here for the new Egypt was sovereignty from which national dignity flows. The Egyptians, in whom sovereignty resides, have become, with their relevant institutions, co-makers of foreign policy. This, at times, poses difficulty in dealing with foreign powers, as in this case, the U.S.

However, to be allied with the people of Egypt is a more durable alliance than with their former dictators. A writer by the name of Baher Shaarawi chose this apt title for his recent article on people's power, **"People are more durable than their rulers."**

Wael Ghoneim, is the young Egyptian and Google Executive who ignited the Egyptian street by the means of social media. It was fitting to honor him in Boston in June 2011 by bestowing upon him the annual John F. Kennedy prize for courage.

Between the Egyptian Army and the Revolution: What is the Deal?

Friday, October 7, 2011

Nobody knows for sure, except that the revolutionaries are impatient. They want a date certain for the transfer of power from the Supreme Council of the Armed Forces to a civilian government. They want an immediate lifting of the state of emergency law which has been in effect for nearly the entire reign of "El-Askar" (the army) from the early 1950s till now. Under these laws, detainees can be held without charges or trial for an indefinite period of time. They want to abolish trials before military tribunals. They want jobs with salaries commensurate with the inflationary pressures. The want... They want... They...!!

Revolutions are never tidy affairs. They are, as in all countries in the region affected by the Arab Spring, cascading events, popular explosions, sudden upheavals where there is hardly any planning or any recognizable leadership. Euphoria is the result especially, as in the case of both Tunisia and Egypt, the dictator either flees (the case of Tunisia's Ben Aly) or is prevented from leaving the country and is put on trial (the case of Mubarak of Egypt). In Egypt, the guns of that one-million man cohesive army remained silent, and the generals were invited to rule in an interim capacity (ruling by the Supreme Military Council under Field Marshal Tantawi, and governing by a technocratic government led by Prime Minister Dr. Essam Sharaf) until after elections, both parliamentary and presidential.

Although the honeymoon between the protesting public and the military seems to have lost a part of its steam, but the bond between these two poles of power seems to survive in the following manifestations:

The fear of a pro-Mubarak conspiracy to sour that relationship persists;

The responsiveness to the public demand for a definite time-table for parliamentary elections (with 38 parties in the competition), now set for November, to be followed by presidential elections on the basis of a new constitution to be drafted thereafter;

The declaration by Field Marshal Tantawi that the military would not offer a candidate to be Egypt's next president. This declaration had a calming effect with regard to the new Egypt becoming, once more, a secular democratic polity;

The trumpeting of the completion by the Egyptian army corps of engineers of a speedway stretching for 309 kilometers (192 miles) from Giza, at the foot of the pyramids to Assyout, the de facto capital of southern Egypt, nearly halfway from Cairo to Aswan;

The pomp and circumstance attending Armed Forces Day, October 6, in which the public came out in strength to celebrate;

The avoidance of showering praise in the Egyptian media on the generals for fear of a slide-back to the military dictatorship which collapsed on February 11, 2011 after 60 years of oppressive rule;

The call by leading opinion-makers in the Egyptian media for the armed forces to show more muscle in dealing with the chaotic conditions resulting from the continuity of demonstrations in Tahrir and elsewhere in Egypt;

The rejection by the public of foreign criticism of the slowness of the pace of Egypt's transition from military to civilian rule as interference in Egyptian internal affairs;

The repeated assurance by Tantawi and other leaders on the Egyptian Supreme Military Council that once the acts of instability cease, and the re-organized police forces are back to the business of maintaining law and order, emergency laws will be lifted.

These are indications that both the military and the Tahrir throngs are adjusting to a basic revolutionary reality: filling the vacuum left by the defunct regime takes time. And solutions for the economic downturn cannot be fashioned by decrees alone. But the anxiety about the speed of the return of the military to their barracks is catalyzed in an old Arab proverb reflecting the fear of the return to military rule. The proverb says:

Those who have once been bitten by a snake suffer a jolt upon seeing a twisting rope being dragged.

This proverb explains why a frenzy of speculation gripped the entire Egyptian political spectrum because Field Marshal Tantawi was seen recently for the first time out of uniform walking the streets. His mere appearance in a civilian suit and tie evoked the grim speculation of yet another military officer grooming himself for the post of president. Tantawi was quick to respond to the rumors by saying humorously, **"Would it have been better if I wore a torn up civilian suit?"**

Egyptian Blood on Egytpian Hands: The Maspero Massacre

Friday, October 14, 2011

The email came to me, fast and furious. It was from a young Coptic lawyer, one of my collaborators. It was dated October 11 on a horrific disaster which befell all of Egypt on Sunday, October 9, at Maspero. That is where the Egyptian Television is located, facing both the great Nile and also thousands of mainly Coptic demonstrators.

On that eventful day, perhaps the most eventful since Dictator Mubarak was chased out of office, 26 demonstrators were killed, 329 injured. The cause of the Maspero uprising: an attack in upper Egypt on an Egyptian Coptic church in the most southern of Egyptian provinces, Aswan

Province. It was the spark that ignited the Copts who marched from their area of mostly Coptic concentrations in Cairo, called Shubra, on the symbol of Egypt's newly found freedom of expression, the state-run Egyptian Television at Maspero.

In his email of October 11, my Coptic lawyer friend said: **"Egypt is crying blood and all the reason for that is the selfishness of some political parties and internal/external groups that want to see Egypt in this catastrophe. I am really wondering why this is occurring for our dear country which really does not deserve all of that. I also bring this tragedy to the lack of rule of law (for) which we all should work to strengthen (it.)"**

Reflection of this extreme anxiety about the future of the Revolution of January 25 was through a cartoon in a government-controlled newspaper called **"Rose Al-Youssef"** which made the rounds throughout the Arab world. The gifted cartoonist by the name of Anwar, had 2 persons wading into a pool of blood: one representing the military, the other, the civilian Prime Minister, Dr. Essam Sharaf. On top of these two figures, the ominous words read: **"Do you think we should open an investigation in where this blood came from, or is that not necessary?"**

That bloody confrontation was between Coptic demonstrators on one side and security forces bolstered by military police on the other. Muslims seem to have been split into two factions: one group sided with the Copts, the other with the forces of the Government. The first group was rewarding the Copts for their principled stand for national unity during the anti-Mubarak uprising; the second was rewarding the army for keeping its powder dry when Tahrir was aflame in quest of Mubarak's removal form power.

Who is to blame? All parties. Who are the winners? Nobody. Who are the losers: EGYPT. In an email, my dearest niece told me from Cairo: **"My heart is breaking for Egypt."**

What are the consequences? The honeymoon between the army and its people seems to have evaporated -at least for now. There is suspicion that the military is angling for overstaying their welcome by extending the period of military rule, with a facade of a supine civilian government.

Yet actions by the Government were swift as were mutual recriminations. Partial night curfew was declared for central Cairo; the

Supreme Council of Armed Forces instructed the Government to conduct a thorough investigation and to bring to justice all those who were the cause of that mayhem; the Prime Minister called for national unity; the Copts called for the internationalization of sectarian strife, accusing the army of complicity.

In such complicated event, the conspiracy theory takes a front seat in the drama of the new Egypt taking its first baby steps towards democracy. PM Sharaf declared: **"There are criminal internal and external fingers which played their part in the violence in central Cairo to impede the establishment of a democratic system in Egypt."** Then he went on to tell the nation on TV: **"The worst dangers confronting Egyptian security are the attempts to disrupt national unity; to sow disunity (between Muslims and Copts); to drive a wedge between the people and their army... It is difficult to characterize what happened as a sectarian conflict."**

PM Sharaf seemed to have a boost for his theory from Pope Shenoudah, the head of the Coptic Church. His Eminence, through the Holy Clerical Council which included 170 bishops, declared: **"Christian faith rejects violence. Outsiders penetrated Coptic demonstrators to commit those atrocities and then point the finger of blame at the Coptic community."**

As for Al-Azhar (the Glorious) (Seat of Islamic learning for more than 1000 years), it declared through its Grand Imam, Sheikh Dr. Ahmed El-Tayeb: **"The Egyptian military was and shall always be the expression and manifestation of the principle of Egyptian citizenship."**

The root cause of Coptic unrest was also tackled: The Council of Ministers is slated to approve within two weeks a new law for standardizing the zoning rules of the construction of both mosques and churches.

If it does, then the flames at Maspero, which were ignited from a small church in Aswan Province, might have been converted into light guiding Egypt in the near future towards civilian and democratic rule.

Gaddafi's Bloody End As Seen from Cairo

Friday, October 21, 2011

The headlines in the Cairo press screamed "Gaddafi's Assassination." It was not in glee on the part of the Egyptian printed media. It was in reflection on the end of the life of the Libyan dictator of 42 years who once waged war on Egypt only to be hit back by Egypt's airforce as ordered by Sadat.

Then there was this quiet satisfaction in the Egyptian street as it compared between how Gaddafi was pummelled then shot to death, and how Mubarak was being wheeled on his sick bed into open court in Cairo with his doctors and lawyers in tow.

Within this spectrum of emotions and soul searching, there was no mistaking Egypt's sigh of relief that Gaddafi's end meant a new beginning in neighboring Libya. There was no dancing in Egypt's streets, yet there was quiet humming of glee for the Libyan masses erupting in song and dance.

The editorials celebrated what promises to be a new beginning in Tripoli. The theme in the main editorial in the Egyptian Government newspaper Al-Ahram (established in Cairo by the Takla Christian Lebanese brothers 136 years ago), in its issue number 45609 summed up Egypt's mood.

"Yesterday, the curtain fell on the Gaddafi era, in order for a new age to begin. This beginning is not for Libya only, but for the entire Arab region, and perhaps for the world. It was an era marked by dictatorship, oppression, suppression of the freedoms and rights of the citizen, and murder. The Gaddafi period was characterized by disrespect for the people's destiny, by frittering away national wealth in order to feed personal ambitions and external whims. In this, the Libyans, the legitimate owners of that wealth, were permitted no say, no opinion, not even a whisper.

More than any other leader in this area , Gaddafi personified this dark period in Arab history. Since his assumption of power in 1969, he pushed his behavioral antics to grotesque limits... Those antics included his strange theories which he posted in his book "The Green Book" in which he developed a philosophy of governance all his own. Through that philosophy, he made the Libyan people his field of experimentation from populism (jamahiriya), to socialism (ishtirakia), to rule by "popular committees."

Gaddafi swung wildly from the concept of Arab unity, to divorcing that concept in preference for African unity. Throughout his reign, he tried to impose his views on his people and their neighbors. This he did through money, weapons, terror and intervention in their internal affairs. This led him to wars with Chad, Sudan, Egypt and Tunisia.

His mischief had an overreach beyond North Africa. He got involved in conflicts in Northern Ireland and in Latin America. Then abruptly, in later years, he tried reconciliation (after Lockerbie) with the West, by giving up his nuclear material and allowing western companies to pursue investments in Libya.

But the Arab Spring, armed and determined, flared up, ending his reign -a reign which was based on family and tribe, through he clothed it, once in nationalism, then in socialism.

No doubt, the post-Gaddafi world will be both different and better. It is our fervent hope that, in its new era, Libya shall open a new page based on democracy, respect for human rights, and responsiveness to the Libyan people's aspirations.

During the long Gaddafi period, these were all values which were nowhere to be found. "

A Tahrir Refrain: "Raise Your Head Up High, You are a Copt"

Friday, October 28, 2011

When the Egyptian masses rose up on January 25, 2011 to throw off the yoke of the Mubarak regime, they raised in Tahrir both the crescent and the cross. That is Egypt at its best: inclusive, cosmopolitan, moderate and diverse. As of that date, all of its population (90 million - one fourth of all Arabs) aspired to a bright tomorrow, with Egypt, both of its Muslims and Christians (Copts) charging forward, leading the region towards democracy, development, and, above all, dignity.

Then came the Maspero massacre of Wednesday, October 19 (see our earlier blogs). Thousands of Copts clashed with security and armed forces guarding the Egyptian TV building in the area of Cairo called Maspero. Several from both sides; more were wounded. It was the Egyptian Revolution darkest hour. Egyptian blood on Egyptian hands. Some expatriate Copts even called for internationalization of "the Coptic question." The unthinkable became almost thinkable. It was a jolt which caused Egyptian leadership and institution to spring into action.

Consequently on October 24, Field Marshal Hussein Tantawi, the de facto and interim Egyptian Head of State, met with Pope Shenouda, the Pope of Alexandria, and the head of the Coptic Church -one of the most learned personalities whom I know of in that part of the world. The agenda carried an assuring message: Egyptian Copts and Egyptian Muslims are one and inseparable body politic.

At that historic meeting, there were issues to be discussed, solutions to be put in place, national harmony to be strengthened. The purpose was to emphasize that Egypt's national interest was supreme, and that Coptic grievances which resulted in the Maspero massacre needed to be addressed. On top of the list was, not only to investigate the events and the wrong-doers of the Maspero massacre. But also to deal with the perennial delays in the construction and refurbishing of Coptic churches all over Egypt. The triggering events which flared as a result of the attack on the Marynab Church in Egypt's deep south had to be addressed.

For his part, Pope Shenouda was eloquently reassuring at this meeting with Tantawi. The spirit of amity and peace should always govern all dealings between Egypt's Muslims and Copts. They are, as the Pope of Alexandria said, the sons and daughters of the Egyptian homeland. Sedition was a danger that should not confront Egypt.

The following day, the Egyptian Cabinet considered a new law governing the zoning, construction and authorization of all places of worship, both churches and mosques all over Egypt. This law was the product of committees on social justice and legislation, and of "the Family's House" (Bait Al-Aaelah) -an interdenominational institution created by the Grand Imam, Dr. Al-Tayeb, of Al-Azhar, the citadel of Islamic learning located in Cairo for more than one-thousand years.

How is this reflected within the Egyptian community in the U.S.? In the monthly newspaper entitled Voice of Belady (My Country's Voice), its editor-in-chief, Mr. Mouhib Ghabbour (a distinguished Copt) celebrate with members of the New Jersey Egyptian community, both the end of Ramadan (the Muslim month of fasting) (in August) and the feast of the Virgin Mary in one sitting. The motto of his more than 70 pages in both English and Arabic is fascinating. It reads:"Separation Between Religion and State -No Turban Is Above the Law." AMEN, Mr. Ghabbour!!

These expatriates have now been given a potential voice in running the new Egypt. By a decision of the Egyptian Court of Administrative Justice in Cairo, the Government were instructed to allow Egyptians abroad to vote at their respective Consulates and Embassies.

Said Al-Azhar, through its delegation to Pope Shenouda on October 25: "The Maspero event shall be the last of Egypt's deep sorrows."

7 NOVEMBER 2011

When the Headlines in Egypt's Press Tell the Whole Story

Friday, November 4, 2011

The press in Egypt after Mubarak had found its mouth: loud, uninhibited, and very personal.

The news of the forthcoming elections for Parliament later this month are dominating. Why not? There are more than 38 parties in competition and the cartoons humorously reflect that intra-Egyptian race for a piece of the pie very cogently.

In the newspaper Al-Gomhouriya (the Republic), the distinguished cartoonist Ahmad Toughan has an interesting caricature. A candidate in these highly-contested elections comes by accident upon a poorly-dressed man, thrusts his hand forward in a forced hand shake and exclaims to the bewildered man: **"Where have you been, Man!! I have missed you for a long time! In fact I am running for a parliamentary seat - ONLY FOR YOU!!"**

But electioneering by the parties spawned of the Muslim Brotherhood, and the more to the religious right, the Salafis (see our earlier blogs) issue an assuring election devise: No banners carrying religious symbols. The Muslim Brotherhood-oriented political party "Al-Horriyah Wa Al-Adaalah" (Freedom and Justice) carries in its newspaper an interview with the Secretary-General of that party, Mr. Saad Al-Katatni states:

"The Democratic Coalition For Egypt shall enter this race under the motto, *We Bring Good Things to Egypt*. This indicates the great aspirations of the parties in that Coalition for serving Egypt and its public during this important juncture in Egypt's modern history."

What about the motto **"Islam is the Solution"**?, asked the interviewer of Mr. Al-Katatni. His response was:

"This is the historic motto of the Muslim Brotherhood which established the party and which it uses since 1987. But the party will not use this motto because it does not wish to impose it on its partners in that Coalition. But the party may use it in future elections."

Not all of the headlines in the Egyptian press were devoted to those historic elections for the House of Representatives.

Some of those headlines dealt with the attendance of Field Marshal Tantawi, Chairman of the Supreme Council of the Armed Forces and the de facto President of Egypt during this eventful transition, at the naval exercises conducted by Egypt in its territorial waters.

Other headlines featured the news of the meeting held by the Prime Minister, Dr. Essam Sharaf, with the President of the Supreme Judicial Council, Counsellor Hossam Al-Gheriani, and the President of the "Judicial Club," Counsellor Ahmad El-Zind to solve the problem of the Egyptian Bar. The problem revolves around what constituted disruptive behavior of some Egyptian lawyers in the Courts. The Egyptian Bar, located in Cairo, is a member of the Federation of the Arab Bar Associations, also located in Cairo. The lawyers are claiming immunity from what they regard as harassment by judges presiding over court litigation These issues are not yet resolved.

While on judicial matters in the new Egypt, the headlines also dealt with the appearance by deposed President Mubarak and his two sons, Alaa and Jamal, together with former Minister of the Interior, Mr. Habib Al-Adli and others, before the Criminal Court. The trial has been instituted on the basis of charges of corruption, abuse of authority, theft of public funds, illegal ownership of land and real estate, torture and the killing of peaceful demonstrators by government security forces, during the historic uprising in Tahrir and elsewhere in Egypt which began on January 25, 2011.

The fear from an unwanted return to military rule or domination of the politics of post-Mubarak Egypt was also palpable in these headlines. The newspaper Al-Masri Al-Yom (The Egyptian Today) had an article raising dark suspicions regarding the ultimate intentions of Egypt's Supreme Military Council. It said in part:

"The Council is an integral part of a regime which lost only its head, but not its body."

The article written by a woman journalist, Sahar Al-Jaarah, opined that:

"The continuity of our revolution is our biggest cause for faith in the future. This is *Revolution Until Victory*. There are no other alternatives."

In a Slow Motion Towards a Constitution

Friday, November 11, 2011

In his seminal book in Arabic, The Future of Culture in Egypt, the great Egyptian philosopher, Dr. Taha Hussein wrote: "Power derives from the people. Thatpower does not issue from either ignorance, or distraction, or stupidity. Nor does it issue form submissiveness, nor servitude." (p.94)

He was blind, a graduate of Al-Azhar University (The Glorious), educated also in France, married a French woman, and became in the late 1940s Egypt's Minister of Education. Above all, he was the father of free education including university education, as he espoused the principle that constitutionalism and democracy needed for their protection an educated public. Taha Hussein saw clearly, though he was blinded since age 5, the indelible link between liberty and education.

Now with the resurrection of democracy in Egypt from the ashes of military rule from 1952 to 2011 (Mubarak was made to abdicate power on February 11, a mere 9 months ago today), Egypt, in a slow motion, is inching towards the drafting of a new constitution for a secular Egypt.

In spite of that slow motion, the excitement is palpable. On November 10, I received the following email: *"Dear All: I am very proud today that I was able to register myself to vote abroad in the upcoming elections. The process was very easy and did not take more than 5 minutes. Hurry up!!"* That email was sent to many persons including myself by a young physician (radiologist), Dr. Osama Raslan, a friend and the son of friends. It was in reference to the parliamentary elections which will take place later this month in all the 27 provinces of Egypt. In these elections, 38 political parties are competing in a broad spectrum from liberals to Islamists emerging from the suppression of military rule. And what a rainbow of diversity!!

What is emblematic about that forward motion, from parliamentary election, to a constituent assembly, to drafting the new constitution for post-Mubarak Egypt is that the present Cabinet of Egypt includes a Deputy Prime Minister, Dr. Aly Al-Salami. His portfolio is entitled **"Democratic Change and Political Development."** In his attempt to convene a conference of all the parties competing in the upcoming parliamentary elections, the Deputy Prime Minister was rebuffed by the "Freedom and Justice Party" which has spun off the Muslim Brotherhood. Said the Secretary-General of the FJP, Dr. Saad El-Katatni that all Islamist-oriented parties (which include 4 parties made up of Salafis -the farthest to the right of those Islamic groupings):

"This is an attempt to confuse public opinion by busying it with principles intended to freeze the upcoming drafting of the new constitution within the framework of those principles. It is a sabotage of the popular will."

The secular parties disagreed. They were led by the historic party Al-Wafd (akin to the Congress Party of India) which hoisted the banner of Egypt's independence from Great Britain in the Revolution of 1919. They said that the proposed conference will have before it no less than eight documents dealing with "Constitutional Guidelines." The sources of these documents are diverse, including one authored, for debate, by the Supreme Military Council which governs Egypt at present on an interim basis.

The essential debate is driven by the fear of sabotaging the march of the new Egypt towards democracy, dignity and development (the 3 Ds). Thus the opposition to those constitutional guidelines can be seen from the lense of suspicion of authority engrained in the public psyche over more than half a century of army rule. The term "guidelines" was read "trusteeship."

Egypt's road map towards constitutionalism have these road signs: from parliamentary elections this November; to a new Parliament; to the selection by the new House of Representatives (Majlis Al-Shaab: the People's House) of a hundred "personalities" forming the Constituent Assembly; to the drafting within 6 months from the date of convening the Constituent Assembly of the new post-Mubarak constitution; to a plebiscite to be held within 15 days of completion of that draft on a consensual basis for its approval; then finally to the promulgation of the new constitution.

Against this background, the voice of secular Egypt was raised by one of the new parties "Al-Messriyoun Al-Ahrar -the Free Egyptians" established by Naguib Saweeris, a prominent Copt.

A member of the Political Bureau of the AA, Dr. Muhammad Hamid declared:*"There is fear from any form of control or domination by the extreme religious right over the Constituent Assembly!!"* Then in support of the preparation of guidelines for that Assembly as of now, Dr. Hamid added: *"We need a constitution which provides for a secular State, for the protection of civil rights and liberties including the protection of minorities, and for principles reflecting a broad consensus."*

STAY TUNED!! WATCH FOR THE ACCELERATION OF THAT SLOW MOTION

The Road to the Future Runs Through Reconciliation

Friday, November 18, 2011

In Cairo, the Council of State adopted earlier this month a historic judicial ruling. It stated that former members of the now defunct Democratic National Party (DNC) (the one party which ran Egypt under Mubarak) were eligible to compete as independents or members of newly-formed parties in the parliamentary elections to be held later this November.

The ruling signaled that the Egyptian Revolution, in spite of anxiety about the future role of the SCAF (the Supreme Council of the Armed Forces) in Egypt's governance, is shunning revenge. It was a declaration of revolutionary modernity whereby the Tahrir uprising is seeking to be inclusive of all Egyptians. What added to the significance of the action taken by the Council of State is that its ruling overturned a prior judgment by a lower court in Mansoura (the Delta, west of the Suez Canal) which banned all those who belonged to the DNC from all forms of political participation. The lower court has reasoned that the DNC, having been the tool of "political corruption" (i.e. dictatorship) under the Mubarak regime, all of those who carried its membership card were culpable.

It is to be noted here that one of the first acts of the January 25 revolutionaries was to burn to the ground the headquarters of the DNC, a magnificent building overlooking the Nile. With that building went the hypocritical sign on it that declared to all Egyptians, **"We Are for You."** Interpretation by the Egyptian masses: **"They Are Not for Us."**

The Deputy President of the Council of State, Dr. Mahmoud El-Attaar, in explaining the legal underpinning of that historic act of national reconciliation referred to an earlier decision by Egypt's High Constitutional Court issued on June 1, 1986.

In that decision the Constitutional Court nullified the constitutionality of an earlier law adopted in 1978 through a plebiscite declaring all those who belonged to any political party prior to the 1952 Revolution (the Nasser Coup d'etat) are disenfranchised. The reasoning for the 1978 law was the same as the reasoning for the ruling of the lower court (in Mansoura) which was stricken out of the books by the Council of State in November 2011, namely: **corrupting political life**.

But the giants of the Egyptian judiciary and the great judicial publicists like the late Dr. Waheed Raafat and the late Dr. Farouk Abdel-Barr, who belonged to the school of our beloved and departed Dr. Al-Sanhouri objected to the 1978 law, disregarding the results of that plebiscite as pure dictatorial manipulation of the popular will.

The line of Egyptian judicial continuum from nullifying the law of 1978 to striking down the ruling of a lower court in Mansoura was as follows: **"These laws deprive Egyptian citizens from exercising their civil and political rights under the Constitution."** It went on to say in the words of Counselor Mahmoud El-Attaar: **"That deprivation is very broad in nature, and is based not on specific inculpation of political corruption, but on theory and suspicion not anchored in a specific legal provision."**

Nothing could explain the wrongful disenfranchising of a broad sector of Egyptian society under the recently-abrogated ruling, like providing the case of one member of the now dissolved Egyptian Parliament. It is the case of House member Alaa Makady, Number 333, of Samalloot, province of El-Minya, in upper Egypt, and one of our Regional Representatives of SUNSGLOW - Global Training in the Rule of Law.

Mr. Makady had occupied that parliamentary seat from 2005 to 2010 succeeding to a long line of the Makady family who were always voted in by the public to that seat since 1958. The Makadys are a proud clan which played throughout modern Egyptian history a critical role in the independence of Egypt from Great Britain and in the development of economic, political, and social life in that part of the great southern Egypt, called Al-Ssaeed. I have personally witnessed the results of their charitable contributions to the poor in their area of the Province of El-Minya, and their incessant work for interfaith harmony between Muslims and Christians/(Coptic) in southern Egypt.

The Makadys role in Muslim/Coptic harmony has no clear parallel in the Nile Delta (Northern or Lower Egypt) for one simple reason. Al-Ssaeed works on the basis of alternative dispute resolution (ADR) which we, as law professors in America, teach in law schools. Upper Egypt acts on Coptic-Muslim disputes, which usually implicate land boundaries rather than religion, on the basis of inter-clan conciliation. The Nile Delta is not so deeply engaged in that quick dispute resolution mechanism which costs very little and lasts for generations. I have personally made presentations before the Makady - created "The National Society for Human Rights" where Coptic priests sat in large numbers, next to Muslim Sheikhs, as brothers.

Alaa Makady won his family seat in 2005 not as a DNC member, but as an independent. So how can he be prevented from exercising his civil and political rights only because he sat in a parliament, now dissolved, which was dominated by the DNC. I asked Alaa by phone: "Are you now going to run as an independent?" His answer was a "No" with a hearty El-Minya/Samalloot laughter of satisfaction!!

In Egypt, Is There a Revolution II?

Saturday, November 26, 2011

Yes. The volcanoes in Tahrir and elsewhere have erupted again. And with clashes came casualties. The scenes give the impression that the January 25 Revolution has not yet spent itself. But why?

The only clear answer which may not be the only answer is that "the Mother of the Arab Spring" is weary of the intentions of the SCAF (the Supreme Council of the Armed Forces). Having lived under a military dictatorship since July 23, 1952, the 90-million strong Egyptians are trying to show the SCAF the exit door. They are hungry for the pre-1952 Egypt: a multi-party democracy which was anchored in the 1923 Constitution, but this time without the King.

But the SCAF has not said that it wants to stay beyond the elections, perhaps in 2013, of a President. What seems to have caused the eruption is the ambiguity of the SCAF declarations. That ambiguity has expressed its content in rumors. It is well known that in the absence of credible information, resulting from dictatorship, rumors acquire the force of established facts.

Other factors have compounded the dangers of the November 18 eruptions or Revolution II: the hesitant decision-making by the civilian government of Dr. Essam Sharaf, whose resignation might become a reality. The populace accuses it of being a rubber stamp for the SCAF. Though the Sharaf Cabinet includes a Minister for Democratic transformation, Dr. Aly El-Salamy, the march towards the promised land of democracy looks to the anxious public as moving at snail's pace.

On top of that, one finds a genuine apprehension of the emergence of the new Egypt as a religious entity. Though the Egyptians, whether Muslims or Copts, are by nature a religious people (monotheism began in Egypt under Akhenaton thousands of years ago), there is fear of the eventual assumption by the so-called "Islamists" of power through the upcoming elections. Both the Copts and the liberal parties are genuinely concerned about this eventuality. Such a development would also be abhorrent to women who have reasserted their role, through the Arab Spring, in Egyptian civil society.

It should be also noted that Al-Azhar (the Glorious) has asserted in its document of August 17, drafted by both Muslim and Coptic leaders, that "Islam does not recognize State based on religion." But such assurances have been overwhelmed by yet other immediate concerns, namely, the role of the military in the Egypt of the future.

Suspicion of the SCAF, whether rightly or wrongly, is rooted in an article in what is now called "The Declaration of Principles of the Constitution of Modern Egypt." That article, "Article 9" states among other things that: *"... The Armed Forces have a special status and have their own detailed concerns which relate to national security, and which have to be taken into account when considering their technical matters and budget... The Armed Forces shall have their Supreme Council which is charged with the exclusive responsibility of considering all their concerns. The views of that Supreme Council shall be sought in all legislation affecting the Armed Forces before the promulgation of such legislation..."*

Article 9, therefore, looks to the millions in Tahrir and elsewhere in Egypt, as creating an exceptional status for the Armed Forces by putting them either above civilian authority or parallel to that authority. Democratic Egypt rejects such interpretation although the document containing it says that these articles are only "Constitutional Guidelines." This is again another cause for concern agitating the masses which call for the establishment of a Constituent Assembly after the parliamentary elections. The task of the Constituent Assembly is the drafting of a new Constitution. Thus Tahrir asks: "Why have Guidelines at all" to the basic law document which should be left for its elected authors?

There are even further concerns for the Tahrir masses. These masses say: "Why has that Document replaced the term a *secular State* by the term a *democratic State*?"

In the midst of all these ambiguities, arguments, demonstrations and casualties including fatalities, the biggest concern now is: **"In which direction is the Egyptian Revolution --- the Mother of the Arab Spring --- heading??"**

8 DECEMBER 2011

In Cairo Recently, I Was First Unable To Read The Street Signs

Friday, December 30, 2011

For 16 days recently in Cairo, I was unable to read the street signs. I mean the signs of where the Egyptian revolution was heading were confusing. But one thing I was rather sure of: the Revolution which toppled Mubarak on February 11 was succeeded by Revolution II which was pitting the demonstrators of Tahrir against the SCAF (the Supreme Council of the Armed Forces) of Abbasia - also in Cairo.

Revolution I demonstrated in Tahrir; Revolution II demonstrated in Abbasia. Rev. I called on the SCAF to step in the void left by 60 years of dictatorship; Rev. II was asking the SCAF to let go with governing Egypt through a supine Egyptian civil government. While three Prime Ministers (Shafik, then Sharaf, and now Ganzouri) succeeded one another, the SCAF kept on sending mixed signals as to the length of its tenure as the supreme executive and legislature of the land.

From Tahrir, the demonstrators marched on the symbols of Egyptian institutional continuity: the Parliament, and the seat of the Prime Minister and his Cabinet. Nervous about menacing statements by a member of the SCAF regarding the future power of the civilians over the military, they ignited Rev. II to disastrous consequences. Clashes took place; the two sides, civilian and military cum security forces engaged in stone throwing and Molotov cocktail hurling. Causalities resulted on both sides.

While the SCAF tried to calm the situation down, promising handing over of power to a civilian President and government on July 1, 2012, Rev. II was suddenly infiltrated by children of the street who had neither knowledge of nor loyalty to institutional Egypt. In most cases, the street urchins were no older than 15 years of age.

They torched L'INSTITUT which housed Egypt's history and which was established by great French scholars who accompanied Napoleon I when he invaded Egypt in 1798 to cut off Britain's imperial lines to India. More than 200,000 books and rare manuscripts were in grave danger of being forever obliterated by fire, and the world, especially UNESCO, rushed in to reconstruct that historic trove. I saw people weeping in anguish for what happened, and the headlines in the Egyptian press screamed in anguish: "Egypt's Heart is Burning!!"

Prime Minister Ganzouri, a great economist, called on the country to help stamp out the chaos. And the SCAF hurriedly put together a Consultative Council made of 30 civilians to help it, together with the Cabinet, run the country whose January 25 Revolution was supposed to be the model for the Arab Spring. And with a tough-minded new Interior Minister, the call went out that peaceful demonstrations and hooliganism do not mix. Thus the see-saw between peaceful demonstrations and forceful suppression went into high gear.

In spite of all of this uncertainty, and in fact in the midst of, fair and orderly elections for the lower house of Parliament were held. Sixty-seven percent of participation by men and women was recorded. The Islamists who were harvesting close to 50% of the contested seats rushed to assure the Copts, women and the tourists that Egypt shall not be a theocracy, like Iran. The principles of Al-Azhar declared on August 17 to the effect that Islam does not call for a State based on religion were stressed. The elections for the upper house of Parliament, the Shura, were to be held in early Spring and a constituent assembly of 100 was to be established with a membership of 100 to draft the new constitution to be submitted to a national referendum. Subsequently, a President is later to be elected. The Muslim Brotherhood, through its newly-established political party (Freedom and Justice) declared that it shall accept the people's choice for President, even a Copt or a woman.

So by the end of my 16-day stay, I found myself hopeful that Revolution II would not be able to destroy Revolution I. The problem of Revolution II is that its goals remain unclear except for its call for the SCAF to depart immediately. Trying to find some answers while in Cairo from December 6 to December 21, I was advised by my friend Aly to accompany him to Kasr El-Aini Hospital. There the victims of those clashes before the Cabinet's seat lay while being treated by under equipped doctors and nurses. I stopped by 2 beds, on each of which lay a young man in his early 20s. Each one of them had the same name; Nabil. One was a Muslim, the other was a Copt. They had been shot by security forces with live ammunition. I asked each of them: "Why were you demonstrating?" The answer was the same: *"I want to claim Egypt back!!"*

Suddenly, the Cairo street signs began to be clearer.

9 JANUARY - FEBRUARY 2012

The Al-Azhar Freedoms Charter: The Egyptian Magna Carta

Tuesday, January 24, 2012

On January 11, 2012, I heard my fax singing. The sweet song was faxed to me by the Egyptian Council for Foreign Affairs, an NGO which I represent at the U.N. Over the signature of ECFA's Executive Director, Ambassador El-Sayed Amin Shalaby, the covering note stated:

"Knowing of your interest in Al-Azhar and its mission, I am sending to you as attached hereto Al-Azhar's document entitled "The Basic Freedoms Document" which was issued on January 8, 2012. You will realize the importance of the timing of its issuance in view of the increasing apprehension felt in regard to the basic freedoms, particularly religious and cultural freedoms."

Al-Azhar "Freedoms Charter" of January 8, 2012 has built upon the earlier Al-Azhar document of August 17, 2011. Co-signed by Pope Shenoudah, the great Coptic Patriarch and Egyptian Scholar, the January 8 Charter states in its preamble in Arabic:

"Following upon the liberational revolutions from which sprang freedoms and which gave impetus to a comprehensive renaissance amongst all sectors of society, the Egyptians, together with the rest of all Arabs and Muslims look to the Nation's scholars and thinkers to define the relationship between the over-arching principles of the tolerant Islamic Sharia and the bundle of basic rights unanimously recognized by international conventions."

Then the document goes straight on to the definition of the basis within which "the civilisational experience of the Egyptian people" is framed. These are:

"the freedom of opinion and expression, the freedom of scientific research, the freedom of literary and artistic creativity, taking into account the observance of the objectives of Sharia and the recognition of the spirit of modern constitutional legislation, and the requirements of humanitarian and informational progress."

So to what end does all this lead? The Charter's response is:

"...in order to enable the Nation to transition to the establishment of its constitutional structures in peace, moderation, and in a spirit of consensus, moderation and with God's blessings. This is while guarding at all times against the false calls which use as a pretext religious injunctions for doing good and the avoidance of evil. Such a pretext enables these false calls to intervene in public and private freedoms; thus contravening the civilisational and societal development of modern Egypt at the very time when the country needs unity, and a true understanding of moderation in faith. This is the Al-Azhar's religious mission and its responsibility towards society and the homeland."

From thence follow the various freedoms promulgated by that historic document. These, in summary, are:

First: "Freedom of Faith":

Stresses the relationship between freedom of faith and the right to full equality in citizenship for all on the basis of equality. The document refers to the verse in the Quran "no compulsion in faith," and moves on from there to criminalize any aspect of such compulsion or religious discrimination. It calls for the right of everyone to adopt whatever thought they may espouse, without aggressing against society's obligation to protect the sanctity of the three "religions of the Book" (i.e. Judaism, Christianity, and Islam).

It ends with the adage espoused by scholars of ijtihad (the application of reason to faith) and legislation in regard to the "golden rule" which states "if reason and adherence to what is written collide, reason should prevail, and adherence to the written should be reinterpreted."

Second: Freedom of Thought and Expression

The Al-Azhar's Magna Carta describes this freedom as being at the root of all freedoms, as is manifest in the utilization of all means of expression in writing, artistic production and digitized outreach. It incompasses the right to assembly, to the establishment of parties and other civil society organizations, freedom of the printed, audio, visual and digital press as well as access to information necessary for informed consent.

This freedom, the Charter cautions, does not include the right to inciting violence, sectarian discord or radical calls for discrimination. It quotes the maxim of the great historical Muslim scholars which states: "My view is correct but is subject to error, and the opposing view is wrong but is subject to rectification."

Third: The Freedom of Scientific Research:

The Charter describes this freedom as encompassing social, humanitarian, physical and mathematical sciences. It defines this freedom as the engine of the train of human progress. It cites the Quran's emphasis in many of its verses on the need for examination, reflection, extrapolation and analogy in regard to universal and human phenomena.

On these bases, the Document calls for total academic freedom allowing for experimentation, hypotheses and probability. It cites some of the names of the great Muslim scholars such as Al-Razi, Ibn Haitham, and Ibn Al-Nafees who contributed in their time to the advancement of knowledge and science in both East and West.

Fourth: The Freedom of Literary and Artistic Creativity

The Charter ends with this type of freedom as covering all types of literature, poetry, song, drama, narration, theater, personal oral histories, visual arts, cinema, TV, music, together with all derivative types of this freedom.

This freedom, the Charter states, is boundless, and is premised only on the ability of society at any given time to absorb it and assimilate it. It is, the Charter says, the mirror of society's conscience, and its aspiration for a better future.

This equivalent of the Magna Carta was issued a mere 17 days before the first anniversary of the January 25 Revolution – a date which is now celebrated as the new national date of the New Egypt. Thus it is correct to see in the Charter of January 8, 2012 a direct link to the ideological basis of the freedom of faith which is at the heart of global diversity.

Happy Rebirth to Egypt: Her Sphinx is Rising!!

Saturday, February 4, 2012

January 26, 2012

It is one year old, when democracy was reborn in the ten thousand year old country. So on January 25 this year, I could almost see the great sculpture of Mokhtar rising. The sculpture is called "Egypt's Renaissance" (Nahdhat MISR). Sitting majestically against the great dome of Cairo University, the black marble Sphinx is made by the Sculptor to rise with a peasant Egyptian woman placing her gentle hand on the head of the colossal Sphinx. With her lips slightly parted, you can almost hear her whispering to the rising Sphinx, "Rise up. Your awakening is overdue."

And so it was with 10 million Egyptians rising in Tahrir and elsewhere in Egypt, wrapped in the Egyptian tri-colored flag, and shouting on January 25, 2011 "Leave" "IRHAL" to Mubarak. On February 11 of last year, he did, as an Egyptian young woman, holding aloft a crescent and a cross, ecstatically yelling in disbelief, "No More Fear!!!" The reverberations of those chants must have been pleasing to the ears of historic Egypt (the Sphinx), and of modern Egypt (the peasant woman). A phenomenal rebirth of the heart of the Arab homeland has finally happened.

Following Tunisia and Egypt, the Arab Spring sprang to Libya to end another dictatorship of long duration. Poetry is integral to the Arab psyche and oral history. Witness what the great Egyptian poet, Hafez Ibrahim, said in 1912 in his memorable poem regarding Fascist Italy's invasion of Tripoli, now the proud capital of Libya.

The first 2 verses of his 45-verse epic poem is entitled "The War on Tripoli." Translated from Arabic, that great Egyptian nationalist said

"Greed has unmasked the West, O East, rise up and beware of sleep O Sun, carry to everyone,Your rays of peace throughout the East"

Again the great theme of rebirth and renaissance. No more fear!! The first salvo in the rebirth of Egypt as a democratic State was the seating of Parliament. The members came to that historic Chamber, located near Tahrir, through free and fair balloting. The specter of one-party rule has mercifully disappeared. On January 24 of this year, as the members of the lower house of Parliament, both bearded and well-shaven, took their oath of office, the populace outside gave them upon arrival bouquets of flowers. Some of those parliamentarians were even hoisted over the shoulders of the Tahrir young demonstrators. Another graphic symbolism of the New Egypt rising.

Inside the Chamber, discord erupted. No surprise!! At birth, the newly re-discovered democracy was uttering its first cry. Democracy is not a tidy business. Its discord is a signal of vibrancy. January 25 has become the national day of the New Egypt. In this, I could discern another symbolism. On January 26, 1952, the so-called "Free Officers" whose leader was Nasser burned Cairo. It was the spark that ended democracy in Egypt and ushered in the Nasser coup of July 23, 1952. Sixty years later, Tahrir destroyed the 60 year old military dictatorship in Egypt, with the unceremonious toppling of Dictator No. III – Mubarak.

Yet, the Egyptian Revolution, the mightiest uprising of the multi-faceted Arab Spring, is not yet over. That unfinished symphony which is keen on ending the subjugation of Egyptian sovereignty to outside powers still has unfulfilled demands. The major demands of all the Tahrirs in Egypt are:

Ending military rule and the handing over of power from the SCAF (Supreme Council of the Armed Forces) to a civilian government even sooner than the declared date of July 1, 2012;

Speedy trials for Mubarak, his family, and their cohorts;

Full accounting for the martyrdom of nearly 1000 demonstrators, and the injury of thousands;

Acceleration of the rebuilding of the Egyptian economy, now threatened with collapse and reclaiming all public resources to which Mubarak and Company laid false claim;

Speeding of the drafting of the new Egyptian Constitution through a yet to be chosen constituent assembly;

The re-assumption by the police forces of their duties, assuring the safety of the Egyptian street;

Cleansing of the judiciary and other institutions from corruption;

Elimination of military tribunals for the trial of detained civilians.

The list of revolutionary demands goes on and on. In the meantime the SCAF, through Field Marshal Tantawi declared on the first anniversary of the Egyptian Revolution the rescission of emergency laws, except from thuggery (baltagah). *If sculptor Mokhtar was still alive, his Sphinx would have fully risen on its four legs.*

In the Midst of the Arab Spring: A Russian-Chinese Deep Winter

An Occasional Commentary by the Blogger - (Sunday, February 5, 2012)

February 2, 2012

Around the horse shoe table of the UN Security Council, a deep cold winter wind blew from the seats of Russia and China in the face of the Western and Arab representatives attempting to have the Council adopt in early February a resolution to slow Al Assad's killing machine deployed for the past ten months against the Syrian uprising for dignity and democracy. Having closely observed the tumult in Tahrir Square in Cairo since early 2011, there is little doubt in my mind that the winds of the Arab Spring are destined to destroy that family business, the Al-Assad dynasty, which has endured since the early 1970s. The game of the Syrian dictatorship, supported by Iran and politically sustained by strange bed-fellows like Russia and China, is doomed to come to a tragic end. It is only a matter of time.

The fiction openly advanced by Russia at the UN Security Council and elsewhere that "regime change" shall be the result of a resolution demanding that violence against peaceful protesters all over Syria should stop is laughable.

Such a stance ignores several vital facts. Too much blood has already been shed all over Syria, sucking the oxygen out of the lungs of any legitimacy left for the Syrian butcher regime. The regional organization, the League of Arab States, exercising its legitimate role under Chapter 8 of the UN Charter had intervened. It has suspended the offending regime; it has dispatched a monitoring team, though ineffectual, to Syria; it has submitted, through Morocco, a draft resolution for a peaceful transition in Damascus akin to the Yemen model. The Libyan model has very little resemblance, if any, to the Arab League's plan for Syria as it does not provide for military intervention. The Syrian masses are demanding, at the cost of their blood, that Al-Assad should go.

The hypocrisy of the Russian-Chinese position towards the present Syrian civil war is transparent. In essence, both Moscow and Beijing are trying to protect their fire walls against an Arab Spring-like somersaulting over their backyards. These protective walls are built around their own oppressed minorities and hyper-sensitive monolithic regimes. This is not to mention their considerable economic interests, including the sale of armaments and the purchase of energy from Syria.

A so-called regime change in Damascus could beget a regime disarray inside the Russian-Chinese protective walls. While touring Asia, Russia's foreign minister, Sergey V. Lavrov has recently told the Australian Broadcasting Corporation that "we are not friends or allies of President Assad." Really? If so, then who are the beneficiaries of Russia's blatant obstruction at the UN Security Council?

At this very moment the Syrian National Council, Syria's government in Turkish exile, is describing the Moroccan draft resolution before the Security Council as "extremely important." Why? Because as Qatar's Prime Minister told the Security Council on behalf of the Arab League: "The Syrian government failed to make any serious effort to cooperate with us."

Out of this historic re-alignment of friends and alliances resulting from the Arab Spring, through the Syrian upheaval, the West, especially the US, the UK, France and Germany, are occupying the high ground. Russia and China are fast becoming the enemies of the Arab masses which are searching for the three Ds: Dignity, Democracy, and Development. It was historic to see the US and French flags unfurled by the masses in Libyan squares in recognition of the NATO campaign against Qaddafi.

Both Moscow and Beijing, whose icy winds are blanketing the Arab Spring in Syria, seem to ignore the changes in the concept of sovereignty. Since the tragic Holocaust of the late 1930s and 1940s, human rights have steadily grown through international humanitarian intervention. This recent doctrine provides that when a government is killing its people, who are the real sovereign, domestic jurisdiction must give way to international intervention.

This doctrine has in fact trumped Article 2(7) of the UN Charter which has given the State the right to define what domestic jurisdiction, is except where international peace and security are involved. The main purpose of this international law evolution is to save that sovereign from its insane government. The Assad regime continues unabashedly to manifest its insanity. And the League of Arab States, whose present Secretary-General is the venerable jurist, Dr. Nabil al-Araby, a former Justice of the International Court of Justice, is pleading with Moscow and Beijing to heed the calls for mercy from every corner of Syria, across all sectarian divides.

Appeasing Russia and China through watering down the Moroccan draft resolution before the Security Council is not likely to stop the bloodbath caused by Al-Assad dynasty's iron-fisted dictatorship. Better force Russia and China to veto the original Arab League proposals, on which Morocco's draft is based, than to drop references to the urgency of having the Damascus butcher surrender power. A watered-down resolution by the Council may avoid a Russian and a Chinese possible double veto. But it will end the traditional obfuscation by both Moscow and Beijing that the West, not they, are the enemies of liberal democracy.

The exact opposite is true. It is patently ironic to have the Global Times, a Chinese publication, extol the virtues of Russian and Chinese open opposition to democracy. On December 5, 2011, it editorialized that "The West doesn't really have an interest in promoting democracy to the world... Its scheme is to expand its interest hidden behind that process."

A weakened UN Security Council resolution could not fail to provide Al-Assad, supported by the enemies of the Arab Spring, with a renewed license to go on killing the oppressed Syrian masses.

It behooves free Syria and the rest of the Arab world to remember who stood with them in their darkest hour and who stood with their tormentors.

The Domino Theory in the Arab Spring

Saturday, February 18, 2012

On February 11, 2011, Mubarak as the Pharaoh of Egypt, fell. Before that, the former President of Tunisia, Ben Ali, had fled to Saudi Arabia, and the fall of Mubarak was shortly followed by the bloody end of the reign of Qaddafi of Libya. A few weeks ago, the former President of Yemen relinquished power, and now the President of Syria, Bashar Al-Assad is trying, in the most brutal fashion, to destroy his people and his country in a hopeless attempt to stay in power. The Arab Spring is proving the existence of a domino theory which is expected to apply in short order to Bahrain. The rest of the Gulf oil rich countries may soon follow.

We therefore pose the question: What makes the domino theory work its magic in all these Arab countries? The answer lies in monolinguality -the Arabic language and its rich culture, more than in Islam as a faith, or history as a shared tradition. The Arabs adhere either to Islam or Christianity.

The Arabic language, the language of the Quran, in its highest classic form, is the lingua franca of nearly one third of a billion population. Its cadence and rhythm are nearly hypnotic. Its intonation is gripping. Its poetry and prose have galvanized populations from the Atlantic Ocean to the Gulf to rise up in war or to follow the lead even of unworthy tyrants.

It is sung in recitation of the Quran, and through the lovely voices of great singers like Umm Kalthoum and Abdel-Wahhab and Fairooz. It is used in all Arab Courts and from pulpits in mosques and churches. It is even known to Arabic-speaking populations as the "language of the DHADH" - one of the 26 letters of the Arabic alphabet. Like another semetic language, Hebrew, it is written from right to left.

Regarding the origin and dominance of the Arabic language, the great Egyptian philosopher, Taha Hussein has a theory. In his seminal book in Arabic entitled **"About the Pre-Islamic Literature,"** he says: "The Arabian Tribe of Quraish located in the Hedjaz (western Arabian peninsula) possessed a form of Arabic which then became the Classic Arabic Language. Quraish (from which the Prophet Muhammad descended) imposed its Arabic on all other tribes, not by the sword, but through the intersection of mutual relationships, religions, political, economic. Quraish in whose midst Mecca is located also used the Pilgrimage (Al-Hadj) to make its Arabic dominant."

It will be noted that the cry of the millions in Tahrir Square, Egypt, resulting in collapsing the Mubarak regime, was **"The People want the Regime to Go" (Al-Shaab Yorred Issqat Al-Nizam).** For the other Arab revolts that slogan became the equivalent of the Marseillaise to the French Revolution. That unity of language has been at the heart of the domino within the Arab Spring.

An Iraqi celebrated poet, Maaroof Al-Russafi, once wrote (in Arabic) about Arabic as a harmonizing inter-faith factor:

"If we(the Arabs) are one national unity. What does it matter that we adhere to various religions? Our people are bound together through three values: One tongue, various countries and a belief in God."

Al-Russafi penned that poem in the early 20th century. When I asked a modern Iraqi woman, Dr. Hend Shnayen, my Executive Assistant: **"What do you like most in Classic Arabic?"** Without hesitation, she said with deep conviction:**"Its multiplicity of synonyms."**

Absolutely correct!! In Arabic, God (Allah) is known by 99 names. A cry for freedom in the west of the Arab world quickly reverberates in many synonyms throughout that vast area which is now being forever transformed. That domino for dignity works.

As a student of the psychology of education in Egypt in the late 1940's I was offended by a decision taken by a Deputy Minister of Education regarding teachers' salaries. As head of the student teachers union at that time, my criticism of that decision, which denigrated the status of teachers, was swift. During that period, since I wrote songs and poetry, my attack was in poetry which brought about a general strike for higher salaries. The Deputy Minister expelled me from the Teachers Institute, thus causing the prolongation of the strike. That strike was eventually settled by various measures including bringing me back from my village to my seat at the Institute, fully rehabilitated.

Ah!! For the power of classic Arabic which has moved millions to action and caused dictators to disappear!!

Who Are the World Losers In The Arab Spring?: Russia, China, Iran, and Hezbollah

Monday, February 27, 2012

The TELY group (Tunisia, Egypt, Libya and Yemen) have won the first stages in their march towards democracy. Their populations were able to change the regional geostrategic map through toppling their dictators. We are now waiting for Syria and Bahrain to do the same: Syria, through collapsing the fascist system of the Baath party heady by a family business which may be called Al-Assad, Inc. That system was established in 1970 through a bloody coup. Bahrain, through modification of its system of governance, possibly a la Morocco, might enable its Shii majority to participate in a democratic system, while staying safe from the grip of a theocratic Iran.

The Arab Spring is a variety of seasons. Its most ominous chill is not in its variety of directions. It is in its most determined adversaries, namely, Russia, China, Iran, and Hezbollah. We may call this quartet the anti-democratic axis. An axis is a group of partners sharing the same objectives through a variety of methods. An axis is not a community of commonly-accepted values. It is a bundle of sinister objectives pursued through a diversity of national or sectarian policies.

The anti-democratic axis which is standing in the way of the Arab Spring cannot be victorious. The Arabs of Syria and Bahrain, together with the West assisting them in a variety of ways, cannot but ultimately prevail. For the anti-democratic axis is using the kind of obstructionist tools which are hopelessly outdated.

Examples: the double veto by Russia and China prevented the adoption earlier this month by the UN Security Council of a resolution intended to stop the grisly slaughter of protesters by the huge death juggernaut of Bashar Al-Assad. Arms from Russia, acquiescence from China, intervention on behalf of Al-Assad by Iran and Hezbollah are all necessary adjuncts of the most brutal suppression of the Syrians search for freedom. But the external supporters of Al-Assad reign of terror are bound to fail because they are on the wrong side of history.

Both Iran and its Lebanese proxy Hezbollah (the Party of God!!) are military, ideological and logistical supporters of a dying Syrian regime. Neither the Iranian Revolutionary Guard, nor the Iran-Syria mutual defense pact, nor the attacks by Hezbollah operatives on Syrian refugees in Lebanon are a match for the massive march for freedom by millions in Homs, Deraa, Aleppo, Hama, Lathakia, Idlib, Damascus and Ain Al-Zoor. It is a massive wave determined to bring the Assad regime to its pre-destined end. The Syrian National Council has been legitimated by 60 States which met earlier this month in Tunis. Even dictatorship has a shelf-life; the love of liberty is an eternal human quest.

How does the quartet of evil (Russia, China, Iran and Hezbollah) justify its unprincipled stand against the pro-democracy hurricane in the new Middle East? They say that the pro-democracy wave is engineered by both the West, some members of the League of Arabs States, and outside saboteurs and terrorists!! They say that the Libyan model has proven that the West is riding the crest of the Arab Spring to effect regime change. They say that Syrian sovereignty is under attack. They say that only through dialogue could the Syrian mess be taken care of, and that peaceful methods are the only means to reconciliation.

Let us briefly examine the hypocrisy of all these fake arguments. Like a sudden earthquake, the Arab Spring sprang suddenly through years of combustible suppression of dignity and human rights. Its engineers are the millions gathered, largely unarmed to demonstrate against totalitarianism. The West, through legitimation by the League of the Arab States and eventually by the UN Security Council, came to the rescue of Libyans when crazy Qaddafi was on the verge of slaughtering the Libyan masses in Benghazi. Better a change of regime which has lost its legitimacy, than a systemic and prolonged aggression against the principle of "rule by the people for the people", and not by a corrupt dictatorial cabal.

Regarding Syrian sovereignty, the anti-democratic quartet is following its own bankrupt ideology which puts the State ahead of the individual who is the true repositor of sovereignty. And what dialogue are they seeking? What kind of dialogue should we expect between a mass murderer and his Syrian victims?

The hypocrisy of the anti-democratic quartet is manifest: Both Russia and China fear an equivalent of the Arab Spring ripping through their oppressed Muslim and non-Muslim populations. Iran and Hezbollah are blind to the reality of their isolation in a progressive Middle-East.

10   MARCH 2012

The Theory of Conspiracy in Mubarak's Bed

Friday, March 2, 2012

You would never see a defendant being rolled in a cage in a court room in a bed, except in Egypt. Mubarak of Egypt is on trial, and the bed on which he lays has ignited the rumor mill and has helped sustain the theory of conspiracy.

Whenever his name is called by the presiding judge, Mubarak's response "present" is loud and clear. His hair is black - so he must be attended to by someone who dyes his hair - sitting.

According to the theory of conspiracy, Mubarak was advised by SCAF (the Supreme Council of Armed Forces), Egypt's present de facto Government, not to appear in court standing. Lying in bed, it is rumored, is intended to lessen the shock of showing the deposed dictator of Egypt standing in a cage before civilian judges. The bed prop may also generate some sympathy towards him in a public that is traditionally emotional and forgiving to those who have fallen from power. An Arabic proverb sums it all up: **"Respect those who were mighty until their days of power have come to an end."**

The demonstrators of Tahrir have wished to hear Mubarak defending himself against charges of corruption, use of deadly force against peaceful demonstrators, torture, and illegal diversion of public funds and State land. Some of those demonstrators want to see him hang. Their vengefulness is an outcome of thirty years of misrule and suppression.

In this context, the present plans to have Mubarak join his 2 sons and other fallen high-level defendants at the Tora Farm prison is under constant attack. "Why treat Mubarak differently from treating any other common criminal?!"

The rumor mill in Egypt goes on its merry way, conjecturing that may be, when he is not lying in bed, "like a mummy" in court, he plays squash - his most favorite sport. The conspiracy theorists also posit that the trial of this modern day "Pharaoh" is a mere show whose scenario has been written by SCAF. In essence, they are busy spreading the word that even moving their former dictator from "the International Medical Center," where he is pretended to be in intensive care, to the Tora Farm prison where his two sons, together with the rest of Mubarak & Sons, Inc., shall be accompanied by superb amenities.

The appeals motion submitted by the Mubarak defense team to have their client and his two sons released, with all what they have accumulated by way of illegal wealth divested to the State treasury, has been summarily dismissed. Their other motion calling for trying him before a military tribunal (after all, he is a military man who had headed the Egyptian Air Force) was debunked by the Chief of Military Justice, General Adel Al-Morsi. On what grounds? At a press conference held in Cairo on Wednesday, February 29, Al-Morsi declared that "Mubarak does no longer enjoy any military status enabling Military Justice jurisdiction to attach to him." But was not Mubarak the Egyptian Commander in Chief? General Al-Morsi responded brusquely: "that title was merely honorific!!"

The attempts by the Mubarak defense team to separate the most grievous charges against him, namely ordering the killing of 850 demonstrators in January/February 2011, from the lesser charges of corruption, was behind the failed move to have their client appear before a more sympathetic judicial military panel.

No one yet knows what the Mubarak trial will produce by the way of a credible verdict. The SCAF seems to be distancing itself from him, in spite of the narrative of the conspiracy theorists. The Islamists seem to be more concerned with how to develop, through their parliamentary majorities in the two houses of Parliament, their skills to govern an Egypt of a historic diversity. The Tahrir demonstrators are bereft of a coherent ideology, except, at least for now, to get the SCAF back to the barracks. The Government of Dr. Al-Ganzouri is struggling to slow the free fall of the Egyptian economy.

With or without his bed, Mubarak's sympathizers are mainly outside Egypt - in Jordan and the Gulf area. While in Jordan last week before a Jordanian Court to defend an international client, I heard people wondering aloud: "Why subject an 83 year old man, a former president of the most populous Arab State, to those indignities?" The answer lies in the 60 year old history of an Egypt ruled by the iron fist of a brutalizing military dictatorship. That era is over!!

The Salafi With A Bandaged Face

Friday, March 16, 2012

It was 3:00 AM on Wednesday, February 29, 2012, when a man with a long beard, a Salafi member of the newly-elected Egyptian Parliament, walked in a police station to file a criminal complaint. His face was nearly completely bandaged. His report caused that police station to come to full alert. Soon a wide dragnet was in full swing.

A Salafi is supposed to be a Muslim man of God; a strict observant; a traditionalist who claims to live and act as Muslims lived and acted 1400 years ago in Arabia. Salafis are a copy of the Wahabbis in Saudi Arabia. To them, Sharia in its most unevolved interpretation should be the law of the land. They were nurtured by the Mubarak regime to counterpoise the Muslim Brotherhood, which ,by comparison to the Salafis, is a moderate Muslim grouping.

The bandaged face of the complainant conveyed to the police the perpetration of a heinous crime. That Salafi, they were convinced by his story, was a victim of an armed robbery. It was a highway robbery between Cairo and Alexandria. The Salafi alleged that five masked assailants had intercepted his car, beat him up with the butts of their guns, messed up his face, robbed him of 100,000 Egyptian pounds ($16,666) then sped away in their black Cherokee Jeep.

Later the Salafi with that bandaged face repeated his story before TV cameras as his distraught wife looked tearfully on. In the meantime, the Police, fanning out in search of the criminal offenders, brought back to their station 30 black Cherokee Jeeps to investigate the whereabouts of their owners at the purported time of the alleged crime against "a man of God," and a "member of Parliament" to boot.

National security and economic resurgence were the priorities of the new Egypt. Thuggery (baltaga) had to be stopped. The bandaged face was to be the face of strict police reaction to the security deficit of which all Egyptians are complaining.

Suddenly people in white coats were presenting themselves to the police investigators, with shocking evidence. A senior physician explained to the police the reason for the bandages on the face of the Salafi complainant. The physician, through hospital uncontroverted records of his specialized establishment, had earlier that day released the Salafi from hospital following surgery for a nose job!! The bandages were those of the "Salma Hospital for Specialised Surgery." They were not there because of a hate crime against the Salafis.

Soon the Salafi block in the Egyptian Parliament scrambled to save face -a face without bandages. Dismissal from Parliament of that liar with a freshly straightened nose job was the only response from national scandal. The 30 black Cherokee Jeeps and their owners were released; parliamentary immunity was lifted in order to clear the way for the Ministry of Interior to press charges for lying to the authorities; and apologies from the Salafi to his party, his movement, his Parliament, and his nation, followed in succession.

The nose job which had cost that liar eight-thousand Egyptian pounds ($1,333) had a greater cost -the credibility of the Salafi movement. That movement was mercilessly ridiculed at the national level. For that movement, with which the Muslim Brotherhood adamantly refused to be allied, had defied the moderateness of Islam as called for by Al-Azhar, the historic seat of Islamic learning in Cairo for more than one-thousand years.

The national program of the Salafis became a rich subject for cartoonists. Calls by the Salafis from their headquarters in Alexandria, for covering ancient Egyptian monuments with wax, for stopping and teaching of English, and for the full niqab (full face cover) became the subjects of ridicule. "Nose-gate" has just entered the vocabulary of post-Mubarak Egypt.

LIAR LIAR, YOUR PANTS (OR NOSE) ON FIRE!!!

He is Dead But His Crown Shall Always Shine on His Head

Friday, March 23, 2012

This issue is being written on Tuesday, March 20, 2012. At this time, the first day of Spring, an Egyptian military plane was taking off from the Cairo Airport. Its destination is Wadi Al-Natroon, northwest of Cairo. It is carrying the body of a truly historic figure - Pope Shenouda III. Two more military planes were taking off, carrying Coptic Clergy, to the same destination. The Egyptian flags are at half-mast. So is the flag of the League of Arab States. It is a day of national mourning.

All of Egypt was mourning Pope Shenouda, the patriarch of Alexandria, and the spiritual leader of the Coptic Church whose roots are embedded in Egyptian soil since 200 years AD - well before the establishment of the Church in Rome. The Greeks gave Egypt its name, which means the land of the Copts. And the Nile gave it life for thousands of years. Herodotus described Egypt in the most succinct way: "Egypt is the Gift of the Nile."

So was Pope Shenouda, for 40 years, a gift to our world. He stood for tolerance, for the rights of minorities, for compassion towards Christians and Muslims and Jews alike. Through it all, including an internal exile imposed upon him by President Sadat, (Shenouda dared to have truth speak to power) Shenouda stood tall, majestic and smiling.

That historic figure, that fount of learning, that defender of the continuity of Egypt as an undying civilization, was born on August 3, 1923 in Asyut, southern Egypt. His name was Nazeer Gayed who attended Cairo University; then, in 1954, at the age of 31, he became a monk. His ascent to the Papacy was remarkable. He had always combined church learning together with an incredible memory for both Ancient Egyptian history, world politics and world diplomacy. Shenouda's cosmopolitanism was one of his many hall marks.

At the time of the rise in Mubarak's Egypt of the Salafis (Muslims to the extreme right), Pope Shenouda stood shoulder to shoulder with Al-Azhar's

Rectors, especially with the late Sheikh Tantawi who was succeeded by the present Rector, Sheikh El-Taiyeb. Together they faced down sectarian violence. During the Mubarak regime, I saw Shenouda on TV standing up during a State function to cheer a Mubarak historic announcement. January 7, the day when the Copts celebrate Christmas, was declared as a national Egyptian holiday. In response to Shenouda's cheers, Mubarak quipped: "We, Muslims, did not want you to have all the fun by yourselves!!"

People who knew Pope Shenouda at a close range revelled in his wit and self-deprecating jokes. I recall an event at the Egyptian Consulate General in New York City which was held by the then Consul-General, Ambassador Sherif El-Kholy. The occasion was held in honor of Pope Shenouda who visited the US frequently to tend to his flock in North America, and to see his physicians. About a hundred people were invited, most of whom were prominent Copts.

Before the Pope could begin his remarks, the audience, including me appealed to him to delight them with some of his famous jokes. He smiled and responded by a joke about the Egyptians of southern Egypt (Al-Saeed) of whom he was one. He said: "Do you know why God created the southern Egyptians?" We laughed but offered no answer. Shenouda's response which arouse loud laughter: "He created them only to entertain the rest of Egypt!!"

On his last visit to the U.S., the present consul-General of Egypt, Ambassador Youssef Zada, went to the JFK airport to greet him. There was a throng of Egyptian Copts in attendance including a lady who was lavishly dressed in red and black. The Egyptian flag is of 3 colors: red, white and black. As she approached to kiss the Pope's hand, the Patriarch of Alexandria smiled broadly and asked her: "Where is the third color of our flag?" Perplexed, that lady did not respond. As Ambassador Zada later related to me in his offense, the Pope came to her rescue: "The white must be in another place."

Mourning his passing, on behalf of all Muslims, Dr. Ahmed Al-Taiyeb, Al-Azhar's Rector hit the mark in his official eulogy of March 19. The Sorbonne educated Rector said, in part:

Al-Azhar Al-Shareef with all its institutions, including the Supreme Council of Al-Azhar, the Consortium of Islamic Research, the Al-Azhar University and Bait Al-Aailah (the House of the Family, grouping together all creeds) grieve for the passing of this great son

of Egypt. We recall his great national stances, his pure love for Egypt and of all Egyptians, and his unwavering commitment to the establishment of communal harmony and security amongst the sons and daughters of our homeland."

Prophetically, Pope Shenouda was being flown to Wadi Al-Natroon on March 20, the first day of Spring, the season of rebirth.

Though he is dead, Shenouda III shall always have his Papal Crown shine on his head!!!

For the First Time, Egypt Is Choosing its President, So Why Is Egypt Laughing?

Friday, March 30, 2012

The Supreme Commission for Presidential Elections in Egypt issues application forms to Egyptians desiring to run for the highest office of President. It has been swamped by applicants. Its Chairman, Counselor Farouk Sultan, said that they had expected 150 such applicants. Instead, by March 20, the number of applicants had reached 900 and counting.

Looking at the identities of some of the would-be Presidents of the nearly 90 million Egyptians is a Nubian who came from Aswan seeking that high honor. When newsmen asked him what his program for post-Mubarak Egypt might be, his answer was: **"to fight poverty; to ban the national food of Falafel and Foul (beans) and replace it by meat."**

Any Egyptian may ask for a form stipulating the provisions authorizing the entry into the race for the Presidential office. A candidate for that Office, if not sponsored by one of the political parties represented in the new Parliament, must have a certain number of authorized signatures of citizens (30,000 such signatures) from 15 out of the 27 Provinces (Governorates) throughout Egypt. These procedures have created a stampede to collect signatures if party backing is lacking. The form is called "a deputizing form," on which the signer names his or her candidate for President. The stampede, in turn, has led to new forms of corruption. An illiterate woman, while asking for the form at an authorized office, threw it away when told about possible violations leading to a jail term. **"What?"** she screamed. Then went on to say tearfully: **"This was not what we agreed upon with that candidate. I do not need his bags**

of rice and sugar if my support leads me to prison!!!"

In the meantime, another citizen, a male from the Governorate of Giza, South of Cairo, where the Pyramids stand to attest to Egypt's durability, was on his way to jail. That individual entered the offices of the Supreme Commission for Presidential Elections to get the necessary documentation for entering the presidential electoral races. The police immediately placed him under arrest. For in his possession, there was a large amount of drugs, a hashish-derivative called Bango.

Truth be told, not all Egyptians were laughing at this avalanche of high office seekers or publicity seekers. At the entrance of one of the many "forms distribution centers," a taxi driver left his cab running at the curb to voice his indignation at the media. Looking straight at TV cameras which were focusing on the out of ordinary office seekers, he shouted: **"Shame on the Media. You are giving our beloved Egypt a terrible name. You are making of all of us a laughing stock. How can the world believe that great Egypt allows a coffee vendor or a simple laborer to run for President? In America, the limit is only two."** Hey!! Welcome to popular democracy. Love it or leave it!!

So what is behind the nearly one thousand aspirants to the Egyptian Presidency? Oh, yes: there goes the conspiracy theory again. But this time, it is not in Mubarak's bed, as one of our previous blogs had indicated. It is in the now dissolved National Party -the party through which Mubarak had governed Egypt as a security State for 32 years. How does the National Party (Al-Foloul: in Arabic, the Remnants) get involved in this unwieldy Egyptian presidential race? Aha!! The presumed answer was said to have been discovered by Dr. Medhat Khafagi, a candidate for that office. He claims that, **"The Dissolved (in Arabic: "Al-Monhal") -the National Party- is trying to give the glorious January 25 Revolution a bad name!! Therefore the Dissolved pushed the rank and file from the endless corners of Egyptian poverty to run for President including a baker, a hair dresser, and a doorman.!! Even if such unqualified individuals have no chance to be President, the fact of their applying for the job would accomplish the goal of showing the Revolution as mob-oriented!!"**

11   APRIL 2012

Needed in Egypt: A Crash Course in Anger Management

Wednesday, April 11, 2012

In the Constitutional Declaration, an interim legal measure acting as a stop gap pending the drafting of a permanent Constitution for Egypt later this year, there is an important provision for those who are now aspiring to run for president of Egypt. It says that a candidate for the highest office in this important Arab country, must prove that neither he nor she, nor their parents have ever carried a non-Egyptian passport.

This provision is proving very troublesome to two potential presidential candidates whose orientation is Islamic. They are: Hazem Salah Abu Ismail, a Salafi (extreme Islamist) and Muhammad Saleem Al-Awwa. The rumors flooding Egypt now is that the late mother of Abu Ismail had a US passport, and that the father of Al-Awwa was a of Syrian nationality. Oops!!

A flurry of angry responses, for and against, erupted. Abu-Ismail declared that his own group was stabbing him in the back. They were, the would-be candidate charged, a bunch of liars. Only his sister, who resides in America, carries a US passport, he retorted. His late mother, he claimed, had only a green card, and was never a US citizen.

In rebuttal to Abu-Ismail, Sheikh Tarek Youssef, an Imam of a mosque in Brooklyn countered as he shook with anger in an interview with an Egyptian cable channel called Dream. "Abu-Ismail is lying about his mother's nationality. She was an American citizen, thus her son cannot be a candidate for the Egyptian presidency."

At long last, the Supreme Commission for Presidential Elections, stepped in the sea of mutual recrimination. It said that Egypt's Ministries of Foreign Affairs and Interior had been requested to check on the backgrounds of all aspirants to the presidential post. Until those investigations are completed, no one should presume what the results might be.

In the meantime, rumors were flying hard and fast about attempts by the Muslim Brotherhood to have Abu-Ismail cede his campaign in favor of its own would be candidate Khairat El-Shatter, a millionaire businessman. The price for Abu-Ismail's withdrawal would be a vice-presidential position in an El-Shatter administration. "Absolutely, No," Abu-Ismail's campaign declared. A vice-presidential candidate is not subject to the same restrictions noted above with regard to a non-Egyptian nationality. He ended up being excluded from running for president.

Yet in the first mass rally for El-Shatter, there were voices of support which were drowned by counter voices in opposition. Those opposed to the nominee of the Brotherhood declared on its Facebook page that the nomination of El-Shatter was a disaster. The Muslim Brotherhood, with a 50% of parliamentary seats,**"should not have presented a nominee. It is a dangerous trap!! It is wrong for the Brotherhood to shoulder alone the entire heavy burden of ruling Egypt, by cornering for itself both the legislative powers and presidential power as well. This is a recipe for disaster."**

Let us now turn our attention to the Constituent Assembly of 100 which is charged with the awesome responsibility of drafting a post Mubarak constitution. All eligible voters would say "yea" or "nay" on it in a national referendum whose result would establish a legal baseline for the presidential elections. The Islamists (the Brotherhood and the Salafis) control 70% of seats in the new Parliament.

In a move to deny the Islamists the exercise of those monopolistic powers in the legislature, in the drafting of a Constitution, and in connection with the election of the president, members of the liberal secular parties simply walked away from the Assembly of 100. This put the onus on the Islamist majority to fill that critical gap in order to legitimize the constitutionality of the Assembly of 100.

Feverish attempts at compromise followed: "Please come back. We need you. OK?? The vote in the Assembly shall not be 50% + 1; it shall be 60%. We shall also abide by Al-Azhar declarations about diversity, inclusiveness, and representativeness of the entire rainbow of Egyptian society including the Copts. Would you please come back??" "No!" said the secularists. "Your Assembly has no legitimacy because it does not reflect the shades of the entirety of Egyptian public opinion."

Rage On, Egypt!! Democracy lives on intelligent compromises. So find your way to a middle ground!!

Mirror Mirror on the Wall, Who is the Fairest of Them All?

Wednesday, April 11, 2012

Four front runners competing for the post of President of the largest demographically Arab country: Egypt. The time is short, and the elections are to be held around mid-May. At this time, out of nearly 1000 would be candidates, only four of them are in the lead.

These are: Amr Moussa, former Secretary-General of the League of Arab States; Abdel-Monim Abu-Elfotouh, formerly of the Muslim Brotherhood, now the head of the Freedom and Justice Party of Egypt, with Brotherhood solid connections; Khairat El-Shatter, the economic and financial brain of the Muslim Brotherhood; and Omar Soliman, former head of Intelligence and former Vice-President of Egypt in the days leading to the collapse of the Mubarak regime.

Who is the Fairest of Them All? The mirror on the wall is a bit foggy and this blogger cannot read the tea leaves. Beyond the four front runners named above, there are others who are still in the race, and yet others who are being pushed out of the race. In the first category, the numbers are too many to count; in the second category (the pushed out), there is the Salafi would-be candidate, Abu-Ismail whose credentials were called into question from his late mother's grave (she was a U.S. citizen -a disqualification). In the same category, there is Dr. El-Baradie, former Director-General of the UN-affiliated International Atomic Energy Agency (IAEA) who pushed himself out of the maddening melee.

Had the Revolution of January 25, 2011 been true to itself, Muhammad El-Baradie, a Noble Peace Prize Laureate, should have been declared presidential candidate by acclamation. But like every revolution, with the US Revolution of 1776 against British domination the only exception, the Egyptian Revolution has swallowed up those who planted the first seeds. Thus the first potential leader who, under Mubarak's nose, called for freedom and democracy in the then-dictatorial Egypt, El-Baradie was side-lined. In fact I was afraid that the Mubarak regime might "rub him off," to use the language of the Mafia. Perhaps, his high world-wide visibility saved his life. Charisma, his opponents, especially Amr Moussa, claimed was a Baradie-deficiency; his long career abroad, others alleged, made his connection to a complex Egypt rather weak.

Looking into the magic globe at the four front-runners for candidacy for the top job in Egypt, one can see potential problems overwhelming their election by a clear majority. Amr Moussa had served under Mubarak as a foreign minister. Abdel-Monim Abu-Elfotouh does not have the backing of the Muslim Brotherhood which commands 50% of seats in the new Parliament. El-Shatter's candidacy was like a Johnny-Come-Lately. The Muslim brotherhood hurriedly pushed that candidacy forward, just a few days before the deadline for papers filing was upon them. It was a sudden switch, which began with "no nomination from the Brotherhood for President," to "our concern for Egypt caused us to nominate El-Shatter for president."

As to ideology, Abu-Elfotouh is ideologically to the left of the Brotherhood and is an advocate of diversity. El-Shatter is calling for a modified application of Sharia (Islamic Law). And Oman Soliman seems destined for failure in his bid, having been the face of a brutalizing Egyptian intelligence for most of his tenure under Mubarak. As a military man, a General, he is suspected to have the backing of the SCAF (the Supreme Council of Armed Forces). Yet the SCAF days may come to an end on July 1st of this year.

The mix of presidential aspirants is a bit confusing. The walls of Egypt everywhere is plastered by electioneering ads. In fact the traffic in Cairo is super-snarled because of street closures when a candidate is campaigning. And the Copts, especially after the passing of Pope Shenouda, are guessing at what the future might hold. So are women, together with the creators of Egyptian art and films. Egypt desperately needs tourism and trade.

Who is the fairest of them all? Who knows!!

The only certainty is that neither Amr Moussa, nor El-Shatter nor Abu-Elfotouh nor Soliman was in Tahrir Square on Day One when the Revolution of January 25, 2011 erupted. They seem to have waited to see whether it would topple Mubarak before they decided that the time was ripe to surf the wave to the highest position in the land. Each one of the above-named gentlemen has a revolutionary deficiency.

The young who made that epic Revolution, the first popular one since 1919, seem, at least for now, to have gone under that wave.

In Tahrir: Divided We Stand

Friday, April 27, 2012

There is a fierce battle raging in Egypt in connection with the approaching presidential elections. Battles of this sort need flags, symbols and throaty screams amplified by microphones. There are also signs, photos, music, and speeches in Arabic. This is the way the millions who occupy Tahrir Square in Cairo are pursuing their dreams in post-Mubarak Egypt.

But the ghost of the Mubarak collapsed regime still haunts these diverse factions whose collective dream is to shape the future of Egypt. With the Islamists garnering 70% of the seats in the new Egyptian Parliament, the only power zones left for contention are: the Constituent Assembly of 100 which has yet to take shape before it delves in to the formulation of the new constitution, and the election of a President.

Egypt is today divided over which direction to take: a State with an Islamic orientation, or a state with a secular orientation. There are no model in the Arab/Muslim world to follow. Because of the balance between its ideological/historical forces, the new Egypt can never emerge this summer as another Saudi Arabia (a Wahhabi policed-State). Nor as another Turkey (a State whosesecularity is guaranteed by the armed forces). Nor as another Iran (an Ayatollahs theocracy).

The colors of the various flags in Tahrir reflect that noisy search for road signs in the most populous Arab State, Egypt of 90 million of 350 million Arabs. The green flag represents the Muslim Brotherhood which controls 50% of the seats in the new Parliament; the black flag belongs to the Salafis, the Islamic movement which enjoys 20% of parliamentary seats who look to the Wahhabi failed governance model for guidance; and then the tri-color flag of Egypt, official Egypt, with the yellow eagle (the Quraish falcon) stamped on it to declare that Egypt is an Arab country –The Arab Republic of Egypt.

Missing from the parade of flags is a flag for Al-Azhar, the most moderating Islamic institution in the entire Muslim world of nearly 1.5 billion people, most of whom are non-Arabs. Nor is there a flag with a cross on it, except that of the liberal Wafd party of Saad Zaghbol, Mustapha El-Nahaas, and Makram Obeid (a Copt) who had all passed away from the scene. The Wafd flag which is still raised proudly at their beautiful building in Cairo shows a crescent hugging a cross –a great symbol of an Egypt made up of both Muslims and Coptics.

The ingathering by the millions in Tahrir and other equivalents all over Egypt, including Alexandria and Suez, took place last Friday. They were all united by a fear that the Supreme Council of Armed Forces (the SCAF) whose head is General Tantawi, the de facto Head of State since the removal of Mubarak from power, would overstay its welcome beyond June 30, 2012. "Yasqott Yasqott Hokm El-Askar!!" (Down Down with Military Rule!!) was their unifying chant. Beyond that, their chants reflected the facts in Tahrir today: the Egyptian body politic is divided, fractured, polarized, and confused. At least for the present.

What is all the divisions about? A panel of Egyptian judges, called the Egyptian Election Commission dismissed the applications to run for president of three contenders. These were Omar Soliman, former Intelligence chief under Mubarak, regarded as a symbol of that collapsed security regime; Khairat El-Shater, candidate of the Muslim Brotherhood, as a person who had served time in jail under Mubarak; and Hazem Salah Abu-Ismail, candidate of the Salafi movement, as a person whose mother was an American citizen and thus disallowed from that race by post-Mubarak enactments.

To the Tahrir masses, the motives for those disqualifications by the Election Commission were suspect. The Commission is headed by Judge Farouk Sultan, the head of the Supreme Constitutional Court, the country's highest. He had enjoyed a meteoric rise in the judicial ladder under the

Mubarak regime. Prior to that, he had sat on the military and state security courts, a badge of dishonor in the perception of the new Egypt. As a neutral agent, Judge Sultan's problems were compounded by an allegation leveled against him by another senior judge, Zakaria Abdel-Aziz, a former president of the court of appeals. He called Sultan "a big part" of the former regime. Hence the suspicion that the SCAF was a co-maker of the decisions adopted by the Farouk Sultan's Election Commission.

The divergence of views and suspicions were fueled by the fact that decisions adopted by the Sultan Commission were non-appealable. Who closed the door to such appeals? Article 28 of the Constitutional declaration promulgated by the SCAF after Mubarak's departure, pending the formulation and approval of the new Egyptian Constitution.

Presidential candidates who ostensibly remain approved by the Election Commission number, as of now, between 10 to 13. Leading that pack are: Amr Moussa, former Foreign Minister under Mubarak –a secularist; Abdel Moneim Aboul Fotouh, a liberal Islamist who had split from the Muslim Brotherhood and formed the Freedom and Justice Party; and Hamdeen Sabbahi, a secularist in the mold of the failed pan-Arabism of Gamal Abdel-Nasser who in 1952, led the coup that destroyed Egypt's old traditional multi-party system.

This is the tip of the iceberg (though it hardly ever snows in Egypt, let alone forming icebergs!!). There are 20 parties, movements and coalitions, not counting student, labor, professional, university syndical organizations, and artistic groups.

They all competing to be heard, struggling to be visible, and regularly competing for "OCCUPY TAHRIR SQUARE!!"

12   MAY 2012

Egypt to the Salafis: "YOUR MOMMA!!"

Friday, May 4, 2012

When Mubarak was in power, he feared the counter power of the Muslim Brotherhood. In response to this fear, he, prior to the January 25, 2011, followed the path of his original mentors, Nasser and Sadat. Those military dictators who had shackled Egypt for 60 years had a recipe: fight the Islamists by other Islamists. The Mubarak weapon was pre-ordained: fight the Brotherhood by an extremist Islamic movement called the Salafis.

The term "Salafi" in Arabic means "the return to the age of their co-religionist ancestors, the Islamists of the 7th Century A.D." That return to the Islamic governance of nearly 1980 years ago is ideologically and practically flawed. Islam of the age of the Prophet Muhammad and his four successors (Khalifas) was democratic (based on Shura-consultation). It was based on women integration in decision-making and in other public life aspects. It was also based on treating non-Muslims as equal in rights and obligations ("Lahom Ma Lana wa Alaihom Ma Alaine" – Arabic for: They have the same rights and obligations as us Muslims). It was respectful of art and culture.

How far removed are the present-day Salafis from this formula of what Islamic Law (Sharia) is all about?! Very far to the point of being unrecognizable. Long beards and long worry beads are characteristic of the

Salafis in Egypt of today. In their utterances and practices, they made Islam unrecognizable except for rituals. But Islam is defined, not in the solitary context of rituals. It is defined by the way you treat others, especially the others who happen to be non-Muslims.

The Mubarak Salafi creation, with its base in Alexandria, burst into the open only after the original revolutionaries, gathered by the millions in Tahrir Square and similar squares all over Egypt, got rid of Mubarak. The Salafis felt that it was time to harvest the fruits from the trees of freedoms which they did not plant.

The result has been the establishment of a political party called "Al-Noor" (The Light) which gained 20% of seats in the new Parliament. Those elections were fair and free, and the anti-Salafi forces accepted those results. No problem. Now emerges a problem for the Salafis who, in effect, look for guidance not within cosmopolitan Egypt. They look for it from across the Red Sea – the wabbi police practices of the Arabian Peninsula which at times parallel the extreme Taliban ideology in Afghanistan.

The problem is that the Salafi leader, Hazem Salah Abu-Ismail, wishes to run for the highest post in Egypt in the forthcoming May elections. He was disqualified by the Supreme Elections Commission under laws enacted during the Mubarak regime. These enactments stipulated that an Egyptian presidential candidate must be an Egyptian citizen who neither he/she, nor his parents have ever carried a non-Egyptian passport. Abu-Ismail's Momma, who had passed away, was found to have been an American citizen who in fact had been registered to vote in US elections. Trouble in paradise for Abu-Ismail and his Salafi movement!!

That disqualification was not the only one. It parallels other disqualifications affecting other would-be candidates including Omar Soliman, the former spy-in-chief for Mubarak, and Khairat El-Shater of the Muslim Brotherhood for having served time in jail for political reasons.

Yet the Salafis would not let well enough alone. Reared on the conspiracy theory, and trusting in their throaty numbers, they attempted to besiege the Defense Ministry, where the Supreme Council of Armed Forces (the SCAF) has its headquarters. In very late April, in Cairo, the Salafis rumbled and their adversaries counter-rumbled. The Salafis lost and Abu-Ismail's hopes for the Egyptian presidency evaporated.

Who are the counter-Salafis? Nearly everybody else, including the

Muslim Brotherhood whose public stance is decidedly more moderate. In this, the Brotherhood, especially the Freedom and Justice Party (FJP), is joined by the General Union of Artistic Syndicates (Cinema, Drama and Music) which is assisting the FJP in the quest of Abdel-Monim Abu-Elfoteuh for the presidency.

These anti-Salafi forces have resorted to public demonstrations at the Headquarters of the Court of Cassassian (Naqd) in Cairo (where this blogger conducted hearings five years ago regarding compensation for the estates of the victims of the Egyptair crash of 1999).

Other anti-Salafi responses are taking place in Egypt's public squares and in the secular media. Among those direct and indirect responses are:

Demonstration against Saudi authorities before the Saudi Arabian Embassy in Cairo for having arrested in Jedda an Egyptian activist, Lawyer Ahmed Al-Gizawi, for insulting Saudi Authorities while in Egypt; the Saudi Ambassador to Egypt was recalled by his Government;

The present efforts to exclude the Egyptian Parliament from joining in the drafting of the new Egyptian Constitution;

The formation by Dr. Muhammad El-Baradie, who during the Mubarak dictatorship was the first to call for constitutionalism and democracy, of a new party. His party is devoted to constitutional protections with the predictable name of "The Constitution Party" (Al-Dostour Party);

The defense of Al-Mufti of Egypt, the progressive Sheikh Dr. Aly Jomaa for his religious visit to Al-Aqsa Mosque in Jerusalem. The defenders charge his attackers, especially the Salafi's, of desiring to replace the enlightened Jomaa by a Salafi obscuranist; and

Counter-attacking Abu-Ismail by alleging that he had lied about his credentials when applying to run for president by not revealing his mother's US citizenship.

In effect, the new Egypt is telling the Salafis: "YOUR MOMMA!!"

A Heap of Brotherly Confusion

Friday, May 11, 2012

In Cairo, the underground (the Metro) runs perfectly well. Clean, on time, cheap, non-congested. At the Suez Canal, the southbound and the northbound, between Port Said on the Mediterranean (north) and Suez on the Gulf of Suez (south) runs as a Swiss watch. If these events happen in Egypt as symbols of modernity and connectivity, why does not the revolutionary aftermath run similarly smoothly?

The answer lies in a beautiful quote from *National Geographic* in a recent incisive article headlined **"Egypt in the Moment."** It goes like this: **"Before, there was no dialogue about the future. Now there is one."** Herein lies the brotherly confusion. For the dialogue raised basic questions whose answers lie dormant in the minds of those who toppled Mubarak, as well as of those who rode the crest of the revolutionary success at no cost or at a little cost to themselves. The former group fragmented; the latter group split in caucuses each claiming to be "the guardians of the revolution."

Here we begin with the Supreme Council of the Armed Forces (the SCAF). With no government in place on February 11, 2011, when Mubarak was pushed out of power, the SCAF assumed or was invited to assume power over demographically big and culturally diverse Egypt. Field Marshall Tantawi, from his office at the Ministry of Defense in Abbasiyah, Cairo, became the de facto Head of State. In effect, the SCAF protected the revolution at birth, then, as a unique midwife, took over the role of a stern mother. Tantawi is the face of official Egypt and also its substance.

That role was truly beneficial. It saved Egypt from the calamitous predicament of Syria where civil war is raging in spite of Kofi Annan's understated descriptions. It also provoked endless series of demonstrations in many Tahrir Squares all over Egypt. While in Libya, where the country is bathed in competing city-state militias, Egypt is bathed in competing ideologies, Islamists and secular, and in all kinds of squabbles by professional syndicates and labor unions. All of these forces are demanding instant political and economic solution and benefits.

How about the signal success of holding those fair Parliamentary elections in which a whopping 67% of the electorate, men and women, participated? Here lies the SCAF's boast of its good intentions of moving a complex Egypt toward the promised land of democracy and development. To the anti-SCAF forces which want to force their way, in despite the structures of the provisional constitutional scheme promulgated under Mubarak, the SCAF says: we protected you from our guns; we shall leave on June 30 of this year; our role in protecting Egypt from chaos, after a civilian president is elected this May and a new constitution is drafted and approved in a plebiscite, must continue.

Both the Muslim Brotherhood and the Salafis (no coalition between the two is possible because the Salafis adhere to a literal and unworkable interpretation of the role of Sharia in governance) hold 70% of parliamentary seats. But the weight of secularism in and out of Parliament is crushing the Brotherhood's old motto of "Islam is the Solution."

The Islamists demand of an ouster of the Ganzouri Cabinet of technocrats has been rebuffed by the SCAF and by the secular parties and parliamentarians. The Brotherhood's initial selection of a would-be presidential candidate, Khairat El-Shater, and the Salafi's selection for the same role of Hazem Salah Abu-Ismail were aborted under applicable legal rules. El-Shater had served time in jail under Mubarak's rule; Abu-Ismail's mother was an American citizen, a disqualifier under the rules of that bygone era. In fact, the SCAF bared its teeth by putting down a rowdy demonstration by the Salafis who besieged the Defense Ministry in Abbasiyah in a failed attempt to get their candidate un-disqualified. The SCAF said: "How can an Egyptian attack his/her own Defense Ministry? We are acting on the basis of court decisions, not on the basis of a desire to stay over beyond June 30, 2012." The majority of the populace seems to join the SCAF in support of this argument.

Within a few days from now, and definitely before the end of this May, a new President of Egypt will emerge in spite of the heap of brotherly confusion. The three leading candidates are: Amr Mousa, a secularist; Abdel-Moneim Abu-ElFotouh, formerly one of the brain-trusts of the Muslim Brotherhood; Muhammad Morsi, now the formal candidate of the Muslim Brotherhood; and Hamdain Sabbahi, a Nasserite.

The role of the judiciary has been decisive. Thirteen-thousand judges shall oversee the fairness of that fierce competition for the highest office in Egypt. Fifty-two million Egyptians have the right to vote at twelve-thousand polling stations. Campaign financing is limited to ten-million Egyptian pounds ($1.7 million approximately). Under the leadership of Judge Farouk Sultan, who presides over the Supreme Commission for Presidential Elections, the presidential race is predicted to be fair. It shall also be protected by massive security forces backed up by the SCAF.

By the end of June, the heap of brotherly confusion is expected to gradually evaporate. It shall then be the time for the mighty River Nile to swell in its annual flood season. Then the voice of the late Um Kalthoum, that departed great lady of the Arab song shall ring out again in praise of that mighty river in these words:

"If it was not for the Nile, neither Egypt nor the Sudan would have found their place in human history."

The Cairo Buzz About the Future Prez

Friday, May 18, 2012

By the end of May 24, 2012, Egypt would have chosen, for the first time in its 10,000 years of recorded history, its future President. That historic person could be one of thirteen personalities, each with an electoral symbol. These symbols help guide the nearly 53 million electorate in making that unprecedented choice. There are no elephants among the symbols (elephants inhabit the great Cairo Zoo), nor are there donkeys (in the Arab culture calling someone "a donkey" means "very stupid.")

The symbols for the front runners are "the horse," for Abdel-Moneim Aboul Fotouh (former member of the Muslim Brotherhood); "the sun," for Amr Moussa (former foreign minister under Mubarak); "the scales," meaning justice, for Muhammed Morsi (candidate of the Muslim Brotherhood); and "the falcon," for Hamdain Sabbahi (secular Nasserite). There is little doubt that as of July 1, 2012, the coup perpetrated by Nasser on July 23, 1952, would officially come to an end.

Like in every electoral campaign, electioneering is waged by rallies, debates, demonstrations, TV interviews, songs, jokes, and the flow of money. The Cairo buzz has been focused on the televised debate between Aboul Fotouh (60 years old) and Moussa (75 years old); the former was jailed for a total of 6 years during the Mubarak regime, the latter served Mubarak and his regime in various capacities for many years.

Being the first such debates in the history of the Arab world, the whole region watched that lively spectacle. Aboul Fotouh was attacked by Moussa for having been an Ikhwani (a member of the Muslim Brotherhood); Moussa was hit back for having voted for Mubarak's continuation in office in the fraudulent elections of 2010. Aboul Fotouh retorted by saying "But I was expelled by the Brotherhood for my moderate stances," and Moussa tried to downplay the stigma of voting in support of a dictator by saying: "At that time, the choice was between Mubarak or a worse alternative - Mubarak's son Gamal."

In his 80 page political manifesto, Moussa presents his priorities as would-be President: end of the emergency laws which have lasted since 1954; elimination of illiteracy; acceleration of development; and the attraction of foreign investments.

Aboul Fotouh's focus is on "the average Egyptian citizen, whether Muslim or Christian (Copt); Islamic jurisprudence; rebuilding of a strong Egypt with strong armed forces; and increased funding for public education and public health." The pillars of his platform (he is a Physician) are the safeguarding of the Revolution of January 25, 2011, and the observance of "whatever is good for society as a whole," including the right of a Copt or a woman to run in the future for the post of president of Egypt.

Throughout this presidential campaign which is fast heating, the political jokes are mobilized. Dr. Muhammad Morsi, the candidate of the Muslim Brotherhood is called "the spare tyre." The reason is that when the Brotherhood feared that its chosen candidate, Khairat El-Shater, might be disqualified (for serving a jail sentence of a long duration during the Mubarak regime, they nominated Morsi as an alternative.

Another candidate, General Ahmed Shafeeq, was called "the candy candidate." He had promised to distribute lots of candy to the Tahrir Square demonstrators. And Moussa who declared his candidacy in the midst of a dilapidated section of Cairo to show his determination to abolish poverty, was called "the cigar candidate." Unfortunately for him, he was photographed in the midst of poverty smoking an expensive cigar.

From "the spare tyre," to "the candy candidate," to "the cigar candidate," to ten other candidates, the Cairo Buzz regarding the future Prez makes for a great reality show whose outcome shall define the outcome of the Arab Spring in this pivotal Arab country - Egypt.

13 JUNE 2012

Narrowing the Field of Choice

Friday, June 1, 2012

Voting for a president for the first time in 5000 years, the Egyptians narrowed the field of choice from 12 to 2. The two who are slated for a runoff in June are Dr. Muhammad Morsi of the Muslim Brotherhood and former Air Force General Ahmed Shafik. No choice could be more stark: Between an Islamist of the moderate type, and a military man who had upraided the January 25 revolutionaries as insolent children as they rose against Mubarak.

In effect it is a duel between the Freedom and Justice Party (FJP) and what is perceived as the old order of Mubarak and military rule attempting a comeback. The daily newspaper of Cairo *Al-Akhbar* summed it up: *"It is between a Sheikh and a field marshall."* Each of the two has burst on the national scene with heavy baggage of the past -a contest between the Islamists who are untried in governance, and the old hands (Shafik was the last Prime Minister under Mubarak) who had unfortunately made of Egypt a security State.

In comes the art of compromise to win the hearts and minds of 53 million Egyptians who will have the rare chance of elevating one of these two controversial candidates to the presidency. For Morsi, the assurances of a government of national unity, and a readiness, if elected, to have a prime minister from outside the Muslim Brotherhood. And for Shafik, a renewed commitment to the principles of the January 25 Revolution, a non-reintroduction of the defunct regime, and non-interference in the upcoming criminal trials of Mubarak & Sons.

With the Brotherhood controlling 50% of seats in the new Parliament (the Salafis have 20%, but no coalition is expected to emerge between the moderate Islamists and the Salafis who are regarded as Wahabbi-oriented), the Morsi campaign is busy assuring the country that concentrating power in Parliament together the Presidency would be bad for Egypt. Their declarations focus on the following themes: the Government should reflect the views of all political forces in Egypt; there shall be a presidential advisory group including Copts and other parties representatives with a role in decision-making; and a revolutionary front to confront the remnants of the now-dissolved National Democratic Party of the Mubarak era.

Shafik seems to have a more difficult time assuring the electorate that, as president, he would turn his back completely on the Egypt of Mubarak. His main appeal is that his law and order background would ensure the augmentation of security, nationally and on the street. He cites his experience in executive matters, together with his military background as necessary ingredients for assuring the outside world about the secularity of Egypt and for attracting foreign investments.

Yet attacks on Shafik continue unabated (his campaign, headquarters was recently attacked and was partly damaged by arson.) Some of these attacks take an extreme form such as the claim that Al-Azhar had issued a fatwa (religious advice or edict) that voting for Shafik would be un-Islamic. Al-Azhar, the Cairo-based venerable citadel of Islamic moderation and inclusiveness for more than a 1000 years, quickly denied that news. Beyond these efforts by Morsi and Shafik to attract votes and secure victory later this month in the second and final round of voting, the political scene in Egypt keeps on producing assurances for a future democratic Egypt:

A new charter called **"The Obligation"** or **"The Commitment"**(Al-Aahd) promulgated by the new Egyptian Democratic Party and endorsed by several other political parties, called for the formation of an inclusive presidential group to advise the new president. It also called for the formation of a coalition government of national unity which would include youth, woman and Copts.

Parliament Legislative Committee has approved a draft bill for general amnesty applicable to political malfeasants whose infractions do not rise up to the level of criminal activity.

Seven political groupings in Assiut, Upper Egypt, have decided to boycott the run-off elections. They felt that neither presidential candidate has met their expectations. But the Mofti of Egypt, the progressive Dr. Aly Gomaa, issued an appeal to all Egyptians to vote and to stand behind whoever wins this month.

In the meantime, Mubarak & Sons will be back to the Cairo Criminal Court to face the consequences of their past.

Where are Those Millions of Egyptians Going With The Revolution? So Far Nowhere!!

Friday, June 8, 2012

The Song of Soroor "KHALAS" means two things: "It is over," and "Deliverance." Very appropriate to the revolutionary go-around which has plagued Egypt's march towards a functioning democratic State - toward the Indian model of the Arab world.

What is wrong? Egypt is electing a president whose powers are still written in the sky - non-defined. Why? The permanent Constitution is not yet drafted, let alone approved in a national plebiscite. So, are there any provisional constitutional bases for either of the two run-off candidates for president (Morsi, the Muslim Brotherhood; and Shafik, the last Prime Minister under Mubarak) to operate? Yes: in the revised provisional Constitution promulgated by the Supreme Council of Armed Forces (SCAF).

OK!! So it looks as if the new Parliament, with 50% of the seats held by the Muslim Brotherhood, and 20% of those seats held by the Salafis -the Egyptian version of Wahhabism, together with Morsi, the most likely candidate to become president, might turn Egypt into an Islamist State. Not likely, but possibly.

But why then are we assuming that Shafik, the secular candidate might lose? Well, because several of the candidates who did not make it to the run-off are now throwing their lot with Morsi. While Shafik brandishes the fear from the emergence of an Islamist State, Morsi reminds his supporters of the possibility of a return of the old regime through Shafik.

Consequently, millions of demonstrators poured into Tahrir Square for a variety of reasons. The triggering event was opposition to what the masses considered a light sentence which a judge imposed on Mubarak and his former Interior Minister, El-Adly. The judgement called for a life sentence for both men, but absolved Mubarak's two sons, Gamal and Alaa, and several Interior Ministry top officers of corruption and other charges. Some demonstrators carried nooses to symbolize their demand for tougher sentences including capital punishment. Mubarak, El-Adly and others are accused of direct responsibility or complicity in the killing of more than 800 peaceful demonstrators in Cairo, Alexandria, Suez and other Egyptian cities.

Yet other segments of those demonstrators in Tahrir had different though supplementary agendas, supported by former presidential candidates who were unsuccessful in reaching the run-off echelon. Prominent among those run-off failures are Hamdain Sabbahi, a leftist Nasserite, and Abdel-Moneim Aboul Fotouh, a liberal Islamist. Their call was, and continues to be, to disqualify Shafik, a run-off presidential candidate, on the basis of excluding all those, like Shafik, who served Mubarak in prominent positions.

The Islamist dominated Parliament had adopted a law on political exclusion of all those who symbolized the face of the Mubarak regime. Though the law in theory applies to Shafik, yet he was permitted by the Supreme Presidential Elections Commission, headed by Judge Sultan, to enter the presidential race. To disqualify him after millions, including the majority of Copts who are fearful of an Islamist State, had voted for him, would be tantamount to disfranchising all of those millions. Not only that. Such unheard of action would give Dr. Morsi, the Muslim Brotherhood candidate, an uncontested victory which might sow the seeds of later delegitimation.

Summing up the overall picture of this stuttering revolution, tracing it from its root, it could be said that the constituent assembly of 100 should have been established to draft the permanent constitution well before the presidential elections were held. But now Egypt shall have a president by the end of this month with powers undefined except through make-shift

Constitutional provisions promulgated by SCAF. SCAF is still grappling with the issue of selecting those 100 members of the Constituent Assembly, and Parliament is still considering whether it should get involved in that selection.

By July 1, SCAF is expected to retire from governing, handing over executive powers to a President with ill-defined powers. Stay tuned!!

The Egyptian Revolution: It is Stuttering Not Sputtering

Thursday, June 14, 2012

By this weekend, Egypt, though stuttering, would have elected by popular vote a President. It shall be a historic choice not available to the presumably oldest State on earth for 10,000 years. Whether it shall be Muhammad Morsi of the Muslim Brotherhood or Ahmed Shafik who was the last Prime Minister under Mubarak will determine the course of the Arab Spring well beyond Egypt's borders.

The age-old struggle to determine the identity of Egypt, whether Arab (Muslim or Christian), or Islamic, or Mediterranean (secular and African) is back. With more than 10% of Egyptians being Coptic, the adherents of the first Christian Church, the Church of Alexandria, nervous about the new Parliament with 70% of its seats being occupied by adherents of political Islam, the struggle for Egypt's identity is destined to have international connotations.

As of January 25, 2011 when the flame of the Arab Spring jumping from Tunisia, where it started, to Egypt, Tahrir Square in Cairo hoisted a flag where the Crescent and the Cross embraced. But as the Revolution attained its immediate objective, the toppling of Mubarak which occurred on February 11, 2011, the super-organized Muslim Brotherhood stepped in. The Governance void was filled by the Supreme Council of the Armed Forces (SCAF); a group, less tolerant of diversity, called the Salafis, came in from behind; and more than 36 other movements and political parties, mostly secularists, liberal and Nasserite, kept the revolutionary legitimacy alive through occupying Tahrir Square.

The collapse of the old regime, an extension of 60 years of military dictatorship, brought with its two clear and present dangers: a security void, and an economy in a free fall. Scrambling for a modicum of order, and responding to the demand by millions for a democratic system of government, 70% of 53 million eligible voters cast their ballots in March 2012 for a new bi-cameral Parliament. The two major Islamist parties, the Brotherhood and the Salafis, routed their secular opponents who now hold only 30% of parliamentary seats. Al-Azhar's efforts to moderate that result, through its various declarations for inclusiveness, went largely unheeded.

Looking at the source of legitimacy in the new Egypt, we find multiple and competing sources: for revolutionary legitimacy, we find it in Tahrir Square; for law and order executive governance, we find it in the SCAF; for the people's corporate will, we find it in Parliament; for the interpretation of laws enacted both during and after Mubarak, we find it in the Egyptian judiciary; for a constitutional sanction, we find it, not in a permanent Constitution which is yet to be drafted, but in a patch work of the old Constitution as amended in a plebiscite after January 25, 2011, and promulgated by SCAF. It is in the temporariness of the constitutional design that we find the stuttering voice of the Egyptian Revolution.

The body charged with drafting Egypt's, basic law is not yet set up. Its prospective 100 membership is supposed to reflect all shades of Egyptian public opinion. The role of Parliament , with its present Islamist majority, in the selection of the constituent assembly is the focus of secularist opposition.

The squabbling political parties were brought together by SCAF with a deadline for agreement on the standards for selection. SCAF issued an ultimatum: if you do not agree on those standards, we shall re-promulgate the 1971 Constitution. Agreement was reached, but when Parliament, with its two chambers convened on June 12, twelve parties defected from the consensus on selection standards.

Why the lack of consensus? The secularists felt that the Islamists in Parliament wanted to shape the constituent assembly in its Islamists image. They declared that their withdrawal was due to the absence of a broad agreement guaranteeing that the new constitution, which shall be voted upon after a new President has been chosen, should be **balanced and expressive of all sectors and colors** of the Egyptian rainbow. Even Dr. Muhammad El-Baradei, the first voice to oppose the Mubarak one-man rule, attacked the method of that selection describing it as **the burial of the Egyptian Revolution.**

In the midst of that confusion, Egypt's Supreme Constitutional Court added its own dose: a review of the legitimacy of presidential elections in response to a challenge to Shafik being a run-off candidate. This happened only two days before Egypt votes for selecting either Morsi; the Islamist, or Shafik, the Secularist!!

Coupled with the re-imposition of martial law by SCAF, that Court upheld the results of the run-off between those two personalities. Stuttering goes the Egyptian Revolution forward to anoint a President whose constitutional powers are yet to be written.

Egypt Between the Beards and the Bayonets

Monday, June 25, 2012

No easy choice. For Morsi of the Muslim Brotherhood and Shafik, a general of the old regime, the post of President is a huge prize which each of them is already claiming. But the Supreme Presidential Elections Commission is yet to declare a winner. That Commission, headed by Judge Sultan, who also heads the Supreme Constitutional Court, is still deciding on more than 400 charges of voting irregularities levelled by the two men and their supporters.

In the meantime, the Supreme Council of the Armed Forces (SCAF), the de facto executive of Egypt since the deposing of Mubarak, has dissolved Parliament, reinstated emergency laws, promulgated an interim constitution, decided upon which powers cannot be vested in a new President including civilian oversight over the military, and warned that Tahrir Square cannot be permanently occupied by protesters.

As a result, the expected happened. The Brotherhood demonstrated; the dissolution of Parliament was challenged as illegal; the Constitutional Court was called an instrument of manipulation in the hands of SCAF; the Beads declared that they would surly protect the January 25 Revolution from the Bayonets; and the Bayonets barricaded Parliament pending the holding of new parliamentary elections based on a constitution which is to be drafted by its own chosen 100 member-strong constituent assembly. Add to all of these destabilizing factors the possibility of Mubarak's death in the short term.

The question thus arises: is Egypt hovering on the brink of a civil war? In human affairs, nothing is impossible. But an Egypt plunging into a classic civil war is highly improbable.

The factors militating against that grim prospect are too numerous to count, Foremost among these factors are: orderly governance is an ingrained habit in Egypt for thousands of years; the armed forces are conscripted, representing all of Egypt, with loyalty belonging not to regions but to Egypt as both a homeland and a concept; Egypt's cosmopolitanism is enduring, thanks to the country being at the cross-roads of Europe, Asia and Africa; the recent moves by SCAF (some call it 'the soft coup d'etat') is a reminder to the Muslim Brotherhood that its newly-won freedom could be extinguished and Al-Azher's weight cannot be discounted in keeping the Copts, especially after the passing of the great unifier Pope Shenouda, integrally engaged in Muslim/Christian harmony.

The adage inherited from Pope Shenouda, in whose honor an Egyptian postal stamp has been issued, goes like this: **"Egypt is not a country in which we live. Egypt is a country which lives in us."**

Yes the stalemate resulting from the need to preserve the Revolution and the need to ensure the security of Egypt is very unsettling to millions of Egyptians. Rumors have therefore crowded out credible information. Even the repeated declarations by the SCAF that they are keen on handing over powers to an elected president are met with deep scepticism. The date for the transfer of power to a civilian government is now said to have moved from June 30 to "after the election of a President."

The big question is: would that President be a representative of the Beards or of the Bayonets? The answer shall determine the future of the Arab Spring, not only in Egypt, but also within the Arab homeland.

The cover pages of two Egyptian newspapers reflect the views of the majority of Egyptian masses. The cover of Al-Mossawwar reads: "We shall not be governed by the Supreme Guide (of the Brotherhood). And the cover of Sawt Al-Azhar (the voice of Al-Azhar) declares: "The Al-Azhar Rector says: Egypt is a democratic State: Neither Secular nor Religious. The people need to banish the world 'exclusion.' Women's rights should be observed. Eliminate any difference between a Muslim and a Copt."

14 JULY 2012

The MORSI CODE: Reading the Tea Leaves of the MORSI Presidency

Monday, July 9, 2012

He is a historic figure. Not because of charisma, but because in him Egypt found its first-ever elected President. You may not call him "Abu-Ahmed" (Ahmed's father). Only his wife may be called "Umm Ahmed" (Ahmed's Mother). Their oldest son is called Ahmed. President Muhammad Morsi hails from the Sharkia Province (Governerate). I know the Province well, having myself hailed from there. In Zagazig, its capital, located about 175 miles northeast of Cairo, I was educated till graduation from high school. The large El-Ayouty clan is sprawled over there, especially in a town near Zagazig called Kanayat. Known to all Egyptians for its extreme generosity, it is rumored that when the railroad from Cairo to Ismailia and Suez was built, the villagers of one hamlet invited all the passengers of one train to a meal.

Already there are indications that Morsi, a member of the Muslim Brotherhood and an engineer who received his Ph.D. from California (two of his sons are Americans by birth), will try to assert his presidential powers against the Supreme Council of Armed Forces (SCAF). SCAF has symbolically, on June 30, turned power over to him, but retained residual powers causing the Arab press to call him "fat-free President."

From his early pronouncements, one can read an early Morsi Code. His priorities are the needs of the masses: alleviating traffic congestion in Cairo; subsidizing the price of bread, sugar and cooking oil; alleviating the burdens of life in the slums which have over years of neglect by 60 years of military dictatorship smothered the access points to once beautiful Cairo.

His first meetings as President were with the families of those who lost their lives during the January 25, 2011 revolution; with the Coptic leadership; with the young revolutionaries; with women groups; and with nearly all the leaders of the active political and religious spectrum which has sprung to existence from Tahrir Square. In Tahrir, he took his first oath of office, calling that historic Square the birthplace of legitimacy of people's power.

Morsi is stressing Egypt's respect for international agreements, obviously including the 1979 Treaty of Peace between Egypt and Israel. He is showing strong inclinations toward selecting an independent personality (meaning outside the ranks of the Muslim Brotherhood) for Prime Minister. Two of the Deputies to the President might be a Copt and a woman. The main thrust is towards a government of national unity.

Huge gaps remain unfilled in Egypt's governance. Parliament has been dissolved by a judicial decision enforced by SCAF prior to June 30; the constituent assembly of 100 members has not yet begun its drafting of a constitution for the new Egypt; and elections for the lower chamber of Parliament have not yet been decided upon. It is still unclear whether the dissolution of Parliament applied to both the lower and upper Chambers. President Morsi's powers and prerogatives in this period of constitutional no-man's land are undefined.

In the meantime, there is plenty of symbolism to fill some of these gaps: Moving from a modest apartment to the opulence of Mubarak's palace was jarring, especially for Umm Ahmed; having the Presidential guard standing in the hot summer's sun was ended by Morsi; praying in the palace for security reasons on Fridays, was negated by Morsi in favor of praying at Al-Azhar; taking his second oath of office before the Supreme Constitutional Court was effected, following much debate against it. Those who were against that venue cited that all the judges were Mubarak's appointees. Those who were for it insisted that taking the oath before that Court manifested respect for the law.

The Morsi administration seems to be searching for identity which would not be characterized by Islamism. So far, it seems to be free from the urge for revenge for past oppression. In fact nothing has been said so far in regard to the trials of Mubarak and sons. But a famous Arab poem says: *"The coming days shall reveal to you what your knowledge did not encompass."*

In Egypt, Islamism Comes in Three Flavors

Monday, July 9, 2012

First, there is the Islamism of Al-Azhar: Moderate, inclusive, with legitimacy going back 1050 years ago. That was when the Fatimides, the Shii reign which established Cairo itself, in 975 AD, then built Al-Azhar University. Its scholarship covers Sunni as well as Shii schools of Islamic thought.

Second, there is the Islamism of the Muslim Brotherhood, founded by a charismatic school teacher, Hassan El-Banna, in 1928 in Ismailia on the Suez Canal. Born as a reform movement, it soon spread from Egypt to other Arab countries east of Suez and west of Alexandria. As of 1947, its suppression became a tool by the pre-Nasser and the post-Nasser governments for the maintenance of Egypt as a secular State. Its ideology fluctuated between militancy and moderateness in accommodation of the complex nature of cosmopolitan Egypt.

Third, there is Islamism of the Salafis, who are to the extreme right of the Islamic spectrum in Egypt. For inspiration, they look to Wahhabism in Saudi Arabia. Their rise to notoriety in Egypt could be dated to the early years of the Mubarak regime in the early 1980's. That defunct dictatorship, wishing to keep the Muslim Brotherhood under check, encouraged the rise of the Salafi movement as a counterpoise to the vastly bigger and more articulate Brotherhood.

Thus it could be said that the Salafis constitute the extreme right of Islamism in Egypt, with the Brotherhood occupying a centrist position, and Al-Azhar constituting the most liberal, the most neutral, and the most influential in matters of faith interpretation, as compared to the other two types of Islamism in post-Mubarak Egypt.

When it comes to decision-making in Egypt after the January 25, 2011 Revolution, it could be said that Al-Azhar provided quiet guidance through its Rector, Sheikh Ahmed Al-Taiyeb.

But the Brotherhood, through its recently-formed political party, the Freedom and Justice Party, was able to gain 50% of the seats in the lower house of Parliament. Subsequently it gained the upperhand in the presidential run-off of late May 2012. As a result, its candidate, Dr. Mohamed Morsi became Egypt's President. The Salafis were able to muster enough votes in the Parliamentary election of March 2012 to gain 20% of the seats in the lower house. Now Parliament has been dissolved as a result of a judicial decision enforced by the Supreme Command of the Armed Forces (SCAF).

As of June 30, 2012, the SCAF turned to President Morsi the reigns of government, if not the reigns of actual power. Yet there are indications of gradually clothing President Morsi with specific prerogatives and other symbols of presidential powers. Examples on this trend are multiplying.

The SCAF invited Morsi this month to hand the new graduates of the Naval Academy and the Air Force Academy their commissions upon graduation. Morsi has been left free to select his Prime Minister who is expected not to be from the Brotherhood. He has been able to declare that he intended to have a Copt (Christian) and a woman as two VPs. The Salafi opposition in this regard was to no avail. Even prior to the drafting of a new Constitution, he has decreed the formation of a high commission to investigate and hold accountable those who might be charged with causing the death of nearly 1000 Egyptian demonstrators in various parts of Egypt, as of January 25, 2011.

And if beards have become ID cards for Islamists in Egypt as well as elsewhere, the Court of Administrative Justice has disallowed the freedom of members of the Police force to grow beards as being against regulations.

A presidential decree was also promulgated by Morsi on July 4, 2012 constituting a committee to scrutinize all judgements issued by the military from January 25, 2011 until the SCAF retirement on June 30, 2012 against civilian detainees. The jurisdiction of the Committee, under that presidential decree (Decree No. 5, 2012) also extends to judgments issued by civilian courts against detainees during the same period indicated above. The Committee is required to submit to President Morsi its findings within 2 weeks dating from July 4, 2012.

In a further assertion of his presidential powers, Morsi, in a bold move whose consequences are not yet clear, decreed the convening of the Parliament dissolved by SCAF prior to its retirement on June 30. The move does not seem to be a challenge to the Supreme Constitutional Court which ruled that one-third of Parliamentary seats was bereft of a legal basis. Morsi is now challenging the SCAF interpretation of that judicial decision whereby the entire lower chamber was dissolved.

Commenting on the general trend of the Islamists accommodation of secularism in the new Egypt, Dr. Abdel-Monim Abo-Elfotouh, one of the presidential candidates prior to Morsi's selection, and a former leader within the Muslim Brotherhood declared: "In Egypt, there is now no religious State nor a military State."

It also seems that Tahrir Square is gradually losing its magnetism to the demonstrators following Morsi's taking the oath of office for the first time in the Square. On that occasion, he declared that "Tahrir Square is the source of popular sovereignty, and that sovereignty resides in the Egyptian people."

Now those who want to voice their grievances do not go to Tahrir. They congregate before the Qubba Palace in Cairo, Morsi's official residence, which is the equivalent of the White House in Washington D.C.

From the three flavors of Islamism, emerges a democratic value - FREEDOM OF CHOICE!!

Mirror Mirror on the Wall: WHO IS THE FAIREST OF THEM ALL? The Court, the Palace or the Barracks?

Friday, July 13, 2012

The grade is a passing grade, but there are no flying colors!! The month of June 2012 witnessed three historic events in Cairo:

First: The Supreme Constitutional Court issued a judgment casting constitutional doubts upon the legal basis for electing one-third of the lower house of Parliament. In Egypt there are three high court systems: The Supreme Constitutional is charged with reviewing the constitutionality of laws; the Court of Cassation is the highest court of appeal from judgments rendered by lower courts; and High Administrative Court is a court of appeal from administrative, executive decisions taken by any government administrative authority.

Second: On the basis of the decision of the Supreme Constitutional Court, whose judges are all appointees of the defunct Mubarak regime, the Supreme Council of the Armed Forces (SCAF) dissolved the Islamist-led Parliament. That was before SCAF, as per its prior pledge, surrendered all of its executive powers on June 30 to the newly-elected President, Dr. Muhammad   Morsi.

Third: With the departure of SCAF from governance, which it assumed since the ouster of Mubarak, President Morsi issued a presidential decree calling the dissolved Parliament into session. By that decree, the President, who ran in the May elections as the Muslim Brotherhood candidate, nullified SCAF's order of parliamentary dissolution. Simultaneously, Morsi's decree put the legality of the judgment of the Supreme Constitutional Court in doubt.

So who is the fairest of them all? The Constitutional Court, the presidential decree, or the SCAF order of dissolution? To answer these questions, a million people marched, each to his or her tune; countless constitutional lawyers entered the fray; and writers, most of whom seem to have little training in conflict of laws, penned down long opinions about who is legally right and who is legally wrong; and judges, in a country where the judiciary since the days of the pharaohs are nearly at par with religious authorities, got also in the act.

While the SCAF maintained discreet silence except to admonish that no one was above the law, the Constitutional Court reaffirmed its earlier judgment. But Morsi, in an attempt to soften the blow of his decree, said through a spokesman that his decree is intended to find a legal mechanism for putting the contested judgment into operation.

Responding to the presidential decree, 347 members of the People's Assembly, the lower house convened in their chamber for only 20 minutes, while 161 members did not show up. Gavelling the lower house into session, Dr. El-Katatni, its spokesman/presiding officer/Islamist, the House referred the controversial judgment to the Court of Cassation to determine "the mechanism for implementing the Constitutional Court decision." Then it adjourned, after transferring its legislative powers to Morsi pending Cassation's decision (Egypt's permanent constitution is still being drafted).

The move thus accomplished a number of primary objectives of the Morsi Administration: it bestowed on Morsi temporary legislative authority. A banned House of Representatives cannot legislate while its legitimacy is in doubt. It also manifested at least a pro forma respect for the judiciary and the laws. It reframed the judicial question into one of separation of powers -the Constitutional Court cannot dissolve Parliament, a co-equal branch of government. More importantly it tended to clarify the fog surrounding the decision of the Constitutional Court. The decision did not call for the dissolution of Parliament. It had merely put in question the legality of electing one-third of the membership which had been allocated to individual (non-party affiliated) candidates, a restriction which apparently was not observed by the political parties.

So who is for Morsi's decree and who is against it? Of course, the Islamists (70% of seats -both Brotherhood and Salafis) were supportive. Cassation, they maintained, has jurisdiction over questions of legality of parliamentary representation. Liberals and others derided the reconvening of the House of Representatives asserting that the Constitutional Court decision is final, non-appealable; and that that judgment needs no clarification of implementation mechanism. Amongst them was Dr. Yehia El-Gamal, the former Deputy Prime Minister of Egypt after the fall of Mubarak.

In a colorful interview with one of Egypt's popular TV channels, Dr. El-Gamal, who is considered one of the foremost constitutional lawyers in the Arab world, quipped: "Parliament is dead. Even President Morsi cannot bring the dead back to life!!!"

AL-WASAT (Middle of the Road): Egypt's New Ideology Between Islamism and Cosmopolitanism

Thursday, July 19, 2012

President Morsi seems to have 82 million advisors!! They constitute the entire population of Egypt, as per the recent census. We have here a bit of exaggeration intended to depict the advisories avalanche which continues to swamp the Presidential palace.

There is a historic Arab proverb that says: "The best position is the Middle." This is backed up by a peasant adage which advises the holder of a club to show his non-threatening intentions by "Hold your club from the middle." This preference for the "Middle of the Road" is also reflected religiously in the Quran where, in describing Muslims, it says: **"You are a middle-road nation: _ummattan wasatan._"**

Unfortunately this centrism has been buried under the tsunami of Islamic militancy. Under Islamic Sharia (Law), jihad does not mean aggression. It means either fighting inner negative urges to do bad things, or self-defense when aggressed against territorially. The maniacs who perpetrated 9/11 have been terribly misguided. In Islam, war cannot be for aggression; only for self-defense.

In post-Mubarak Egypt, the forces of 38 organizations, movements, political parties and others are vying for prominence. The spectrum stretches from the Salafis, the extreme Muslim right, to the socialists and Nasserites, on the left. The Muslim Brotherhood had moved inexorably from the right to the center to accommodate Egypt's cosmopolitanism which is watched over by the Supreme Council of the Armed Forces (SCAF).

Handing power over on June 30 to the newly-elected President Mohamed Morsi of the Muslim Brotherhood, does not mean a full isolation of the military from governance. The return to the barracks is so far only symbolic. The Turkish model of the army being the protector of the secularism of the State since 1923, is indelibly imprinted in the minds of SCAF which commands vast human and economic resources. In a recent statement by Field Marshall Tantawi, while ordering disbanding the Islamist-led Parliament, he followed up by saying: **"We shall never allow Egypt to fall in the hands of one faction."** It was a clear signal to the Brotherhood: Don't push us too far!!

Signals pointing to centrism, middle of the road, cosmopolitanism as a guiding principle in post-Mubarak Egypt are multiplying. Here are some of these road signs as gleaned from the Egyptian street and the Arabic-language media.

A new Egyptian party, crystallizing the middle of the road ideology, has been formed. Its name is "AL-WASAT" (Middle of the Road).

Al-Azhar has regained its dynamic role in declaring that moderation is its historic creed. In this case, moderation and inclusiveness go hand in hand. Al-Azhar insists on having the Copts and women play energetic roles in shaping the future of Egypt.

President Morsi referred to the Court of Cassation the SCAF decision to disband the Egyptian Parliament, together with his decree defying that ban. This case of a ban and counter-ban began with a judgment by the Supreme Constitutional Court which cast doubts on the constitutionality of the laws under which Parliament was elected. Legal experts, reflecting the Egyptian mentality of moderation, predicted that Cassation and the Constitutional Courts shall never stand in defiance of one another. These experts reasoned that Morsi's decree is an executive order and, as such, is referable to Cassation, while the Constitutional Court judgment did not call for the dissolution of Parliament.

Only 50% of eligible voters cast their votes in the run-off for the Office of President (Morsi v. Shafik), with Morsi getting slightly more than half of these votes. Absence of a landslide. Thus towing the line in the middle of the road in presiding over Egypt is a natural course of action.

A huge conference on the ideology and the merits of the "Middle of the Road" was held in Cairo where Al-Azhar played a prominent role.

The constituent Assembly which is charged with drafting the Egyptian Constitution is said to be keeping unchanged the text of Article 2 of the 1971 Egyptian Constitution. This article states interalia that the "principles of Sharia are the primary source of legislation." Principles are not legal provisions. They are only guidelines.

The Salafi attempts to make Sharia the only source of legislation have faltered as those attempts were totally rebuffed by the Rector of Al-Azhar, Dr. Ahmed El-Tayib. His declaration was met with enthusiastic approval by both the Muslim Brotherhood, the Copts and women. The first part of that Article reads "Islam is the official religion of the State, and the Arabic language is its official language."

AL-WASAT IS EGYPT'S ROAD TO RECONSTRUCTION AND RECOVERY FROM SIXTY YEARS OF MILITARY DICTATORSHIP WHICH BEGAN ON JULY 23, 1952 BY COLONEL NASSER. THAT

DARK PERIOD IS NOW OVER!!

HERE COMES A LANTERN: Kandeel (means lantern) is now Prime Minister

Friday, July 27, 2012

Dr. Hesham Kandeel is now PM of the new Egypt. Chosen by President Mohamed Morsi for that post, he is a technocrat of 50 years of age. Like Morsi, he is an engineer, with extensive training in the U.S. As promised by Morsi, Kandeel was picked up from outside the ranks of the Muslim Brotherhood.

One of the gravest problems facing Egypt is the possible reduction of its quota from the water of the Nile. That quota was set by a treaty concluded in 1929 when Egypt was a semi-protectorate of Great Britain which had a final say not only in Egypt, but also in the Anglo-Egyptian Sudan.

The Blue Nile runs from Ethiopia through the Sudan causing the great annual flood in Egypt; the White Nile runs from Lake Victoria, Uganda, also through the Sudan, up north. From Khartoum, the Sudan, the two rivers combine in the majestic Nile River which empties in the Mediterranean after leaving its bounty to give life to Egypt. Now 7 African States, which are also Nile reparians, having become independent since the 1960's, demand a revision of that treaty. They aim at benefiting from better quotas of the waters of the mighty Nile. So far Egypt and the Sudan have been reluctant; but their stance cannot possibly trump agreed needs of these sister States for more Nile water for development.

Against this complex watery background, the selection of Dr. Kandeel to lead the first Egyptian Cabinet, following the heady days of the January 25, 2011 revolution, assumes special significance. He has been the Minister of Irrigation and Water Resources in the interim cabinet of Dr. El-Ganzoury. Africa, the NileValley, and infrastructure are expected to become new ministerial portfolios in the about to be announced Kandeel Cabinet.

Comments by politicians, academics and the youth made to various

Arabic language media reflect enthusiasm for the emerging character of the Kandeel Cabinet. Prominent among those are statements made by Dr. Mustafa Elwi, distinguished professor in the Cairo University Faculty of Economics and Political Science.

Dr. Elwi stresses the importance of the technocratic nature of the new Cabinet with ministers chosen, not on the basis of political or party considerations. The main criterion for selection, he pointed out, should be meritocracy which is the only way to lift the new Egypt out of the present primal chaos.

In the same vein, the liberals represented by Al-Wafd party, which is much older than the Muslim Brotherhood, gave an unqualified support to a Cabinet of technocrats. In this respect, Al-Wafd party expressed its good wishes to Kandeel whose Cabinet is expected to include at least one Coptic minister, the present Minister of Tourism, Munir Fakhr El-Din, a member of the Wafd.

The burdens of the new Cabinet, which is expected to include a broad spectrum of a variety of Egyptian parties, forces, and organizations, cannot be underestimated. Its most pressing problems are the economy and the restoration of tranquility and peace to the Egyptian street.

As to the issue of relations with the Supreme Council of the Armed Forces (SCAF), an active process of dialogue and consultation is afoot since June 30. That is the date when SCAF handed most of the reigns of power to the newly-elected President of Egypt, Dr. Morsi. Here the main issues of these consultations between the civilian administration and the SCAF are the selection of the Minister of Defense, the degree of scrutiny over the military budget, the SCAF's concern for the balance of powers between the three branches of government, and the continued secularity of the new Egypt.

A few hours from the posting of this blog, the new Cabinet of Kandeel would have taken the oath of office before President Morsi. Following that historic event, a new Presidential Advisory Council would also be declared. It is expected to include a leading Coptic political thinker, Samir Morkos, in a newly created position of decision-making, called Assistant President.

The new Egypt is finally taking shape. A Kandeel (a lantern) is throwing some light into the fog which has enveloped the country since January 25, 2011. Said Prime Minister Kandeel (not Kandil): **"My Cabinet shall be an integrated team, and shall include at least one woman. The new ministerial portfolio**

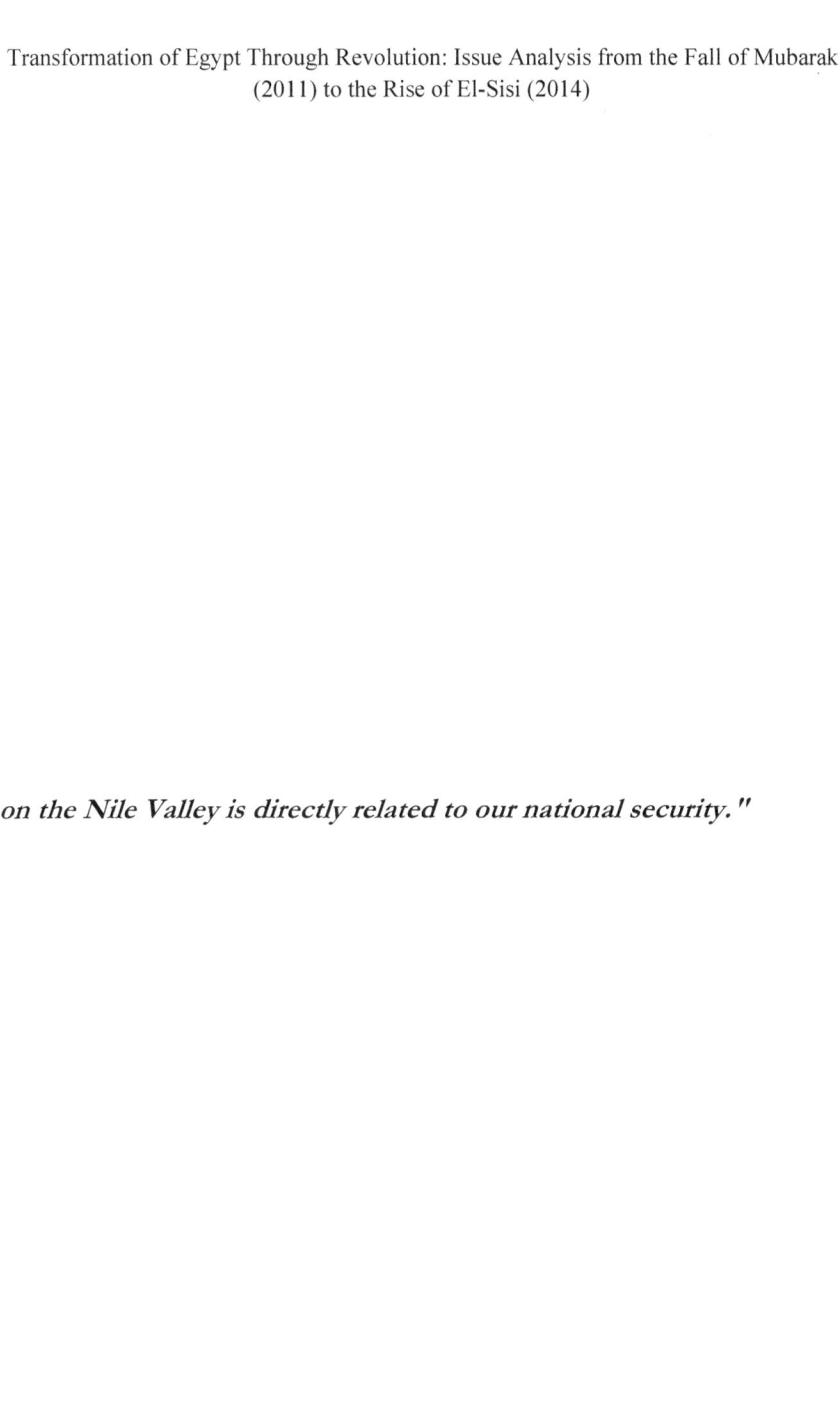

on the Nile Valley is directly related to our national security."

15 AUGUST 2012

Dahshoor, Giza Governorate, Egypt, and the New Egypt

Friday, August 3, 2012

Dahshoor is south of Giza, which is west and south of Cairo. If the name of Giza stands for the greatness of ancient Egypt as symbolized by the great Pyramids, Dahshoor, one of the villages of that Governorate, shall always stand for the decline of modern Egypt as symbolized by the Muslim-Coptic clashes of recent days. Those clashes epitomize the civilizational wreckage bequeathed to the new Egypt by 60 years of military dictatorship.

Sameh and Wael Youssef are two Coptic brothers who own a cleaner shop in Dahshoor. Emad Ramadah Daher, a Muslim client brought a shirt to their shop for cleaning and ironing. Due to equipment malfunction, the shirt was damaged by burning. Soon, the Daher shirt accidental burning blossomed into a violent confrontation between the Muslims and Copts of Dahshoor. In turn, this led to the burning of the house and shop of the Youssef family at the hands of Muslim hooligans. Molotov cocktails were the weapon of choice.

Coptic families fled for dear life, and Dahshoor entered the annals of ignorance, bigotry and ethnic tensions, the wounds of which shall obviously take years to heal.

The Dahshoor events took place on July 25, eliciting formal statements from the Giza Coptic Diocese and from the Egyptian Government, from President Morsi down to top police officers of the Giza Governorate. The Diocese, in its traditional efforts to foster normalcy between Muslims and Copts, stressed the efforts of the police and security forces at containing the crisis, and at apprehending the wrong-doers. Yet the Giza Diocese could not avoid measuring the depth of the Dahshoor crisis.

So its statement pointed to the burning and looting not only of the house and shop of the Youssef family. It went on to describe how other Coptic homes were torched, how the Coptic church in Dahshoor was vandalized, and how other shops owned by Copts, including a jewelry store and a soft drinks shops were also attacked.

Such acts were perpetrated following the burial of a Muslim victim of these riots who had died as a result of his being accidentally hit by a stray molotov cocktail.. The statement ended by appealing to the Government to bolster security in the area, to bring the outlaws to justice, and to apply the force of law equally to all. Property losses have been estimated in the millions of Egyptian pounds.

For his part, President Mohamed Morsi said, through his official spokesman, that the law shall be applied to all malfeasants. The goal, he stressed, was to maintain the customary harmony and amity between Egypt's Muslims (approximately 90% of the population) and Copts (10%).

And Mostafa Bakri, a former member of the Egyptian Parliament (now dissolved), described the Dahshoor sectarian upheaval as resulting from a vast conspiracy intended to destabilize the new Egypt. He estimated the number of Coptic families who fled Dahshoor and its environs, at 120 Coptic households. On his Twitter, Bakri posed a central question which must be on the minds of all fair minded Egyptians:

"There is a vast difference between freedom and anarchy. For how long must Egypt await the arrival of a savior? Anarchy must be arrested, otherwise Egypt might become a failed State. If anarchy, such as what happened in Dahshoor, persists, together with the present economic free fall, the door shall be wide open for a revolt by the hungry hordes which shall devour everything in Egypt."

The Sinai Massacre and the World of the Underground

Friday, August 10, 2012

In the annals of the Egyptian Revolution, Sunday, August 5, 2012, shall remain a day of infamy. Jihadists, said to be Palestinians, attacked an Egyptian army garrison based in Rafah at the border between Egypt and Gaza. It was a sneak attack with assault weapons, at the time when those Egyptian military sat at sunset for the break of their fast during this month of Ramadan.

The devastating ambush resulted in the death of 16 army personnel, including officers and the wounding of 7 others. The ostensible purpose of the treacherous attack inside Sinai, Egypt, was to strike at Israeli positions through Gaza. The Jihadist endeavor was foiled, but it unleashed a host of consequences which shall surely redefine a series of relationships. It could be said that, in a domino-like style, the affected network of relationships includes those between: The Morsi regime and the Hamas authorities in Gaza; the Egyptian-Israeli collaboration under the terms of the Egypt-Israel Peace Treaty of March 1979; the delicate balance of power between the civilian Morsi regime and the Supreme Council of Armed Forces (SCAF); and the outlook of the Egyptian masses upon the rule by their Islamist-oriented government.

The most immediate result of the Sinai massacre is the remilitarization of Sinai and the development of its infrastructure. Sinai is Asian Egypt and its security and Egyptian sovereignty over it trigger huge reaction by the Egyptian masses towards any perceived weakening thereof.

As typical of the Egyptian Revolution so far, the pendulum can swing abruptly from one extreme to the other. Until the Sinai massacre took place, the most important concerns for the new Egypt were the economy and security on the Egyptian street. But after August 5, security from external threats trumped concern for Egypt's present economic woes.

In that context, easing passage by the Gazans into Egypt was seen as a threat. President Morsi and the Qandeel cabinet were lambasted in the

Egyptian street for being soft on the Gaza Palestinians. The shared Islamist orientation between Cairo and Gaza was blamed for the Sinai massacre.

The masses yelled for closing the official entrance checkpoints between Sinai and Gaza. The armed forces were called upon to destroy all tunnels dug up clandestinely by the Palestinians to overcome the hardships imposed upon the Gaza inhabitants by the Israeli blockade. But the tunnels became new underground highways for smuggling weapons, jihadists, commercial items including cars from Egypt into Gaza.

Thus Egypt, following the Sinai massacre, began to look hard at its security from brother Arab terrorists and from any military intervention from the outside into the suddenly-constructed program to overcome lawlessness in Sinai. The calls for a cooperative review by both Egypt and Israel of the security protocols annexed to the 1979 Peace Treaty became vociferous. They made the strengthening of the might of the Egyptian army, security and police units, in order to effectively decimate the pockets of anarchy and terrorism, a primordial necessity. New areas of cooperation on the Israel/Gaza/Sinai borders may have been grudgingly opened up by the very events that caused all of Egypt to mourn its martyrs.

As the funerals for the massacred 16 Egyptian army personnel proceeded all over Egypt, most of the mourners showed hostility toward the new rulers of Egypt, excepting the military. Prime Minister Qandeel was booed as he finished praying for the dead; President Morsi cancelled his appearance at the main military/civilian funeral; flags were lowered at half mast all over Egypt for the 3-day period of official mourning; each Governerate which lost someone in the Sinai massacre had provincial funerals and counted their martyrs as victims of the treachery of Palestinian jihadists.

While the Gaza administration declared that "the liberation of Palestine cannot come at the expense of Egypt's security," the Egyptian airforce scrambled its fighter jets and gunship helicopters which took to the air to bomb and strike suspected pockets of terrorism and anarchy in Sinai. As they seethed with rage, the Egyptians applauded the show of force. The flow of Libyan arms to the Palestinians in the east became a focus of attention by the huge Egyptian military establishment.

Suspicion of the ultimate objectives of the Palestinian jihadists was fueled by all kinds of rumors: some said: Those elements were keen on destabilizing the new Egypt which they wanted to be dragged into an unwanted war with Israel. Others devined that the goal was to declare Sinai an Islamic Emirate.

The first page of Al-Ahram newspaper, the oldest Egyptian daily (first issue is dated August 5, 1876) of August 10, 2012, headlines: **"Destruction of 150 tunnels. Liquidation of 60 Terrorists." The government bedouim informants estimate that there are 1200 tunnels. Welcome to the dark world of the Sinai underground, where the owner of each tunnel is called "the King," and the tunnel supervisor is called "the Prince." This is an Egypt which is largely unknown even to its people. Now the battle against "the underground" has begun, and the nation has risen up insisting on avenging the victims of the Sinai massacre.**

Ending the Nasser Coup of July 23, 1952 By a Soft Coup of August 12, 2012

Thursday, August 16, 2012

On August 12, 2012, President Morsi of Egypt ended the military hegemony over Egypt which began with the Nasser coup of 60 years ago. The Nasser coup ended the monarchy in Egypt; the Morsi soft coup began the Second Egyptian Republic on a sound footing. The action by Morsi, by which he ousted Field Marshall Tantawi from his post as Defense Minister, and General Anan from his post as Chief of Staff, marked the real return of Egypt to civilian rule.

Since the Nasser coup, the armed forces have controlled the destiny of Egypt in every walk of national life. Decisions on war and peace, foreign policy and development, agricultural reform and industrial transformation, were dictated from above. Nasser, Sadat and Mubarak, in succession, held unchallenged sway over Egypt. Meaningful opposition, in any form, did not exist. The word of the President (El-Rais) was the final word, and the successive constitutions were no more than words on paper. Two of the great institutions of Egypt, the judiciary and Al-Azhar became mere government departments. A big chunk of the economy, perhaps 30% of the GDP, became the preserve of the armed forces. Accountability and oversight with regard to the armed forces were non-existing.

Since the fall of Mubarak on February 11, 2011, Field Marshall Tantawi, as head of the Supreme Council of the Armed Forces (SCAF), ruled Egypt.

With the election of Mohamed Morsi in June, 2012, as President of Egypt, the SCAF, on June 30, nominally turned over its powers to the Morsi regime. However, prior to the election of Morsi, the SCAF dissolved Parliament, arrogated to itself powers which normally would have devolved upon the President, and insulated the military budget and the armed forces economic preserve from civilian oversight. Egypt's new President was expected to be largely a mere figure head.

But Morsi had other plans. He ordered the dissolved Parliament into a brief session for the purpose of bestowing upon him legislative powers, pending elections for a new Parliament. And he, in the manner of non-confrontational challenges, gave the Constituent Assembly brief deadlines for the completion of drafting Egypt's new constitution. His choice of a Prime Minister (Dr. Qandeel was so anointed) signaled his preference for a technocratic administration and for some distancing from the Muslim Brotherhood where he had his political upbringing. At the table of the Qandeel Cabinet, Tantawi sat as Defense Minister, but not for long.

Then came the tragic events of the Sinai massacre of August 5, in which 16 Egyptian soldiers lost their lives. But the massacre also gave Morsi the chance to cut the power of the military down to size.

The Sinai massacre was a huge embarrassment to the military and to the intelligence. Morsi wasted no time to rid Egypt of the last vestiges of the Nasser Coup of 1952 through those forced retirements. Even before the dismissal of Tantawi and Anan and other top military brass from their posts, the voices of the millions had arisen in Tahrir Square: **"Down Down with the Military."** Keen on affording the old military guard a soft landing, Morsi invited both Tantawi and Anan to serve in his Presidential Council, and gave them the highest decorations for services rendered to Egypt.

Reactions to the soft coup were immediate and positive. The replacements of the retired military top brass came from the ranks of a younger generation. The post of Defense Minister was given to General Abdel-Fattah El-Sisi. Huge crowds went to public squares to demonstrate in favor of having the military establishment accountable to civilian rule. To those masses supporting Morsi's decisions, the Sinai massacre was attributed to a military which was distracted by its undue involvement in political affairs.

The soft coup had other far reaching ramifications: the constitutional amendments which had been put into effect by SCAF were abolished. The Minister of Justice, Ahmed Makki provided a legal justification. He said: *"The President's decision in this regard draws its legitimacy from the sovereignty of the people who chose him to be President. He shall exercise legislative powers until a new Parliament is elected. The Presidential executive decrees shall be subject to review by the new Parliament."*

Minister Makki also declared another important measure to insure judicial independence. His declaration in that respect was to transfer Judicial Inspection from his own ministry to the Egyptian Supreme Judicial Council. The Egyptian judicial establishment was gleeful. The soft coup expressed itself in other various ways. **The January 25 Revolution seemed to have found its true path which began in Tahrir Square, Cairo, which is bounded on one side by the great Egyptian Museum. From the windows of that historic Museum, the mummies of the great Pharaohs of Egypt seemed to look upon the youth of the New Egypt smiling.**

16   SEPTEMBER 2012

Without Fanfare Egypt Resumes Its Regional Leadership Role

Friday, September 7, 2012

One of the most memorable songs of the Broadway Musical, *"How to Succeed in Business Without Really Trying"* is *"I believe in You!!"* In it, the singer, down on his luck for a long time, looks at himself in the mirror and sings that song of self-assurance. The Egyptian Revolution of January 25, 2011 is a historical musical of self-assurance.

Yes, the economy is in tatters; women and copts are still concerned about their civil rights in an Egypt where the Muslim Brotherhood is ascendant; the bedouins in Sinai are restless; tourism is only a trickle; and the infrastructure has been crumbling for a long time.

But this is not a permanent scene. The potential is quite different. Egypt's huge demographics (nearly 90 million) will gradually have their impact on development. The marginalized bedouins of Sinai top the list for infrastructure enhancement. The crowded Nile valley will systematically be drained from human congestion, eastward to Sinai and westward to the great western desert all the way to the Libyan border. The problem of sharing the Nile waters between nine riparian States will be solved through renegotiation of the Treaty of 1929. In all of this, the security of the Egyptian street is being ensured.

Of equal importance, the Hisham Qandeel Government is seeking economic and financial and technological partnership everywhere - from the shores of the Red Sea and the Gulf, to China, Japan and Australia, to the US and the European Union. President Morsi's first trip outside of Egypt was to China where cooperation agreements for $6 billion were concluded.

Nearly simultaneously, large business delegations organized by the U.S. Government and the Chamber of Commerce representing fifty U.S. corporations, descended upon Cairo. They have their aspirations as well as their concerns. These concerns revolved around Egyptian bureaucratic barriers inherited from the past and impeding foreign investments. And the Morsi regime was ready to oblige. The U.S. Government, encouraged by the present progress toward democracy, was also keen on reducing Cairo's debt to Washington, D.C. by $1 billion, coupled with other grants and debt rescheduling.

Moreover, the International Monetary Fund moved in the same direction of helping the Egyptian economy. Until now, negotiations are proceeding between the Egyptian government and the IMF regarding Egypt's request for a $4.8 billion loan. Judging by the past performance of the IMF (who can forget the 1977 bread riots during the Sadat regime because of the stringent demands of the IMF?), opposition arose against the IMF loan project. Leading the popular charge against dealing with the IMF was the Muslim Brotherhood's Freedom and Justice Party (FJP). The FJP was calling on Prime Minister Qandeel not to proceed with those negotiations until all "internal alternatives" are exhausted. A romantic idea, in the face of the realities of present day Egypt!! Thus the opposition was ignored, especially when the Islamic concept of "necessity" was invoked as a response to silence that criticism.

In the midst of this euphoria, Egypt's march towards democracy was being assisted by civil rights organizations. Among those NGOs was the National Council for Human Rights which submitted to the new Justice Minister of Egypt, Ahmed Makki, no less than ten proposed bills. All of those proposals aimed at enhancing personal freedoms and civil rights. Topping these proposals were: a unified law for the construction of places of worship: mosques, churches and synagogues; a law governing NGO's; a law on the freedom of assembly and the right to peaceful demonstration.

Included in that bundle of proposed laws was a bill dealing with equal opportunity and non-discrimination. It provided for non-discrimination on the basis of religion, language, gender or social status in education and employment. Violators, the bill stated, would be punished by 6 months to a year of imprisonment, together with monetary fines reaching up to two-hundred thousand Egyptian pounds ($34 thousand).

As to family values as advocated by some members of the Muslim Brotherhood, such as extolling women subservience to men, this advocacy is expected to go nowhere. A non-starter!! For the first popular demonstration in Cairo in the 1860's was the historic march by women during which they ripped the veils off their faces and trampled them under foot.

The new Egypt is finding its post-revolutionary feet internally and regionally. Its natural leadership role is being resumed without fanfare. In Iran, the only regional ally of the killer regime of Bashar Al-Assad of Syria, President Morsi, at the meeting of the non-aligned States, called on Al-Assad to step down. In the context of the newly-found freedoms of the Arab masses, consultations regarding a sub-regional alliance of post-dictatorship States are taking place. The deal with Egypt, Libya and Tunisia which are a geographic continuum from west of Gaza to eastern Algeria.

A new Arab world is being born, with Cairo, the headquarters of the League of Arab States, is showing the way towards internal development and external independence from the sway of big powers. Egypt seems to be looking at itself in the mirror, singing out, despite its present difficulties, "I believe in you!!"

When Ignorance of Values Prevails Catastrophic Tragedies Occur

Friday, September 14, 2012

Out of a small church in Gainesville, Florida, came Pastor Terry Jones. Consumed with ignorance about Islam, he judges it, not by its moderation and universalism. He sees it through the prism of Bin Laden, the huge tragedy of 9/11, and the cutters of hands and legs in Northern Mali. To Jones, the Quran, the holy book for 1.5 billion Muslims, is a book of evil. Burning it at his church of only 300 congregants, is both a religious and a patriotic duty.

In his ignorance, as he burnt his copy of the Quran, inflaming passions of both Muslims and Americans, he incinerated also a central part of his own faith. For the Quran, in its full recognition of both the Torah and the New Testament, glorifies the name of Jesus 25 times, and the name of the virgin Mary 34 times - the only mention of a woman in more than six thousand verses.

Nor did Pastor Jones presumably know that among the 6487 volumes which Thomas Jefferson sold to the Library of Congress, was his own two-volume English translation of the Quran which the Muslims revere as God's (in Arabic, Allah) words revealed to Muhammad. The cover of that historic text reads: "The Koran: Commonly Called 'The Alcoran of Mohammed,' Translated into English immediately from the Original Arabic." Jefferson had purchased his Quran in the 1780's in response to the conflict between the US and the "Barbary States" of North Africa - today Morocco, Algeria, Tunisia and Libya.

From Jones, past forward to the American-made video entitled "The Innocence of Muslims." It ridiculed the Prophet Muhammad and caused the senseless killing of a distinguished U.S. diplomat, Ambassador Chris Stevens, at the US Consulate in Benghazi, together with 3 other fine US foreign service officers, and several Libyan security guards. But the catastrophe did not stop there. Between September 18 and September 21, a mere four-day period of Muslim rage at that video, the capitals and other cities in 22 States, from Morocco to Indonesia, have been rocked by attacks on American missions, and violent clashes between the police and enraged Muslim demonstrators.

This is a real anti-American tsunami engulfing two dozen countries, some of which have just emerged from the reign of brutal dictatorships and are now governed by Islamic-oriented regimes. Their sense of euphoria has outpaced their ability to grow in to governance. Nor have they mastered yet how to balance between internal pressures, and external needs for assistance from the outside world, especially the USA. Even without that video, the Arab street in Tunisia, Libya, Egypt, Yemen, Bahrain is not yet safe. And the Syrian civil war with nearly 25000 dead, and a huge number of Syrians living in tents outside Syria as refugees, has transformed Syria into a huge patch of killing fields.

The video producers are an Egyptian Coptic rabble rouser with a police record, named Nakoula Basseley Nakoula, a gas station owner. His coschemer is a man by the name of Steve Klein, an insurance salesman. Justifying the production of that incendiary film, Klein is reported to have said that the intent of the film was to get extremist Muslims to stop killing. The coptic church in the US has denounced that hallucinating video.

When it comes to Egypt, the tragedy assumes gargantuan proportions. Egypt's new partnership with the US is still in its infancy. President Morsi is US-educated and educator, and two of his sons are US citizens. Under his leadership, the Muslim Brotherhood, which had put him forward as its presidential candidate, is kept at a healthy distance. His Government, headed by Hesham Qandeel, is made largely of technocrats.

But when the Egyptian mob (the Muslim Brotherhood did not take part), angered by that video, replaced the US flag over the Cairo Embassy by a black flag of the Salafis, Morsi was a bit late in condemning that attack. Balancing between the internal constituency and the need for US assistance and friendship is an art which apparently needs time for Morsi to master.

Two-hundred and twenty Egyptians including 20 security officers were injured at the Embassy's perimeter. Twenty-four person were arrested. Egyptian tanks surrounded the US Embassy for protection. As Morsi, prompted by President Obama, denounced the violence, his Prime Minister Qandeel declared on September 13 that Egypt's highest national interest was being harmed. Only then did the flame subside, and the "Million demonstrators" did not materialize in Tahrir.

The ignorance of values also extends to the Muslim World, now fully enraged by the attacks on the Prophet Muhammed. When lecturing one day at the Cairo University School of Law on the tragedy of 9/11, I discovered from the questions that many still felt that that criminal acts could not have been perpetrated by Muslims. In the new Arab World, with its rediscovered freedoms, I wonder how many people are familiar with the First Amendment of the US Constitution, especially with its reference to "the freedom of speech, or the press."

Their experience is that government can suppress both, and they demand that Washington D.C. should suppress that video. But how can it do so? The new authority over that video is Google. And Google is not beholden to the U.S. Government. With the video being disseminated by YouTube, its owner Google has blocked access to it in only Egypt and Libya. Here Google misses a main tenet: hate speech is defined by it as against individuals, not against groups. Since the video mocks Islam but not Muslims, Google believes that it falls within its guidelines. An aspect of ignorance: In Islam, Muslims, those who submit their will to God, are one with their faith. There cannot be any Muslims without Islam.

OK!! Turning to the Muslims, one could see in those combustible demonstrations an element of ignorance of the Quran, the primary source of Islamic law. Several verses in the Quran call for giving a cold shoulder to that video which is based on both malice and ignorance. By all means, hold the Prophet Muhammed close and dear. But also remember God's words revealed to him-May Peace Be Upon Him. To the likes of Terry Jones, Nakoula Basseley Nakoula and Steve Klein and their ilk, remember what Allah says in the Quran regarding dealing with those who are ignorant of or inimical to Islam and the Muslims.

In the Quran, Chapter No. 7, Verse No. 199 says: "Keep to forgiveness (O Muhammed) and enjoin kindness, and turn away from the ignorant" And the Quran, Chapter No. 25, verse No. 63 says: "and when the foolish ones address them (the Muslims) they answer: Peace."

It is a pity that we in the 21st century, do not have a Geneva Convention making insulting any faith an international crime (Prime Minister Qandeel has called for that). It is even a greater pity that a bunch of hoodlums in Florida and California can ignite such havoc across the globe. It is even the greatest pity that when ignorance of values **prevail, catastrophic tragedies occur. May the souls of these four diplomats who were killed (martyred) in Benghazi rest in heavenly peace.**

International law calls them "protected persons." Now in their heavenly abode, they, by the grace of God, are eternally "protected."

The Mountain and the Ram

Friday, September 21, 2012

There is an Arab poem about an angry ram. The poem narrates that a ram has somehow perceived a mountain to be its enemy. So it kept on attacking that mountain till the ram's horns were broken. The messages you cannot punish someone or something by losing a part of your body without in the least harming your adversary.

How does this poem apply to the endless saga of denigrating Muhammad, the Prophet of Islam to which millions of Muslims respond by angry demonstrations? I wonder if the Muslim demonstrators were to respond in more peaceful ways, whether the defamers, cartoonists or film makers, might give up on the stupid blackart of insulting the Prophet!!

Were this miraculously to happen, the poem would fit perfectly: The denigrators would be the angry ram whose horns would be broken as it keeps on attacking the mountain (the Prophet Muhammad) without getting any rise from the Muslims.

Thus to the Muslims I say: "Don't get angry!! Get even!!" I know that this may be nearly impossible. Muslims are enjoined by their faith to believe in all God's prophets, in all scriptures, and to respect other faiths. **The Quran, in chapter 16, verse 36, states: "And verily, we have raised in every nation a messenger, proclaiming: Serve Allah and shun false gods."**

So it is out of the question for a Muslim to depict either Moses or Jesus in a disrespectful way. After all, in a secular sense, Moses, Jesus and Muhammad were all born and ministered in the same region. In that sense, the three of them may be regarded as "compatriots"!! "Getting even" in the context of insulting either Moses or Jesus is therefore out of the question for Muslims.

So let us think of other ways to "get even" without being destructive. How about giving up on endless demonstrations, with their attendant destructive consequences, including disruption of international relationships, and get in the film industry? Make a good film about Nakoula Basseley Nakoula, that crazy Egyptian Copt with a police record in California, and depict him as the buffoon he really is!! Write a good script for that movie, hire some gifted actors and actresses (do not forget memorable songs) and call the film: "The Abbasiyah Graduate!!" (Abbasiyah in Cairo is the equivalent of the Bellevue hospital for the mentally-disturbed in New York City).

Now dub the film in several languages and market it everywhere. I am almost sure that the film would draw millions to the box office as a form of revenge, and lots of money would be made for charitable causes. Basseley's puny 14-minute video would be eclipsed, and "The Abbasiyah Graduate" would stigmatize that idiot for a long time.

The same may be done to the French editor of the weekly "Charlie Hebdo" in Paris. There are millions of Muslims in Europe, especially in

France, who would love to fund that "Get even" enterprise. Crowds would have fun, money would be made, France would not need to close all its missions and schools in 20 Muslim countries for fear of violence, and that ignorant editor would live in infamy pour sa vie!!

Yes, the Muslims are angry at the video and the caricatures insulting the Prophet of 1.5 billion Muslims. How about "Getting even" by also putting forth the great story of Muhammad's message, in print, online and in all types of visual imagery? In my weekly seminar on "Islamic Law in the 21st Century" which I teach as an adjunct professor of law at Fordham University School of Law in New York City, I, in 15 minutes out of 2 hours summed up that message as follows:

Muhammad's message advocated freedom of conscience; rule by consultation and consensus; justice in governance; the rights of women as equal partners in society; respect for contracts; mercy towards the weak; freedom from enslavement; amity towards non-Muslims; freedom from fear; the importance of education; and the value of truth and honesty. To the Muslims, mankind is one in, God.

Friday, a day of prayer, has become a day of rage. About that day's group prayer: the Quran in chapter 67, verse No. 10, says,**"When the prayer is ended, then disperse in the land and seek Allah's bounty."** Seeking that bounty is the essence of "sustainable development." It is not to be sought in endless destruction. In Islam, piety and working for the commonweal go hand in hand.

In Egypt, the Muslim Brotherhood's political party "Freedom and Justice" has called for the enactment of an international law "for the protection of religious symbols." Good!! In my humble estimation as an attorney, that call would need decades for its implementation. Here are some of the reasons:

Where are we going to get a broad international consensus regarding: (a) What is a religious symbol?; (b) What do we mean by protection?; (c) Who will do the protection if not sovereign States within their own boundaries?; (d) To what extent can we differentiate between symbols and practices?; (e) How would this protection affect the laws in some European countries against the Niqab and veil in public places?; (f) Is the minaret a universally-acceptable religious symbol?; (g) Would such a law affect the freedom of expression enactments including the 1966 U.N. Convention on Civil and Political rights?; (h) How could a case be constructed and brought before a court of law of competent jurisdiction?; (i) Who might the plaintiff be and what injury could that

*plaintiff prove to have suffered?; and (j) What is the sentencing range and what form of
compensation?*

Am I complicating things? Yes. Because I am looking at an issue which
is very complex.

*Only by education, and cool-headedness could we shrink this problem. Getting angry
is understandable. Getting destructive of life and property is not. Fighting a wrong with
wrong is not a solution. For a Muslim faced with such provocations, it is better to be the
mountain, not the ram. Turn the whole episode into a farce, a spectacle of the absurd.
Put Terry Jones, the Quran burner, on a broom with a cone over his empty head, flying
one way into an eternal sunset as the wicked male witch of the west.. Lighten up!! Make
your tormentors the laughing stock of this world of rage!!*

The Freedom of Expression: A Clash of Interpretations

Friday, September 28, 2012

It is English common law - and plain human logic: You are in a crowded
theater. Some idiot stands up and yells out a falsehood: "Fire!! Fire!!" The
audience panics and rushes aimlessly in every direction, seeking an exit. As
they run for their lives, they trample under foot several others. Death and
injuries occur. Was that free speech? No!! The perpetrator, if found,
would be led away by the police on criminal charges!!

A rabid anti-semite scrawls on the tombstones of a Jewish cemetery in
Queens, Long Island, the despicable swastika. Was that free speech? No.
It is an incitement to hatred!!

A KKK clansman, under the cover of night, burns a cross on the lawn
of an Afro-American family to express his racist hate for the blacks moving
in his neighborhood. Is that an exercise of his constitutional right under
the First Amendment which states:

*"Congress shall make no law respecting an establishment of religion, or prohibiting
the free exercise thereof; or abridging the freedom of speech, of the press..."*

That offending clansman cannot get away with it under the cover of this
first article of the American Bill of Rights. Why? An incitement to racial

hatred in a society which prides itself on diversity.

A woman, during the 2008 presidential campaign (Obama vs. McCain) tells Senator McCain why she was going to vote for him and against Obama. "He (meaning Obama) is an Arab!!" McCain disagrees with her at a minimum level. "He is not an Arab?!," he admonishes. McCain's message would have been a great lesson in American diversity had he added: "So what if he was an Arab?!!"

A bunch of criminals orchestrate the deadly attack on the U.S. Consulate in Benghazi on September 11, 2012. A great U.S. (and world) Ambassador, Chris Stevens, together with three other U.S. diplomatic and consular personnel, are martyred. Does that inconsequential little nothing of a video insulting the Prophet Muhammad, put together by a renegade Copt who is now back in jail for parole violation, reason enough for that heinous crime? Absolutely no.

That video, together with the satire expressed about Muhammad in the weekly French "Charlie Hebdo," resulted in ugly upheavals in more than 2 dozens of States, Members of the Organization of Islamic Cooperation (OIC). In these rage-full demonstrations, people died, property was destroyed, U.S. flags were burned, and a price of $100,000 was placed on the head of the video producer by a Pakistani cabinet member. Did the provocative causes justify those dastardly effects? No. They simply painted Islam with a color with which it had absolutely no relationship.

What we are faced with today on a world scale is a very ominous clash of ideas competing for interpretation. For the Muslims, the provocations which, since 9/11, took the form of a patriotic response to those events, are manifestations of anti-Islamism. For the West, especially in the U.S., they are protected speech by individuals over whose actions the government hand is stayed.

The two sides are reading the same events, but justifying their responses on the basis of a variety of different texts, different value systems, different historic traditions, and different historical experiences.

To an American, the U.S. Constitution has settled the case in favor of the freedom of expression. President Obama affirmed those beliefs when he told the UN General Assembly 67th session on September 25, 2012:

"I know there are some who ask why we don't just ban such a video. The answer is enshrined in our laws: our Constitution protects the right to practice free speech. Here in

the United States, countless publications provoke offense. Like me, the majority of Americans are Christian, and yet we do not ban blasphemy against our most sacred beliefs."

But the Muslim world is reading a different text. The Universal Declaration of Human Rights, Article 29, paragraph 2, states:

"In the exercise of his rights and freedoms, everyone shall be subject only to such limitations as are determined by law solely for the purpose of securing due recognition and respect for the rights and freedoms of others and of meeting the just requirements of morality, public order and the general welfare in a democratic society."

The Muslim world is also turning to Al-Azhar's historic document of January 11, 2012 which, in my blog of January 24, 2012, I described it as "The Egyptian Magna Carta." In addressing the "Freedom of Thought and Expression," Al-Azhar, as per my words in that blog:

"describes this freedom as being at the root of all freedoms, as is manifest in the utilization of all means of expression in writing, artistic production and digitized outreach. It encompasses the right to assembly, to the establishment of parties and other civil society organizations, freedom of the printed, audio, visual and digital press as well as access to information necessary for informed consent.

This freedom, the Charter cautions, does not include the right to inciting violence, sectarian discord or radical calls for discrimination. It quotes the maxim of the great historical Muslim scholars which states: "My view is correct but is subject to error, and the opposing view is wrong but is subject to rectification."

On the day following Obama's speech at the UN, Egypt's President Morsi, in a clash of interpretation of the freedom of expression, told the same General Assembly in Arabic, translated by me into English as follows:

"Egypt respects the freedom of expression. By that we mean an expression which is not exploited to incite hatred for anyone. It is not the freedom of expression which targets for attack a particular religion or a particular culture. A freedom of expression which confronts extremism and violence. It is not the freedom of expression which enshrines ignorance and denigrates others. But, at the same time, we stand firmly against the use of violence as a means of expressing rejection of these imbecilities."

Again in connection with making fun of Muhammad, the Prophet of Islam, a general call issued forth calling for a Trial of Muhammad World Day. The Mufti of Egypt, Dr. Aly Gomaa, a renowned leader of moderation in Islam, condemned that call as well as the video produced in California. An American newspaper charged Gomaa of incitement to violence and terrorism. And in response, Gomaa publicly denied that false charge and called on the UN to enact an international instrument criminalizing attacks on any religion and on its symbols.

So goes the clash of interpretations of the valued principle of freedom of expression. Who is right and who is wrong? This is an impossible question to answer in any definitive manner.

However, the long range response might be for world leaders, educators and foundations to encourage learning about and respect for all faiths, cultures and values. There is also a crying need for mass knowledge of foreign languages such as Arabic, Farsi, Turkish and Urdu. We need to bring our continents closer together through all types of exchanges, trade, tourism and the performing arts.

From the point of view of one of the newly democratically elected Arab presidents, President Moncef Marzouki of Tunisia, a Salafi is as dangerous to world peace as is a westerner ridiculing Islam.

17   OCTOBER 2012

The New Egypt "Oktoberfest": A Parade of Ills and Attempted Solutions

Friday, October 5, 2012

There is hardly an easy transition from dictatorship to the magical world of democracy. After the "Silence of the Lambs," for sixty years, the lid is off that boiling pot of discontent. So if you wish to observe a unique Oktoberfest, we suggest that you don't go to Munich. Your destination, we propose, should be Cairo. There you will find a nation of 90 million being reborn, with all the attendant noises of a difficult birth.

The parade which you shall witness is that of ills and attempted solutions. First you shall observe a bunch of drummers obstructing major railway junctions demanding higher pay. Under Mubarak, security forces, backed up by a mighty military, would have been on the scene, breaking those demonstrations up, notwithstanding the number of human casualties. But in the New Egypt, democracy calls first for negotiations which may or may not be backed up by a measured level of force. The historic love for Mother Egypt - "Mother of the World" - would be invoked, and the drums, drummers, and throngs of discontented workers would eventually go home. Next you shall hear armored personnel vehicles rumbling towards Northern

Sinai in pursuit of bedouin marauders who, under Mubarak, have been marginalized.

The result of 30 years of neglect is that plundering and attacks on army posts and natural gas pipelines have become a way of life. These events do not permit of negotiations, as security in Sinai is not only an internal issue; it is also a transborder headache. Thus force is applauded, including capital punishment for the loss of innocent lives. However, force only without more cannot solve an endemic problem stretched over a vast frontier. So at the end of the columns of military might, comes in the parade a big sign raised by the first Sinai dweller to be appointed Deputy-Governor for North Sinai. His name is Dr. Adel Qatamesh, who declares:

"We hope to restore Sinai to its natural place in Egypt's priorities. We shall develop its huge natural resources in accordance with well developed plans. Sinai possesses huge potentialities which have been neglected for far too long. We intend to recreate in Sinai an engine for economic development for all of Egypt. Unlimited jobs will be created."

Our parade of ills proceeds along a twisting road of hopes, struggles, expectations, and a big dose of hyperbole. This time, the parade's segment is made of representatives of more than 25 liberal and secular parties. They have been largely squeezed out of central stage by the unique device of fair elections. The Islamists, both the moderate Muslim Brotherhood, and the ultras, called the Salafis, registered majoritarian gains in Parliament. This sector of the parade is fronted by "the April 6 Movement," "the Free Egyptians," "the Popular Current," and "the Constitution Party." What do they want? Political Diversity!! What do they mean by that? The creation of an accountability lobby to keep the Islamists under secular scrutiny.

Now, with the sun setting down over the Great Pyramids of Giza west of Cairo, our parade of ills and proposed solutions accelerates its pace.

The Constituent Assembly which is still in the midst of drafting a new Constitution is under continuous criticism. The screams mix and mingle around some of the new articles dealing with: Sharia being "a primary" (not the primary) source of legislation; Al-Azhar's restoration to its traditional independence as the main source of interpretation of questions of Islamic faith; the renaming of the upper house of Parliament "the Senate," to replace "The Shura Council" (a nod toward secularity); and the judicial mechanism for suing the State (i.e. appealing Government executive decisions).

The journalists want to draft a code of ethics to be administered by a National Information Authority.

The Labor Unions gushing forth with several grievances, including the quickening pace of privatization of inherited public sector establishments.

Then comes thousands of children seeking proper school buildings for their proper education, instead of tents set up in certain localities because of lack of funds.

The parade of ills goes on. But it seems to roll by in a diminished state of agitation. Hope in the New Egypt springs eternal. As Egypt struggles through its difficult transition, including combating corruption and insecurity on the streets, a new spirit of this Egyptian Oktoberfest asserts itself:

National reconciliation including President Morsi honoring the late President Sadat posthumously. It was under the military regimes of sixty years, including the Sadat era, that the Muslim Brotherhood of which President Morsi was a presidential candidate, suffered the unmitigated pain of suppression. The Mandela pattern of national reconciliation seems to accord more with the spirit of historic Egypt.

Mahmoud v. Morsi: "The Battle of the Camels"

Friday, October 12, 2012

Mahmoud (Egypt's Chief Prosecutor, Abdel-Meguid Mahmoud) and Morsi (Egypt's President Mohamed Morsi) are battling it out. Morsi has ordered Mahmoud out of his job and to the Vatican, as Egypt's Ambassador. Mahmoud is refusing on the grounds of judicial independence, and Morsi is sticking to his authority, as the democratically-elected President who has been on the job for a little more than 100 days.

Now Tahrir has again been engulfed in demonstrations, led by the two factions: pro-Morsi and anti-Morsi. In essence, the Mahmoud v. Morsi is the straw which broke the camel's (Morsi's) back. The Chief Prosecutor has just exonerated the symbols of the defunct Mubarak regime from any

149

wrong-doing in early February 2011 in what has entered the annals of the Egyptian Revolution of January 25, 2011 as the "Battle of the Camels."

In that engagement, as the Mubarak regime was fighting for its life of 32 years of outright dictatorship, the Tahrir demonstrators were suddenly and brutally attacked by Mubarak thugs. The attackers descended upon the pro-democracy demonstrators, riding camels, horses, and horse-driven carts. The attackers brandished swords, knives, and long bamboo sticks in a hopeless last-minute gasp to enable Mubarak to hold on to his dictatorial power.

The Battle of the Camels of February 2011 was quickly and decisively settled in favor of the pro-democracy movement, though after suffering fatalities and injuries. There was no assistance from the security forces which have fled Tahrir. When I was in Cairo shortly afterwards, I was told by some eyewitnesses that the role of the Muslim Brothers in vanquishing the pro-Mubarak mounted attackers was crucial. They were experts in street combat, tightly organized, highly motivated, and fearless as they brought horses and camels down with their mercenary riders.

Confessions documented that "the Battle of the Camels" was ordered by the former Presidents of the two Chambers of the then-Parliament: Fathi Sorour, of the People's Assembly, and Safwat El-Sherif, of the upper Chamber, the Shura Council. Both men are now in the Tora jail, south of Cairo, having been inculpated on charges of corruption. Their alleged roles in "the Battle of the Camels" were still pending investigations on the more serious charges of killing and maiming peaceful demonstrators.

Out of a sudden, the Chief Prosecutor, Abdel-Meguid Mahmoud, declared those prominent figures innocent of wrong-doing in "the Battle of the Camels," a development which caused popular uproar and precipitated the attempted dismissal by President Morsi of the Chief Prosecutor.

While the highly secular Egyptian judiciary sided with Mahmoud, the President's supporters, especially the Islamists, saw in that verdict the continuing influence of the "foloul" -the remnants of the Mubarak regime who were already pre-maturely celebrating that verdict in the Tora prison.

In reality, Mahmoud v. Morsi, is a larger battle between the Islamists and most of the secularists. The majority of the occupants of the senior ranks of the judiciary and the Prosecutor's Office are holdovers from the Mubarak regime. Confronted by the Morsi presidential decision of terminating his high profile position, Mahmoud cited a law barring the

President from firing him. To many Egyptian observers, the struggle which is now taking place between Mahmoud and the President is highly politicized. During the Mubarak era, the judiciary was Mubarak's cat's paw in subduing the Muslim Brotherhood from whose ranks Morsi has emerged to win the presidency of Egypt last June.

Dr. Essam Al-Erian, who heads the "Freedom and Justice" Party of the Muslim Brotherhood called Mahmoud's ruling "very dangerous." He also called upon Morsi to convene the Presidential Council (advisors to Morsi) to examine the political implications of declaring the wrong-doers innocent.

The Salafis also called on the President to order "the retrial of the killers of the demonstrators." They, together with the Muslim Brotherhood, are accusing the investigators of not examining the totality of the evidence.

In this campaign of attacking the Chief Prosecutor, they were joined by a large segment of the secularists, especially "The Popular Current." (P.C.) The P.C. claimed that not all evidence inculpating those who ordered the mounted attackers in "the Battle of the Camels" into battle was presented. They went as far as describing that episode as "a massacre." The P.C., together with "the Youth of April 6," called for parliamentary intervention to overturn Mahmoud's ruling.

More importantly, a prominent member of the Constituent Assembly which is still drafting the new Egyptian Constitution, Mahmoud El-Said, declared, "The blood of the martyrs shall not be spelled in vain." Contributing to this argument, the spokesman for "The General Union for the Revolution," Mustafa Younes El-Nagmi, called upon Morsi to prevent those accused of fomenting "the Battle of the Camels," from leaving Egypt pending a retrial.

In the meantime, Tahrir is witnessing clashes between the pre-Morsi and the anti-Morsi forces (the latter campaigning against the rise of Islamism in Egypt). The sad result so far has been nearly a 100 demonstrators being injured.

The saga of "The Battle of the Camels" of February 2 and 3, 2011 is not over yet. The mass exoneration of 24 suspects accused of committing those atrocities is indeed the straw which broke the camel's back. **Even the Director General of the Presidential Office, Ahmed Abdel-Atti, confessed that "the general situation in Egypt is perplexing and is difficult to separate its intertwined components one from another."**

Democracy and Faith: Not for Foreign Exportation, Dictation or Reinterpretation

Monday, October 22, 2012

Look it up in any dictionary!! I did, in English, French, Spanish and Arabic. No precise definition, except for the generic terms: "by the people." So please stay away from imposing any definition, except "by the people" on that term. Your yardstick should not be one measuring various shapes, forms and practices which, by historic necessity, change from one environment to another.

The Arab Spring is giving birth to democracies; that is to say again "government by the people" at various stages of maturation. Take Egypt, for example, demographically at least, the center of the Arab world. Democracy is moving by baby steps. Messy steps, yes. Backward to the old bad days of dictatorship, the phenomenon of absolute rule, no.

Therefore, if you believe that absolute rule is oppressive due to its suppression of human rights, as in the days of the Nasser/Sadat/Mubarak, whom would you prefer: Mubarak, the secularist dictator, or Morsi, the so-called Islamist, the democratically-elected President of Egypt? Before you answer this question, use your "rule by the people" yardstick.

If you throw "stability" in the mix, you, as some commentators are prone to do, might say: "Mubarak was an age of stability." Really? What kind of stability, and for whom, and through whom? If you mean by stability, tranquility and predictability, so is the nearest cemetery. The people of Egypt voted for Morsi.

They have never voted in a fair and open election, not run by "the Ruling Party" since 1950. After 62 years, they, through the chaos of Tahrir Square, toppled Mubarak, put him judicially in jail for his abuse of power and elected Morsi, the candidate of the Muslim Brotherhood. You may then argue that only 50% of the Egyptian electorate of 53 million men and women voted. And I would say: In any democratic practice, the result is decided by those who are "present and voting." There is no vote for the so-called silent 50%. They chose not to have a voice. And that was a run-off, preceded by 70% + participation which narrowed the field to two candidates: Shafik, the military man (a holdover from Mubarak days -rule by the Air Force pilots), and the Islamist, Morsi. Shafik lost; Morsi won.

Was that a victory for Islamism in Egypt? Yes it was. Is this good or bad? It was good for the principle of democracy. This is providing that: (a) secularity in Egypt is not smothered; (b) minority rights pertaining to the Copts, women, bedouins of Sinai, and Nubians of upper (southern) Egypt are respected; (c) all forms of freedoms of expression in dress, art, film, songs, dance and theater are protected; (d) international treaties are respected; (e) opposition parties, whose number exceed 30, exercise the freedom to organize and to voice their views of the conduct of their government (the heart of "by the people"); (f) rebuild the economy, through investment, indigenous and foreign, trade and tourism; (g) keep the Salafis away from trying to impose their nearly 1500 years of interpretation of Sharia, which has never stopped to evolve, towards accommodating "the public good" at any given time; (h) maintaining the principle of sovereignty by not being subservient to special interests, domestic or foreign; and last but not least (i) safeguarding the core of democratic rule through respecting the Constitution which is now being drafted by the Constituent Assembly, especially the peaceful rotation of power through the voice of the people, freely expressed in open and fair elections.

Have I exhausted all criteria? No. The list is open and can go on and on, without forgetting the principles of "judicial independence," of the dictum issued by Al-Azhar, namely that "Islam does not recognize a State based solely on religion." And this is where Sharia and the US Constitution converge (the First Amendment on the separation between State and religion). I had the opportunity of stating that convergence at a panel organized in New York City at the Waldorf Astoria hotel in 2006 by the American Bar Association which dealt with "Law and Religion."

The two values, the State, underpinned by democracy, and religion, are not mutually antagonistic. For each of them serves the people within its own domain. Mixing between the two is not only confusing. It is also combustible as it leads to a sinister form of racism, discrimination, hate, and unchannelled rage. Yet they both share one common characteristic: they issue from their own environment, and defy dictation and/or definition from the outside.

The Difficult Birth of the Egyptian

Constitution: Will a Caesarian Be Necessary?

Friday, October 26, 2012

The noise inside the meetings of the Constituent Assembly and outside goes on. It is truly a difficult birth for the new Constitution of post-dictatorship Egypt. It is a struggle for the soul of the January 25 Revolution. That soul is basically whether Egypt shall be secular, Islamist or a combination of both. I am betting on the third alternative. And nearly 90 million Egyptians are watching very closely. So is the rest of the Arab world and beyond.

What is the problem? Who are the actors? Which articles have emerged from the Assembly's Drafting Committee only to be opposed by the Governance Committee? And who will arbitrate between the factions and under what authority? Could the judiciary step in?

These questions would have never arisen if the popular parliamentary elections in which 70% of the huge electorate of 53 million did not produce an Islamist majority of 70%. But they did, and 70% of the parliamentary seats were gobbled up by the Islamist parties with 50% for the Muslim Brotherhood, and 20% for the Salafis.

The heart of the battle is Article 2 which is being copied from the old Constitution of 1971. It refers to **"the principals"** of Sharia being the principle source of legislation. The Islamists, especially the Salafis, are opposed, since the term **"principles"** is ill defined. **Dr. Issam Dirbalah**, the President of The Shura of Al-Jamaah Al-Islamia expressed on October 25 his opposition in these words: **"It is obligatory to provide a clear definition of that term and then place it in a separate article."**

Confronting that call of **Dr. Dirbalah**, the independent Cairo daily **"Al-Sabah,"** delegitimated the entire Constituent Assembly. Its executive editor,**Wael Lotfi** said: **"History shall remember that that Assembly has no legitimacy, either constitutionally, or politically, or morally...It consists of a small group of Muslim Brothers and their allies."**

In response, the Editor-in-Chief of **"Freedom and Justice,"** the mouthpiece of the Muslim Brotherhood party countered: **"Our national duty enjoins us to urge our brothers who constitute the liberal and leftist currents to apologize to the Egyptian people for their attempts**

to impede the building of the State's institutions."

In spite of its centrality to the warring factions, Article 2 is not the only subject of contention. There are of course the articles dealing with the President's powers and prerogatives, the rights of minorities especially the Copts, gender equality, the independence of the judiciary and broad civic and individual rights. All these articles are now thrown for a historic public debate in the streets of the new Egypt, before the final text is brought before the entire electorate for approval in a referendum.

This is the first time ever in the very long history of Egypt to have the public at large debate its national charter, its Constitution. It is also the first time that one hundred and one civic society organizations call for the incorporation into the yet-to-be approved Constitution of an article dealing with the role of civil society in the drafting of the new Constitution. Athenian form of democracy being practiced in Egypt across the Mediterranean from Greece!!

But the secularists resorted to what amounts to an overreach. They instituted a case before the Administrative Law court challenging the legality of the institution and composition of the Constituent Assembly. The court issued a ruling referring the case to a higher court, the Supreme Constitutional Court. Well, this is the very court whose judges were hand-picked by Mubarak. But strange things happens in any revolution or transitional period in any State in post World War II.

The referral of that case to a higher court was seen by the Islamists as a victory - a victory through delay. The Assembly now could rush its work towards completion before the Supreme Constitutional Court would be ready to dispose of that historic case. This is although the Constituent Assembly is still grappling with the draft articles dealing with several important issues, such as Article 36 which guarantees gender equality. This formulation is inherited from the Sadat-era Constitution of 1971. Even the Salafis are content with that Constitutional inheritance because the article ends with words to the effect that equality should be observed in a way not contradicting to Islamic Law. The secularists want these words removed.

The issues do not just end there. There are supplementary articles dealing with the rights of women, the child and the family - the family being the core of society. Emphasis is made on mutual observance of the rights and obligations of a husband and a wife towards one another.

These are matters of crucial importance to the new Egypt and beyond. Problems surrounding that birth abound. Perhaps a Caeserian might be needed!! One thing is certain: In about two months from now, the Egyptians will see the birth of a new dawn through a new text of their new Constitution.

18 NOVEMBER 2012

Obama's Four More Years: The New Egypt Reacts

Friday, November 9, 2012

They proudly call him "the black American President." They devote to his success miles and miles of print. They attend in droves the celebrations held at the U.S. Embassy in Cairo. They openly show great relief for Romney's exist. Why?

Interest in America and its ways has never been more palpable. This phenomenon is fully shared by both the Islamists and the secularists. It is an interest which reflects general hope in a reinvigorated American involvement in the New Egypt, economically, educationally, technologically and in selected areas of foreign policy, especially in the Israeli-Palestinian conflict. "Hope and Change," borrowed from Obama, has become an Egyptian mantra. Egyptian resentment toward America's support for Mubarak has practically dissipated.

Cairo's attitude toward Russia has sunk to a new low. The New Egypt feels abhorrence toward Moscow's support for the Assad regime in Syria. In this regard, Egypt, historically, has always looked west, not east.

Contemporary Egypt was first developed by the French as of the early 19th century.

Egypt, taking a brief holiday from the woes of its transition from dictatorship to democracy, celebrated the onset of Obama's second term in adulatory terms. They highlighted Obama's call for healing the wounds of the bitter presidential campaign. "Tahrir" wishes that a similar reconciliation would be possible with the remnants of the Mubarak regime.

Cairo saw humility in Obama's declaration in his victory speech in Chicago that he had become "a better President." It wishes that its leaders would show the same strength of character. Though the challenges facing Washington, D.C. and Cairo may not be the same, but the Egyptians perceive in Obama's reference to "the challenges ahead" a reflection of what their new leaders keep on repeating.

Even Romney's speech conceding defeat and wishing Obama's success in the coming four years was a reminder to Egypt that it does not yet posses this tradition of congratulating your adversary.

There is also in Cairo that sense of quick pride in the enhanced importance of the minorities in America. The Egyptians also saw in the small margin of victory for Obama a reflection of what happened in the competition between Morsi and Shafik in June for the post of the presidency.

As to the expected "gridlock" in U.S. governance, well, that is nothing new to Cairo. This is although the Egyptian gridlock has different poles. In Cairo, it is between the judiciary and the other branches of government.

What did the New Egypt fear in Romney? **First**, they do not know Romney. Romney did not even define himself. Romney was defined by his adversaries. **Second**, they were hostile to his references to the rise of the Islamists to power as "chaos in the Middle East." The Egyptians also saw in Romney a man of war. In Obama, they saw a man of peace, especially as regards Iran.
It also greatly helps that Obama's middle name is "Hussein."

From the Pharmacy to the Papacy: Pope Theodoros II of Alexandria

Friday, November 16, 2012

His sure medicine is a dose of love and an equal measure of unity. That is the prescription of His Holiness Pope Theodoros, the 118th Pope of the venerable Orthodox Church of Egypt. He comes to the headship of a very historic Church in the annals of Christendom the first church after Christ. Elevated to that exalted position by a unique election system which goes back 2000 years (a process of selection followed by drawing a lot among four clergymen), the new Pope inherits the mantle of the great Pope Shenouda III.

The date of his elevation to the Papacy was November 4, 2012, his 60th birthday. His Egypt has changed since the revolution of January 25, 2011. A historic change has come to his land, the land of the Copts (Egypt), and so his message is a mixture of love, the creed of that Church which boasts of having the hiding place of the Holy family in Old Cairo, and unity, which has become quite elusive in this age of rage.

Theodoros II has a 1975 baccalaureate in pharmacy from the University of Alexandria. This was followed, ten years later, by a World Health Fellowship from the UK. For His Holiness, it was an 1985 double graduation. In that year, he was also able to graduate from the Coptic Clerical College in Egypt. After a period of seclusion as a monk at the Anba Bishoy Convent in Wadi Al-Natroun in 1986 in the western desert, he was ordained a Coptic priest in 1989. Within 8 years thereafter, he became a Bishop.

This new spiritual leader, whose original name was Wagih Sobhi Baqi Soliman, had a father who was a land surveyor. The family kept on moving in Egypt from east (Mansourah), to south (Souhag), to west (Damanhour). It was as if fate was offering the future Pope a broad look at his beloved Egypt.

On this Pope's shoulders lie the new burdens of remelding the Coptic community into one community with their Muslim brethren. It is not by numbers or a ratio of one Copt to 10 Muslims, forming the demography of 90 millions, the largest Arab State. It is by the shared history which began in the 8th Century since the time of Amre Ibn Elass led the Muslims westward from Palestine into the Nile Valley. The new arrivals were under strict instructions from Khaliph Omar who, from Medina in what is now Saudi Arabia, ordered them in no uncertain terms: "No forced conversion. And learn from your brothers, the Copts."

This eventuated into Egypt becoming a model for the Islamic Law persistent call for diversity and respect for the other. But the ill wind of extremism, which cloaked itself in an Islamic garb, began as of the Khomeni revolution in Iran to blow westward blanketing Egypt in its path. Those ominous developments ignored the great patriotic stance of the Coptic church in regard to Egypt's gradual liberation from Great Britain in 191
9, 1936, 1946, and in 1954 when the British troops evacuated Egypt.
With incidents of conflict between the Copts and the Muslims multiplying in Egypt, the call of the new Pope for national unity acquires added significance. After all, his great predecessor, Pope Shenouda III, was described as "Egypt's safety valve." In the same vein, Pope Theodoros sees in Egypt's Coptic heritage an avenue for preserving, through his medicine of love, a great antidote to Egypt's inter-religious anxieties.

"The Egyptian Coptic Church, "the new Pope declared," is a model for all churches, and for the Egyptian Community, in regard to the separation between State and Church."

At Crossroads in Egypt: One Sign Reads: "To All Directions;" The Other Sign Reads: "To All Other Directions"

Friday, November 23, 2012

President Morsi now has it all: Executive, legislative and ... not judiciary, but something else called "absence of judicial review." It happened on Thursday, Nov. 22, a day when the whole world was grateful for that Gaza cease fire. Morsi, the engineer and the first elected president of Egypt since the birth of ancient Egypt, has, with the US managed to stop, at least for now, the senseless carnage between Gazans and Israelis. During those anxious hours of negotiations, the world looked at Morsi as the voice of reason. President Obama spoke to him at length concluding: that man with roots in the Muslim Brotherhood was indeed a pragmatist. The accolades from all over the world rained on Morsi once the fighting stopped.

Then came Thursday, Nov. 22, a fateful day in Egypt's halting march towards democracy: Morsi promulgating a decree granting himself broad powers. Before that decree was issued, the sign reading **"To All Directions"** signaled a deadlock in the efforts to draft a new constitution. After the issuance of that decree, the sign reading **"To All Other Directions"** signaled the unknown.

The dilemma is rooted in the following facts: a split between the Islamists who control the majority of parliamentary seats and the secularists; the haggling in the constituent assembly (the Assembly of 100) over the few yet-to-be-drafted articles of the constitution, resulting in the withdrawal of most of the secularists, including the Copts, from those deliberations (about 25% of the membership); and the fear that the Supreme Constitutional Court, whose judges are hold-over Mubarak appointees, was poised to dissolve that constitutional assembly. Members of that Assembly were chosen by the Islamists-dominated and now dissolved parliament.

Was Morsi correct in issuing that decree? "Correct" is a subjective term which is subject to all kinds of interpretations. Those who support Morsi say: that decree is an emergency enactment of limited duration ending with the plebiscite on a new constitution and the setting up of a new parliament vested with full legislative powers.

Morsi opponents claim that Morsi, using his accolades for his role in the Gaza crisis, is assassinating democracy, tipping the delicate scales in favor of the Islamists in whose ideology his roots run deep, and is anointing himself as the new Pharaoh.

Perhaps the reality is buried under a ton of rhetoric and counter-rhetoric. In spite of that situation, a central fact emerges: the two sides of that schism fear a return to the past leading to an early abortion of the January 25 Revolution. However, each side wants to own that revolution, interpreting its progress on the basis of its ideological perspective.

There is another central fact in the battle of reading the signs at that historic Egyptian crossroads. There is no love lost between Morsi and the Supreme Constitutional Court. That Court had dissolved Parliament, only to have Morsi reconvene it for 20 minutes to have it grant him "temporary" legislative powers. Ancillary to the suspected powers of the Supreme

Constitutional Court was the suspicion towards the Public Prosecutor, Abdel Meguid Mahmoud, for failing to win stronger sentences against Mubarak and his associates.

So now, President Morsi, who had returned the army to its barracks, has, through the November 23 decree, freed himself, his decrees and the constituent assembly from judicial oversight. **Free at last? Not so fast.** The battle between the Islamists and the secularists, signalling an open wound in the Egyptian body politic has begun to intensify. Tahrir Square is again the huge podium from which arguments and counter arguments, as well as rocks, tear gas canisters, and more dangerous projectiles, are exchanged.

In response to those who say that Morsi abhors judicial independence, we find Morsi appointing a new Public Prosecutor, Talaat Ibrahim Abdullah, a former leader of the movement for judicial independence under Mubarak.

To those in Egypt who say that Morsi now represents a continuation of the 60 years of dictatorship under which Egypt has suffered, Morsi has addressed his nation on Nov. 23 saying **"my actions are for the protection of that revolution."**

As the counter-Morsi protesters burned down Muslim Brotherhood offices in Alexandria and elsewhere, in response to the frightening amassing of powers in the hands of one man, Morsi, he responds that he was **"the President of all Egyptians."**

The masses, while pleased with Morsi's plans to retry Mubarak and his cohorts (against the principles of **"res judicata"** -the thing has been decided), the opponents still scream that **"Morsi wants to make of himself a God."**

Al-Sharkawi of Cairo University, an advisor to Morsi says: "This is mainly a political conflict. Egypt needs to move forward. The life of that decree is from 2 to 4 months. Egypt cannot wait anymore. The judiciary did no reflect the will of the people."

For now, I tend to agree. But I was educated in Egypt until the age of 24. There I learnt from my Scottish professors at Zagazig High School in the Province of Sharkiah, a British adage: "Nothing is more permanent that the temporary."

162

19   JANUARY 2013

Under the Sails of Its New Constitution: The New Egypt is Launched

Friday, January 4, 2013

On December 26, 2012, the New Egypt was launched under its democratically-adopted constitution. Some called it "the Second Egyptian Republic." Wrong. The Nasser Coup of 1952 did not launch a First Egyptian Republic. It inaugurated a dictatorship which coopted the name of "republic" to clothe it with legitimacy.

It **is also wrong** to call the new Constitution "flawed." No constitution is born perfect. It is amendable.

It **is also wrong** to call it "an Islamist constitution." We in the U.S. do not call our constitution "Judeo-Christian." It is an American constitution.

It **is also wrong** to conjure whether Egypt is going to be a "Pakistan" or an "India." This is blatant ignorance. Countries and their systems have to be evaluated on their own terms. No two countries are ever alike.

It **is also wrong** to say that the Egyptian Constituent Assembly lost its legitimacy because one third of its members walked out. If you are absent, you have no vote.

It **is also wrong** to say that the new constitution lacks credibility, because only about one-third of the eligible voters participated in the plebiscites of Dec. 15 and Dec. 22. In legal terms, we only count those who are "present and voting."

It **is also wrong** for the opposition in Egypt to call for a restart from square one. This means disfranchising all those millions who voted for going forward.

It **is also wrong** for some of the elite (Al-Nokhbah) to describe the voting majority as "illiterate." It is the Nokhbah which needs to be schooled in the art of democracy.

It **is also wrong** to characterize President Morsi as totally beholden to the Muslim Brotherhood. He, in June 2012, emerged as the winner in free and fair elections, regardless of the genre of his political roots. He was not the first choice of the Brotherhood. El-Shatter was. But he was disqualified, and Morsi was put forward by the Freedom and Justice Party of the Muslim Brotherhood as their alternative choice.

It **is also wrong** for the opposition to continue its campaign of nullification after the results of the plebiscite were announced. **Enough is enough.** If you are unhappy with Morsi, or with the Brotherhood, and or with the Constitution, you nonetheless should allow the country to go back to work. Then reorganize and challenge them in 2016. But, please get out of the way, and go back to rebuild that collapsed security and economic system.

It **is also wrong** for the opposition to theorize about certain articles in the Constitution or to say that the document should have "a societal consensus." In a democracy, you take decisions by a majority vote. There is no precise definition for "a societal consensus." Even in Islamic Law, Ijmaa (or consensus) does not mean a total meeting of the minds of all Muslim scholars in a given geographical area.

It **is also wrong** to say that the Constitution is too detailed. Refining a constitution is through application and, if necessary, an amendment. Now that the Shura Council (the upper Chamber of Parliament) is in place, it has all legislative authority and could propose amendments to the lower Chamber when elected in two months.

It **is also wrong** to claim that Morsi is waging war on the judicial system. On the contrary. The Supreme Constitutional Court fired the first shots. It dissolved the lower chamber of Parliament on a technicality, and manifested interest in also dissolving the Constituent Assembly for the second time in a row. Now the Constitution governs the principle of separation of powers.

There are other blatant wrongs which the fragmented opposition is committing: Calling on the armed forces to intervene after the people had approved the Constitution; unfurling the banner of a possible civil war; scaring off the Copts that under the new Constitution their position in Egypt shall be precarious; and calling on outside powers and international institutions either to intervene or to withhold their economic and moral support for the New Egypt.

These wrongs are not only seditious. They are proving that the political thought of the so-called liberals about democracy in Egypt is nearly a black hole. One does not advocate democracy through the stifling or denigration of the popular will.

Thus it was right for Morsi to declare to the nation on Dec. 26, 2012 that the Constitution "reflects the spirit of the January 25, 2011 revolution; that is based on respect of the rights of citizenship regardless of religion; that the polemics which preceded the adoption of the Constitution by nearly two-thirds of the voters were a healthy democratic sign; that he, prior to that adoption, committed errors (an allusion to his November 22, 2012 constitutional declaration putting him temporarily above the law); and that

"Egypt and the Egyptians now have a constitution which is freely accepted, and which was not a grant from a king nor an imposition by a president, nor a dictation from an occupier."

As I sat in my seat in Egypt Air returning from Cairo to New York City on Dec. 23, a fellow traveller to my right, asked me anxiously about my opinion of the new Constitution. I provided the above analysis. Yet I was joyed by that critical question coming from a beautiful young Egyptian woman who was dressed in an Egypt Air uniform. "What do you do for Egypt Air?," I asked. "I am a pilot on a brief vacation!!"

Now this is the new face of Egypt, young, professional, confident and concerned about her country which she sees from above as she flies, as well as from below as she navigates the Cairo crowded streets.

Thus under the sails of its new Constitution, the New Egypt is

launched, hopefully towards a destiny of national unity.

Why Did Egypt Revolt?: The Facts Through the Fact Finders (Part I)

Friday, January 11, 2013

On Tuesday, January 1, 2013, the Egyptian Fact Finding Commission announced at a press conference in Cairo, its findings into the events which led to the Egyptian Revolution of January 25, 2011.

This blue ribbon commission, which was set up by a decision taken by Egypt's Prime Minister (Decision 294, 2011), was headed by Egypt's past Chief Justice, Dr. Adel Qura. Its work which covered 400 pages in Arabic dealt with the events from January 25 until Mubarak's fall from power on February 11, 2011.

In this series, beginning with Part I, this blog will highlight the facts as seen by the fact-finders and neutrally reported nearly 2 years later.

The Qura Commission, while analyzing the events as testified to by hundreds of witnesses and backed up by documented of all types of visual, audio and printed material, has in effect produced a unique document. This report should be studied on a world-wide basis. Reason: It contains a careful and judicious cause and effect of why people, anywhere, revolt.

We begin with the findings into the role of social media in that historic revolution whose course is still undetermined.

The Commission analyzed the ways and means whereby the Mubarak regime, during its dying days, attempted to shut down the Internet. It said that the three cellular phone servers operating in Egypt have simultaneously cut off their service to certain provinces. That blackout was in response to orders to them from the Mubarak security services.

Social media, including Facebook and Twitter, have played a crucial role in bringing hundreds of thousands of protesters to Tahrir Square and to other public squares all over that country of nearly 90 million people. As those means of communication were cut off by governmental design, the blackout also impacted negatively on the means of communication used by the police and other components of the huge security apparatus in Mubarak's Egypt.

The result of that cut-off, while temporarily affecting the means of galvanizing the millions of Egyptians streaming into the public squares, was more devastating to the forces of the so-called "law and order." This was manifest in severing the links between various chains of command of police and Ministry of Interior chains. With the chain of hierarchy command disrupted, large police units fled from the streets, decision-making became personalized, police conduct descended into hit and miss, and responsibility for those uncoordinated actions became impossible to determine.

Testifying before the fact-finding Commission, Dr. Amre Badawi Mahmoud, the Executive Head of the National Organization for Communication Coordination, stated in Arabic:

"On January 23, 2011, the top representatives of National Security called the heads of the 3 cellular phone servers to a meeting with them. An Emergency Operations Headquarters was set up. Its role was to issue special instructions with regard to both operation and interruption of communications in accordance with the provisions of Article 67 of the Law on Communications. The reason was given as being the developing of a severe state of emergency in Egypt, affecting the core of national security. Thus service was ordered to be cut off on January 27, 2011 at 10:00 AM, and was instructed to be resumed on January 29, 2011 around 9:30 AM. As to the Internet, it was ordered to be suspended on Friday, January 28, 2011 and was resumed on February 5, 2011.

However in the case of the Internet, that interruption did not affect the special frequencies used by the Police. With public pressure mounting on the Mubarak regime to depart, the blackout was finally ended. But the fact that it was put into effect has harmed Egypt's world wide reputation as a civilized State. That is not to mention the negative effects suffered by the cellular phone servers."

This series shall be continued subject to the exigencies of the fast developing news from Tahrir.

Why Did Egypt Revolt?: The Facts Through the Fact Finders (Part II)

Saturday, January 19, 2013

Mubarak and his crew are going to be retried again. Either acquittal, which is not likely, or a stiffer sentence, which could be capital punishment. The decision is a legal anomaly. It subjects the defendant(s) to retrial for the same charges in which a legal decision was already rendered. But revolutions are not known for adhering to recognizable legal procedures.

Mubarak, his two sons, his former interior minister and others associated with the fallen regime, are still facing charges including allowing their security forces and "baltagiahs" (thugs) to kill peaceful protestors.

The recent Report of the Fact-Finding Commission of the prestigious Egyptian jurist, Adel Qura, has found those charges to be credible. The order of an Egyptian appeals court, issued on January 13, 2013, for a retrial reflects the seriousness in which the Qura report is held.

In Part I of this series on that report, this blog dealt with the role of the social media and public information in influencing the events of the first 18 days of the Egyptian Revolution (January 25 to February 11, 2011). Now Part II deals with the issue of what the Commission describes as "Shooting with Live Ammunition and Death by Being Run-Over by Vehicles."

The Commission confirms that as of January 25, 2011, police forces began using live ammunition against peaceful protestors in Suez, the city for which the Suez Canal is named. It goes on to state that the illegal and inhuman practice soon spread to nearly all of the other Egyptian provinces. In particular, the Fact-Finders named Cairo, Giza, Alexandria, Ismailia, Dakahliah, Qaliubiah, Gharbiha, Sharkiah, Faiyoum, Beni Suef, Assiut, Aswan, and Sinai North. There are 27 provinces (called Governorates) in which Egypt is administratively divided.

On the matter of death-by-vehicles, the Report states that armored police vehicles were intentionally sent to run over protestors for the purpose of killing or injuring them. It presented visual evidence on these actions recorded by TV and by networks of social communication media. In one such recording, a police car is shown veering in the direction of a protestor who was flung to the ground by that vehicular action. Another similar recording shows another police vehicle backing up against another demonstrator. The victim was killed.

A third security vehicle with diplomatic license plates was shown speeding towards Tahrir Square and ploughing into throngs of demonstrators, cutting down whoever was in its way.

The Fact-Finders found two such instruments of death parked behind two police stations in the greater Cairo area. Those vehicles were discovered being dismantled in order to hide their identities. But the investigators were able to record finger-prints found on the bodies of those vehicles.

Neither the Traffic Department nor the Customs Department could verify the owners of the vehicles. But the Report referred to an emissary from the U.S. Embassy in Egypt who had filed a report on one of those vehicles as having been stolen from the Embassy.

The Fact-Finders were informed by the Ministry of Health that as of February 20, 2011, the total number of casualties resulting from those practices had reached 384 fatalities and 6467 injured citizens. Since the tally of fatalities based on reporting by all provinces had reached 846 by February 16, 2011, the Qura Report disputed the veracity of the lower figure. On that basis, it confirmed that at least 846 deaths had occurred.

The Report also confirmed that among those who met with death in the police ranks were 26 officers and police recruits during the period from January 25 to February 9, 2011.

Summing up their findings on this sector of the Report, the Fact-Finders concluded that:

The Police has unnecessarily used lethal force in a failed attempt to disperse the demonstrators;

That the orders to use those methods had to be authorized by the highest level of authority as decreed by standing directives to the Ministry of Interior;

That the right of protestors to peacefully assemble and voice their grievances is a basic human right as based on the Egyptian Constitution and laws, as well as international law including UN resolutions. The Report thus cited Egyptian Law No. 109 of 1971 which, in Article 102, provides that:

"A Police Officer should only resort to force to carryout his assigned duties if the use of force is the only method left for him to fulfill his duties."

Only the Interior Minister could exercise that authority, under the Egyptian President giving the green light for such draconian measures.

Thus the grand stage for retrying Mubarak and those who had basked in the sun of his autocratic role was set, although the outcome remains unclear.

This series shall continue in future weeks with Part III.

Why Did Egypt Revolt?: The Facts Through the Fact Finders (Part III/Last Part)

Friday, January 25, 2013

The historic Report of the Fact-Finding Commission which was issued in Cairo at a press conference last month draws its importance from two factors: It is a complete analysis of why people revolt, and it is done under the leadership of one of the most prestigious judicial authorities in the Arab world, Judge Adel Qura.

Part I of this series which ends with this Part III, dealt with the role of the media, Facebook, Twitter and other means of social mobilization. This was followed by Part II which dealt with the role of the police and other security forces in regard to "Shooting with Live Ammunition and Death by Being Run-Over by Vehicles." Now this Part III deals with 3 issues: (a) Thugs (Baltagiahs) intimidating peaceful protesters; (b) Extra judicial arrests; (c) Security break-down.

Taken in its totality, the Fact-Finders have unmistakeably placed the onus on the old regime for these gross infractions of constitutional rights of the Egyptian citizen to peacefully demonstrate. The weight of evidence of all kinds, including visual evidence, is overwhelming. The direct impact of that Report could be seen in the recent court of appeals ruling to retry Mubarak, his two sons and other suspects for their alleged commission, directly or indirectly, of actions whereby nearly 900 demonstrators were killed and more than 6000 were injured in various Egyptian provinces.

The Report of the Fact-Finding Commission covers the critical period from January 25 to February 11, 2011, with the latter day signaling the fall of Mubarak from his 32-year old position as Egypt's dictatorial President.

With regard to the thugs (Baltagiahs; quasi-militias), the Report focuses on the period from February 2, to February 3, 2011. During those 24 hours, bloody confrontations took place all over Egypt. The locales were Tahrir Square and its equivalents in many of the Egyptian Provinces.

The Report calls that Wednesday "Bloody Wednesday." On that morning, the Mubarak regime supporters poured into Mustafa Mahmoud Square located at the Arab League Avenue. Other supporters came from other Cairo quarters, thus swelling the numbers of counter-protesters. As per the testimony of some leaders of the National Party (the Governing Party), those activists were instructed to prevent the anti-Mubarak demonstrators from entering Tahrir Square.

How about the throngs of anti-Mubarak demonstrators who were already camped inside Tahrir? The orders were to besiege the occupiers of Tahrir within whose ranks, elements of the secret Egyptian police were infiltrated to commit intimidation and anarchy. But since that iconic public square is surrounded by high buildings, both business and residential, the anti-democracy infiltrators also ascended to rooftops.

To the anti-Mubarak elements, rooftops became the high ground from which they threw stones, marble tiles, and molotov cocktails on the heads of the unarmed demonstrators below. Simultaneously, the Fact-Finders state, the police and thug elements within Tahrir Square used their guns, rubber bullets, and tear gas canisters in attacking the pro-democracy throngs.

The scene gets more horrific with the invasion by a group of riders of camels, horses, and mules, driving their animals at top speed into the packed crowds. The Report goes on to describe those events which it calls "The Camel Battle" as the most frightening of all the other illegal acts committed by the fallen regime. The riders of those animals, most of whom came from Nazlet El-Samman, near the Giza Pyramids, were armed with thick bamboo sticks, long knives, swords and iron bars. They breached the iron barriers which were erected to protect the Tahrir occupiers, and proceeded to cause indiscriminate death and injury.

In self defence, the demonstrators ripped up street pavements and hurled their broken stones at their attackers. During that melee, the demonstrators detained some of the camel riders and other infiltrators. From their IDs they found that they were either police forces dressed in civilian clothes or were members of the National Democratic Party, the then-ruling party of former President Mubarak. The detainees were delivered by their civilian captors to the armed forces with whom the Fact-Finders were in communication to document that important report.

The Fact-Finders also documented what was beamed by bullhorns. The leaders of those anti-deomcracy throngs described the peaceful demonstrators as mercenaries, turncoats, traitors and non-thinking hordes who were misled by Dr. El-Baradei, Ayman Nour and other anti-dictatorship icons. The anti-democracy throngs were urged, the Fact-Finders pointed out, to "liberate Tahrir Square from the traitors who want for Egypt only destruction."

The Report contained a copy of a document carrying the logo of the Interior Ministry under the heading: "Secret and Very Important." The document, which is not yet authenticated, is said to contain orders "to hire Baltagiahs (thugs) to create chaos and to be generously paid." That document was referred to Egypt's Attorney General for further investigation.

Dealing with the remaining issues, namely extra judicial arrests and the security breakdown in Egypt, the Fact-Finding Commission declared in its Report the following:

The Police placed under arrest without legal cause many of the demonstrators and media personnel who were reporting on the events of those history-changing 18 days in early 2011. Those detainees were kept for varying periods at various detention centers.

The security breakdown was brought about through the use by the Ministry of Interior of Baltagiahs who were activated in various areas of Cairo and Giza. The regular police forces have left the scenes of these clashes between the thugs and the pro-democracy protesters Thus the Baltagiahs were enabled to destroy public and private property, after committing acts of pillage. Some of the police stations were reported to have been burnt by arsonists from within the ranks of those hired thugs.

All these findings by the Qura Fact-Finding Commission are now in the hands of Egypt's Attorney General. Those occurrences shall no doubt be taken into account during the retrial of Mubarak and his crew in the months ahead.

January 25, 2013 marks the 2nd anniversary of the Egyptian Revolution. Two years have already gone by. Yet the revolutionary cataclysm and its reverberations are not yet over. When would they be over? Nobody knows!! But barring interference by the army, the march towards freedom and democratic rule shall eventually be impossible to reverse.

20 FEBRUARY 2013

The State of the Egyptian State: Collapse, Never; Change of Regime, Not Unthinkable

Friday, February 1, 2013

Chaos, chaos, everywhere!! Official reports are the equivalent of the writing on the wall. Just compare the statistics of 2012 to those of 2011: Homicide: up by 130%; armed burglary up by 350%. Crime, overall was at a record of 5814 in 2012, compared to 2778 in 2011; felonies doubled to 40,220; kidnapping accounted for 258; rape for 109; arson: 632; burglaries: 9284; car theft: 20,375. Those ominous statistics were culled from all provinces. This is not to mention 20,000 recorded criminals who took advantage of this security collapse and fled from jail.

The managing editor of Al-Ahram newspaper, the official newspaper of the regime, Ahdel-Nasser Salameh, headlined on January 25, 2013: **"Our Revolution is in the Balance!!"** That was the date of the Revolution's second anniversary. Collaboration turned into a day of mourning, especially at the major cities of the Suez Canal (Port Said, Ismailia and Suez). Mr. Salameh summed up Egypt's dilemma in few sub-headings: **"We are confronting a huge disappointment. The Revolution failed to be convincing to large sectors of our population. The people are now asking whether January 25 ushered in a revolution. History may**

shame us all. The ruling authorities cannot govern alone by themselves."

From a beautiful dream to an ugly nightmare. And on January 26, 2013, President Morsi declared a state of emergency from 9:00 PM to 5:00 AM in the Suez Canal area. Then when the public defied the curfew hours, the president blinked. He left the management and the duration of the curfew to the local authorities in the Suez Canal area. Wild and uncontrollable demonstrations had erupted in Port Said and Suez. The chaos in Egypt took various forms: thousands of protesters were against sentencing those accused of killing soccer fans a year ago in Port Said; celebrating the second anniversary of the Egyptian Revolution by major riots in support of the Morsi regime and in rebellion against it; denunciation of the Muslim Brotherhood by the secularists and counter-denunciation of the secularists by the Islamists; continuation of the conflict between the judiciary and the executive authorities; and the economic collapse of the largest Arab country, namely Egypt.

Where did the beautiful dream of a transition to democracy in Egypt go? The country of 90 millions was thought to be preparing for parliamentary elections shortly under its new Constitution. The upper chamber, the Shura Council, is now reconstituted and is wielding legislative powers pending the results of those elections. President Morsi is thought to have had wrestled power from the Supreme Council of the Armed Forces (SCAF), and the military position in the power structure of the new Egypt is now defined by the Constitution. So has been the judicial authority whose independence was detailed in that Constitution.

Events on the ground is proving that sovereign power cannot be solely guaranteed on paper. Not even on the parchment of the new Constitution. Nobody seems to be happy with their share of power. Morsi is accused of being subservient to the Islamists; the National Salvation Front (NSF), representing the opposition and coordinated by Dr. El-Baradei, is hopelessly fragmented; the security on the Egyptian street remains unattainable; the infrastructure is in dire straits; the young remain unemployed; and the Copts are doubtful about their future security and their freedom of practice in the new Egypt.

How about a dialogue amongst the antagonistic factions? President Morsi has been calling for such a dialogue. The NSF had rejected these calls declaring that they were intended to buy time for a regime they abhor.

Then came a dire warning on January 29. 2013, issued by General Abdel-Fattah El-Sisi, Egypt's Minister of defense. In a speech at the Cairo Military Academy (Egypt's equivalent of West Point in the U.S.) he said, **"The political, economic, social and security challenges which face Egypt today represent a veritable threat to its security and cohesiveness. The persistence of conflict among the various political forces and their disagreement regarding administering the country may lead to *Egypt's collapse.*"**

Then in pointed remarks to the basic mission of the Egyptian armed forces, the General said: **"The Egyptian army will remain the solid and cohesive rock and the strong pillar on which Egypt rests. It is the army of all Egyptians, regardless of their group affiliations."**

One does not have to be a mind reader to decipher what El-Sisi was hinting at: The possibility of a military intervention which would suspend Egypt's march toward democratic rule. *Now it was the turn of the opposition to blink. The National Salvation Front agreed to sit with the Islamists and the other forces to sort out their differences in order to save Egypt's transition to democracy.*

Summing up the state of the Egyptian State, one has to conclude that with regard to Egypt of 10,000 years:

COLLAPSE NEVER!! CHANGE OF REGIME NOT UNTHINKABLE!!

IN THE CONTEXT OF THE EGYPTIAN REVOLUTION, AHMADINEJAD OF IRAN CALLS FOR PAN-ISLAMISM

Thursday, February 14, 2013

International conferences serve also bilateral ends. So is with the 12th Summit of the Organization of Islamic Cooperation (OIC) which took place in Cairo on February 5 and 6. Nearly 50% of the membership of 57 States attended. But the only Head of State whose presence eclipsed all others was Ahmadinejad of Iran.

This is significant in the context of the Egyptian Revolution. No Iranian Head of Sate had set foot in the largest Arab State, Egypt, since the signing of the Egypt-Israel Peace Treaty in 1979. That treaty caused Tehran to sever its diplomatic relations with Cairo. And when President Sadat, who had taken that bold step, was assassinated in 1981, a main thoroughfare in Tehran was renamed after the killer (Al-Islambolly). Mubarak, who succeeded Sadat, never forgave the mullahs in Iran for those transgressions.

With Mubarak now in jail, and Morsi, who came from the ranks of the Muslim Brotherhood, in the Presidential palace, the new Egypt felt it was necessary to break with the past. Egyptian diplomacy in the post January 25, 2011 revolution lost no opportunity to assert Egypt's divorce from the era of military dictatorship. Thus Iran was one of those priority areas where Cairo could declare from the top of its hundreds of mingrets its independence from the old quiet alliances.

There is another layer to the cultural archeology of Egypt. Though largely a Sunni State, Egypt remains warm to the Shiis. Cairo was established in the 10th century by a great Shii regime, the Fatimides. (Their name came from Fatima, the daughter of the Prophet Muhammad; the wife of Aly, Muhammad's cousin and protege; and the mother of two of the shining lights of Shiism, Hassan and Al-Hussein).

The historic mosque and university, Al-Azhar, was also built by the Fatimides in Cairo about the same time. (It teaches the Shii main school of thought side by side with the four main Sunni schools. It is no accident that Al-Azhar and the great mosque of Al-Hussein, where Egyptian tradition holds that Al-Hussein's head is buried there, stand next to one another. Millions of Sunni Egyptians flock to that magnificent shrine to pray and invoke the glorified name of Muhammad's grandson who was martyred in Iraq. Next to those great edifices, one finds a section of old Cairo called "Fatimide Cairo."

Now back to Ahmadinejad in Cairo. After being welcomed on February 5 by President Morsi, his first two steps were, predictably, to pray at Al-Hussein shrine, meet with Dr. Ahmed Al-Taiyeb, the Al-Azhar Rector, and hold a press conference to extol the historic relationships between Iran and Egypt.

It was Al-Azhar's Rector, El-Taiyeb, a graduate of the Sorbonne, who articulated a framework for a new relationship between Cairo and Tehran.

Though Ahmadinejad flashed the V sign to the media prior to the Taiyeb-Ahmadinejad mini-summit, Al-Azhar called upon Iran to act on the following issues:

to respect the Sunni veneration of the three Caliphs who preceded Imam Aly (Shii means Partisans of Aly) in leading he then emerging Muslim nation after the passing of Muhammad, the Prophet of Islam;

to accord equal rights to the Sunnis in Al-Ahwaz, the Iranian western province populated largely by Arabs and overlooking the Gulf;

to refrain from interfering in the internal affairs of the Gulf States, especially the State of Bahrain, a member of the Gulf Cooperation Council of six States; and

to fully cooperate in stopping the blood bath in Syria where the present civil war has left more than 60,000 Syrians dead and 2.5 million refugees displaced either internally or externally.

For his part, the Iranian President declared at a press conference that **"I came to Al-Azhar to advocate unity between Sunnis and Shiis. We want to fix together what divides us. This is our solemn duty at present. Like riders in a bus, they can differ in their views, but the bus is moving towards one destination."**

Meanwhile, Egypt's Foreign Minister, Muhammad Kamel Amr, hurried to calm down the nerves of the Gulf States. The new Egypt, in its external relationships, he declared, shall not act at the expense of the security of other States. Then pointedly he added, **"For Egypt, the security of the Gulf States is a red line. Their security is integral to the security of Egypt."**

Accentuating that call for keeping the Gulf States safe from Iranian interference, the Egyptian Salafis (Sunni extremists) declared that Egypt, the largest Sunni state, has the duty and obligation to protect "the Arab Gulf" from any undue influence from outside, being it political, cultural, or military.

Beyond all those declarations lies a factual certainty: The relationship between Iran and Egypt are inching ever closer to one another. Morsi of Egypt began the process of warming up to that relationship. He was the first Egyptian Head of State to visit Iran since the Khemeini Islamic revolution of 1979. That took place when he attended the summit of the

Non-Aligned Movement held in Tehran in August, 2012.

With Iran now being the object of severe western sanctions because of its present nuclear program, Tehran needed to show its public and the world that its foreign affairs outside that wall of sanctions were not impaired.

Reflecting that dynamic was a significant interview granted by Ahmadinejad in Tehran, prior to his Cairo visit, to Al-Ahram newspaper which speaks for the Egyptian Government. In that interview, he made the following declarations in order to frame his global outlook:

Iran has now become a nuclear power. And soon it shall be a State with advanced outer space capabilities;

Sanctions have "affected somewhat our economy." But through Iranian productivity, Iran shall make up for any deficit;

Egypt and Iran, the two States with civilizational depth, should unite their effects to ensure regional and world peace;

Islam is "our path to unity"

The Muslim Brotherhood Versus The Salafis: Divided They Stand at the Helm of Power In Egypt

Friday, February 15, 2013

Together they won 70% of the seats in Parliament. Though the Parliament (the lower chamber) has been dissolved by the Supreme Constitutional Court on a technicality, the forthcoming parliamentary elections promise the same results. Through the highway of democracy, an era of Islamist rule has begun in Egypt .

What does this mean for Egypt? Though nothing can be certain in any revolutionary setting anywhere in the world, there are a few road signs.

First: The Brotherhood and the Salafis say that they are friends, but they are not united. The former are largely moderate, the latter are definitely extremist. There respective political parties (the Brotherhood's

Freedom and Justice Party, and the Salafis' Al-Nour Party) are at loggerheads with one another. Divided they both stand for the term "Islamists." That division has so far not been bridged even by the fact that Morsi, with his roots in the Muslim Brotherhood, is now the popularly-elected president of Egypt.

Second: If healed, the division within the ranks of the Islamists could lead to a functional rapprochement with the secularists. Without that, the Egyptian street could remain chaotic for a long period. And with chaos, the new Egypt shall not be able to shake off its economic misery. It is the economic decline that has been propelling the young and unemployed to the streets to cause destruction and mayhem.

Third: Thrown in the mix of the endless cycle of violence are two main factors. The Egyptian police and the security forces, who are traditionally distrusted, are hated by the masses since the Mubarak days. Their task in quelling mob action has been made more complicated by the recently-acquired capability of the demonstrators to fight tear gas with tear gas, and bird shots with home-made Molotov cocktails. The other factor in that deadly mix is the understandable reluctance of the armed forces to get dragged in those street battles.

By staying above the fray, the armed forces have remained the darling of the masses, and the only cohesive force in the largest Arab country whose population has now surpassed 90 millions.

From the reality of political division within Egypt, to the ideological thinking which is now taking hold in the land of the pharaohs, we see the Arab Spring's inability to fulfill its promise: dignity, democracy, and development.

The Brotherhood espouses the mantra of "Islam is the solution," while the Salafis adhere to the necessity for "the return to the practices of early Islam." (Salaf means ancestor, in this case in the spiritual sense). On the surface, the two ideological principles may look the same. In reality, they are not. For the Brotherhood, Islamism accommodates evolution in interpretation; for the Salafis, literalism of the text defines Islamism. Thus one can visualize the Muslim Brotherhood as standing for evolution, and the Salafis as the party for creationism. In governance, the gulf becomes even larger as it impacts on the daily life of a cosmopolitan country like Egypt.

At least for now, the Brotherhood and the Salafis look more like the most durable political forces in Egypt. Both groups have emerged from the street and have remained the closest of the entire political spectrum in Egypt to the street. They, especially the Muslim Brotherhood since its inception in 1928, have known what makes the street tick, what basic services does it need, what language does it understand. Al-Azhar, for the last 1040 years, has always been the fount of Islamic learning and the Mecca of interfaith, especially in regard to the great Coptic church. But Al-Azhar has always remained an educational institution and a lightening rod for patriotism, but not a vehicle for street organization.

Thus, the Egyptian revolutionary experience in the post-Mubarak era, may eventually parallel the Turkish experience: Islamist rule which tolerates diversity, with the armed forces keeping watch over internal and external security.

Within this framework, the call for a dialogue between the various political forces in Egypt, whose only organized element is the Islamist, remains elusive. The secularists are calling for the return to square one of the Egyptian Revolution. This in effect means the delegitimation of the previous popular votes including the referendum on the new Constitution. The Islamist, comfortable at the helm of legislative and executive power, are calling for respect of the popular will, the status quo.

Neither the Islamists nor the secularists shall be able to make the daily demonstrations go away. In the meantime, the Egyptian street, though weary of the split within the ranks of the Islamists, is more weary of the altercation amongst the seventy political parties and movements. But progressively, the voice of the secularists is losing its resonance with the millions who are hungry for stability, and a better life.

The only strong thread which is holding the ship of the Egyptian State Egypt, together, regardless of affiliations is the slogans. "WE ALL LOVE EGYPT"

Soliloquy of a Dictator: "Whenever I thought of relinquishing power?!"

Friday, February 22, 2013

This blog deals with something different. It is a poem by the famous Syrian poet and songwriter, Nizar Qabbani. The original is in Arabic, translated into English by this blogger. It is intended to focus on the magic of folklore in the Arab Spring, and on why people revolt.

It shall be read by this blogger at an event in Toronto, Canada, which is co-sponsored by SUNSGLOW - Global Training in the Rule of Law and the Toronto University Club. The date of this event is February 27; the topic is: "The Arab Spring and Human Rights." The format is a panel to be chaired by William Horton, Esq., who heads SUNSGLOW's Regional Liaison Center in Toronto, the most recent addition to our ensemble of regional liaison centers around the world.

Now to the Nizar Qabbani poem:

WHENEVER I THOUGHT OF RELINQUISHING POWER?
Whenever I thought of relinquishing power
My conscience stood in the way

After I am gone
who will rule these good people?

After me
who will cure the limp
the leper
the blind?
who will raise the dead?

And from whose overcoat
will the light of the moon shine?

And who will bestow on
the people the gift of rain?

And who will whip them
ninety lashings?

And who will hang them
from the limbs of trees?

And who will force them
to live like herds of cows?
And perish as cows perish?

Whenever I think of

relinquishing power?

My eyes fill out with tears
as if they were a rain cloud.

So let my fate to rule stand, for it is
my destiny

And it shall be from now until
the end of time.

Poem about dictatorship and liberty
By Nizar Qabbani (in Arabic)

Translation into English
By Yassin El-Ayouty

21 MARCH 2013

The Question That Needs to Be Answered in Egypt: What Does the Word "DIALOGUE" Mean?

Friday, March 1, 2013

Time for a simulation exercise in the art of dialogue between the Islamists and the secularists in the new Egypt. The January 25, 2011 Revolution is broken. Its only hope for repair, which is the only road to a successful transition to democracy, is through reaching an important understanding. That is an understanding of what the word "dialogue" means.

So here we go with an imaginary setting. We prepare a conference room with a long table and several comfortable chairs lined up on the two sides of that table. Please do not forget to place the same number of seats for each side. We think that 12 seats for the Islamists and the same number of seats for the secularists would suffice. Oh!! Don't forget to place bottled water and flowers and pads and pens for the participants. No recording please. Only one flag, the flag of Egypt, shall be placed behind the moderator of this imaginary dialogue.

The participants enter the conference room. Instinctively the Islamists, in long robes and overgrown beards, seat themselves on the right; the secularists, equally divided in number between men and women in various attires, are now seated to the left. Whispers amongst each group abound until the moderator gavels the conference to order, then begins:

Moderator: *"In the Name of God, the Merciful and the Compassionate!! Brothers and sisters: we are here today to help the new Egypt move forward. I wish to thank the Muslim Brotherhood and the Salafis for calling for this dialogue with their opponents, whom I also thank for agreeing to attend. I now call on the Islamists to briefly state their case."*

Islamist: *"Our country, Egypt, is beloved by all of us. We won the parliamentary elections and also the presidential elections. The goal of the Egyptian Revolution is to attain democracy and development. We did not stage a coup. We now govern Egypt under a new Constitution approved by a majority. Our brothers and sisters across the table from us do not like the results of the ballot box. They are trying to prevent Egypt from going forward."*

Secularist: *"The Islamists are trying to steal our Revolution. They were not at the frontlines in Tahrir Square on January 25, 2011. They only came in from the cold when they found us, both Muslims and Copts, men and women, young and old, rich and poor, winning..."*

Another Islamist (interrupting): *"This is nonsense!! These are blatant lies. They..."*

Moderator: *"You are interrupting her. Let her make her case. Let her..."*

A third Islamist: *"They have no case, we are the majority which..."*

Moderator: *"Excuse me. You want a dialogue? Yet you are turning it into a monologue. You either stop or I shall adjourn this meeting."* (Turning to the secularist speaker, a non-veiled young woman in a pant suit) *"Please continue..."*

Secularist: *"What has taken place right now makes our case. The Islamists say they want a dialogue. But in essence, they lack the understanding of how to deal with those like us who oppose an Islamist regime. Egypt is too cosmopolitan and too diverse to be governed by the rule of numbers."*

Moderator: *"What do you mean? But democracy is primarily the rule by the majority!!"*

Another Secularist: "*We are not sure that the results of the elections, whether parliamentary or presidential, have reflected the popular will.*"

A fourth Islamist: "*There they go again!! The secularists, who do not even speak with one voice, want Egypt to scrap the results of all elections and referenda, including those approving our New Constitution. They are demonizing us for having won. They are resorting to civil disobedience, strikes and work stoppages in order to prevent President Morsi and Prime Minister Qandeel from getting Egypt back on track.*"

A third Secularist: "*As a Copt, I feel threatened by the Salafis who look upon the great Coptic Church as a strange object in Egyptian society. While Islam calls for tolerance and the acceptance of the other, the Islamists go on describing those who do not see things their way as being against Islam.*"

Moderator: (*Seeing a Salafi focused on shaping pieces of paper into little paper boats*) "*Sir!! Aren't you interested in what the opposition is saying? Why did you join us today? Please show some respect for your opponents.*" [*The Salafis protest:* "*This is democracy!*"]

Moderator again to the Salafi: "*This is a disgusting abuse of your newly-found freedom.*" [*The Salafi ignores the Moderator*] {*This has actually happened and was on the air.*}

A fifth Islamist: "*We know that the street is with us. And we know that there is no way that the results of the ballot box are going to be nullified by the judiciary. That judiciary has come about through dictatorial manipulations by Mubarak and his National Democratic Party (DNC). The secularists are now joining hands with the DNC in their common cause of scuttling our newly-found democracy.*"

A fourth Secularist: "*What he has just said proves our point. We demonstrate peacefully, and the Salafis besiege the Information Production City to prevent the new Egypt from free expression. They use the Police and the security forces to club us into submission. We are not against Islam, but we are against the Islamization of governance in Egypt. We...*"

Moderator (pointing to his watch): I am sorry that the time for this conversation is up. Neither side has reconciled with the other. Frankly, I am startled by the chasm dividing Egypt into two currents: Islamism and secularism. For the sake of Egypt, let us try to meet again. Otherwise, all shall be lost. This meeting stands adjourned.*"

[Blogger's Note: Some of the material in this blog has been inspired by a brilliant article dated December 22, 2012 by Essam Abdel-Aziz, Editor-in-

Chief of ROSAELYOUSSEF, an Egyptian political magazine established in 1935 by Mrs. Fatima El-Youssef. The interpretation of that material and the flow of this imaginary dialogue is the sole responsibility of this blogger].

An Egyptian Republic of Port Said? You Must Be Crazy!!

Friday, March 15, 2013

The Port Said declaration of independence from Egypt is the latest dangerous turn in Egypt's transition to democracy. And the call by that presumed minister on the Minister of Defense, El-Sisi, to assume its presidency is nothing but a provocation of the military. It is a hoax which puts the entire Arab Spring to the test, not only in Egypt but also throughout the Arab world.

The anger shown by the fans of Port Said's soccer team, El-Masri, at a court decision in Cairo that 21 of those fans should face capital punishment may be understandable. The accused have been inculpated in the wanton death of 74 fans of the rival El-Ahli team of Cairo at the end of a game in Port Said. With the judiciary in Egypt being at loggerheads with the regime of President Morsi, attacking the court decision in this case, commonly called "the Port said massacre," seemed to fit in with the present pattern of chaos in Egypt.

At Port Said, as well at the other major cities on the Suez Canal, the protection of safe international passage through the Canal has always been the responsibility of Egypt's armed forces. But as the inhabitants of Port Said rose up in indignation against the judiciary, the dangerous by-product has been the prolonged attacks by the public on nearly all government installations. The police cannot cope with that massive surge of lawlessness. So the army is now filling the security gaps left by the yet-to-be reorganized police and security forces in the post-Mubarak era.

Unfortunately, things did not stop there. Both the army and the police came under fire emanating from the throngs besieging government and private installations and other properties. On its Facebook page, the Ministry of Interior which is in charge of the police issued a startling declaration on March 4. It claimed that unknown persons are trying to sow armed conflict between the police and the army. Some members of those forces were injured in that spasm of indiscriminate shootings.

In such a situation, Egypt's armed forces could not possibly stand idly by. This claimed provocation has come on the heels of arsoning of the Port Said Governerate Building by the mob using Molotov cocktails. Until now, the casualties have been 3 dead and more than 400 injured. Two army soldiers died as a result of these uncontrollable clashes. In the meantime, the spokesman for the armed forces, Ahmed Muhammad Aly, denied the rumors that police elements and armed forces elements were locked into battle against one another in Port Said.

Even without these clashes, Port Said has witnessed for the past 3 weeks a state of civil disobedience. As a result, most of the city's productivity has come to a standstill. The only activity which has proceeded unabated is the throngs of unemployed marauding in Port Said, shouting against the Morsi regime and against the country's miserable economic situations.

Manifestations of the persistent chaos of revolutionary Egypt abound:

The Egyptian International Council for Human Rights addressed a call to General El-Sisi to assume supreme power in Egypt until the country transitions from the present upheaval to stability. This is obviously a call for unseating President Morsi.

Fifteen thousand forms calling on El-Sisi to lead the country have been distributed to the inhabitants of other cities, like Ismailia and Port Said.

Calls for civil disobedience have gone out to the inhabitants of major cities like El-Mansoura and Alexandria.

Clashes between the demonstrators and the security forces continued in Cairo and centered on the area of international hotel chains, such as the Semiramis in Cairo.

The general parliamentary elections which were scheduled to take place this April throughout Egypt for the lower Chamber have been postponed by a judicial decision.

Earlier in March, the secularists staged noisy demonstrations against what they described as the "Islamization" of the Egyptian armed forces, and for the removal of President Morsi, and the nullification of the new

Constitution

Throngs surrounded the statue of the unknown soldier in Cairo on a Friday called "Support the Armed Forces Friday." Women and Copts were in the lead of those vociferous demonstrations.

Against the background in this security collapse, all the pronouncements of General El-Sisi and his spokesman have been to affirm the armed forces commitment to Egypt's internal and external security. It is important to note that the oath of the inductees into the huge Egyptian army stresses the loyalty to Egypt and the armed forces. No loyalty is affirmed for the crazy notion of an Egypt made up of city states. Even Mubarak, from his jail cell and through his attorney, has issued an appeal to his countrymen who deposed him to stop the madness and to rally around Morsi, the elected President.

Whatever You Do In Tahrir or Elsewhere, Do Not Mess with the Armed Forces!!

Friday, March 15, 2013

On March 14, Egypt's Minister of Defense, **General Abdel-Fattah El-Sisi**, issued another warning to the demonstrators and conflicted political forces in his country. As usual, the warning was indirect, but could not be misunderstood. **"We are going to confront anyone who threatens Egypt's peace or Egypt's army!!"**

Expanding on this verbal shot across the bow of the street forces which has disrupted life and normalcy in Egypt, El-Sisi, who was addressing Egyptian border forces, added: **"The armed forces have been working at their highest levels of fighting preparedness for the restoration of the country's sovereignty, the guarding of its territorial and sea boundaries, and the rebuffing of everyone who might even think of threatening Egypt's peace or the security of its armed forces."**

El-Sisi was not only addressing Egyptians. He was also baring the teeth of Egypt's army, a huge professional force whose traditions go back to **Muhammad Aly**, the founder of modern Egypt in 1805, to all other Arab nationalities involved in the smuggling into and out of Egypt of arms, drugs and humans. Against that geostrategic background, the General promised continued modernization of the border forces, stretched from the borders of the Sudan (south), to Libya's (west), to the Mediterranean (north), to Gaza's and the Red Sea (east).

The armed forces had contributed massively to the destruction of the **Mubarak** regime through telling the dictator that they belonged to Egypt, not to its President. Thus they could not open fire on the Tahrir demonstrators who were shielded by their national army from destruction. Egypt was neither Libya under Qaddafi, nor Syria under Assad.

By the same token, the armed forces, in their oath of service, do not pledge loyalty except to **"Egypt and the Armed Forces."** This is not the oath of a sectarian army, or of a militia, or of an Islamist force or of a secular force. It is a pledge to serve Egypt as a whole. That is especially so under the new Constitution of November 2012 which provided for a special status for the armed forces, under a system of civilian oversight.

The gist of all those declarations was **"DO NOT MESS WITH THE ARMED FORCES!!!"** The results were nearly immediate:

The mutiny within the ranks of police officers evaporated.

All police precincts and related offices were back to work.

The Minister of Interior pledged better armament and other equipment to the police forces.

The chaos in Port Said which needed intervention by the armed forces came to an abrupt end.

The calls on **El-Sisi** to assume power disappeared. That call by the secularists for an army coup was disregarded.

The public seems to have awakened to a central fact of Egypt's difficult transition to democracy: **The armed forces were not going either to replace the police or to stage a coup.** The armed forces were not going to be manipulated by the new political forces continually contending for power in the new Egypt.

Commenting on the return to near normalcy to the Egyptian Street, **Muhammad Hassanain Heykal**, the writer/statesman of the **Nasser** era, and the oracle of Egypt at that time said:

"The religious and the secular forces in Egypt, being on a collision course, have realized that the armed forces have refused to be dragged in the quagmire of the politics of the public square. But if public safety and the functioning of the State are in peril, then the armed forces will come to the rescue."

Tunneling Under the Walls of Egyptian Sovereignty

Friday, March 22, 2013

The walls of sovereignty are mythical. But in international law they are real whether they are between the borders of the State of Arizona, and Mexico, or between Sinai of Egypt and Gaza of Hamas.

Due to the Israeli blockade around Gaza, the Gazans have dug up hundreds of tunnels through which all kinds of goods are smuggled. From cars to cement; from vegetables to armament; from person to equipment. However, it seems that Egypt's tolerance of these very lucrative tunnels, lucrative to Palestinian tunnel owners and diggers, has now come to an end.

From the succession of events and the official and non-official declarations of the Egyptian armed forces guarding Sinai, it appears that secular Egypt under Mubarak had turned a blind eye to the tunneling under Egypt's sovereign boundaries. By contrast, the leadership of Egypt's armed forces does not entertain such tolerance. Sinai has become a priority security concern.

President Morsi has deep Islamic (Muslim Brotherhood) roots. Thus he may have been expected by Hamas, an offshoot of the Brotherhood, to be in favor of the tunnels even more than before. Events are now proving the contrary, at least as far as the armed forces are concerned. Their primary duty is to ensure secure borders, and the tunnels are nothing but a form of invasion.

The attack on Egyptian armed forces in the Sinai region late last year resulted in the death of 16 armed forces personnel and a greater number were injured. **"Intolerable and shameful"** screamed the Egyptian media.

And now the finger of accusation is pointed by the armed forces to suspects from Gaza.

The main headline in **Al-Ahram** newspaper which speaks for the Government headlined on Tuesday, March 19, **"The Army Fortifies Sinai."** Then, in a sub-heading, it added **"Unprecedented Security measures. The arrest of 3 Palestinians accused of unlawful entry."** The Governorate (Province) of North Sinai has recently been flooded by heavy equipment for the destruction of the tunnels leading from Gaza into Sinai. We have also been witnessing large concentrations of armed forces and police personnel in that region. The change of military uniforms of the Third Egyptian army which is based in Sinai, had been the result of impersonating these forces.

Egypt's armed forces have discovered large quantities of the cloth from which Egyptian army uniforms are made. Those goods were about to be smuggled through the tunnels from Rafah, Egypt, into Gaza. That discovery was followed by a stern warning by the armed forces against insinuating persons bent upon creating mischief into Sinai. The immediate background of that episode was a deadly clash against the police during the civilian uprising in Port Said. During that clash, shots were fired which were later falsely described as clashes between the army and the police. **Nonsense!!** --said both the army and the police. The engagement included persons dressed in Egyptian army uniforms.

General Osama Askar, commander of the Third Army declared that army uniforms have been changed to foil the plots of smugglers who use the tunnels to create conflict between the army and the Egyptian masses, or between the army and the police.

Questions about the Egypt vs. Gaza case arose also on the diplomatic front. It seems that General El-Sisi, Egypt's Minister of Defense, has refused to see Khalid Meshaal, Hamas political chief, when he was recently in Cairo. The media attributed this rebuff to the still to be proved involvement of Hamas operatives in the murder of those 16 Egyptian army personnel, last year. The Egyptian street is abuzz with the rumors that El-Sisi has vowed to bring those accused of that heinous aggression at the Egyptian-Gaza border to justice.

Thus when Ismail Haniyah, head of the so-called Gaza government, called for security coordination between Hamas and Egypt, his call fell on deaf ears in Cairo.

The Arab Spring has brought about an Egyptian regime with an Islamic orientation. But Islamism on one side of the border does not translate into a religious/ideological orientation on the two sides of that border. The sovereignty of Egypt is standing in the way of such a coalition based on religion. The hundreds of illegal tunnels between Rafah (Egypt) and Gaza seem now to be doomed. They have stood for underpasses which in effect undermined Egypt's control over its troubled border to the east.

Raping Women in Egypt Is Raping the Egyptian Revolution

Friday, March 29, 2013

Islamic law equates in many respects between men and women. Muhammad, the Prophet of Islam, encouraged women to offer counsel at his councils. Article 4 of the Egyptian Constitution of December 2012 provides for: **"Equality before the law and equal opportunities for all citizens, men and women, without discrimination or nepotism, especially in the areas of education, employment, political rights..."** The majority of the drafters of that historic document were Islamists.

Women have spearheaded the revolution of January 25, 2011. They were in Tahrir Square and in field hospitals. They were the cheerleaders for the rebellion against Mubarak; the attackers of the security forces. Some of them were martyred, while other women became graffiti artists. In their long robes, and in western attire, women stood for hours to cast their votes enthusiastically.

In the early days of the revolution, the Muslim Brotherhood and the Salafis stayed on the sidelines for 3 crucial days. It was only on January 28, 2011, that advance elements of the Islamists, seeing these millions in every public square in Egypt clamoring for the Dictator's downfall, joined in. The occasion was the infamous **"Battle of the Camels"** when Mubarak's thugs thought that fear was a winning tactic. It backfired, and a few days later, Mubarak was history.

While in Cairo last December observing the process by which the Egyptian Constitution was approved, I interviewed women revolutionaries. These included young women pilots who fly for Egyptair. What a jump in the status of women in the new Egypt. No longer are women **"half the sky"**; they seem to be destined to be **"most of the sky."**

There is even a **"Voice of Egyptian Women,"** an informal advocacy group that, to quote from their petition to Egyptian President Morsi and to the Cabinet of Dr. Qandeel, **"wishes to promote and safeguard the rights and interests of Egyptian women."**

Then suddenly, the new Egypt seems, especially as of 2013, to speak about the status of women through two uncoordinated voices. At a panel organized in early February in connection with the 44th Cairo International Book Fair, veiled women, representing the Islamists, insisted that **"the status of women in the new Egypt was better than before."** But the non-veiled participants, representing the secularists, the liberals and the Copts, countered that **"the new regime has taken Egyptian women back to the dark ages."**

These contradictory statements were followed by pointed accusations by the liberals that women have become the targets of sexual harassment aiming at preventing them from participating in demonstrations and other activities of political involvement.

The door to an ugly deterioration in gender equality and to the enhancement of women's role in Egypt's political life was suddenly flung open -the rise of rape and sexual assaults. The clarion was sounded on Egyptian TV by Ms. Hania Moheeb. It was a first in the Arab world for a rape victim to appear for all to see describing in details her ordeal. That defiance of social taboos was made the more historic by the appearance of Ms. Moheeb's husband next to her to lend support. **"She did nothing wrong!!,"** he declared in defense of his spouse.

Hania detailed to the entire Arab world how a group of men attacked her during a public protest. The Egyptian National Council of Women declared that by its count, there were 18 such cases which were tallied by other human rights groups. Ms. Moheeb, 42 years of age and a journalist, made of her ordeal a cause celebre in order to graphically describe the breakdown of social order in generally conservative Egypt.

*Hurriedly, the Morsi government embarked upon drafting legislation to criminalize sexual harassment. Whether that measure shall cure the problem remains to be seen. But what Hania Moheeb has done by going public with the full backing of her husband is akin to an earthquake which collapsed the wall of silence. At a recent women demonstration, the marchers held long knives above their heads and chanted: **"Don't***

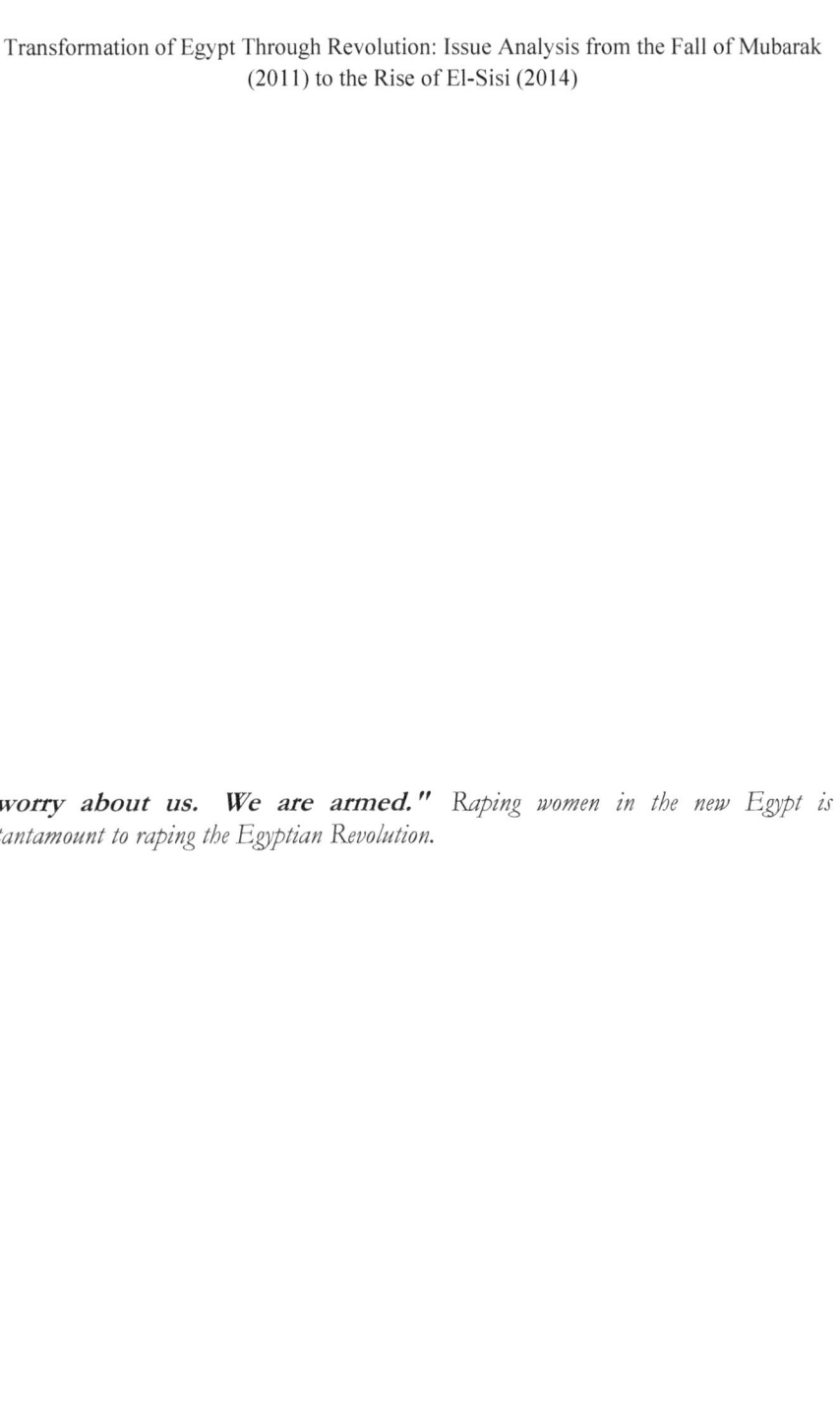

worry about us. We are armed." *Raping women in the new Egypt is tantamount to raping the Egyptian Revolution.*

22 APRIL 2013

In Egypt's Valley of the Kings, The Pharaohs are Angry Tonight

Friday, April 5, 2013

From Ramses, to Tut; from Nefertiti to Hatshepsut: along the western edge of the great Nile, the Pharaohs are angry!! In the stillness of the desert night, brightly lit by the moon and the stars, they wake up from their slumber. A soft but angry whisper is passed amongst them, from tomb to tomb; from mummy to mummy. Then the whisper becomes a quieter rage carried north to Cairo on the wings of the desert winds. It reverberates and grows into a hurricane of protests in which Cheops of the Great Pyramids, and the Sphinx join in a maddening scream:

"WHERE HAVE THE TOURISTS GONE? WE ARE ETERNAL, AND WE HAVE RIGHTS TOO!! WE ARE LONELY, DESERTED, EVEN DESPISED BY SOME OF THOSE WHO ROSE IN REBELLION AGAINST MUBARAK. MUBARAK PRETENDED TO BE ONE OF US. HA, HA, HA!! WE BUILT A STABLE AND A GREAT NATION. EGYPT IS OURS. WE STAYED AND IT STAYED. BRING US BACK OUR TOURISTS, OUR TRUE WORSHIPPERS, OUR THOUSANDS OF FOREIGN

FRIENDS WHO TAKE PICTURES AND PROVIDE MOTHER EGYPT WITH HUGE INCOME. GO BRING THEM BACK. AND IF YOU DON'T, OUR CURSE SHALL BE UPON YOU!!"

Twenty percent of Egypt's foreign currency earnings have evaporated. The income from tourism is probably more stable than the income from the Suez Canal. But with the chaos in the Egyptian street, the tourists are staying away. In December last year, I got accustomed to have breakfast alone at my Cairo hotel. The cook and the helpers were my only companions. They looked sad, even frightened as they tell me: **"Dr. Yassin, we are at only 20% capacity!! No more tourists except the occasional backpacker who cannot spend too much. We have to feed our families and keep this place open!!"**

In their frustration, they are not alone. From the Minister of Tourism, Zaazou, to the Head of the Egyptian Tourism Authority, Nasser Hamdy, to the idle guides, the great city of Luxor now looks like a ghost town. Ninety percent of its population depend on tourism for their livelihood. Guides have tours but only three or four a month. The guards of those great monuments are also idle. Cruise ships are moored together in bunches along the Nile. The smell of death, death of a great Egyptian industry, is unmistakable. Neither Indian nor Iranian tourism can replace the traditional western, Russian, Japanese, and Australian tourists who are the big spenders.

In 1949, one year after college graduation, I wrote a play in Arabic, one of a total of 17 which in 1952 garnered for me a Fulbright Scholarship to the U.S. My plays, which were also used as methods of teaching Egyptian history, had songs in them. I was reminded of one of them at the Valley of the Kings, west of the Nile in Luxor. Here is how it happened:

I was standing with a group of American friends at the entrance of the tomb of King Tut. Our young guide was an Assistant Professor of Antiquities in Cairo. His name is Tarek, a bright young man whose mother was German, and who loved his subject. Suddenly Tarek told the group:

"We have among us today the author of a play in Arabic which my University Department has used as a part of lively teaching material. The title of the play is 'Conflict Among the Gods.' Here is the author!!" His finger was pointing at me. It was a play on the original ancient concept of the Holy Trinity: Father (Osiris), mother (Isis) and son (Horus). Horus, depicted in monuments as a falcon was avenging the brutal death of his father at the hands of the malevolent, Seth, Osiris' brother. **Osiris stood for ancient Egypt as the great just ruler. He also stood for the concepts of resurrection and victory over death.**

The love of ancient Egypt was drilled in us as of primary school. At the age of 8, my father, an Islamic scholar, took me from our village northeast of the Nile Delta to Cairo. It was my first time in that historic capital. Our first destination was the Pyramids and the Sphinx. There I stood speechless gazing upon those timeless attractions. Suddenly my father started to recite a secular prayer -a poem extolling the nexus between Egypt and its monuments. In my translation, the poem goes like this:

"These are our monuments;
 After we are gone;
 Don't forget to come gaze upon us."

But today, the Pharaohs are angry!! No more tourists to gaze upon them!!

Death at the Cathedral - St. Mark's Cathedral, Cairo, Egypt

Friday, April 12, 2013

Gone are the days in the late 1960's. Nasser was in power; the dictatorship kept the streets safe; and Muslim-Coptic conflict was unheard of, in fact unthinkable. That great Cathedral where St. Mark of Alexandria is interred had stood at that time unfinished. Nasser noticed and asked his escort why had construction stopped. The answer came crisp and clear: **"Mr. President: the Coptic church ran out of money!!"** Nasser's response was historic: **"The State should fund the project"** And it was done!!

As we know, St. Mark was one of the great four Gospel writers: Matthew, Mark, Luke and John. Through St. Mark, and through history, including the flight of the Holy Family to Egypt, the land of the pharaohs has always enjoyed a special place in the history of Christianity. In fact, the word Egypt in Greek means the land of the Copts. **"Blessed is Egypt my People"** (Isaiah 19:25); **"Out of Egypt I called my son"** (Matthew 2:15); **"Egypt is not a country in which we live. It is a country that lives in us"** (His Holiness, Pope Shenouda III, who joined his creator on March 17,

2012).

The Vatican released the remains of St. Mark to Egypt, 2 years before Nasser died in 1970, for reburial in his homeland, which lived in him. St. Mark's return to **"the land of Copts"** for reburial at the great Cathedral named after him in Abbasia, east of Cairo, was a great national day. In fact it was international, as Emperor Haile Selassie of Ethiopia and many other world dignitaries also attended. The Ethiopian Church was, and continues to be, a branch of the great orthodoxy of the Eastern Roman Empire from which emerged the Russian, Greek, Syrian and Armenian churches.

Tradition holds that the first church in Christendom was that of Alexandria -established a mere 200 years after Christ. Christ had stayed in Egypt, together with the Virgin Mary, for four years. Hence the title of the heads of the Coptic church as **"The Pope of Alexandria and the Patriarch of St. Mark's Bishopric."**

That was and remains the indelible link of Egypt to Christianity, as well as to monotheism in general, including Judaism through Moses who was Egyptian-born. But with the destruction of dictatorship in Egypt as result of the Revolution of January 25, 2011, something else was born as an unwanted companion to democracy -chaos. With chaos in the Egyptian street, came the Muslim-Coptic conflict. The Morsi regime was pulverized by the events which began at a village north of Cairo called (Al-Khossouss) on Sunday, April 7, which resulted in the death of 4 Copts, one Muslim, and the injury of many.

But the tragedy of the newly-introduced sectarianism in Egypt did not end there. As the Copts and Muslims were processing from St. Mark's Cathedral for the burial of the 4 Coptic youths, additional blood was spilt. Details of the tragedy are still unfolding. What is clear so far was that the Cathedral was the scene of an ugly confrontation. At the beginning, security was nearly absent. But as additional security forces arrived, the intensity of the melee increased as tear gas canisters were hurled by officers haphazardly into the Cathedral compound. Lack of training? Perhaps.

Morsi called for a prompt investigation and called the attack on St. Mark's Cathedral **"an attack on me personally."** Al-Azhar, as well as all stripes of political and other institutions, organizations and movements, including the Muslim Brotherhood, raised their voices in anger condemning that dastardly attack. Al-Azhar also cited a prior attack on its own headquarters by "thugs." The very fabric of Egyptian society seems to be coming apart.

One wonders about the Arab Spring as it unfolds in Egypt. Several questions arise: Is there a sectarian conflict in post-Mubarak Egypt? Yes. Are the Copts, who constitute perhaps more than 10% of a population of nearly 90 million anxious about their future? Yes. How do they express that anxiety? They point to their marginalization, especially under an Islamic-oriented regime. That marginalization has been eloquently expressed by a great Coptic writer in New Jersey, Francois Basili. Francois is the son of a famous Coptic priest by the name of Bolus Basili who, though a cleric, was a member of Parliament during the Sadat era, representing both Muslim and Coptic residents of the Cairo district of Shobra.

Have the Copts materially manifested their fear about the ominous trend toward Islamic-Coptic animosity? Yes. One of the great families of Coptic entrepreneurs, the Sawiris Group, has left Egypt, together with their huge investments in telecommunications.

The attack on the Coptic Cathedral is not the only instance of of the vanishing tolerance for diversity and cosmopolitanism in Egypt. Other examples abound. There is a rise in anti-Shiism as manifested by the recent Salafi attack on the residence of the Iranism diplomat in Cairo who is charged with overseeing Iranian interests in Egypt. (There are yet no diplomatic relations between Tehran and Cairo.)

There are constant verbal attacks on the liberal Mufti of Egypt, Sheikh Aly Gomaa. Furthermore, there is a spike in acts of sexual harassment intended to shove women out of public life. In a sign of palpable anger, the Pope of Alexandria has left for self-exile in the western desert where the Wadi El-Natroon Convent exists. It is an act intended to say, as the late Pope Shenouda used to say: **"God hears our silence!!"**

The future looks ominous. But it is not yet definitively desperate. For the land of the Copts, the homeland of St. Mark, the country which lives in the Copts (as well as in the Muslims) is probably trying to rediscover its historic and authentic identity. With revolutions, patience is a great virtue. May the blessings of St. Mark and the moderation of true Islam heal those wounds.

From Behind Bars Mubarak Smiles

Friday, April 19, 2013

On April, 13, the former dictator of Egypt was wheeled into court. The occasion was his retrial on charges related to the killing of protesters in January and February 2011, prior to his forced abdication on February 11 of that fateful year. So why was he smiling from behind those iron bars?

His two sons, Alaa and Gamal were next to him as co-defendants. Some of his supporters showed up and cheered him. Nattily dressed, Mubarak sat up in his hospital bed, no more the laid-up sickly person with his finger in his nose as on prior occasions. In recognition of those cheers, he raised up his hand in a gesture of confident greetings for his supporters. The families of the victims of early 2011 were outnumbered and looked sullen.

Outside that Cairo court, more Mubarak supporters showed up in buses, private cars and on foot. Shouting slogans of acclamation, their signs in Arabic read **"THE PEOPLE WANT TO HONOR THE PRESIDENT."** That was a slogan debunking the anti-Mubarak slogan of 2 years ago which reverberated through Tahrir and throughout Egypt and the rest of the Arab Spring countries: **"THE PEOPLE WANT TO COLLAPSE THE REGIME."**

Back to the court, another big surprise: As Mubarak smiled, (or was it a smirk?), the presiding judge, Mustafa Hassan Abdulla, unexpectedly ended the session as quickly as it began. Recusing himself, he cited conflict of interest, whatever that meant in this context. Those events scarring the progress of the Egyptian Revolution, the mother of all Arab Spring revolutions, may be pointing to the emergence of a new theory of revolutionary relativity. It may be briefly expounded in one basic question: "Between the Stability under the Mubarak dictatorship and the chaos under the Morsi democracy, what should the average Egyptian choose?"

This is a huge question which can only be answered on the ground in Egypt by Egyptians who are the only party that could define their own expectations. For now, there is no clear definition for those expectations except through hurling insults by the secularists at President Morsi, and by the Islamists calling the secularists all kinds of names. That verbal war, though not an answer to the lack of security or to the economic near-collapse, might be a catharsis for the 60-years of imposed silence on the Egyptian masses by the former security State.

Other questions are now thrown into the mix and are generated by the Mubarak smiles from behind bars. That smile and that wave by the hand in greeting his supporters in that Cairo court room conveyed what the Germans call SCHDENFREUDE - malicious enjoyment of others' misfortunes. The others are, of course, all those whose revolt brought down the throne of that latter-day pharaoh. Mubarak, for the duration of his 30 years of rule (1981-2011) has told the world: **"Either I or chaos!!"** For the moment, with chaos rampant in Egypt, his demeanor in court conveyed an unmistaken message: **"I told you so!!"**

Mubarak supporters are now repeating the same mantra. I asked an Egyptian businessman in New York City about his feelings regarding post-Mubarak Egypt. His swift response was **"I yearn for even one day of Mubarak's rule. He made the streets safe and business vibrant."**

The Egyptian judiciary, at least its Islamist segment, felt differently. The Attorney General (AG), Talaat Abdullah, has now ordered Mubarak's removal from the comfort of the Armed Forces Hospital overlooking the great Nile in Maadi, south of Cairo, to a hospital bed at the Tora prison where Mubarak's two sons are held. The AG's office announced that the return of Mubarak to the prison's hospital was recommended by a medical team which, after examining the deposed President, concluded that his robust health merited such transfer.

Simultaneously, the President of the Appeals Court (a lower court as compared to Egypt's highest court - the Court of Cassassion), Counsellor Samir Abu-Elmaaty, fixed a new date for the retrial of Mubarak and his sons - May 11. The venue of that trial is the Criminal Court of Cairo North (the 2nd Chamber). The charges have remained the same: Complicity in the death of nearly 900 demonstrators in early 2011, and corruption represented by the conversion of public wealth into private wealth.

Those who smile (or laugh) last, smile (or laugh) longer. Yet the smiles of the anti-Mubarak forces in Egypt - a country united by the pharaohs and the Nile, and split by the January 25 revolution by the Islamists versus the secularists including the Copts - are also an expression of SCHADENFREUDE!!

23 MAY 2013

The Egyptian Revolution Adrift

Friday, May 24, 2013

The great Egyptian Revolution of January 25, which toppled Mubarak's dictatorship is adrift two and a half years later. Democracy has not yet been established, except in form only; chaos has not yet subsided; the Egyptian street is not yet safe; the economy is in a free fall; and a bread and butter revolt of the millions who are under the poverty line, seems to be in the making.

The main features of this stalled revolution is *the antagonism between the Executive and the Judicial authorities; a disorganized secular opposition; the resurgence of the backers of the defunct Mubarak regime; and the pressures on the Morsi regime to resist the stringent conditions of the International Monetary Fund for providing Egypt with a sorely needed loan.*

Taking up the alienation between the Morsi regime and the Judiciary, we note that the new Justice Minister, Ahmed Soliman, has announced on May 8 that his first priority was to rebuild the bridges between the Government (a new Cabinet was sworn in by Morsi on May 7) and the Judiciary. One of the many sticking points in this issue is a draft bill supported by the

Government providing for the retirement of judges at the age of sixty instead of seventy. If adopted, the result would be the retirement of more than 3000 Egyptian judges.

The judiciary, backed up by the opposition, suspect that retirement at 60 would aid the Morsi regime, which has sprung from the womb of the Muslim Brotherhood in appointing a new generation of judges who are in favor of the Brotherhood. If this happens, which now seems unlikely, the Brotherhood would claim control or exercise influence on the legislature (for now, the Upper Chamber of Parliament called the Shura), the executive, and the judiciary. A recipe for a reversion by Egypt to an unwanted autocracy.

Still more on the judicial crisis: the new Minister of Justice, in his commitment to supporting judicial independence, draws his strength from his former opposition to Morsi's so-called **"Constitutional Declaration"** of November 22, 2012 which, prior to its nullification, had virtually placed Morsi above the law. Minister Soliman, in a balancing act, is trying to convince his judiciary brethren not to press for the removal of Attorney General (AG) Talaat Abdullah. The appointment by Morsi of the AG has been declared unconstitutional by a court decision.

Turning now to the opposition to the Morsi regime which is viewed by them as too Islamist, one finds it plagued by factionalism and a short-sighted abstention from participation in governance. The opposition, secular and liberal, seems to adopt the dead-end motto of **"my way or the highway."** That group, fragmented as they are and headed by two men, Mohammed El-Baradei and Amr Musa, was invited by both President Morsi and Prime Minister Qandeel to nominate persons to assume some of the Cabinet posts in the newly reshuffled Cabinet. They refused.

That refusal was short-sighted in two ways: allowing the gaps to be filled by ministers who are allied with the Muslim Brotherhood; and impeding the march of the Revolution towards diversity and stability. Explaining that attitude of rejectionism, Amr Musa said: **"We have refused to be partners because the new Cabinet lacks vision!!"** An excuse which is worse than the wrong for which the excuse is offered.

In his statements to the *Ashrak Al-Awsat*, a Saudi Arabian daily, Amr Musa went on May 7 to expound on the opposition's intractable position. **"There is no consensual national program. There are no policies which are transparently formulated. There is nothing new about the newly-appointed Cabinet members. That Cabinet does not reflect**

the urgent need of Egypt for reversing the collapse of the country's security and economy."

Abstention from participation cannot constitute constructive policy. So the bickering goes on while the new Egypt lies prostrate. If the opposition desires a slow down of what it calls **"the Brotherization (in reference to the Muslim Brotherhood) of the State,"** they should practice their opposition from within the Cabinet not simply from the outside.

The stalemate has opened the door to a gradual resurgence of the former backers of the ex-Mubarak regime. The man and woman of the Egyptian street now seem to long for that age of stability. To them, democracy has brought about chaos and economic destitution. They are now asking: **"What price is freedom?"** The retrial of Mubarak and the other members of the "Gang of Ten" has generated sympathy for the ousted dictator which, at its roots, is sympathy for an Egypt that functions.

If the International Monetary Fund (IMF) sees in government subsidies for basic goods and services an economical strain, it is right economically but dead wrong politically. As an international organization, the IMF is slow to learn from its disastrous lessons in Egypt of Sadat (1970-1981). At that time, Sadat had agreed to the IMF conditions for a loan, by eliminating the subsidies for bread, sugar, and cooking oil.

The result was huge demonstrations ("the bread riots") all over Egypt in February 1977. I was in Cairo with my wife at that time and witnessed the tumult. Consequently, Sadat had to rescind his decree and, among other measures, began discreet consultations which led to the Camp David agreement of 1978 with Israel under the tutelage of U.S. President Jimmy Carter.

On the stage of the new Egypt, the IMF is back with the same package of strong remedies for the ailing Egyptian economy. Morsi and his regime are acutely aware of the lessons learnt the hard way from the Sadat era. Egypt and the IMF are at present locked in futile negotiations. Revolt of the masses is a continuous threat to the new Egypt. Fear of further popular hostility to the regime and by extension to the Muslim Brotherhood is palpable.

So the continued drift of the Egypt Revolution goes on. No present safe harbor is in sight. It is the materialization of a theme song in a recent Egyptian soap series called "Zohra and her five husbands." In that fictional soap story, the song goes like this:

> *"From the days of my entering the Sea of Life,*
> *I have found no safe harbor;*
> *Every event in my life begins with a celebration and ends with a catastrophe."*

The Egyptian Army Says: "No to a Coup Against Morsi"

Friday, May 24, 2013

Petitions are being circulated by a movement called "TAMARROD" (Mutiny). Its objective is to effect President Morsi's recall. This seemingly democratic process aims at deposing the first-popularly elected President in the 10,000 years of Egypt's recorded history. It does not matter that that movement is doomed to failure. It is a secularist movement which is leaderless, and is attempting to confront a highly organized Muslim Brotherhood.

TAMARROD is the flip side of earlier petitions calling on General Abdel-Fattah El-Sisi, Egypt's Defense Minister to **"save the country from the present chaos."** On May 12, El-Sisi declared unequivocally that **"the armed forces are far from contemplating a return to governance."**

By saying no to a coup, El-Sisi was also chiding both the Islamists and their fractious opposition for not coming together to end the present stalemate in governance. Speaking at the military exercises of the Ninth Mechanised Division, General El-Sisi addressed the various opposition factions as follows: **"You should reach a consensus formula amongst yourselves. Otherwise, the alternative is very dangerous."**

Simultaneously the Minister of Defense was counter-attacking those who, through manipulation by the media, keep on spreading rumors about a breach between the armed forces and the police. **"This army is like fire with which you should not play."** Then he pointedly added: **"But it is not fire to be directed against its own people."**

In these utterances addressed at various constituencies, El-Sisi was also mindful of the popular affection in which the armed forces are held. After all, it is the only remaining cohesive force in the new Egypt. **"Of course, I am respectful of those who are now calling upon the armed forces to leave the barracks and come down to the street,"** he said. Then he added: **"But the armed forces are not the solution. You should not be impatient, or angry. For standing for 10 or 15 hours in line to cast your ballots is better than going on a rampage destroying your country."**

All of El-Sisi's declarations, though aiming at the internal front, were made at a time when the external front was being threatened by terrorist infiltrators. To the east, the Sinai front was under constant security threats from bedouin marauders and rogue Gazan elements. The gas pipeline to both Jordan and Israel has been repeatedly attacked, and elements of the army and police were constantly ambushed. And through the western borders with Libya, arms and contraband flowed into Egypt without interruption.

In the context of that chaos, the Egyptian Minister of Interior, General Muhammad Ibrahim, announced on May 11 that a terrorist cell with links to Al-Qaeda has been discovered in Cairo. The aim of that cell, he alleged, was to attack the French Embassy (presumably for France's military thrust against terrorists in Mali) in Cairo and to sabotage the Cairo metro.

A Possible Mutiny on the Nile

Friday, May 24, 2013

Is a mutiny against President Morsi possible? Events in Egypt seem to answer this question in the positive. The reasons are many, but the central causes are: **deteriorating economy; unattainable dialogue between the Islamists and the secularists; confrontations between Morsi and the Judiciary; absence of confidence in the ability of the civilian government to manage its relationships with either the police or the military.**

Is that mutiny imminent? No one can tell. What might it lead to? Possible intervention by the armed forces. What form of military intervention? Either a military coup or, alternatively, a larger role for the military in the governance of Egypt. If this happens, what would be the impact on the Muslim Brotherhood in Egypt? Cutting its influence down to size.

Now to the indicators and the triggering events:

Six Egyptian soldiers and policemen were abducted in Sinai by Egyptian bedouins who later released them unharmed. It was a first, even in lawless Sinai: Egyptians on Egyptians. The abductors had demanded release of fellow bedouins who are incarcerated by the Government. Morsi refused to negotiate with the abductors, and the Minister of Defense, General El-Sisi, faced with a huge storm of anger by the Egyptian masses, counselled patience. While military intelligence was securing the intermediacy of tribal chiefs, the armed forces, in a show of unprecedented military muscle, poured into northeast Sinai for a robust response.

The episode generated public media reactions which reflected both the animosity between the Islamists and the secularists, as well as the dearth of informed analysis by the pundits, a dearth verging upon hallucination. Those opposed to the Government and the Islamists opined that that act of abduction was pre-arranged by the Government which they accused of focusing on the islamization of the State, rather than on internal and external security.

It was galling to both the armed forces and the secularists that President Morsi, at a meeting with the Ministers of Defense and Interior, and the Chief of National Intelligence, read out the demands of the abductors. The list reflected what seemed to be a governmental sympathy for Hamas, as it was reported to read as follows: **(1) stoppage of the destruction by the armed forces of the tunnels dug illicitly between the Egyptian town of Rafah and Gaza; (2) Removal of all military checkpoints; (3) evacuation by both the army and the police of certain Sinai locations; (4) release from jail of 65 "jihadis" who had been implicated in terrorist acts at Taba, Sharm El-Sheik (both Red Sea locations) and Al-Azhar; and (5) Presidential amnesty for some of those convicted in absentia and sentenced to capital punishment.**

The public and the armed forces were stunned by what appeared to be the placement by the government of Hamas and its Sinai supporters ahead of the dignity of the State.

On Friday, May 17, General El-Sisi summoned Hamas leaders who are posted to Cairo. He is reported to have told them in no uncertain terms that they were playing with fire, and that the destruction of the tunnels would proceed in spite of Hamas unhappiness with those measures. **"Egypt's security is a priority above all else,"** he warned Hamas.

On the following day, at a meeting with the Ministers of Defense and Interior, and with the Chief of National Intelligence, President Morsi seemed to chide General El-Sisi for his upbraiding of Hamas. Morsi is reported to have told El-Sisi that the Government was very keen on its strategic relationships with Hamas. The General was not to be intimidated by the President. His response is reported to be: **"We have irrefutable evidence that terrorist elements in Sinai have been receiving logistical support from inside Gaza. We cannot allow this to continue under any circumstances."**

In response to that cleavage, leaders of the Muslim Brotherhood attempted to shift the blame for the abduction of the soldiers and policeman to El-Sisi. One such leader, Hamza Zobaa, declared sarcastically that terrorism showed the ineptness of the leadership of the armed forces. The clear aim was to float a veiled threat by the Islamists that El-Sisi might be relieved of his post by President Morsi.

In the meantime, the movement called **TAMARROD** (mutiny) aiming at the removal of the elected President went on collecting signatures from all parts of Egypt. TAMARROD described its actions as an open exercise of the popular will. The movement was pointing up the failure of the Morsi government to reverse Egypt's economic collapse, and indirectly to the need for the army to step in and secure for the country both development and internal security.

The future of that historic revolution of January 25, 2011 remains uncertain. It is quite possible that all of the above are mere manifestations of birth bangs of a new democracy. It is to be hoped that this is the case.

24 JUNE 2013

Sordid Name-Calling in Egypt Is a Malpractice of Democracy

Sunday, June 2, 2013

We can understand!! After 60 years of brutal dictatorship which imposed silence on the masses, the heavy lid on free speech is now off. The steam in the boiling pot has been gushing forth all over Egypt: demonstrations; disruption of public life; hate for the police; crime, including car theft and sexual harassment; calls by every labor syndicate and association for immediate raises in salaries; disruption of rail and motor travel.

With all that noise, a deafening noise, came also confrontations between the presidency and the judiciary; the executive and freedom of the press including artistic expression; the secularists, including the Coptic Church, and the Islamists; the street and the Ministry of Interior. The economy is down; public anger is up. What also occurred was the ability of 53 million Egyptian voters, now including members of the armed forces and the police, to vote in a fair and free elections for a president.

With the wall of fear gone, up went the malpractice of unreasonable vilification and name-calling of the President and his team. The sordid and constant name-calling of the Executive has now become an Egyptian sport.

No reasoned criticism, but unabashed frontal character assassination. No innuendos, but frontal generalized attacks. No alternative programs, but the heaping of scorn on proposed programs. No reading and research, but imaginary hallucination and stupid competition for first place in the language of profanity.

This is democracy run amok!! Samples are numerous:

A woman journalist says in an interview in the daily **"Al-Massri Al-Yom," "In the era of the Muslim Brotherhood, everything in Egypt has declined. Producers are frightened. Business finds no markets. All problems are to be attributed to the Brotherhood. Mixing of religion and politics is a nightmare which shall lead to the collapse of Egypt as a State."** She offers no statistics; no specific instances; no comparative analysis; no field research. This is particularly so when she asserts the veracity of her general criticism when she states: **"The Brotherhood is insistent on the creation of a regime paralleling that of Mubarak."**

In another interview published in the daily **"Al-Wafd,"** another woman opinion-maker proclaims: **"Egypt is now living the worst epochs of poverty -an epoch never before experienced by the Egyptians. Since President Morsi assumed his high office, no good has come to Egypt. Garbage is still in the streets; corruption continues as it was before; incomes have evaporated; people cannot find food to eat; the country is ruined."**

In another article in the daily **"Al-Shorooq,"** a male reporter is sarcastic about Morsi, who was photographed in an Egyptian field of ripened wheat. Since the Government has trumpeted the increase in domestic wheat production, the reporter ridicules that symbolic assurance by saying, **"That photo could have had more significance if it stood for the exit of Morsi from the presidential palace."** Then he goes into a trance by saying: **"That wheat field suffered the loss of a part of its expanse through accommodating the erection of a platform for Morsi to give his speech."**

More from the hate speech by the same reporter: **"Our grand children shall read in the history books that "Morsi has lived his tenure behind enhanced security protection. If the Muslim Brotherhood is serious in their calls for nullifying the citizenship of any Egyptian opposed to Morsi, they should begin with Morsi who he has been the** first in causing the public to lose confidence in him." Then he goes on to say: "Mubarak built his legitimacy on caring for Egypt's infra-structure. But the Islamists wish to build their legitimacy on their preoccupation with women's infra-strucuture."

Another journalist writes in "Al-Yom Al-Arabi," chiding President Morsi for ignoring the fate of seven Egyptian soldiers who had been kidnapped by Sinai Bedouins (now released): "The person who occupies the Presidential palace is afraid to pray in the mosques without a ring of guards around him. But he did not make a move to free those hostages, thus hurting the dignity of Egypt and the honor of his presidency which he shall never uphold."

Thus goes the sordid name-calling under the guise of democracy which espouses free speech. All that material has nothing to do with assessing the Morsi presidency which is only one year old. The avalanche of criticism would have had some constructive merit if it was backed by cause and effect, objective comparison between what was Egypt like during the Mubarak dictatorship and what it is like today. A dose of civilized patience is called for, thus allowing this fledgling democracy to take shape. The noise of idiotic hate and name-calling is its seed of destruction. This is not in support of Morsi. It is in support of an enlightened opposition.

Those who wish for democracy to succeed in Egypt should remember what happened during the Mubarak regime to an editor-in-chief of the daily "Al-Destour." He was hauled to prison for merely reporting that Mubarak was ill. But now the wall of fear is gone. Let the so-called opinion-makers avoid constructing in its place a solid wall of ignorance that threatens to undermine the newly-found freedom of expression.

Those who, by their thoughtless utterances, cannot wait for the democratic process to mature and to run its normal course to future elections are the perpetrators of the possible abortion of a democracy whose birth was difficult and whose course is still being charted.

Islamic Law and Global Security Course Syllabus

Friday, June 7, 2013

Fordham University	**Islamic law**	Prof. Yassin El-Ayouty
School of Law	**and Global Security**	Thursdays, Fall 2013
Course Syllabus		9:00-10:50am

Since the late 2010, the Arab Spring is still going on. The course for this Fall has to take account of that. It is a historic transformation, which has an impact on our understanding of Islamic Law (Sharia) in the 21st century in the context of global security. Thus the focus centers on the areas, which may guide you to your selection of a good topic for your term paper: (a) Authority in Muslim Society; (b) The impact on corruption; (c) The use/abuse by dictators of Islamic Law; (d) The role and place of political parties with Islamic orientation in democratic rule; (e) The importance of women's participation in governance; (f) The role of diversity and the acceptance of "the other;" and (g) the distortion by Al-Qaeda of the meaning of Jihad under Islamic Law.

1. **Goals:**

   -To understand the source and principles of Islamic Law, as they relate to global security

   -To comprehend how Islamic Law is applied in the 21st century, and to learn the basic vocabulary

   -To see how you can integrate it in your future practice

2. **Methods:**

   -Brief presentations by the instructor, especially on material in Arabic

   -Weekly presentations by the students on pre-assigned topics

   -Discussion of term paper topics.

   -An outside speaker or group attendance at an event relating to Islamic Law (tentative)

3. **Texts:**

   A. Books:
   - i.   Wael Hallaq, A History of Islamic Legal Theories (Paperback: 2005)
   - ii. Abdullahi Ahmed An-Naim, Islam and the Secular State (Paperback: 2009)
   - iii. Tarek Ramadan, Islam and the Arab Awakening (2012)

   B. Handouts: handouts relevant to the selected course topics below. If in Arabic, English translations by El-Ayouty. In particular, Al-Azhar documents (El-Ayouty's blog: http://tahrirforever.blogspot.com)

4. **Course topics:**
   - i.   Islam and Diversity
   - ii. Islam and Social Justice
   - iii. Islam and Authority
   - iv. Islam and War

v.   Islam and Human Rights

vi.   Islam and Ijtihad (Reasoning for the application of the mind to the te͓ of the Quran and the Sunna)

vii.   Islam and Jihad

viii.   Islam and Terrorism

ix.   Islam and the Judiciary

x.   The impact of the rise of Islamists to power as a byproduct of the Ara͓ Spring

5. Grade Distribution:

75% for a term paper (20-25 pages, including footnotes, double spaced); 15% for participation; 10% for meritorious contributions. **You may use the͓ term paper to fulfill the writing requirement by completing the appropriate paperwork with the Registrar's office by the Drop/Add deadline.** NO FINAL EXAM

6. Attendance:

Sessions begin promptly at 9:00 am and adjourn at 10:50 am. You must attend at least 80% of class sessions

7. Office Hours:

Thursdays after class from 11:15 am to 12:15 pm.

8. Deadline for Paper Submission:

By the last session of the Fall semester. No online submissions. Must submit two copies.

9. For First Session:

Professor El-Ayouty will present an overview. Presentation for subsequent sessions will be announced in class each week.

10. Pre Class Readings:

Specific students shall be assigned to lead the discussion on pre-assigned readings. Discussion leaders shall distribute one to two page summaries of the required reading on the day of their presentations. This activity, together with the Q&A period that follows, are integral parts of your "participation." The quality of the student's questions or comments counts towards "meritorious contributions"

11. A course Coordinator:

Selection of a student volunteering assistance in the coordination of course activities. Minimal time requirement. Counts towards "meritorious contribution." You may email me abut your interst (and please include your graduation date) at yelayouty@sunsglow.com, or yelayouty@gmail.com.

Has Egypt's Foreign Policy Changed?

Friday, June 14, 2013

This blog draws for its material from various sources in Egypt. For this issue we quote the full text of an article by **Ambassador Dr. El-Sayed Amin Shalaby** on the impact of the Egyptian Revolution on Cairo's foreign policy. A diplomat and a scholar, Dr. Shalaby occupies an important niche within the spectrum of information on Egypt's international relations. He is the Executive Director of the **Egyptian Council for Foreign Affairs** which I have the privilege of representing before the U.N. Economic and Social Council. The title of the article is **"Has Egypt's Foreign Policy Changed?"**

"So far, in regards to foreign policy, geopolitical constants are transcending any differences between Egypt's prior and new regime. But this may not always hold, writes Al-Sayed Amin Shalabi

During the 18 days of the 25 January Revolution, demands for overthrowing the regime and ending all types of domestic grievances were constant. But foreign policy seemed to recede into the background, at least until protesters gathered in front of the Israeli embassy and demanded the ambassador's expulsion.

Soon afterwards, researchers and experts fired off a barrage of criticism against Egyptian foreign policy under Hosni Mubarak, noting that Egypt forfeited its regional status, that it took its cue from the US, and that it was too chummy with Israel.

At which point, it became clear that the revolution had another goal, which was to set Egypt's foreign policy straight. Accordingly, Egypt's first post-revolution foreign minister, Nabil Al-Arabi, began criticising Egypt's closure of the Rafah Crossing, considering it a breach of international law. He also pointed out that Egypt would remain committed to the peace treaty with Israel, but only on the condition that Israel does the same. Al-Arabi called for opening a "new page" on Iran and wanted the country to sign several outstanding international agreements, including that of the International Criminal Court.

The ruling Supreme Council of the Armed Forces (SCAF), by nature averse to major changes, took a cautious attitude to foreign policy. It asserted Egypt's commitment to all its international obligations, including the Israel peace treaty, a position it conveyed to various US delegations that came to Cairo after the revolution, which suggested that post-revolutionary Egypt may not be much different from pre-revolutionary Egypt after all.

After the election of Egypt's first civilian — and Islamist — president, the question of foreign policy surfaced once more. In the first months of his term, President Mohamed Morsi visited Ethiopia, Saudi Arabia, Iran, China, Belgium, Germany, Italy and Brazil.

In all his talks with foreign officials, the president underlined Egypt's commitment to the Israel peace treaty. He offered to ease tensions in relations between Israel and Hamas, and successfully brokered a deal between the two. Israeli sources say that Egyptian-Israeli security cooperation has improved under the current regime.

America was a top priority. It was clear from the start that President Morsi's administration aspired for positive and cooperative ties with Washington. Several presidential delegations made trips to the US to discuss "strategic partnership" and "common values".

When it comes to Iran, several attempts at rapprochement took place after the revolution. But it is hard to speak of a breakthrough, since the US, Gulf countries, Egyptian security services, and the (ultra-Sunni) Salafis are all opposed to improved ties with the Iranians.

Surveying the scope of Egypt's foreign interests, one can identify similarities with the 1952 Revolution. In both cases the country's diplomacy centred on the Arab, African, Islamic and non-aligned planes.

Today's Egypt, just as the 1952 Revolution once was, is eager to establish a balanced and diversified set of international friendships, generally geared to meeting the domestic needs of the country.

One can also glimpse similarities with the early phase of Mubarak's presidency, when the quest for balance and diversification was paramount. Mubarak was fully committed to the Israel peace treaty, but he strove to restore Egypt's ties with the Arab world, something that Egyptian diplomacy managed to achieve after persistent efforts.

Mubarak was eager to maintain the close ties with the US that Anwar Al-Sadat managed to build. But he also sought to rehabilitate ties with the Soviet Union. Early in his presidency, Mubarak invited the Russians to resume working in various industrial projects in Egypt, especially those in which they had been involved in the past, such as aluminium and steel.

Mubarak, it is to be recalled, visited China nine times, and repeatedly asserted Egypt's belief in the principles of the non-aligned movement.

Mubarak's rule may have ended in clear bias toward the US and its plans in the region. After all, he tried to placate the Americans by forging close ties with Israel (the QIZ agreement and the natural gas deal). But he made sure that Egyptian diplomacy remained active in various regional and international forums, albeit not as assertive as some would have liked it to be. Still, the last foreign minister in Mubarak's time, Ahmed Abul-Gheit, criticised Egyptian foreign policy for lacking focus, and for neglecting Africa.

One must keep in mind that some aspects of Egypt's foreign policy are immutable. For example, the country's geostrategic position, its historical legacy, and its demographic weight, all of these are basically the same. Egypt cannot but take account of the international order and the shifting balance of power in the region and the world. This has always been the case, and nothing is going to change in this regard.

One development, however, is new. Since the 25 January Revolution, public opinion has begun to exercise considerable influence on the country's policies. So, from now on, expect foreign policy makers to pay close attention to public perceptions and demands."

In Egypt, Islamists Versus Secularists: The Process of Reciprocal Nullification

Friday, June 14, 2013

He, President Morsi, entered the big hall where his supporters, the Islamists, have congregated. Thunderous applause; a standing ovation; and a deep throated chant: **"We All Love You,!!!"** **(Kollena Binhibbak!!!)** That was in Cairo on June 10. Morsi's response to his cheering supporters, led by the Muslim Brotherhood, was: **"I call on all political parties and groups to national reconciliation. The process should be based on a unified vision for the new Egypt. No more sloganeering!! No more auctioneering!!"** At that point, the beards and worry beads shook with shouts of approval.

President Morsi is keenly aware of the approaching ominous date of June 30. Millions of Egyptian secularists are expected to converge on every public square calling for his recall. They are demonstrating under the banner of **"Millions for the Red Card,"** meaning: You are out of the game. Legally there is no basis in Egypt for recalling an elected president.

Of course, there is Article 152 of the new Egyptian Constitution promulgated in December 15, 2012. It reads, in part:

"A charge of felony of treason against the President of the Republic is to be based on a motion signed by at least one-third of the members of the House of Representatives. An impeachment is to be issued only by a two-thirds majority of the members of the House of Representatives."

No reference to a recall. And, at present, there is no House of Representatives, pending elections later this year, with no specific date set as yet. Recall is a process of relief from the continued rule of a malfeasant. It is a form of a no-confidence vote to be taken indirectly by the people via their elected representatives. The days of Athenian democracy where the entire populace gathered to vote in an amphitheatre are long gone.

Such legal facts are overlooked by the movement **"TAMMARROD" (Mutiny)** which claims to have already gathered ten million signatures for recalling President Morsi. They seem to forget that the street is for electioneering. The ballot box is for elections through which they can vote Morsi out of power if they win in the next election, even by a simple majority.

Other legal hurdles face the June 30 uprising: (a) signing a petition, a non-verifiable process, cannot and should not disenfranchise the 51.5% majority who voted for Morsi, **(b)** Morsi may have not delivered on his campaign promises. So have many heads of State around the world who find themselves in the same position. Election promises constitute no contract. At best, these are **"illusory contracts,"** aspirational in nature, vacuous in legal merit. A wish list which is subject to all types of frustration, including **"acts of God."** Morsi committed neither a felony nor a treason.

Now the secularists, though divided and fragmented, have come up with what I call **"the new doctrine of rejectionism."** In turning down Morsi's repeated calls for a dialogue with the "Front for National Salvation" headed by Dr. Mohamed El-Baradei, they now have what appears to be a set of beliefs expounded recently by the **"General Secretary of the Egyptian Socialist Party."** He is an engineer by the name of Ahmed Baha El-Din who, on Tuesday, June 11, defined that **"doctrine of rejectionism"** in an interview with the United Press International in Cairo.

What are the elements of the doctrine, if one might call it a doctrine?

(1) The Egyptian masses should regain their revolution on June 30, which marks the passing of one year of Morsi's presidency, through massive demonstrations;

(2) Their objective should be to secure their liberty, social justice, and human dignity, which the Islamist rule of Morsi has failed in attaining;

(3) The Muslim Brotherhood has totally failed in ruling the country, and have manifested hunger for more intrusive powers. That hunger is being satisfied through repressive measures which are now leading the populace to call for the fall of the Morsi regime;

(4) The downfall of Morsi has become an urgent necessity which also calls for early presidential elections to replace Morsi;

(5) The phenomenon of using Islam for political ends must be vanquished as it reflects a continuation of Egyptian policies during Mubarak;

(6) The veil of Islamist governance is a pretext for ignoring the needs of the poor; and

(7) Any governmental opposition or suppression of the June 30 demonstrations shall be confronted by a robust response

While the secularists are busy drawing their lines of battle against the Islamists, the latter were getting their forces ready. The head of what is called **"The Sharia Organization,"** Dr. Ahmed Al-Saloos, has called for the various Islamist parties to unite. The goal is to defeat the secularists who are less organized than the Islamists in the forthcoming parliamentary elections for the lower chamber. Al-Saloos whose organization is considered a political arm of the Muslim Brotherhood, and an umbrella for a broad Islamist alliance, called for unified support for any Islamist candidate in any electoral district in order to defeat the secularists in the upcoming elections.

June 30 is looming as a possible turning point in the troubled history of the Egyptian Revolution. Let us hope that democracy in Egypt shall survive this process of reciprocal nullification. Diversity and zero-sum games are anti-thetical to one another. Here I pose one question that has always troubled me for lack of a clear answer:

How could Egypt of old have given the world so much, whereas Egypt of today is still searching for itself?!! Amazing!!

The Broader Arab Civil War For Which Egypt Should Be An Improbable Party

Friday, June 28, 2013

In their international relationships, the Arab States are better at attacking one another than at reconciling peacefully their differences. The late American Professor Malcolm Kerr of UCLA wrote in 1958 a distinguished treatise entitled **"The Arab Cold War."** If he were still alive today he would have been the author of a book on a much devastating inter-Arab ware. The coming Sunni-Shii war, for which Egypt should be an improbable party. Such conflict is expected to have cataclysmic consequences for regional stability and world peace.

This broader civil war is ironically one of the consequences of the Arab Spring, on which this blog has focused in regard to its Egyptian sector. Triggered by the Syrian civil war, the Sunni majority of that troubled country has seen the ruling Alawite (Shii) minority, led by the killer regime of Bashar Al-Assad, drawing its fighting strength from Shii troops from outside Syria. From Iran and Shii-majority Iraq to the east, to the Lebanese Hezbollah to the west, the Syrian bloody landscape witnessed militarized Shiism pinning the Sunnis down.

The embers of conflict between Shii Islam and Sunni Islam which have simmered east of Suez for the past 14 centuries have now been allowed to shoot up its flames. The intense Arabism of Syria which made Damascus boast of its continuous resistance to western influences and to Israeli claims to the entirety of historic Palestine has become, under Bashar dictatorship, largely a Shiism on the defensive. The stalemate in the largely Sunni fight for an Assad-less Syria prompted a realignment of Islamic sectarianism. Turkey, Saudi Arabia, Qatar and other Gulf States have been pouring in armament and volunteers -in aid of the Free Syrian opposition. Their ideological conviction is that a Shii triumph in Syria would be a net Sunni loss to all these Sunni States.

The complications leading to that religious/Arab versus Arab/Muslim versus Muslim broad civil war do not stop at that. Religion in armed conflicts has always meant the prolongation of these conflicts as each side sees itself fighting on behalf of God. These complications in the present Syrian civil war can be discerned in the entry of Al-Qaeda and its affiliates like Al-Nassra into the field of battle. These latter groups, with agendas of their own which have become more pronounced after the liquidation of Bin Laden are, as to be expected after 9/11, labelled terrorist organizations.

Thus the so-called **"war on terror,"** having become intertwined with **"regime change"** saw a Russia assisting Bashar; a China on the sidelines; an America hesitant to provide lethal arms to the **"free Syrians"**; a Britain and a France reluctantly drawn into the conflict without a clear sanction from the European Union; and a United Nations which, in civil wars, can contribute no more than a limited humanitarian assistance and a heap of toothless resolutions condemning blood-letting.

Into this unholy mess, post-Mubarak Egypt has found itself in the unenviable situation of doing nothing except to kick the Syrian embassy out of Egypt. In mid-June, President Morsi declared that rupture with Syria's Bashar before throngs of his Muslim Brothers.

The Morsi declaration at the Cairo stadium quickly galvanized the secular opposition which so far found no unifying theme amongst its components except to try to force Morsi and the Islamists out of power. Both El-Baradie and Amr Musa, the two most prominent leaders of the secular opposition which is now getting ready for massive demonstrations against **"the Islamization of the State"** on June 30, condemned the severing of relations with Syria.

More importantly, the spokesman for the Egyptian armed forces made it clear that **"we shall not be used for war outside of our boundaries particularly in combat against a sister State"** (meaning Syria).

As for Bashar, he taunted Morsi by saying in response to that speech: **"You do not know where to set your feet, because you have no political experience. You need to grow up."**

So where is Egypt now from the looming Sunni-Shii civil war? In all probability, the new Egypt shall largely stand aside. It has its own internal problems. It also is now looking west of Suez to forge an alliance with Libya and the Sudan.

However this assessment does not rule out an Egyptian involvement. The Salafis are trying to push Egypt into that unholy confrontation. In this regard, let it not be ever forgotten that neither the Quran, nor Al-Sunna of the Prophet Muhmmad has denied the existence of a variety of Muslim sects. In teaching Islamic jurisprudence at Fordham University School of Law, New York City, I have not come upon a shred of evidence justifying the demonization by Sunnis of Shiis. Al-Azhar University, established in Cairo by the Fatimides(Shiis) more than a thousand years ago, teaches both Sunni and Shii schools of thought. The expansion of the scope and modernity of sharia has been largely due to Shii ijtihad(the application of reason to the written texts). The great Shii scholar, Sheikh Al-Sistani, observing in quiet anguish the looming Sunni-Shii conflagration, uttered recently in Baghdad the following electrifying words in Arabic (my translation):

"Al-Sunna are not our brothers. They are ourselves. Even if they kill half of us, we shall never condone killing them!!"

Let the demons of sectarian conflict in Egypt, as well as elsewhere in the Arab and Muslim world beware. The fires which they ignite may destroy the hopes of the 1.5 billion Muslims for becoming fully integrated in the world community.

Through Divisions, Egypt is Threatened with Becoming an Orphan

Friday, June 28, 2013

The Muslim Brothers claim Egypt as Islamist. Their Salafi opponents regard Egypt, without the application of the traditions of early Islam, as only a work in progress. The secular opposition sees in Islamism as a threat to the cosmopolitanism of Egypt. The ultra-Salafis look upon the the ancient Egyptian civilization as pagan and on its great monuments as mere idols. The great community of artists, singers, dancers, opera goers, and film makers see in these cultural buffeting winds the early warnings of a devastating storm.

Within this division, which constitutes cultural chasms, stand three institutions which may ultimately save Egypt from being orphaned. An orphan status is a status where either there are no existing parents, or that parentage is claimed by many parties to the point that the child has no identification of specific parents.

The three institutions which today stand for one identifiable, unified and discernible Egypt which the June 30 uprising (TAMMARODD) threatens to tear asunder, are: The armed forces, Al-Azhar, and the Coptic Church. Each of them has a specific historic role in aborting the cultural orphaning of Egypt. The Coptic Church is more than 2000 years old; the Al-Azhar mosque and Islamic university is more than 1000 years old; and the contemporary Egyptian armed forces are more than 200 years old.

The roles of these three institutions are not only anchored in hundreds of years of national Egyptian traditions. They are also proud of their standing up for Egypt at its hours of peril. The Copts have always stood for the country's independence, and have fought the country's attackers, standing side by side with their Muslim brethren. Al-Azhar was, historically, the launching pad of great national resistance movements, especially as regards western encroachments in the 19th century. And the Egyptian armed forces, in spite of chronic deficiency in armament, have valiantly battled the country's external adversaries, since the dying days of the Ottoman empire.

Here we are talking about tangible institutions. But these institutions are also bolstered by intangible cultural factors. Foremost among these are the nationalist songs which we sang out in formation as primary school students, boys and girls, all over Egypt. In my days at that private school in my hometown of Zagazig, Sharkia Province, called at that time **"King Fouad Al-Awwal School,"** we sang, prior to marching to our classrooms: **"Bilady Bilady Fidaki Dammi"** (My country, my country, I shed my blood for thee).

Egyptians, rank and file, never tire of repeating what their sages have often repeated. Two religious scholars of the 19th century, have taught them that Islam was a way of life not particular to a geographic area. Sheikh Rifaa Al-Tahtawi and Sheikh Muhammad Abdoh, educated at both Al-Azhar and France, had proclaimed that the practice of morality under Islamic traditions of tolerance is more observed in the non-Islamic west than in the Islamic east. The collapse of the Ottoman Empire in 1918 is attributed, in part, to the traditional Muslim scholars in Istanbul opposing the training of the Ottoman troops by non-Muslim trainers. And most of the Egyptian banners raised in Tahrir Square during the formative years of the Egyptian Revolution of January 25, 2011 did not proclaim Islamic sayings. On the Egyptian flags, they declared: **"I Love Egypt"** (Baahibb Massr).

Such built-in safeguards, both institutional and cultural, against the orphaning of Egypt through divisions and fractures, are real protective barriers. Ignoring them might result in an historic infanticide -the death and burial of an infant called **"Democracy"** in the most populous Arab country -Egypt. *Diversity (the elixir of historic Egypt) is all for one. Division (the curse of post-revolutionary Egypt) is one without all.*

25 JULY 2013

The Fall of Morsi: The Defects of Definitions and the Dilemma of Realities

Sunday, July 7, 2013

President Morsi, the first elected President of of Egypt was removed by the military from office on July 3. His Islamist reign, backed up by the Muslim Brotherhood, did not last more than 368 days. This is a huge transformational event in the 2 1/2 year old Arab Spring. It shall not affect Egypt alone. It shall reverberate throughout the Arab and Muslim worlds encompassing 1.5 billion people. The swiftness of condemnations, though mostly cautious, by outside powers is ill-advised. Events in Egypt should always be left to the 90 million Egyptians to decide.

The installation by the military, the only cohesive and disciplined force in post-Mubarak Egypt, of an interim president, Judge Adly Mansour, the Chief of the Supreme Constitutional Court, is a fait accompli.

This fait accompli is not yet accepted by the Muslim Brotherhood which calls the events of July 3 a coup, refuses to join the post-Morsi government headed by a judge, and sneers at the new authority as a bunch of **"usurpers."** The divisions within the Egyptian body-politic, which this blog had previously analyzed, have deepened. Egypt's stability is threatened.

The specter of intensified armed confrontations between the supporters of the so-called **"legitimate"** and freely-elected President (now under house arrest) and his opponents numbering 23 millions in all public squares in Egypt is a distinct possibility. Who is right, and who is wrong, are questions which shall be debated, if not settled, for a long long time.

Here follows my own personal debate with myself as if I were two Yassins: Yassin the lawyer v. Yassin the professor. The lawyer is on the side of applying the mechanics of the law; but the professor is applying the dictates of fairness. The law is written, transcribed, objective, and conventional. Fairness is subjective, controversial, debatable, and inchoate. Fairness has to do with values. The professor in me sides with General El-Sisi who led the military ouster of President Morsi. WHY?

Let us start with the defects of definitions in order to lead us to the dilemma of realities. No credible dictionary has ever offered a consensual definition of any of these three terms: democracy, aggression, and terrorism. Customary law and practices vary from one political culture to another, giving each of these terms subjective definitions.

Since we are here dealing with the concept of democracy, let us raise the question of the presidential elections in the US in 2000: Bush v. Gore. In my estimation, as both a lawyer and a professor of law, I find the 5-4 decision of the U.S. Supreme Court stopping the State of Florida from the vote recount a subversion of the democratic process. It gave Bush, thanks to the vote of Justice Sandra O'Connor which tipped the scale, an unmerited presidency.

That vote has changed the course of history. It led the U.S., after 9/11, to two wars: in Afghanistan and in Iraq. That slippery slope also led to the histrionics of legal advisers, such as John Yoo, who devised for the pinnacles of U.S. power, voodoo **"laws,"** setting aside the Geneva Conventions of 1949. In effect, these so-called **"laws"** indirectly enabled world-class criminals such as Bin Laden to claim, with some unmerited justification, that their criminality has duped the U.S. into immersing itself in the so-called **"war on terror."** It took the U.S. 12 years before declaring through President Obama that that "war" was over. It was a declaration of fatigue.

This historic lesson in the imprecision of defining democracy leads

Yassin the lawyer to look at how Morsi came to be President of Egypt. After 60 years of military dictatorship, Mubarak was removed from power in February 2011, thanks to the armed forces. They protected the massive demonstrations in Tahrir. As a lawyer, I would insist that you do not hold presidential elections before you draft a constitution and have it ratified by at least a legislative power. In Egypt, this was not done.

In its rush towards populism, Egypt voted, some say unfairly, for Morsi as President. He was not even the first choice of the Muslim Brotherhood. This was done without a charter defining the powers of the three branches of Government (legislative, executive, judiciary). The cart was thus placed before the horse.

This was followed by another set of legal defects. The judiciary dismissed the lower house of Parliament claiming that one-third of its membership was voted wrongly into office as party representatives. That quota had been reserved for independents. Why not disqualify only that one third, and why did the judiciary which was charged with electoral supervision not stop the vote? It did not happen. And the judiciary at that point was not yet governed by now constitutional provisions. The whole process was plagued by one ad hoc measures, one after another. The pre-Morsi constitution was the only available charter resorted to as expediency dictated. The Morsi presidential advisers were in the mold of John Yoo in regard to the Bush administration.

With 70% of the membership of the House of Representatives belonging to the Muslim Brotherhood and the Salafis (50%; 20% respectively), the Islamists lambasted the judiciary (the Supreme Constitutional Court) as "Folool" (remnants of the defunct Mubarak regime). On this chaotic stage, strode President Morsi with an activism of his own. He instructed the Speaker of the House (Mr. Al-Katatni, a senior member of the Guidance Council of the Brotherhood) to convene the dissolved House in open defiance of judicial rulings. The war between the two camps, the President and the Islamist-dominated House of Representatives, on one side, and; the judiciary on the other side, was now in full swing. It was a war in which the secularists sided with the well established and highly professional judiciary.

The House of Representatives met for only 20 minutes then adjourned. That was enough time to transfer its law-making authority to the President. Thus, Morsi, without Constitutional sanction, became both the head of the Executive and the law-maker at the same time. The declaration that ensued to the effect that that accumulation of power was transitory convinced the opposition that the dictatorial President was marching to the orders of the Brotherhood. Morsi, with no experience in governance, confirmed the worst fears of the secularists. On Nov. 22, 2012 Morsi issued a so-called **"constitutional declaration"** putting himself above the law. The opposition screamed foul. Nobody listened. Absolute power was corrupting absolutely.

The experimentation with democracy was proceeding in the wrong direction. Following the Nov. 22 **"constitutional declaration,"** Morsi became faced with a strengthening wall of rejection. It was diverse, secular and determined. His opponents were bolstered by Al-Azhar, the Coptic Church and the elements of creative Egypt (the arts, the theater, the film industry, the world of song, dance and music of cosmopolitan Egypt). Later that dictatorial declaration was withdrawn, but the damage had already been done. Nobody knew where the cart leading the horse was going. Compounding the legal problems, Morsi's arrogated legislative powers were transferred to the Senate (the Shura) of which one-third were Morsi's appointees, pending the holding of parliamentary elections for the House of Representatives.

These elections did not take place. They were deferred until after the Constitutional Assembly, also dominated by the Islamists, had finished its drafting of the post-Mubarak constitution. That Assembly became also infected with endless confrontations between the Islamists who wanted an Islamic State, and the secularists who struggled to keep Egypt a secular State. The casualty became the art of compromise in which neither the Brotherhood nor Morsi were trained.

Most of the more than 250 articles of the new Constitution were presumed to have been agreed. But other articles defining the character of the new Egypt remained contentious. Suddenly the opposition called it quits; walked out of the Chamber. Without hesitation, the Islamists took advantage of that situation and got their own version of the controversial articles approved. The document became rightly known as **"the Islamist Constitution."** What was the hurry in rushing that charter through a rump Constituent Assembly? Fear by the Islamists that the judiciary would strike again and dissolve the Constituent Assembly.

Morsi and his Qandeel Government were desperate to get that text approved in a hurriedly arranged plebiscite. It became clear to the opposition that the Islamists were engaged in a zero sum game which precluded any meaningful compromise.

The Islamists were deceived by the power of their numbers, not realizing that a large segment of the voting Egyptian public could not even comprehend most of those constitutional articles. I was in Cairo in December 2012 when the plebiscite, in two stages, was conducted. The turn-out was low; Egypt was divided; the Islamists were triumphalist; and the document by the end of 2012 was declared the law of the land -a divided land with a Constitution lacking the consensus of the populace.

The presidential calls for a dialogue with the opposition were premised on **"let us go forward with what we got now."** The opposition turned deaf ears to what they regarded as a constitutional charade. They wanted a new beginning. The experiment in democracy, whatever that meant in the context of Egypt of the Arab Spring, was showing signs of a deepening malaise. As of the end of 2012, Egypt was rudder-less; the Islamist chants all over Egypt was **"Islamiah"** (meaning an Islamist Egypt). That term replaced the slogan of the January 25 Revolution of **"Selmiah"** (meaning peaceful).

Now to Yassin, the professor dealing with higher values of governance and the inchoate notion of fairness. Morsi has inherited huge burdens. Egypt was economically broke; the IMF would not agree to loaning the country close to $5 billion; unemployment surpassed 60%; goods and services were not being delivered. Bread, electricity, cooking oil, gas, diesel fuel and other basic commodities were in short supply. The police was not yet re-organized; the Suez Canal cities had to be subdued by emergency laws; the rate of crime shot up; the young authors of the January 25 Revolution were side-lined. Tourism dried up; various unions went on strike; rail travel was interrupted.

Journalists were being hounded by the authorities for articles putting the new Egypt in bad lights, jewelers emptied their stores of gold for fear of robbing; each neighborhood had its vigilantes guarding its persons and property; some large cities declared themselves **"independent Islamic Republics."** **"L'Institut"** of Egypt, the repository of its historic past, which was established by Napoleon in the early 19th century was torched.

In the meantime, the **"Brotherization"** of Egypt accelerated; 13 out of 27 provincial governors were members of the Muslim Brotherhood; and Luxor, the capital of Egyptian tourism, had a governor, Mr. El-Khyyat, a Salafi, who had been implicated in the bloody murder of foreign tourists in pre-revolutionary days. His appointment was like putting Ayman El-

Zawahri of Al-Qaeda in the position of the Mufti of Egypt. Egypt's great monuments, like the pyramids, and the Sphinx, were declared by some Islamists pagan idols; the statue of Um Kalthoun, the pan-Arab lady singer, had its face veiled; and women were frightened to take part in demonstrations for fear of sexual harassment and rape. The police had disappeared.

Sectarianism reared its ugly head in Egypt all over the country. Islamist incitement of violence became common. All kinds of arms flowed from Libya next door. Copts and Shiis were attacked, and several of their congregants were killed; their places of worship were burnt down. Morsi even sat passively during a sermon in which the Shiis were declared **"unclean apostates."** The call for Muslim prayers sounded in parliament while in session. All sorts of red lines were being crossed by the Brotherhood in total reliance on the results of the 2012 elections. Secular Egypt was fast receding.

The documents of 2011 and 2012 which were issued by Al-Azhar with the imprimatur of the Coptic Church calling for moderation in Islam and respect for minorities remained mere ink on paper. The Coptic question risked being internationalized; the Bedouins of Sinai continued to attack and kill members of the armed forces and the police; and Gazans seemed to look upon Sinai as their hinterland for smugglers of drugs and arms. And foolishly, a meeting held by Morsi with some of the country's leaders on the Nile water issue between Egypt and Ethiopia was aired, carrying threats of attacks on Ethiopia for its construction of a dam on the Blue Nile.

Wishing a Copt **"Happy Easter"** began to be frowned upon as unislamic. On that high Coptic holyday, Morsi did not see it fitting to attend at St. Mark's Cathedral as had been the presidential practice;

The top position of **"Rector of Al-Azhar"** was coveted by the Brotherhood which regarded moderate Islamic advocacy by that 1040 year old institution as a deviation;

The Arab Republic of Egypt became more recognizable as the Islamic Republic of Egypt;

While in Cairo, in December 2012, I witnessed El-Baradie appearing on TV denouncing Egypt's fast descent into dark practices of fabricated values. He pleaded with Morsi and his Islamist minders to **"Take Pity on Egypt;"**

President Morsi, adding to himself at times the voluntary role of a preacher at Muslim prayers, began to be seen as an Imam;

Morsi's interference with security operations against rogue elements of Hamas and marauding Bedouins in cahoots with those elements infringing Egyptian sovereignty was adding to the burdens of the armed forces in El-Arish and Rafah;

Attempts by those criminal elements in Sinai to sow discord between the army and the police proved to the armed forces that the Hamas and Morsi entente was a looming security threat;

The Islamic media, through its calls for an **"Islamic code of dress,"** regulation of hours of alcoholic consumption, and differentiation between Muslim and non-Muslim in the great touristic spots on the Red Sea and upper Egypt were sabotaging tourism in Egypt. Qatar was offering to run Egyptian tourism;

The opposition derided those regulations and measures as socially and economically subversive. It said the authorities were less concerned with the country's infrastructure than with **"women's infrastructure;"**

Morsi's utterances about **"legitimacy"** began to be shrill, rambling, pugnacious, in your face, and sounded to the opposition "putchist." It gave the Morsi concept of **"dialogue"** the connotations of **"my way or else;"**

The presidential palace and the HQ of the Mulsim Brotherhood guided by Khairat El-Shatter began to look interchangeable.

The backlash of TAMMAROD against Morsi proved highly effective. Chants rose all over Egypt: **"Sisi to the rescue!!"** It was akin to France's call upon General DeGaulle, at its hour of near national disintegration in 1958 during the Algerian war: **"L'armee au pouvoir!!"** General El-Sisi publicly warned that Egypt was facing a total collapse. His calls for national reconciliation went unheeded. The opposition, demanding constitutional nullification and a new beginning, would not accept the presidential call for a national dialogue. No compromises were offered, and the Islamists began to call their opponents **"enemies of Islam."** Morsi was made in effect the personification of faith, and his utterances, laden with Islamic phraseology, seemed to bolster that notion. The Islamists road map was no more than the mantra **"Shariah"** (legitimacy); the armed forces had a road map inspired by historically secular Egypt.

To Yassin the professor, the issue boils down to weighing between **"the legitimacy"** emerging from the ballot box, and **"the fairness"** emerging from the dilemma of realities of post-Mubarak Egypt. Put differently, is the ouster of Morsi a coup against **"democratic"** Egypt, or an impeachment of a President who seemed oblivious to the fact that complex Egypt needed a nuanced productive and inclusive leadership? Is democracy mere mechanics with a universally-accepted standards, or is it a process that needs to mature in an Egypt which has not experienced it except during brief periods in the 1920s?

I vote for the actions taken by the military to remove Morsi from power. He has failed to deliver and has lost the trust of his public -his broad public. Islamic jurisprudence which I teach at Fordham University School of Law in New York City sums up the purpose of governance in two principles: Justice (Adl), and Service benefiting the citizens (Ma Yanfaul Nas). Morsi the Islamist has even failed his presumed standards. What happened in Egypt on July 3, 2013 should be looked upon as a revolutionary course correction. Nominal democracy has ended with the end of his regime.

Under any version of the new constitution, a House of Representatives has the power of impeaching a President. Such body does not exist at present. 23 million Egyptian citizens have filled that void. El-Baradie aptly described that mass action as **"voting by their feet."**

Many of those voting for Morsi, including me, were not voting for the candidate of the Muslim Brotherhood. They were voting against his opponent, a military man, General Shafik. The score was 50.5% to 49.5%, hardly a landslide for the winner.

The **"Islamist"** constitution was approved by 22% of an electorate that numbered 53 million voters.

Morsi's defiant speech of July 2 was his last -in effect an abdication speech. The ballot box is a process. Its purpose and substance are good inclusive governance that delivers goods and services. So if you are a devotee of the mere process, you are likely to call the ouster of Morsi **"a usurpation."** But if you value the substance, you would call it a restoration. Morsi has frustrated the purpose of his contract with Egypt. Frustration of the purpose of a contract rightly leads to its nullification.

The military did not "usurp" Morsi's powers. He and the

Brotherhood, who were late in joining the January 25 Revolution, have turned out eventually to be the veritable usurpers. They attempted to usurp the historic character of cosmopolitan Egypt. If they truly want to put Egypt above their ideology and paper-thin legitimacy, they should heed the calls of the interim President Adly Mansour, the former Chief Justice of the Supreme Constitutional Court, to join hands with the new transitional regime to put Egypt back on the right tracks. "Faith is for God: the homeland is for everyone."

The Dark Art of Demonization: How Did the Regime of the Muslim Brotherhood in Egypt View its Opponents?

Thursday, July 11, 2013

They joined the January 25 Revolution late. Sat on the fence, waited for the young revolutionaries to gain a momentum with the armed forces in their defense, then they bounced. The Brotherhood, suppressed by Royal Egypt, then by the so-called Republican Egypt since 1954, was back to the surface. Their reputation unsullied by the corruption of public life in Egypt; their grass roots organizational ability enabling needy Egyptians, and their message simple: **"Islam is the solution."**

When they ran for the post of President, after Mubarak downfall in February, 2011, I voted for them twice from New York City: First for Abdel-Monim Abu-Elfotooh, then, in the run-off between Muslim Brotherhood Morsi and General Shafik, both from my home province of Sharkia, my vote went for Morsi. Why?

Like many like me, I did not wish to have another military man back in the Presidential Palace in Cairo. I was not turned away from the Brotherhood (I have never joined any political party either in Egypt or in America) by their **"Islam is the Solution."** I teach Islamic jurisprudence; follow Al-Azhar definition of Islam as inclusive, diverse and tolerant; value my late father's advice, an Azhari, when he admonished me not to even think of suggesting to my American Catholic spouse to convert ("It is unislamic," he used to say); and I felt sympathy for the downtrodden, the

Brotherhood.

But 368 days of Morsi's rule convinced me that the seeming angels of the Brotherhood were not what I had perceived them to be before they took over the reigns of power. For they turned their slim majority in the presidential elections (50.50% to 49.50%), and their plurality of 50% in the House of Representatives, enhanced by the Salafis to a total of 70%, into a dictatorial iron grip. To them **"legitimacy"** meant excluding the opposition, and inventing a constitution depicting Egypt as an **"Islamic"** State. Democratic means were quickly subverting the democratic ends.

So when Morsi was pushed out of power on July 3 by the screams against him by 23 million citizens, and by the near collapse of the State, I sighed in relief **"Good Riddance."** Some outsiders, judging by pro-Morsi demonstrators, described that corrective reset of the Egyptian Revolution as a coup. Among those was Senator McCain, who has rendered to his country historic services. Such services should not excuse his intervention in Egyptian internal affairs. If he is basing such intervention on the US aid to the military in Egypt, he should keep in mind that such aid is tied to the Egypt/Israel peace treaty of 1979.

Let us now examine the Muslim Brotherhood's outlook on its reign of one year of the Morsi regime. This is not to vilify them as a major mass movement in Egypt. We shall look in their little book in Arabic to discover their failure at uniting Egypt behind the Morsi collapsed presidency. Yes, they issued in early 2013 a little book entitled **"The Achievements of Dr. Mohamed Morsi, the President of the Republic."** Its small size of 24 pages reminds me of the **"Green Book"** of Qaddafi in the early 1980s, and of Nasser's **"Philosophy of the Revolution"** of the 1950s. I read those three tracts in their original Arabic and reached one conclusion: Each one of the three booklets was a harbinger of the fall of their Zaim (Boss/President).

In **"The Achievements"** (Injazat) I found the Brothers demonizing their liberal and secular opponents. Their opponents were depicted as "enemies of the Islamic project." What is the Islamic project? Egypt itself, being folded, with its Copts, its judges, its women, its diversity, its authors of the January 25 revolution, in to an **"Islamic Project."**

That was the tip of the iceberg, or the early hotwinds of the sand storm (khamasin) in the Brothers honing of their dark art of demonization. **"The Achievements,"** published in April 2013, less than 3 months before the uprising of June 30, has one frightening message: "If you are not with us, you are against us." And us meant also Islam itself.

It is difficult to cover all of **"The Achievements"** in one single issue of this blog. We may come back again to it to fathom its weird advocacy of **"The Islamic project 'uber alles' -above all."** Here follow some of its main propositions: (my translation)

Why doesn't President Morsi communicate his plans to the citizens? Because such concern with dialoguing with the Egyptians will keep him away from focusing on solving Egypt's problems!! (p.3)

*What is wrong with sharing with the citizens the President's concerns and aspirations?*Because presidential responses to the dust of public questions and to the fog of accusations and allegations, even by those who pretend to be **"supporters of the Islamic project,"** would be against the Sunna (the path of the Prophet). Then a quote of one of the alleged sayings of Muhammad: **"God does not wish for you three things: polemics, wastage of resources, and an avalanche of questions (addressed to the Ruler)."** (p.5)

How is the conflict between the Islamists and their opponents perceived in the context of the Morsi presidency? That conflict is waged by elements eager to serve their own personal ends. They are sectors of the public which have benefitted from the Mubarak regime, and have united with other elements brainwashed over 60 years. The results is that these sectors of the population do not know right from wrong. (p.6)

What is the ultimate objective of the opposition to the regime of the Brotherhood? Through their coalitions, the opposition intends to confuse the general image of the Egyptian scene, produce an atmosphere of violence, chaos, terrorism, and destruction. Such objectives, if attained by the opposition, are meant to confuse President Morsi and his helpers. The result would be postponing the projected parliamentary elections, delaying the institutional reconstruction of the new Egypt, and convincing the public that Morsi has no achievements. The opposition's goal is to cause the populace to turn their backs on the Islamic experimentation pursued by the Muslim Brotherhood. Rejection of the Islamic project, leading to rejection of the Brotherhoodization, is the path of the opposition to perpetuate the environment of corruption which had enriched those opponents. (p.7)

What shall be history's characterization of the Morsi's presidency? The President shall go forward without giving his opponents any attention to their judgement of his governance. Thus the President shall inflict on them a fatal blow. Out President is going forward with his plans in order to prove that he is a powerful president. History, Inshallah (God Willing), shall regard him as the most powerful President the country has ever known throughout its entire existence." (p.7)

The above reflects only the statements contained in less than one third of the book issued by the Brotherhood on Morsi's achievements. A retired Egyptian senior diplomat told me when I reached him at his home by phone on July 4, following the removal of Morsi from power: **"The Muslim Brotherhood had failed to read the map of the New Egypt."** Indeed they have failed the test of democracy, and thus brought upon themselves not only the collapse of the Morsi presidency. Their calls to violence against the present transitional government are leading to the Brotherhood's gradual suppression and exclusion from the remaking of the new Egypt.

Let those who are mistakenly grieving for the ouster of Morsi as undemocratic and a coup remember an essential fact: What was ousted was the abbreviation of Egypt as "the Islamic Project." There was nothing about it that was truly Islamic. It was a shameful masquerade abusing the banner of Islam and its main tenets of diversity.

Morsi's Foreign Policy and Practices Were Even More Foreign to Millions of Egyptians

Friday, July 19, 2013

Under the freedom of speech doctrine, you are entitled to call the camel a giraffe. But every freedom has a price tag. The price you pay for such a misnomer is that people would call you a **buffoon.** The less kinder among them may even see written on your forehead the word **"idiot."**

It is an idiocy to call the events of June 30 to July 3 of this year a **"coup."** A brief lesson in political terminology might help. When millions of citizens call for a recall, the happening is called a revolution. On January 25, 2011 and on June 30, 2013, millions of Egyptians exercised that right to populist democracy and won. Their first revolution brought together 7 millions; their second, mustered 23 millions. Supported by their armed forces whose personnel sprang from them as conscripts, they were shielded by the tanks of a national army. That army told the losers, Mubarak then Morsi: **"We are the army of the people; not the army of the President."**

It took the American revolution eleven years (from 1776 to 1787) to correct its course, and it took the French revolution even longer to do the same. The two iconic revolutions brought as their supreme leaders, General Washington (in America), and General Napoleon (in France). In Egypt, we had Morsi for 368 days, and we now have Mansoor as an interim President until the 90 million Egyptians settle down on a post revolutionary system. That system should embody diversity, cosmopolitanism, separation between religion and the State, and safeguards, with the help of the armed forces, for the character of the State as secular. Turkey has this model.

The transitional government which was sworn in by President (formerly Justice) Adly Mansour in Cairo on July 16, 2013 reflects that character. Its 34 cabinet members, including General Abdul-Fattah El-Sisi as both defense minister and deputy to Prime Minister Beblawi, count among them three, Coptics and three women. Where are the Muslim Brothers in that technocratic line-up? Nowhere to be found, refusing repeated offers of inclusion in the service of Egypt. The Brotherhood has opted for futile demonstrations and for calling for the return of the status-quo ante. Their abstention means no vote in the future.

Someone at the Cairo-based **"International Institute for Democracy and Electoral Assistance,"** commented on the post-Morsi administration from the two sides of his mouth. On the one hand he says: **"The only institution that can hold government accountable is the people."** Rational!! But then he adds: **"Legitimacy is hanging by a thread."** Irrational, both legally and politically. Why?

Sovereignty resides in the people. It has two pillars defining a sovereign State: **enactment of its laws, and conducting foreign affairs.** Egypt, as a sovereign State, is able to enact laws and to conduct foreign affairs. When I teach law, whether in New York City or at Cairo University School of Law, I remind my students of these two pillars of sovereignty. At present, Somalia is not regarded as a sovereign State because of the absence of these two pillars. That absence or deficiency, makes Somalia **"a failed State."** Since 1922, Egypt has never been bereft of either the competency to make laws for its people, or to conduct foreign affairs in the world outside its borders.

Examining, in this issue, the pillar of conducting foreign policy during the defunct Islamic regime of Mohamed Morsi, I give that regime's performance the low grade of **"F"** for failure. I wish that I could have given it a **"W-P"** meaning **"withdrawal-passing."** Morsi did not withdraw as he had promised the public in Tahrir when he took his first oath of office on June 30, 2012. On that day, Morsi pledged accountability to the people. Then he added: **"If I fail, remove me."** He failed, and 23 millions, on June 30, through **"Tammarod"** backed by the armed forces, forced him out of power.

Morsi's second oath of office was before the Supreme Constitutional Court, whose Chief Justice is now his replacement. The third oath of office by Morsi was at Cairo University where the leadership of the Muslim Brotherhood, his movement and the parent of his party **"Freedom and Justice,"** was given the front seats of honor. That was prophetic: Morsi was gradually distancing himself from the historic character of a secular and inclusive Egypt, and was gravitating towards his Islamist cocoon. A cocoon is a silky case spun by larva for protection. That protection proved unequal to 23 million Egyptians shouting **"IRHAL"** (Go).

At Cairo University, the leadership of inclusive Egypt saw on that day the writing on the wall. Sheikh Ahmed El-Tayeb, the Rector of Al-Azhar, abandoned the Cairo University ceremony protesting the commencement of the Brotherhoodization of Egypt. The opposition to the Brotherhood's coup against the substantive character of the State began to coalesce. The January 25 Revolution to which the Brothers came late was being hijacked in the name of Islam, not as a faith, but as an expedient cover for a blatant political grab for power.

Moving towards analyzing the failure of the Morsi's one-year rule in foreign policy, let us first have a look at my inbox marked: **"Miscellana."** Egypt's Foreign Ministry has been, since its beginning 90 years ago, a superb professional department which has made Cairo's foreign policy a point of reference for global diplomacy. The personnel is highly trained; their educational and linguistic qualifications are above par; their performance, even during the darkest hours of military humiliation, admirable.

However, my **"Miscellana"** inbox, contains embarrassing episodes during Morsi's one movement/one year rule.

For Washington, D.C., his interlocutor was a Muslim Brother spokesman, Gehad El-Haddad - **"the President Foreign Policy Advisor."** An embarrassing lack of knowledge of diplomacy.

At a summit meeting between Morsi and Germany's Chancellor, Angela Merkel, the then - President of Egypt kept on looking at his watch as if he had a train to catch.

Morsi, the engineer who taught the subject of **"the new materials"** on America's west coast in English, could not articulate in English during foreign encounters.

He shouts to his supporters the severance of relationship with Syria as if it were a great achievement. This prompted Bashar, a world class killer, to retort: **"Morsi: Grow up."**

In the context of the Nile water issue with Ethiopia, his meeting was aired, deliberately or not, advocating military action against a sister African State for building a dam on the Blue Nile.

He attempted a rapprochement (a recommencement of harmonious relationship) with Iran -a Shii majority Middle Eastern power. Yet he sat passively at a mosque where a sectarian rabble-rousing Imam called the Shiis **"dirty apostates."** Triple failures as regards the inclusiveness of Islam; the war against sectarianism; and the promise of normalizing relationship with Iran, especially in a revamped Middle East.

From my inbox of **"Miscellana"** to my research notes. Among the sources I perused in the preparation of this blog is the booklet issued by the Brotherhood in April of this year under the title of **"Achievements of Dr. Mohamed Morsi, President of the Republic."** I dealt with that 24-page booklet, published in Arabic in Cairo, in last week's blog under the abbreviated title of **"Achievements"** (Injazat).

Under the title of **"Foreign Affairs,"** (p. 16) there is a list of 12 **"achievements."** None of these twelve items would qualify as a foreign affairs item per se. It is a strange list of grants, loans, and foreign deposits intended to shore up the sagging Egyptian economy. From the contents of that list, the reader is obliged to conclude that the highly professional Foreign Ministry of Egypt had at best a limited input in that amateurish list.

What adds to this **"dehors foreign affairs"** nature of the list is item

10. The item is entitled **"The immediate cessation of Zionist aggression in the Gaza strip."** By definition, an achievement is a completed act. If the Brotherhood means to refer to Egypt's mediation between Israel and Hamas for the prolongation of the present cease fire, this matter is tasked, not to the Foreign Ministry, but to Egypt's military intelligence. On the other hand, if that out of context listing is meant to curry favor with Hamas, that type of Morsiism reflects a lack of reading of Egyptian growing hostility towards Hamas.

For the past 2 1/2 years, the Egyptian masses have looked upon Hamas as an instrument of offensive overreach in Sinai. Sinai, from time immortal, being Asian Egypt, has always been a highly sensitive security/sovereignty issue. There is an undeclared war between Hamas operatives, supported by Bedouin criminal elements, and the Egyptian Second and Third field armies. The top commander of the Second Army, General Wasfi, was nearly assassinated recently while inspecting some check points.

Here I do not wish to go into the present criminal investigation of the presumed role of Hamas in springing pre-presidency Morsi from behind prison bars in Wadi Al-Natrone in Egypt's western desert. Dwelling on the Hamas/Sinai issue is due to the confluence of national security, foreign policy and Egyptian treaty obligations. One of Nasser's misguided plans, which were summarily abandoned, was settling Palestinians in Sinai. At that time, at least Nasser had two excuses for that later aborted project: an Egyptian administration in Gaza (1948-1967) and a so-called war of attrition with Israel.

But under Morsi's Islamic rule, Hamas was looked upon as an Islamist partner of Egypt. At present, Egyptian general public opinion perceives an underground invasion of Sinai by Gazan tunnels through which arms, drugs, terrorists and Egyptian subsidized goods flowed regularly. Under Morsi, Egypt's north-east began to resemble the tribal areas of Afghanistan north-east. Egypt's armed forces were chafing under Morsi's attitude of **"go easy on our Gazan brothers."** Then came Ramadan of last year where no less than 16 Egyptian army recruits and officers were massacred by Hamas and Bedouin elements. El-Sisi declared that the armed forces would bring the assassins to justice, the tunnel invasion to extinction, and Bedouin criminality to an end.

The chasm between President Morsi and Defense Minister El-Sisi began to deepen into a **"Grand Canyon."** Under the special status conferred by the December 2012 Constitution upon the armed forces, the military might of Egypt came into play, especially through the non-declared modification of the protocols relating to Area G of Sinai in the Egypt/Israel Peace Treaty of 1979.

The iron fist of Egypt's armies punching Gazan invaders and Bedouin outlaws in Asian Egypt is a combative replay of an adage used by the American novelist Tom Clancy in his best seller **"The Teeth of the Tiger."** It says, **"If you want to kick the tiger in the (rear), you'd better have a plan for dealing with his teeth."** That is especially so when Hamas has lost its perch in Damascus, its support from Hezbollah, and its leverage with both Tehran and Ramallah. The Morsi regime was politically derelict to turn a blind eye to the rise of the so-called **"jihad"** cum criminality on Egypt's north east -a counter revolutionary movement which also contributed to the drying up of tourism to Egypt.

The Nile water issue between Egypt and Ethiopia was also a glaring foreign policy disaster. Egypt is benefiting from a generous share of the Nile water under a 1929 Nile Water Treaty. That treaty was concluded during colonial times when Britain controlled the destiny of the riparian States from Egypt to the north, to the Sudan and Uganda to the south. Six years after that treaty was concluded, fascist Italy invaded Ethiopia. Now sovereign Ethiopia is constructing a dam over the Blue Nile which carries to both the Sudan and Egypt 60% of the Nile flood waters. That Ethiopian dam is looked upon by both Egypt and the Sudan as potentially limiting their water intake. Ethiopia rebuts this opposition as exaggerated.

So what does President Morsi do in the face of this delicate issue? As mentioned briefly above, he convened a meeting attended by a number of heads of political parties and others to discuss Egypt's options under the uncomprising slogan of: **"Not one drop of Nile water would be lost to Egypt."** The discussions were aired to the whole world, some say by error, others say by design. What were some of the recommendations: **Bomb the Ethiopian dam!!**

A war with Egypt's historic neighbor Ethiopia was proposed as an option at a leadership meeting headed by the Egyptian President. This is at a time when Egypt is struggling to feed its people; big powers are finding that wars are anathema to economic recovery; Egypt is already immersed in a hit and run war in Sinai; and the Sudan is mired in its internal and external armed conflicts. Discovering the historic links between the Egyptian Coptic Church and its Ethiopian sister Church, the Morsi regime, arguably without the benefit of professional diplomacy, sought support from the Pope of Alexandria. The answer was negative.

That was another episode of the Brotherhoodization of Egypt which was running amok. No room for diplomacy, negotiation, conciliation or arbitration -the very tools which Egypt's foreign policy has mastered for a long time. Was General El-Sisi consulted prior to this threat of the use of force, a threat which is legally forbidden under the UN Charter, and the Charter of the African Union? I do not know. But Egypt heard no military voice rising out of that Morsi hallucinating conclave. After the broadcast threat of war, came a quiet and belated visit by Egypt's foreign minister to Addis Ababa. Since then, Ethiopia has been raising the banner of self defense.

The Syrian question was another foreign policy blunder. The greatest majority of the Egyptian public has been horrified by the Bashar killing fields in that sister Arab country. The League of Arab States, whose headquarters is in Cairo, has already given the Syrian opposition the seat of their country. In view of the complexity of that widening civil war, that measure should have been enough. Egypt has been actively trying to get all the parties to the conflict to the table in the framework of the US/Russia plan.

Then suddenly, like a thunder bolt, President Morsi, while recently haranguing his supporters, declared that he had decided to sever diplomatic relations with Damascus. His motley crowd cheered. But it must have been a sad day for the occupants of that magnificent building by the eastern edge of the Nile -the Foreign Ministry. To the Syrian regime, it was like pouring salt into the wound. Bashar was not silent. He called Morsi inexperienced, reminded him of the Cairo-Damascus historic amity, and in effect told him **"shut up."** To Morsi, foreign policy was a matter for the pulpit.

The drift towards the pulpit as a locus for non-digested foreign policy issues, during the Morsi regime manifested that Egypt's secularism was slipping away. A recent fatwa by Al-Qaradawi, who heads the Organization of Muslim Scholars (a Sunni entity) was issued after July 3. It confirmed, especially to Saudi Arabia, the Emirates, and Kuwait, their fear of an Islamist Egypt in the making. This fatwa which, under Islamic jurisprudence has no standing, claimed that Morsi **"was elected to the presidency due to heavenly design." A devine right for Morsiism!!** To those Gulf sources of financial assistance to Cairo, the Arab Spring of Egypt had become a potential tornado against Arab monarchies.

It was on August 17, 2011, that Al-Azhar, with the full concurrence of the Coptic Church and a broad representation of Egyptian political movements, issued eleven basic principles about which there was a solid Egyptian consensus. Its first principle declared: **"Islam, in its legislation, civilization, and history does not recognize a religiously-based State."** (my translation from the Arabic). During the interregnum between Mubarak and Morsi, General Sami Anan, Deputy Chairman of the Egyptian Supreme Council of the Armed Forces declared: **"The secularity of the State is a matter of national security which is non-negotiable."** These pronouncements were not what the Muslim Brotherhood wished to abide by. Power, not principle, was their goal warped in the abaya of **"faith and governance are one."**

Now this is over, hopefully forever. A new transitional cabinet was sworn in by interim President Adly Mansour on July 16. Technocracy, meritocracy and inclusiveness are back. How can the Foreign Ministry, now under veteran diplomat and scholar Nabil Fahay, not be jubilant?

With historic Egypt back, normalcy in Cairo was being politically and financially rewarded. When Burns of the US Department of State was in Cairo he did not even utter the name of Morsi. The calls by the Brotherhood for outside intervention went nowhere. The reign of terror against the judiciary came to an end. Goods and services seem to flow back calming the Egyptian street. El-Sisi, who was recently called by the Brotherhood **"an American agent,"** added to his post of Defense Minister, the post of Deputy to Prime Minister El-Beblawi. Twelve billion US dollars flowed from Riyadh, the Emirates and Kuwait into the Egyptian treasury, thus postponing the day of wrangling with the International Monetary Fund.

Commenting on these developments, former Kuwaiti permanent representative to the UN, Ambassador Abdullah Bishara, the first Secretary-General of the Gulf Cooperation Council, said in a recent article (my translation):

"Whatever one says about the Brotherhood, one cannot escape the conclusion that they are not fit to join the universal march which is guided by certain foreign policy principles. Neither they nor Morsi are equipped with the legitimacy of enlightened leadership which promises that the future shall bring fulfillment of Egypt's big dreams."

The Second Egyptian Revolution of June 30, 2013 Has Waved a Final Goodbye to Exclusive Islamic Rule

Monday, July 29, 2013

Egypt has a durable face, and a changing face. Its durability, expressed in stone, can be seen in the pyramids and the sphinx. The same face is manifested institutionally in the armed forces, Al-Azhar, and the Coptic church. The Egyptian changeable face could also be seen in its secular forces and its Islamist forces.

In this blog, I shall focus on one of the durables in Egyptian life, namely the armed forces. This is in view of General El-Sisi's marshaling the power of the masses in his call made in July 24, 2013. It was a call intended to put the Muslim Brotherhood on notice that the removal of Morsi shall not be reversed, and that the continuation of violence shall be met by force by both the army and the police. In such a confrontation, the army undoubtedly has the upper hand.

Is this situation democratic, undemocratic, anti-democratic, liberal, illliberal street rule, mob democracy? Here descriptions do not much matter. The Egyptian revolution has not matured yet; the transitional government of July 16 is still feeling its way; the Brotherhood and their opponents have shed lots of blood (more than 200 dead); and the terms Selmia (peaceful) and Islamiah (Islamic) are now seen as definite opposites.

The heart of the matter is that the only institution which can save Egypt from civil war or even worse, disintegration, is the armed forces. Since time immemorial, they have been an integral part of Egypt's political life. Some Egyptian experts date that symbiosis to 3000 years B.C.

A good source on this is the book by Ahmed Abdulla, entitled **"The Army and Democracy in Egypt"** (1990, in Arabic). That source is largely built on an earlier source by Anwar Abdel-Malek **"The Army and the National Movement"** (1974, in Arabic).

In my capacity as a guest lecturer at the Nasser Military Academy in 1974, following the October war of 1973 between Egypt/Syria and Israel, I made a discovery. My host, the late field marshal Ahmed Ismail has allowed me to keep the texts of the 73 questions addressed to me by the top leadership of Egypt's armed forces. The questions revealed an Egyptian military which was focused on the future of Egyptian politics. Reflections of this could be found in the book by the very first Egyptian president, following the collapse of the monarchy in 1952. That was the late General Muhammad Naguib in his book entitled **"Egypt's Destiny."**

Therefore it came as no surprise to those who follow this subject closely that the Egyptian Constitution of December 2012 assigns the military a special status. Its task is **"ensuring the safety and security of the country,"** and **"shall be consulted about draft laws related to them"** (Article 197). The Constituent Assembly, dominated by the Islamists, signed on this.

In his call for public demonstrations issued on July 24, General El-Sisi reminded the nation, including the Brotherhood, that three reports had been submitted by the military to the then President Morsi warning against the descent of Egypt into chaos resulting from the President's refusal to compromise with his secular opponents;

expressing alarm at the Islamisation of the State through the merging of religion and the concept of the homeland; and

the rejection by the majority of the public of the Morsi mode of governance whereby that rejection was translated by the Morsi regime as a rejection of Islam itself.

In his call to the Egyptian street of July 24, El-Sisi made it clear that it became clear that **"the conflict within Egypt was morphing into a religious conflict."**

With the war in Sinai against Gazans, Bedouins, Syrians and Hezbollah infiltrators, the armed forces faced a military confrontation to the east, and a security confrontation with the pro-Morsi forces in Cairo, Alexandria, and other urban centers in the heart of the most populous country in the Arab world. The Brotherhood seemed to be spoiling for a confrontation with the national army and the police using the fig leaf of the so-called **"Shariyah"** (legitimacy).

The Brotherhood most serious misfortune, marking the end of its peaceful co-existence with the armed forces, happened on August 5, 2012. In Rafah, northeast of Sinai, a massacre perpetrated on the Egyptian army took place. As troops sat to break their Ramadan fast, they were set upon by a group of terrorists who killed 16 soldiers in cold blood, and wounded 9 others. The Supreme Council of the Armed Forces (SCAF), led by Field Marshal Tantawi, the de facto ruler of Egypt prior to the election of Morsi, issued the following pledge: **"So God be our witness, we shall avenge our martyrs."**

All of Egypt went into national mourning; Morsi's reaction was tepid; the results of the investigation ordered by Morsi produced no results; and the finger of accusation by the armed forces pointed to terrorists and so-called jihadi groups in Sinai who may or may not have affiliation with Al-Qaeda, with some criminal Bedouin support.

Sinai became the real battleground between a secularist Egypt supported by its cohesive national army, and the Morsi regime which acted exclusively on the premise that winning the presidency by 50.50% of only 22% of Egyptian voters in June 2012 was a license for Islamization en masse. That was not Morsi's contract with Egypt.

Morsi interpreted the results of the ballot box of June 2012 as if they were a mandate for politically-cleansing Egypt from the latent anti-Brotherhood opposition. His targets were the judiciary, the liberal media, the House of Fatwas (religious interpretation through non-enforceable guidelines), the independence of Al-Azhar. Also among Morsi's targets was SCAF which, through its support of the January 25 Revolution, had pushed Mubarak out of power, and helped the electorate reach the ballot box.

Sieges by the Islamists of iconic Egyptian institutions such as the headquarters of the Supreme Constitutional Court, the sites of the Egyptian TV and Artistic Production, and the Ministry of Interior whose police forces refused to battle demonstrators constituted an expanding Islamic coup against the soul of secular Egypt.

In the midst of this chaos, Morsi ill-advisedly thought that he possessed some silver bullets. He abruptly sacked the transitional leadership of SCAF (Field Marshal Tantawi and General Anan); ordered the reconvening of a dissolved House of Representatives; and had that rump session of ex-parliamentarians of whom 70% were either Brothers or Salafis resolve in 20 minutes that legislative powers be transferred to him pending the adoption of a new Constitution. To the rank and file of the Egyptian masses, Morsi and Ramses II began to look the same. But Ramses II had kept Egypt united; Morsi was fracturing the land of the Nile.

Former professor Morsi then issued a constitutional declaration in November 2012 declaring in effect that he was above the law -his decisions were not subject to judicial review. That declaration produced a fire storm, as the populace saw in Morsi, especially on the eve of the hasty adoption of the Constitution of December 2012, another Mubarak. Although that ominous declaration was quickly withdrawn, but the specter of Brotherhoodization of Egypt especially at the provincial level, assumed alarming proportions in the public mind.

The president of the Judges' Club, Counsellor El-Zind declared on April 21 that he might sue Morsi through the International Criminal Court, though legally he had no standing. It was a sign of desperation. Out of 27 Egyptian provinces (governerates), 13 had new governors who were members of the Brotherhood.

Analyzing the issue of legitimacy, in the context of the Second Revolution of June 30, 2013, both law and politics lead to the following conclusions:

In June 2012, Morsi was handed an Egypt of diversity, secularism, and protection of minorities both Copts and Shiis; Islamic moderation proclaimed by Al-Azhar; gender equality under the law; a fairly independent judiciary; and an army with an autonomous status whose task has always been border security, and the safeguarding, together with the police, of internal peace. **That was the deal, the contract, the trust and the obligation.**

Regardless what the outside world may characterize the sacking of Morsi on July 3 by the armed forces, in response to the appeals of 23 million Egyptians on June 30 for the intervention by the army, **"the guardian of the nation,"** ex-President Morsi had forged ahead through his base in the Brotherhood, to nullify his contract with his nation.

Through his lack of governing experience, and his reliance on the narrow base of the Muslim Brotherhood and its party (Freedom and Justice), the broad sectors of revolutionary Egypt found their First Revolution of January 25, which, in Tahrir, had raised no Islamist flags, being swallowed by the new regime.

The Brotherhood's continuous waving of the flag of **"Shariyah"** (legitimacy) which calls for Morsi's reinstatement, shall only lead to more bloodshed. Their man has breached his contract in both letter and spirit. The El-Sisi call on the Egyptian Street to rise up again on Friday, July 26, 2013 had resonance with the transitional justice period of Egypt. Thirty five millions answered that call.

In his capacity as Defense Minister and Deputy Prime Minister and in the absence of a functioning homeland both economically and politically, El-Sisi has summed up the country's status: **"The State's national security is facing severe dangers."**

With a war going on in Sinai against terrorism, the army of Egypt is broadcasting the only credible message of the Second Revolution: **"We shall strike with all our might at terrorism in Sinai and anywhere in Egypt."** The Brotherhood is now being labelled by the armed forces as an ally of terrorism, at least in Sinai, which is witnessing a low grade civil war with the Bedouins, and an external war with alleged Hamas operatives.

As of Friday, July 26, the lines of battle with the Muslim Brotherhood have been sharply drawn. And the judiciary has also swung into action. The public Prosecutor has issued an order of 15-day detention against former President Morsi on account of high treason. The charges are expounded below.

With a war raging in Sinai against terrorism, Egypt's armed forces are signalling their unwavering commitment to stamp out terrorism anywhere in Egypt. The term **"terrorism"** now includes the Muslim Brotherhood. Calls by the Brotherhood's spokesmen and other outlets for defections from these armed forces have put the Brotherhood in the defendant's box. The attacks in Sinai against the army and the police have put them in the cross hairs of that mighty adversary. Witness the declaration by Al-Beltagi, a Brotherhood leader, to the effect that the Sinai attacks shall not cease until Morsi is reinstated.

With the battle lines between the armed forces and the Brotherhood so sharply drawn, the whole notion of a compromise has evaporated. Signaling a no return, an armed forces ultimatum was issued to the pro-Morsi forces: **end your disruptive demonstrations by July 27 or else.**

On the civilian side of the crackdown, the Public Prosecutor remanded Morsi to a 15-day detention period. Charges have been filed and investigations begun in alleged criminal activities including his jail break from Wadi El-Natroun prison assisted by Hamas operatives, murderous attacks against security forces, and espionage for Hamas (a foreign power).

The entire Islamist rule is now on trial.

The Brotherhood's response not only led to more bloodshed; it confirmed both the fact and perception of the danger to historic Egypt of an exclusive Islamist governance. Such confirmation came in the form of elevating Morsi by the Brotherhood to divinity. The Brotherhood's Supreme Guide called the unseating of Morsi: **"worse than the dismantlement of the Kaaba (in Mecca where Muslims everywhere turn to prayer) stone by stone."** Morsi's supporters chanted **"For Islam, we are ready to shed our blood."** And at Cairo University, bearded Muslim clerics urged their Muslim supporters to stand firm for **"an Islamic State,"** and against **"a secular State."**

The counter response from 35 million Egyptians who thronged Squares all over Egypt honoring the call of El-Sisi for a mandate from the Egyptian street for the suppression of terrorism signaled where Egypt stood. Those multitudes raised, not the black flags of Islamic governance, but the national flag of Egypt -the secular State. With humor being a part of Egypt's DNA, the chants arose equating the Brotherhood **(Al-Ikhwan)** with sheep **(Al-Kherfan)**. The Islamists appeals for outside intervention were regarded as high treason.

Regardless of the bloodshed which has unfortunately took place since June 30, the criticisms made abroad of the Egyptian military ascendancy, a pivotal point of no return has been reached in Egypt. **Islamic rule in Egypt has been discredited and those who are still visualising its possible comeback are seeing a mirage.**

The Second Egyptian Revolution, which began with Tammarrod in April 2013 and culminated in both the ouster of Morsi and the massive response of Tahrir to El-Sisi call for a mandate **"to end terrorism,"** has also tarnished beyond repair the Brotherhood affiliates in Tunisia, Libya, Syria, the Gulf and beyond.

The reader may be in search of a descriptive label for the June 30 Revolution. Labels are misleading because they gravitate towards a simplistically-conventional description. But I owe it to the reader to dig into my multiple backgrounds in education/history/political science/law to find a label. Let us try this one: **"A Revolt by the Masses Against a Coup."** Translation: The coup was perpetrated by the Islamists against the January 25 Revolution whose premise was secularism.

Secular Egypt is striking back. It is delivering a body blow to extremism in Islam and giving prominence to the Al-Azhar principle:

"Islam does not recognize a State based solely on religion." This is huge!!

26 AUGUST 2013

With Regard to the Second Egyptian Revolution of June 30, The U.S. Should Speak Softly and Carry No Sticks

Friday, August 2, 2013

With apologies to President Teddy Roosevelt who admonished: **"Speak softly and carry a big stick!!"** Mr. President, Sir, allow me as an Egyptian American (I am of dual nationalities) to modify your saying. With regard to the Second Egyptian Revolution of June 30, it is of mutual interest for both Cairo and Washington, that the U.S. refrains from shouting at the Egyptian transitional government. **First:** It will have no effect; **Second:** it is none of the U.S. business; and **Third:** It gives the pro-Morsi forces some false hope that their man should be given a second chance. Nonsense!!

As to the **"no effect factor,"** see the book by Andrew Bacevich: **The Limits of Power: The End of American Exceptionalism** (2010). The same thesis is reflected, though in a different way, in the recent book by Richard Haas, the current president of the Council on Foreign Relations. Under the title of **Foreign Policy Begins at Home: The Case for Putting America's House in Order** (2013), Haas concludes as follows: **"Either the United States will put its house in order and refocus what**

251

it does abroad, or it will increasingly find itself at the mercy of what happens beyond its borders and beyond its control." Well said, Mr. Haas.

With regard to the **"none of the U.S. business"** factor, I begin by the obvious: the sovereignties of nations, large or small, are co-equal. Malta, whose population is less than the number of tenants in the complex where I live in Manhattan, has the same degree of sovereignty as that of China. Why? Sovereignty, in legal and political terms, is not measured by power and influence. It is inherent in a well-defined population within recognizable borders.

Thus Egypt and the U.S. enjoy, each respectively, co-equal sovereignty, No **dictat** and no **Pax-Americana**. From my focus on decolonization, both as an academic and a former U.N. Principal Political Officer in charge of the Africa Division, I have always appreciated two essential values in U.S. politics: support for liberation movements, and the general adherence to Washington's advice: **"No entangling alliances."**

One might say: **"But the U.S. provides Egypt with $1.5 billion in annual aid since 1973. Shouldn't Washington have at least some say in the Egyptian sector of the Arab Spring?"** A fair question; but a wrong premise. For starters, Egyptian sovereignty is not for sale. Waving the stick of withholding that aid would be very short-sighted. That aid, most of which is spent in the U.S. on military equipment and training, is an integral part of the Egypt-Israel Peace Treaty of 1979. An Egyptian President, Sadat, gave his life at the hands of Islamists, for that peace. Playing that card would be tantamount to the possible unraveling of that Treaty which is guaranteed by the U.S.

Note also that the Peace Treaty of 1979 is, in part, a factor in the security chaos in Sinai against which Egypt's armed forces and other security elements are battling. It has restricted the volume and the quality of the tactical armed strength on the Gaza/Sinai borders. Area **"G"** of Sinai has become a veritable ware zone. In that war, where the so-called jihadists, together with Hamas and other marauding terrorist elements, including some Sinai Bedouins, Egypt is daily shedding blood. You cannot put value on human blood.

I stated above a third factor. The U.S. is perceived to be giving, through utterances by Secretary Kerry, Secretary Hagel, and congressional leaders, some hope in the resurrection of the Morsi reign. This is wrong, counter-productive, and cannot be politically or strategically sound. When I teach political science or law, I begin by defining politics as **"the art of the possible."** The chance of a Morsi come back is a mid-summer dream. The culture of **"no second chance"** in a revolutionary context stands in the way of the Muslim Brotherhood.

A second chance might be acceptable in a peaceful American political culture. Witness the **"comeback kid"** phenomenon in the case of Bill Clinton, and in the attempts at similar feats by former New York Governor Spitzer, and former Congressman Weiner. There is a chasm of 6000 miles between **"a comeback"** tolerance in the American culture, and **"a comeback"** utter rejection in the culture of the Egyptian Second Revolution. That geographic distance between Washington D.C. and Cairo has greater vertical depth: the way the Islamist regime has mismanaged Egypt during one very very long year to which the majority of Egyptians put an end in Tahrir on June 30.

Let us now tackle the issue of **"Islamic mismanagement in Egypt"** from June 30, 2012 to June 30, 2013 –when the armed forces, though engaged in war in Sinai, came to the rescue of Egypt. My sources are many, and my evidence is drawn from largely Egyptian voices.

I begin by Dr. Abdel-Monium Abu-Elfotooh, who was pushed out of the Muslim Brotherhood. His views were those of reforming that historic organization which had suffered brutal suppression as of 1948. In 1948, its founder Hassan El-Banna was assassinated by the regime of Ilbahim Abdel-Hadi. The predecessor of Abdel-Hadi, Prime Minister Al-Nokrashi, had been killed in 1947 by the **"Secret Wing"** of the Muslim Brotherhood. One of my several sources is in his book: **"Innovators, Not Spoilers"** (in Arabic, 2005). That book by Abul-Elfotooh, which was published while he was a member of **"The Guidance Bureau"** of the Brotherhood, included his responses to a press interview. On p. 103, he speaks the language of the 21st century.

Abul-Fotooh told his interviewer (my translation): **"I am fully supportive of the freedom of expression, including the freedom of apostasy (ilhad). The Brotherhood is against all forms of exclusion, prohibitions or restraints on freedoms. The Brotherhood is for a secular State not a religious State. They do not reject a president for the Arab Republic of Egypt, even if that president was a Christian. They do not condone anyone who pretends to speak in the name of the Almighty Allah (God). The Brotherhood has no monopoly on Islam."**

Before the presidential run-off of Morsi vs. Shafik, I gave Abdul-Fotooh, as a presidential candidate, my vote. He spoke my language. He also seemed to anticipate my conclusions in the book on which I am working now for publication in New York to counter Islamophobia. The title of this forthcoming book: **"Sharia Legal Principles for the Twenty-First Century."** I am dedicating that work to my late father, Sheikh El-Sayed Muhammad El-Ayouty, a graduate of Al-Azhar who taught Islamic philosophy and history.

My forthcoming book is also dedicated to the late Gamal El-Banna, who, though a brother of Hassan El-Banna, was kept by the clumsy conservatives of the Brotherhood, at arm's length. Gamal, the younger brother, espoused in several of his sources which he had gifted to m, the principle of **"diversity"** in Islam. (I once carried his bags at the Geneva Airport).

One of his many books is entitled **"Islam Is Faith and Community (ummah), Not Faith and a State."** (January, 2003). He rebuts ten years earlier than the chants of the pro-Morsi crowds in Cairo for **"a Caliphate"** which arose as of 2013 following the collapse of the Morsi regime. That chant was repeated on July 3 by El-Zawahri, Bin Laden's successor. It was in the context of a threat addressed by that evil man against Obama.

On the dust jacket of that book by Gamal El-Banna, the author states that, **"the Quran has addressed the Nation (Ummah) as a community of Muslims. Nowhere does the Quran refer to a State."** Then he defines the Ummah as **"a diverse collectivity of mass organizations such as labor unions, political parties, charitable organizations, and civil society institutions."**

Within the two covers of that book by Gamal El-Banna, the central premise is **"freedom of thought and expression is a sine qua non condition."** This is also a rebuttal to the thesis of Bernard Lewis especially in his book, **"What Went Wrong: The Clash Between Islam and Modernity in the Middle East"** (2012)

In effect, Gamal El-Banna is saying: **"Professor Lewis: There is nothing wrong with Islam. The wrong is with the thinking of the likes of the conservative wing of the Muslim Brotherhood."** There is little doubt that handing the books by Bernard Lewis on Islam to US forces on their way to Afghanistan in 2002 could not have served the U.S. interest in reconciling with Islam in the aftermath of 9/11.

That colossal misunderstanding of Islam resulted from seeing that faith of 1.5 billion population through the prism of conservatives and so-called jihadis. It is seeping through the present US assessment of the Second Egyptian Revolution. Secretary of State Kerry, Secretary of Defense Hagel, US Ambassador to Cairo, Anne Patterson, are urging Cairo to release Morsi and to reach out to the Muslim Brotherhood. The civilian and military leadership of the June 30 Revolution responded that the Brotherhood had rejected those overtures. So far it has been a useless **"dialogue of the deaf."** It it takes two to tango.

But we still also have unofficial US voices raising the proverbial stick. Dennis Ross, former Middle East advisor to President Obama yells through the New York Times of July 30, that **"the administration should make it clear that it has red lines that if crossed would result in a cutoff of aid."** Then he goes on to suggest that the US **"should enlist Saudi Arabia and the Persian Gulf emirates to pressure the generals."** I wonder what Mr. Ross is smoking these days!! He is presuming that these sovereign States are no more than US outposts in the Arab world. And he also overlooks the political significance, though not the fact, that these are the very States which have just advanced $12 billion to Egypt.

Summing up the blessing by the Gulf States of the unseating of Morsi, Ambassador Bishara, the first Secondary-General of the Gulf Cooperation Council wrote recently to me that: **"No one ever thought of Egypt under a Mullah."**

And there exists no **"Faustian Pact: Between Generals and Democrats"** in Egypt as claimed by Steven A. Cook, Senior Fellow at the Council on Foreign Relations in the title of his Op Ed page in the New York Times of July 26. Such statements by Ross and Cook exemplify the disconnect between present day Egypt and the American foreign policy establishment. A real shame!!. It was the founder of Saudi Arabia, the Bedouin King Abdul-Aziz Al-Saud who, when approached in the 1930s by the Muslim Brotherhood to allow for a branch of their movement in his Kingdom, refused. His response was succinct: **"Why? We are all brothers and we are all Muslims."**

Official reaction by Cairo to the characterization of the Second Egyptian Revolution as **"the unraveling of Egypt"** was swift. Ahmed Al-Meslemani, the official spokesman of the Presidency declared: **"Egypt is governed by the Egyptian House not by the White House."**

There were also unofficial voices raised in exasperation from what is perceived as US meddling in Egypt's internal affairs. A former dean of an Egyptian Law College told me on the phone: **"If the Americans are enamored with the Muslim Brotherhood, they should give all of them visas –visas to Guantanamo."**

Owners of private micro-buses in Alexandria put up signs in the windshields of their vehicles: **"No Muslim Brothers are allowed. They cause fights to break out with ordinary passengers."** Muhammad Al-Barghouthi, a journalist, wrote in the newspaper **Al-Waltan**, on July 30: **"When it became clear that the political and moral legitimacy of the Brotherhood's rule in Egypt was evaporating, the Brotherhood did nothing but cling to the results of the ballot box which brought them to power."**

Again to Abul-Fotooh's book, **"Innovators, Not Spoilers."** Here on page 113, he says while being a member of the Brotherhood's Guidance Bureau: **"The Muslim Brotherhood has no experience in governance. We are with whatever good they advanced, and against whatever mischief they perpetrated. Don't expect them to follow the example of the Taliban in forcing women to dress their bodies in tents, to destroy monuments or to ban music."** That was before he was forced to quit the Brotherhood which embarked through the Morsi rule on just that perilous path.

So the U.S. should speak to the Second Egyptian Revolution softly and brandish no sanctions. A distinguished Egyptian Ambassador, Dr. Mahmoud Karem, who is attached to the NATO Mission in Rome offered a sober counsel to both Egypt and the US. In an article in English in **Al-Abhram Weekly** of July 9, 2013, entitled, **"Cairo and Washington,"** he states in a conciliating tone:

"We await a strong message from the U.S. anchored in strong ties of partnership with Egypt. The U.S. inspiring constitution that leads with the well-known assertion 'We the People' should act as a harbinger for creating strong ties between both peoples."

Ambassador Karem resorts to the U.S. Constitution as a possible ideological vehicle for a true Cairo-Washington rapprochement. In that context, I, following his example, by resorting to U.S. laws anchored on the Constitution. Therefore, I advance the following Q's and A's:

Is occupancy by thousands of Morsi supporters of at least four main areas in Cairo for days "a peaceful demonstration?"

No! The right to peaceful assembly is governed by three principles: **Time, Place and Manner.** Under US laws which underpinned the break-up of the **"Occupy Wall Street"** movement by the New York Police Department, the State acted on the basis of this tripod of legitimate freedom of assembly. License to assemble is issued for a few hours, at a distance from buildings serving public or private functions, and without disturbing public peace and civilian activities. Of course, no arms or threats of violence are permitted. The sit-ins in Cairo have violated all the three parameters stated above. They have become armed camps controlled by their organization. The Egyptian authorities have the right and the obligation to put an end to that chaos.

Is the Egyptian Government entitled to marshal its armed and security forces to confront those who are abusing the right to freedom of assembly and of speech?

Of course. There is chaos caused by the Brotherhood's hot-heads for the sole purpose of disenfranchising the 30+ millions of Egyptians who demanded Morsi's removal. There is also a war in Sinai. The Brotherhood have characterized the Egyptian Cabinet declaration of July 31 as **"a declaration of war."** No reasonable person should support the shedding of blood of innocent civilians. But the Islamist opposition, which is apparently armed for combat targeting the Second Egyptian Revolution by its own reaction to the call by the cabinet for the restoration of law and order, is inviting a lethal response. This is a declaration of insurrection within Egyptian urban centers which is made more credible by the Brotherhood's declared support for the armed insurrection in Sinai. A veritable civil war is in the making. Let us recall that President Lincoln had to resort to the suspension of certain civil liberties under the Constitution as a means of keeping the Union together during the American Civil War.

Are human rights organizations such as Amnesty International exercising their rightful global functions of enhancing the Rule of Law and the protection of civil liberties when they describe the warning by Cairo to the chaos-makers as **"a recipe for bloodshed?"**

Absolutely negative.

Amnesty International is not a trustee over Egypt. They have overstepped their moral and legal boundaries. Theirs is an ill-advised characterization, thereby weakening their standing in Egypt, not to mention tarnishing the concepts of detachment and neutrality of other human rights organizations. They are out of sync with the popular will manifested by the Second Egyptian Revolution. Their scales and measurements are in sore need of adjustment by competent professionals who know how to balance between civil liberties and national security. Amnesty International could benefit from reading the transcripts of hearings held earlier this week by the US Senate Judicial Committee on the work of the National Security Agency. That organization might also benefit by Secretary Kerry's statement on August 1 in Pakistan. He declared that Egypt's military was restoring democracy in ousting Morsi. His premise was that the "military was asked to intervene by millions and millions of people."

At last, the U.S. is now speaking softly to the Second Egyptian Revolution.

The Abuse of Language as a Means to Sordid Ends

Friday, August 16, 2013

We need a new vocabulary to place the Second Egyptian Revolution in its proper context. A lot of verbiage has been produced especially by the opponents of a secular Egypt. Their language is a mere cover-up to a sordid end. Their end is the resurrection of the Islamist regime of Mohamed Morsi and the marginalization of more than half of the Egyptian electorate who rose up against it on June 30. Words are power, and power should be invoked in support of the popular will. That popular will has been manifested in Tahrir, and the armed forces, under General El-Sisi, have appropriately responded to its call.

The examples on the abuse of language as a means to attack the legitimacy of the Second Egyptian Revolution are legion. Herein below, I shall present the abused language, and follow up by providing the near universal consensual meaning. The purpose is to pierce the veil of linguistic obfuscation through the presentation of selected examples.

The sit-ins at several locations in Cairo are a legitimate peaceful

exercise of the right to assembly:

Not so. Your sit-ins in Rabaa and Nahdha and other central locations have proved to be armed guerrilla camps. You have stored weapons smuggled in to you by your cohorts inside and outside of Egypt, especially by Hamas. You have besieged the residences of the peaceful inhabitants of the sit-in areas; broken and entered those homes to use those buildings as lookouts and sniper positions.

You have also set-up tents and vendor locations for the purpose of endless criminal trespass; built up veritable walls to block access to public streets; committed acts of torture against whomever came within your perimeters with an opposite message; stored materiel for Molotov cocktails for use against the power of the State, including its use of the army and the police; and you have cut down trees and destroyed pavements for use as a stone-throwing weaponry in your armed confrontations with Egypt of June 30.

Your actions have to do neither with the constitutional right to peaceful assembly, nor with the freedom of speech in the new Egypt. In spite of the language you use, you represent a rebellion against secular Egypt. Whoever condones using children as human shields, as you have been doing, is committing a war crime.

The calls for raising the flag of "Allahu-Akbar" are appropriate for the replacement of the flag of Egypt

Really? Your pan-Islamism has no real roots in Egypt. No Islamist flag was ever raised in Tahrir during the January 25, 2011 Revolution whose rightful authors were the youth, both Muslims and Copts. You came late for that uprising against the secular dictatorship of Mubarak and then, through the ballot box, assumed its leadership. But leadership to where? To an Islamic totalitarianism which was thrown out on July 3, 2013. That was because Morsi had violated his contract with the new Egypt.

And guess what? Under Islamic jurisprudence, **Allahu-Akbar** does not mean what you presume it to mean. You use it as a battle cry. But from a Sharia perspective it means that all human beings, of whatever faith, are equal before God. So if you wish to act on the sermon of Sheikh Ahmed Amer in which he said: **"The flag of Egypt should be burnt and replaced by a flag proclaiming Allahu Akbar,"** you shall be proclaiming that you are no longer a part of the Egyptian body politic.

Many of you greeted the seditious call by Ahmed Amer for the destruction of the national flag, by chanting **"Allahu Akbar."** You have thus subverted the lofty call for universalism implicit in **"Allahu Akbar"** for the sordid end of wiping out the identity of Egypt as a State. If you wish for an Al-Qaeda flag, you shall not find it in the land of the Nile. Under your ideology, nationalism and Arabism are not values worthy of your respect. You have placed pan-Islamism, as a political tool, above all else. Your downgrading of Arabism and nationalism is intended to deny that those terms afford, among other things, full protection and equality to minorities, including the Copts.

Those who lost their lives in confrontations with the army and the police, as of the ouster of Morsi, are "martyrs" (shaheed).

We bow our heads in prayer and in grief for them. They were victims of your manipulation of the term **"legitimacy"** (Shariyah). Your leadership pushed those victims to that horrific fate. But as we all grieve for that senseless human loss, we have to correct your abuse of the definition of **"shaheed."**

Islamic law defines **"a martyr"** as a person who lost his or her life while pursuing the legitimate causes of defending the homeland against outside aggression, and fending for oneself against an attack on person, household or property. Shahadah (martyrdom) in Islamic jurisprudence is primarily a defensive mechanism. Thus the shaheeds are those army and police personnel whose lives were lost battling you for the defense of Egypt.

With a heavy heart, we have to note that your supporters lost their lives while threatening and/or aggressing against the security of the Egyptian street and the peace of Egypt which is guaranteed by the armed forces. Warnings to you to disband and to allow Egypt to recover were, over a six-week period, repeatedly flouted by you. Those victims, led by you to their tragic fate, were duped by your calls **"For Morsi and Islam we sacrifice ourselves."** An ugly means to an autocratic end.

In this regard, you became no different from suicide bombers who mistakenly think that the killing of innocent civilians, whether on 9/11 or on the streets of Egypt, Iraq, Afghanistan, Pakistan or Yemen, is a passport to paradise. Islam does not condone self-sacrifice.

Efforts to return Morsi to the presidential palace, through your mutiny against secular Egypt, are your form of worship to be

rewarded in the after-life.

This is a canonization of Morsi and his elevation to sainthood. Your belief in a theocracy on the banks of the Nile magnifies your disconnect with the character, the psyche, and the national identity of Egypt as a State of diversity. An important reason for the collapse of your Islamist regime is that you have not understood the Egyptian public.

Voting for you in the parliamentary and presidential elections was, to a substantial extent, a vote for relief from 60 years of military rule. The Brotherhood has never before been tried as a government for Egypt. Egyptian cabinets before 1952 included ministers and cabinet advisers who were Copts, Armenians, Jews, French, Greeks and British. A true diversity and a modern cosmopolitanism. That is why Egypt before 1952 was a story of success, before it gradually descended to the level of pre-disintegration under secular military dictatorship, ushered in by Nasser.

Solidarity with the aspirations to the creation of a Palestinian State in the West Bank and Gaza should be pursued, among other measures, through collaboration with Hamas

But Hamas is at war with both the Palestinian Authority in Ramallah and with Israel. Egypt, as a State, voted repeatedly at the UN, for a **"Palestine,"** while Hamas spurned all Egyptian and other mediation efforts for reconciliation with the Abbas regime. The failure of efforts to forge Palestinian unity has hampered the Palestinian objective of statehood and has in part thwarted all moves towards an Israeli-Palestinian peace.

Yet the Morsi regime cuddled Hamas (the acronym for the **Movement of Islamic Resistance**) which is looked upon as a Brotherhood affiliate. In an effort to break the Israeli blockade, Hamas has tunnelled into Sinai for the purpose of smuggling arms, fuel, drugs and food stuffs. This tunnel invasion also brought into Sinai jihadi elements for the double purpose of waging guerrilla warfare against Israel, and of harassing, together with the Bedouins, Egyptians security personnel. You seem to forget that the Egypt/Israel peace treaty of 1979, forged under the sponsorship of U.S. President Jimmy Carter, restored Sinai to Egypt. The Islamist response to that Egyptian achievement was to assassinate the President of Egypt - Anwar Sadat in 1981.

With hit and run war going on in Sinai, an internal Islamist mutiny in

Egypt's urban centers, the Egyptian army and police were facing intolerable security threats on two fronts. Their moves to clear the so-called **"peaceful"** sit-ins in Cairo as of August 14 could not have been undertaken during the Morsi Islamist regime. The mutinous Brotherhood declared that the attacks in Sinai and the rebellion in the interior would stop **"the instant"** Morsi is re-instated -a clear inculpation of the Brotherhood in the Islamization of Egypt at the intolerable cost of sacrificing territorial integrity.

Your support of Palestinian rights, through abetting your proxy, Hamas, was not only an incredible foreign policy contradiction. It also amounted to high treason against the State (Egypt) to whom Morsi, in his Oath of Office, had pledged to put its interest above all else. He has violated that Oath.

Your language is not only double talk. It is transparent linguistic acrobatics intended to lead Egypt to a sordid end. Islam is a revered faith. But the Brotherhood is an ideology whose space in this age of globalization and inter-faith communication is shrinking. Unfortunately, you are far behind the 21st Century. You may still catch up with the world of today -Renounce violence and stop trading in Islam as if it were a political commodity. For faith of every stripe, is personal, as Islam itself instructs us.

The Decapitation of the Brotherhood: How the Sit-Ins Had Demolished Their Standing

Sunday, August 25, 2013

Since 1928, their motto included these incantations: **"The Quran Is Our Constitution - And Dying for the Cause of God is Our Most Cherished Aspiration."** A motto expresses a belief. In civilized societies, religious beliefs are personal, not communal, unless you are a member of that community. Islamic law upholds respect for diversity of beliefs. In fact it upholds the personal right to non-belief. For it assigns the power of judging beliefs, not to another human being, but to the Creator.

This is the rock upon which the separation between state and religion rests. It is a powerful instrument for social peace under legislated, not revealed, law. In this principle, one can see the intersection of the U.S. Constitution and Sharia legal principles, progressively interpreted on the basis of their original sources.

It is in this critical area of matters of State, that the Brotherhood failed. Herein lies the fault line in the way the Morsi regime governed Egypt for a year. That year led to the upheaval of June 30, 2013, which took the form of a Second Egyptian Revolution. The First Revolution was that of January 25, 2011 which toppled Mubarak, who is now released on bail from imprisonment.

The task of this blog is not propaganda. It is, to the maximum extent possible, a weekly examination of ascertainable facts. The evidence is based on specific declarations and documents, most of which is in Arabic. The goal is to inform, not to proselytize. I have neither the time nor the inclination to do that. Nor am I the spokesman of either the Egyptian Government, nor a vindictive hater of the Brotherhood. I am my own paymaster, a teacher of law in both the U.S. and Egypt, and am privileged to be a dual citizen of both the U.S., my country of adoption, and Egypt, my country of birth. My only aspiration is to continue being a bridge between the two cultures. If I fail, it shall not be for lack of trying. And if I succeed, the reward shall be limited to the deep satisfaction of having, in a small measure, revealed to the world of America and the world of Egypt (25% of all Arabs) to one another.

There is no escaping the fact that the Muslim Brotherhood, having ascended to power in Egypt in post-Mubarak Egypt, proceeded through Morsi, for whom I voted, to brutalize Egypt through a forced Brotherhoodization. They have declared that **"our rule shall last for 500 years,"** in the way Hitler has aspired to **"a Reich of a thousand years."** To me, who withheld his vote from Shafiq, the military opponent of Morsi, I could see no deliverance from the Brotherhoodization except through the armed forces. More than 30 millions, who engineered the Second Egyptian Revolution on June 30, called on General El-Sisi to act on behalf of secular Egypt. There was no mechanism for recall. In response, he did.

In its hour of national peril in 1958, France, an icon of democracy, called on General De Gaulle to topple the old and bring in a new republic. Their call, not unlike that of the Egyptians in Tahrir, on June 30, was **"L'armee au pouvoir."** Was that a French coup or was it a revolution? I do not care about the semantics. My commitment is to the substance. De Gaulle saved France by ending French colonialism in Algeria. As a result of being sent to Algeria during the war as a UN spokesman, I got hooked on the subject of colonialism which became my Ph.D. thesis at New York University. Furthermore, I acquired substantial field expertise in insurgency and counter-insurgency on which I lectured at NYU in the early 1970s to large classes of U.S. armed forces officers.

With my education being primarily based, not on books, but on field experiences in Algeria, Gaza, Yemen, Darfour and Iraq, I now turn to the Brotherhood sit-ins in Cairo. **Were those sit-ins at Rabaa or Al-Nahda squares "peaceful?" They were not.**

Here is a hypothetical drawn from an imaginary Brotherhood-like sit-in at Times Square, New York City -my city for 61 years.

Imagine a large crowd of American protesters invading Times Square, New York City. Their sit-in is accompanied by the erection of a brick wall across that Square, cutting traffic off, and causing shops, restaurants, theatres and hotels to shut down for days. They set up tents and eateries and field hospitals. The City's authorities then discover that arms are being smuggled in; pavements are broken to provide stones to be slung at the police; nobody is allowed to leave the encampments; and children are dressed in shrouds proclaiming: **"For our President, we are ready to die!!"**

As Americans, they are covered by the First Amendment of the U.S. Constitution: **"...the right of the people peaceably to assemble..."** **"Peaceably"** is a condition. When negated, that right is denied to the protesters and their **"freedom of speech" is "abridged."**

What took place in the Cairo public squares, at the mosque of Rabyaa and Al-Nahdha, prior to their break-up on August 14 after one full month, is by all accounts a mirror image of that hypothetical about Times Square.

Yes --Morsi had breached his contract with Egypt during his 1-year tenure as elected president. Ruling in the mode of representative of the Brotherhood, not as president for all Egyptians, was a negation of his oath of office. Under his erratic rule, the Brotherhoodization of Egypt, a historically cosmopolitan country, became the national hallmark. Out of 27 provinces (he and I hail from the same province of Sharkia), no less than 13 such provinces had Muslim Brothers as their governers. Even Luxor, the capital of Egyptian tourism, suffered the indignity of a governor by the name of Mr. Al-Khayyat as its top executive. A popular firestorm then erupted forcing Morsi to seek his resignation. Al-Khayyat was not only a

Salafi, an extremist movement to the right of the Brotherhood, but also had the blood of 59 tourists on his hands. They were mostly Swiss, Germans, Japanese, Americans, and Australians who perished at the great Valley of the Kings prior to the Morsi regime.

Since the overthrow of Mubarak, by the popular uprising of January 25, 2011, the Egyptian street found its voice. Since then **"Streetocracy"** became the vehicle of popular will. As in the case of the Berlin Wall which came down in 1990, the wall of fear from dictatorship in Egypt came down. Thus when Morsi, who was not even the first Brotherhood choice for presidential candidate, tried to convert Egypt into an Islamic state, millions of Egyptians screamed foul. The decapitation of the Brotherhood, especially with the arrest of its Supreme Guide, Mohamed Badie on August 20, began with those sit-ins -a Brotherhood self-inflicted wound.

Badie's predecessor, Mahdi Akef, upon meeting him at the Brotherhood's HQ five years ago, began the conversation with me with his top advisors by: **"Brother Yassin - Do you speak to the Jews?!"** My answer was crisp: **"The Jews are my brothers and sisters. And my wife is a devout American Catholic. You see, my late father, a graduate of Al-Azhar University and a former professor of Islamic philosophy, provided me with a life road map as he bade me good-bye upon leaving Egypt as a Fulbright on my way by boat to America. It was August 27, 1952, at a pier in Alexandria, when, wearing his Azhari turban, he pulled me aside and said: 'Son! Live as the Americans live. It is the essence of Islam.'"**

Compare this to what Mahdi Akef admonished in a little book entitled **"Muslim Brotherhood Initiative: On the General Principles of Reform in Egypt."** On page 4, he defines reform in Egypt as the application of **"Allah's Sharia (Islamic Legal Code) which is best for this world and the Hereafter."** Compare this Brotherhood call for Pax Islamica with Al-Azhar call in August, 2011 in a document of principles approved by the Coptic Church that **"Islam does not recognize a State based solely on religion."** So as I teach **"Islamic Law and Global Security"** at Fordham University School of Law, I adhere not the Akef interpretation of Islam, which is akin to Al-Qaeda's dogma, but to Al-Azhar's interpretation. In fact **"Allahu Akbar"** means that we are equal before God regardless of our faith or of no faith.

Thus it is mystifying to find in the U.S. unrealistic calls for a compromise with the Brotherhood who have repeatedly rebuffed the calls of the present Egyptian Government for inclusion in the cabinet. The Brotherhood's ideology is not anchored in identifying with Egypt. Badie had declared, **"To hell with Egypt!!"** They identify with what appears to me, as a professor of law and politics, a mythical union with pan-Islamism -a recipe for disaster for Egypt where 25% of all Arabs reside. Going underground has, for the past 80 years, been the Brotherhood modus-operand, which may lead to a full blown civil war.

There has been a lot of blood running alongside the River Nile. A tragic spectacle for which all humanity should grieve. There has been a lot of destruction of institutional Egypt especially Coptic Egypt. I have documents from reliable Coptic church sources indicating that: **"No less than 73 churches and convents have been destroyed. Private Coptic property has been either torched or vandalized including private homes, funeral homes, orphanages, bible schools, 75 shops, 15 pharmacies, 3 hotels and 58 church buses."** Unbelievable!! If that is the Brotherhood's response to unseating Morsi, how could Egypt as a State not welcome the intervention of the army and the police?

In the light of these facts, it is obscene for Senator Lindsey Graham of South Carolina to recently lecture the Prime Minister of Egypt in Cairo by saying: **"Mr. Prime Minister, it's pretty hard for you to lecture anyone on the Rule of Law."** Senator, I humbly suggest that your assumed expertise in ending gridlocks cannot work its magic in Cairo. It may be more effective in solving the gridlock in the U.S. Congress. Financial aid, Senator Graham, does not nullify sovereignties. From my study of imperialism, I learnt that amity between nations is primarily built on mutual respect.

Your proposed sanctions, Senator Graham, may inflict wounds primarily on the dignity of Egypt, wounds which may not quickly heal. Egypt's present fight against terrorism in Sinai and the interior are also America's cause. And please, Senator Graham, you don't have to listen to me. Listen to Israel whose leaders are now assessing the Egyptian crisis in these practical terms: "Either the army or anarchy!!" The Israelis are geographically much closer to the scene in Egypt than you, Sir, in "the sovereign State of South Carolina!!"

And you may have noticed, Senator Graham, that for Egypt, there is now an Arab Marshall Plan in the making, led by Saudi Arabia, Kuwait and the Emirates. Senator, through your and other high-level American utterances and threats, a perception, perhaps faulty, has taken hold in Egypt. The general belief is that the U.S. is, for some

incomprehensible reasons, enamored with the Brotherhood. The anti-Brotherhood forces, opposed to political Islam, both inside Egypt and outside, are striking to roll it back. From my lookout, I believe that the future belong to them, not to the Brotherhood.

A State of Darkness Exists Between the U.S. and Egypt

Friday, August 30, 2013

In Latin, which we study in Egypt, that state is called **"in tenebris."** That state is made up of two opposites: theory in America, reality in Egypt. It also has an outer layer -a rim. The American rim consists of a supposition that an American road map to a Jeffersonian democracy should be a yardstick measuring the developments in present-day Egypt.

Here is my response: throw away that yardstick; stick only to reality as it manifests itself in the facts on the ground in Egypt; then get rid of the so-called experts who are wasting everyone's time by calling Egypt, **"a failed State."** In fact an interviewer of President Obama on TV channel 13 on August 28 described Egypt to the President as **"a collapsed government."** To his credit, Obama stayed away from such characterization.

Here are some examples of theoretical constructs by American public opinion-molders that have no anchor in the cold facts:

Bill Keller rightly says, **"Egypt's fate is, and must be, in Egyptian hands."** But then he leaps, without more, to asserting that **"there is a gloomy sense that Egypt may already be in a kind of death spiral."**

Senator Lindsey Graham of South Carolina, whose Republican Party is threatening to shut down the U.S. Federal Government this October through defunding major programs, has this to say **"Somebody needs to look El-Sisi in the eye and say: You're going to destroy Egypt; you're going to doom your country to a beggar State; you're going to create an insurgency for generations to come; turn around, General, before it's too late."** All that oppressive paternalism was screamed out by the Senator on the **CBS News** program **"Face the Nation."**

A recent editorial in the **New York Times** (August 20, 2013) advocated **"not to help the military, which is making things worse, and could fuel a generation of Islamists to choose militancy over the ballot box."**

Ross Douthat, an Op-Ed page contributor to the **New York Times,** looking down on the new Egypt from a perch higher than the Pyramids of Gaza, admonishes, **"Let Our Client Go."** By client he means sovereign Egypt. His unwise counsel is amplified as he states: **"Client governments are never as tractable as their patrons in far-off capitals expect (meaning the U.S.A.), and great power that thinks it's buying influence is often buying its way into trouble instead."**

The marshaling of theories shall have no effect on the realities of the Second Egyptian Revolution, which have ousted Morsi for good. From the multitude of sources flowing to me from the Egyptian street, I see no **"collapsed Government,"** no **"death spiral,"** no **"beggar State,"** and no **"client"** to patron relationships between Washington and Cairo. These relationships are driven, not by hegemony, but by mutual national interest.

I can see only a mutiny by the Brotherhood against the will of millions of citizens who, with no recall mechanism in place, called for a halt to the radicalization of their country. Yes, there has been a coup in Egypt. But it was a **"coup creep"** by the Morsi regime against the populist achievements of the January 25, 2011 Revolution.

That Revolution was engineered, not by the Brotherhood, but by a broad coalition of people of all ages, Muslims and Christians, well-to-do and the homeless poor, literate and illiterate. They came together declaring the unity between the Quran and the Bible, and hoisting the flags of Egypt on which was inscribed **"We Love Egypt."** In Tahrir, they gave me that flag. No Islamist flags were seen in Tahrir or elsewhere at that time, except after Morsi assumed power and abused his mandate.

On the slim shoulders of 50.50% of the electorate of 53 millions of whom 70% voted, the Morsi regime came. A cartoon in the Egyptian press aptly assessed the meaning of that electoral result. It showed two Egyptians sitting at a cafe with one of them telling the other: **"The fact that General Shafiq (Morsi's opponent) lost does not mean that we love Morsi."**

That cartoon expresses my feelings as I voted for Morsi in order to help Egypt escape another President from the military. The Brotherhood saw it differently. To them, the ballot box became the tip of the spear puncturing the balloon of hopes for an inclusive, secular and service-oriented regime. Morsi failed them and they, on June 30, 2013, struck back with the help of the only other organized force -the military. About that, there is no theory, but a fact-based reality.

I have expounded above on the theories in America. I now turn to the reality of the danger, under Morsi, of the rise of an **Islamic Emirate of Egypt.** I am invariably reading the lips of the Brotherhood through their writings. It should be here noted that by the late 1980's, and within less than a decade of the assassination of President Sadat by the Islamists, Mubarak's Egypt began to see that **"the Brotherhood and jihadist groups were in fact two sides of the same coin."** (Carrie Rosefsky Wickham, **The Muslim Brotherhood** (2013) (page 76).

In his book entitled, **"Jihad is the Nation's Vocation,"** published in Arabic in 2003, a Brotherhood author by the name of Magdy Ahmed Hussein asserts the following: **"This work is a contribution towards arming the Islamic movement inside as well as outside of Egypt with this ideology (jihad) which I regard as an ignored religious duty."** The author is a disciple of the departed **Sayed Qutb** who was correctly described in an issue of the **Sunday New York Times Magazine** as **"the spiritual leader of Al-Qaeda."**

The former Supreme Guide of the Brotherhood, Mehdi Akef, in a booklet entitled **"Muslim Brotherhood Initiative: On the General Principles of Reform in Egypt"** expresses his unbending belief in the Islamization of Egypt. To him, that Islamization is the cornerstone of development as he points out: **"We stand no chance of achieving development in any field of our life unless we return to our religion, apply our Shariah"** (Islamic Law). p.8.

Well, for the past six decades, Egyptian Constitutions including the Constitution of December 2012 have provided for the inclusion of Sharia as **"principal source of legislation."** That means that whatever is not textually prohibited by the Quran and the Sunna constitutes the vast domain of legislated law. **Akef** abridged that domain in order to consist only of revealed law. That is not what Islamic jurisprudence calls for.

The Brotherhood nemesis, Dr. Abdel-Moniem Abu El-Fotooh, also disagrees with his former Supreme Guide. In his book in Arabic **"Innovators not Spoilers"** published in 2005, he attacks that destructive rigidity by saying: **"Faith is lost between immobility and disbelief."** (p.40). He drives his point further home by quoting from the primary source of Islamic Law, the **Quran**, which in **Chapter 43, verse 23,** denigrates those who want to have the Muslims of today emulate their forefathers of 14 centuries ago. The verse reads: **"We found our fathers follow a certain religion, and we will certainly follow in their footsteps."** (Translation by **Abdullah Yusuf Ali**). For his call to innovation and inclusiveness, Abu El-Fotooh, was jettisoned by the Brotherhood. He ran for President, but did not make it to the run-off which produced Morsi.

It now looks that the suppression of that Brotherhood's mutiny, which extends to suspected dealings with jihadi movements, might have influenced Tunisia to declare on August 27 **"The Sharia's Ansar - supporters,"** a terrorist organization. Cairo's resort to curfews and to emergency measures promulgated under **Law 162 (1958)** may one day replicate the actions adopted by Tunisia. There is no other effective way to suppress a mutiny and keep the country safe and functioning. Any calls by the present government for a compromise, through inclusiveness, had one uniform response from the Brotherhood: **No!!**

The problem facing America's theoreticians is of two-folds. On the one hand, they are challenged conceptually. And on the other hand, they are challenged linguistically. **They do not read Arabic.** Thus they are unable to connect with the facts on the ground in Egypt.

What would have they learnt if only they could read the lingua franca of the one-third billion Arabs, including the Egyptians? They would have learnt the following and more:

that **Khairat El-Shatter,** the man behind the Brotherhood's throne, is a co-conspirator in attempting to split northern Egypt from southern Egypt. **The ancient Egyptians united Egypt. Now, the present-day "ancient Muslims" are trying to divide it;**

that the criminal courts in Egypt have before them, among 62 detained Brotherhood members, a Salafi accused of throwing off a child to his death from the roof of a building in Alexandria while hoisting a Qaeda black flag. The name of the alleged suspect is **Mahmoud Hassan Ramadan;**

that the first Deputy of Muhammad Badie, the former Supreme Guide of the Brotherhood, has just issued an attack on the Brotherhood's conduct in Egypt. His critique included: **the Brotherhood's supreme arrogance;**

the unquestioned submission of its members to the dictates of the **Guidance Bureau, and the stipulation that the entire social network of any member should be confined to the Brotherhood social circles;**

that the **New York Times** Cairo reporter, **David D. Kirkpatrick,** has published in the paper's issue of August 30, 2013 falsehoods on the arrest on August 29 of Mohamed El-Beltagy, a Brotherhood leader. The falsehoods in Kirkpatrick's reporting are at three levels: He called that action **"a continuing roundup of Brotherhood leaders;"** he characterized El-Beltagy as **"a former Brotherhood lawmaker considered a moderate within the group;"** and he did not refer to the probable cause for which that fugitive was apprehended. For now, El-Beltagy is facing the following charges in three cases: **incitement to murder; participation in the abduction and torture of police officers; and aiding and abetting of acts of violence including engagements with the security forces using firearms. I submit that such journalism contributes to the state of darkness which exists between the U.S. and Egypt.**

that the Brotherhood's newspaper **"Freedom and Justice"** has within its editorial policy a non-changeable theme: Hatred of the Arabism, exaltation of Islamism. How can this be tolerable in a country which calls itself **"The Arab Republic of Egypt?!"**

These are the realities of post-Morsi Egypt.
Again to a Latin adage: "Inter arma leges silent."(In time of war, the laws are silent). It conforms to the Islamic jurisprudence of "dire necessity." And to the British adage: "Circumstances Alter Cases."

27 SEPTEMBER 2013

Hitler Appointed Joseph Goebbels Propaganda Minister in 1933; The Muslim Brotherhood Graduated Goebbels Successors in 2013!!

Monday, September 9, 2013

For my Masters Degree in history from Rutgers University, New Jersey, in 1954, I chose the history of Nazi Germany as my field. I was fortunate to have chosen Rutgers over Princeton. The former endowed my studies; the latter withheld any financial assistance to a new comer from abroad. My good luck at Rutgers also led me to a mentor, Professor Eyck, a great historian, and a German refugee whose faith was Judaism. Eyck advised me to focus on Goebbels. Why? **"Propaganda is an instrument of war, and Goebbels perfected the big lie technique: "keep on repeating the lie, and in a short time people would believe it."**

The similarities between the Muslim Brotherhood, especially after the ouster of Morsi in July 2013, and Goebbels, in the use of the big lie technique are unmistakable. How do I provide uncontroverted evidence on that? As a defense attorney and a professor of law, I have to build my case on solid proof. This blog does not propagandize and is not paid for. These are two factors leading publishers in America to desire publishing its 110 issues in a book which I shall entitle: **"The Transformation of Egypt Through Revolution: 2011-2013."**

Example (A) : El-Belthagy of the Brotherhood to Al-Jazeera, **Monday, August 26, 2013: "The use by the transitional Government of Hazem El-Beblawi of 'war on terror' is a mere pretext to suppress the Brotherhood, to make the coup justifiable to the outside world, and to deceive the public in Egypt."**

Evidence on That "Big Lie": Let the record show that: (a) the Government after 6 weeks from the beginning of the Brotherhood's sit-ins from July 3 until their removals on August 14, did not, even once, use that term; (b) even after the discovery, through the removals, that the sit-ins were armed little emirates at Rabaa and Al-Nahda, the Government restricted its use of that term to the military confrontations in Sinai; (c) the open support by the Brotherhood, declared and given to the Sinai insurrectionists, who were coopted by Hamas and other Jihadis, enhanced the Government's response through decapitating the Brotherhood without outlawing it so far; (d) the decapitation of the Brotherhood's leadership, including the recent detention of the fugitive El-Belthagy, resulted also from the Brotherhood's repeated rebuffs of the Government's entreaties to them to join El-Beblawi Cabinet.

Example (B): The so-called **"National Coalition for Supporting Legitimacy and Rejecting the Coup" has issued on August 27 to all "honest Egyptians to refuse participation in the Committee of Fifty for constitutional amendments. That National Coalition claims that: the "coup" aims at subverting the popular will; the Constitution of December 2012 was approved by 64% of the voters; the prospective amendments are intended to bring back the Mubarak regime.**

Evidence on That "Big Lie": I was on the ground in Egypt during the two stages of the plebiscite on the Constitution in December 2012. My investigations resulted in 120 pages of hand-written notes on that seminal event. My notes reveal the following: (a) at the Constituent Assembly, the secularists, including the liberals and the Copts, (nearly 30% of the membership), despairing of the high-handed ways of the Islamist majority, withdrew; (b) taking advantage of that withdrawal, the Islamists wrote into the draft Constitution their own version of the contentious articles; (c) fearful of the disbanding by the Supreme Constitutional Court of that flawed assemblage, Morsi declared that that draft would be immediately voted upon; (d) ignoring the popular calls for either a broad national debate or the reconstitution of the Constituent Assembly, the Morsi plans for a two-stage plebiscite went ahead in December; (e) the pleas for resolution of that constitutional impasse was summed up by Dr. El-Baradei's near tearful appeal to the Islamists in his famous TV lament **"Take Pity on Egypt;"** (f) only 22% of the electorate of 53 million voters took part in the plebiscite with the unverifiable result declared on December 31, 2012 by the triumphalist call by Morsi: **"Egypt now has a Constitution;"** (g) amending the Islamist constitution through the Committee of Fifty has to do with the legitimation of the popular will through elections within a few months for a House of Representatives to consider those amendments; (h) these amendments have nothing to do with the re-introduction of the Mubarak regime. That regime is still on trial, as Egypt gears up to putting Morsi also on trial for alleged crimes committed at the gates of his Presidential Palace (Al-Iltihadiyah).

Example (C): Again to El-Belthagy who declared to the correspondent of "Al-Anadoul" (of Turkey) on late August: "The massacre of 25 security officers in Sinai on August 19 was perpetrated by the Egyptian army. The Egyptian authorities are lying in attributing that heinous crime to unknown armed criminals in Rafah, north of Sinai. The coup leaders killed those recruits to divert attention from their problems as an illegitimate government."

Evidence on That "Big Lie": In criminal litigation, which I practice, there is a principle that implicitly tells the Court: **"The Thing speaks for itself."** In Latin, it is expressed in 3 words: **"Res (the thing) Ipsa (for itself) Loquitor (speaks).** It is a rule of evidence, which fully rebuts the Brotherhood's big lie cited-above. This is because the negligence (i.e. the crime) of the alleged wrong-doer may be inferred (legally found) from the mere fact that the accident happened. In this instance, even Master Goebbels would not have gone as far as his presumptive heir, El-Beltagy. This is especially so, bearing in mind that: (a) the Brotherhood had repeatedly manifested its affinity with terrorism in Sinai. The Brotherhood has conditioned the ending of the Sinai terror on the reinstatement of Morsi as President; (b) the Egyptian armed forces are a conscripted military institution with a tradition of cohesiveness going back to 1810. Under the system of compulsory draft, members of those forces identify with Egypt as a national entity. Members of the police/central security forces see in their counterparts in the armed forces their kith and ken; (c) that explains the utter failure of the Brotherhood's calls on the recruits and officers in the armed forces and the police to defect and flee their barracks; (d) there is no way that the army, which in Sinai depends on the police, as its strategic manpower depth, to shoot itself in the foot by killing its own auxiliaries.

Example (D): In **"Freedom and Justice,"** issue of Sunday, August 25, another Brotherhood writer, Shaheen Fawzi, tries his hand at the big lie technique. In that Brotherhood daily, he proclaims the following: First he calls General El-Sisi, the Deputy Prime Minister and Defense Minister: **"The Vanquished, God Willing"** (Al-Halek Bi Amr-illah). Then he asserts that: **"What is happening in Egypt today cannot but be attributed to Zionist and U.S. hands... The secular petro-States have called on their friends in Europe and the U.S. to support the armed forces of Camp David (meaning the Egyptian military) in their aggression against the Muslim Brotherhood."**

Evidence on That "Big Lie": (a) in its first foreign policy proclamation, the Morsi regime had affirmed Egypt's respect for all international treaties already entered into by all previous Egyptian governments. By clear implication, those included the Egypt-Israel peace treaty of 1979; (b) Israel could not have influenced the more than 30 million Egyptians to demonstrate against the Morsi regime; (c) the European Union dispatched Ms. Ashston, whose portfolio is EU foreign policy, to Cairo more than once to broker a compromise between the Egyptian transitional Government and the Islamists to no avail; (d) not to be undone, the U.S. (former Ambassador to Cairo, Patterson; Secretary of State Kerry; and Senators McCain and Graham) tried repeatedly to bridge that gap, but their efforts collapsed; and (e) the U.S., in a show of displeasure at the ouster of Morsi delayed the delivery of 4 F-16 combat aircraft to the Egyptian military, cancelled the already scheduled joint military exercises, and placed the annual financial aid to Egypt under review. From the above, it seems that the Brotherhood, unaccustomed to the art of loyalty, is unable to distinguish between friend and foe, except on the basis of acceptance by everyone of its bidding.

In this regard, I have not touched upon what Shaheen Fawzi outrageously claims in the same **"Freedom and Justice"** article. For he goes on to say: **"The Egyptian military intelligence still throws itself at the lap of the Zionists; fighting the Palestinian resistance in Gaza and elsewhere, and abetting the Israeli operation in Gaza called "Hot Lead" in December 2008.** Even a habitual hashish smoker could not have been carried away in his hallucinations to the extent of that fantasy.

A Final Example (E): The Mufti of the Brotherhood, Abdel-Rahman

Al-Bar issues a fatwa (a non-binding interpretation of a rule in Islamic Law). He calls those millions of Egyptians, who came out in public squares on June 30 to have Morsi ousted, **"infidels"** (non-believers). As to those who call for his reinstatement, they are **"true believers as they support their legitimate ruler."**

Evidence on That "Big Lie": (a) the issuance of fatwas has, since August 2011, been made the exclusive domain of Al-Azhar; (b) in the application of Islamic jurisprudence, a subject which I teach at Fordham University School of Law, New York City, I find Al-Bar to be engaged in a big lie wrapped within his so-called Fatwa. To begin with, Islam does not condone calling others infidels because it provides for a direct spiritual relation between every human and God. In addition, the Quran calls on Muslims to remove an unjust ruler. Moreover, the so-called Mufti Al-Bar is an interested party who, under any legal system, should have recused himself; (c) Abdel-Rahman Al-Bar is a fugitive from justice for his role in attacking the Azbakiyah Police Precinct; (d) the Supreme Guide of the Brotherhood Muhammad Badi; who is now under detention, had preceded his Mufti by declaring it open season on the killing of Egyptian army and security personnel for being **"infidels who do not deserve to live."** His reason: Those forces have refused to defect in support of the Brotherhood's exhortations.

The Brotherhood disciples of Goebbels are failing their departed Nazi master. Through his office as Hitler's Minister of Propaganda, Joseph Goebbels was convinced that he was serving the cause of Nazi Germany, reprehensible as that cause had been. Yet the Goebbels Class of 2013 made up of Muslim Brotherhood spokesmen and publicists feel, like the rest of their movement, no affinity to Egypt. Their Supreme Guide, in fealty to pan-Islamism, had uttered the offensive statement **"To Hell with Egypt!!"** (TOZZ FI MASSR!!)

So, if there is no loyalty to Egypt, one should at least expect from the Brotherhood fidelity to the Quran. Within its nearly 6400 Quaranic verses, the sin of lying is prohibited in 282 verses. In one such verse, the Quran admonishes: **"So hearken not to those who deny the truth."** (Chapter Al-Qalam, verse #8).

This is not to mention the numerous sayings of the Prophet Muhammad against lying, nor the ethos of Islam where it defines faith in the following terms: "Religion is the wise counsel." The big lie technique cannot, under any circumstance be characterized as "a wise counsel." Moreover, Islamic jurisprudence is anchored in "whatever is good for society" **(Ma**

Yanfaul Nas). Using all of these religious parameters as a measure, the Muslim Brotherhood Goebbels Class of 2013 has failed to make its case.

Most of the time, they do not live in the world of facts. The Arabic proverb is "Truth Saves." Lies, whether big or small, perish, leaving their creators, the imposters, naked and on the run.

By the end of this month, my novel in Arabic, which originally appeared in Cairo in 1948, will appear again. It deals with the same issue: the manipulation of faith for the purpose of gaining power. The reader shall find in that novel similarities with today's Goebbels practices by the Brotherhood. Its title is "Dajjal Fi Qariah" (An Imposter in the Village), which is presently being republished by Aalam Al-Kotub (The World of Books, Cairo, September 2013). Our village of today is Egypt where the end for today's imposters shall not be different from the end of the Dajjal (Imposter) in that novel.

Through the Brotherhood's Scorched Earth Practices, a Cairo Paradise Becomes a Wasteland

Monday, September 9, 2013

Their so-called **"peaceful sit-ins"** in Cairo proved to have been arenas for the Brotherhood scorched earth practices. Their enclaves, dismantled by the army and the police on August 14, were later discovered to have been mutinous islands of destruction, desertification and iconic monuments elimination.

This blog is not an anti-Brotherhood propaganda. It serves as a factual antidote to their deceptive propaganda. A case in point is the tragedy of **"Al-Orman Gardens"** where the Brotherhood sit-ins of Al-Nahdha in Giza turned that historic paradise into a waste land. Al-Orman is truly a **"Paradise Lost."**

Testimony by Amre Rabee Raafat, Chief of the Central Management of Forestation testified as follows on September 3: **"Al-Orman Gardens** have suffered considerable devastation at the hands of the sit-in Brothers. These included the cutting down of rare historical imported trees; the theft of 500 ampules containing rare plants, 236 rare paintings of various species of plants; the disappearance of all furniture and computers; the destruction of all telephone and irrigation systems; irreparable damage to two historic pieces of museum-grade furniture donated by King Farouk to Al-Orman Gardens."

The barbarians had swept in under the false protective shield of **"freedom of expression and of peaceful assembly."** These freedoms were subverted by the Brotherhood, following the un-seating of President Morsi, into the freedom to punish historical Egypt. Its icons are not the Brotherhood icons. Their icons are over some mythical horizon outside of the borders of sovereign Egypt. Secular Egypt is not their fatherland. Their frontiers coincide and merge with **Pan-Islamica.**

The same Brotherhood hurricane of destruction did not spare places of worship, whether Islamic or Coptic. Their sit-ins at the Rabaa Mosque in Cairo resulted in deep scars in that historic place of worship. Again to the testimony of the authorities which are now engaged in emergency repairs of Rabaa which ironically gave its tormentors their **"four-fingers"** salute. The word **"Rabaa"** is close to the word in Arabic for **"four"** (Arbaa).

Mr. Tarik Muhammad Sayed is General Supervisor, Corps of Engineers, the Egyptian armed forces. He is in charge of the laborious and expensive process of repairing the extensive damage wrought by the Brotherhood's **"peaceful sit-ins"** on the Rabaa mosque. By the Brotherhood's hands, the beautiful Islamic mosaics, the marble inscriptions of **Quranic** verses, and the wooden carvings which would have been the envy of any internationally celebrated museum, were wiped out. Even the green areas surrounding Rabaa and featuring the historic fountain are now being resurrected. Nor was the Rabaa hospital spared the Brotherhood's scorched earth practices.

As to their respect for human life, there appears to be none. The more than a thousand killed in consequence of the Brotherhood's suicidal confrontations with the army and the police, represented a futile search for publicity through presumed martyrdom. As the leadership hid, fled or was detained, it kept on defying for six long weeks the warnings by the new authorities. The misguided rank and file, though armed but lightly, were the sacrificial lambs. While the **Quran** delegitimates death through self-destruction, the Brotherhood which exalts the **Quran** as their constitution, heavily engaged in it.

Yet Amr Darrag, senior official of the Brotherhood, bold-facedly
announces to Al-Jazeera TV Network as recently as yesterday: **"We
reaffirm our peaceful approach, which is clear in all our protests."**
Give me a break, Mr. Darrag. Your hands are soaked in the blood of the
innocent.

And in a country whose economy is in a free fall at present, the
scorched earth policy and practices of the Brotherhood represent a dead-
end effort to bring Egypt economically and financially to its knees. Their
demonstrations at Bank Misr in Asslout Province, in upper Egypt, had a
battle cry: **"Save your skin by withdrawing your deposits."** When
Egypt fought for its freedom from the British in 1882, 1919, 1936, 1946,
and 1951, poor peasant women donated their golden ornaments to assist
the freedom effort. But that was Egypt which, only after 1948, saw in the
Brotherhood a clear and present danger.

Is it now surprising that a preliminary recommendation by an Expert
Committee of Egypt's Council of State calls for banning the Brotherhood
again? That recommendation might acquire traction especially after the
attempt of September 5 on the life of Egypt's Interior Minister, General
Mohamed Ibrahim, through an Al-Qaeda-style car bombing. If that
proposed ban is judicially-sanctioned, it shall be the Brotherhood's ban
number 3. The first ban of the Brotherhood occurred in 1948 following
the assassination of Judge Ahmed Al-Khazendar. That ban resulted in the
assassination of Prime Minister Al-Naqrashi. That ban was judicially lifted
during the Wafd Party regime in 1951.

Their ban #2 took place in 1954 following the Brotherhood's
implication in the attempt on Nasser's life in Alexandria. That second ban
was lifted in 1974 by President Sadat during the tenure of Prime Minister
Mamdouh Salem. With the lifting of that ban, all Brotherhood's detainees
were released and their property was returned to them. The lifting of that
ban was conditional: they were permitted to function as a civic group
without a license.

Since its inception, many have been the fluctuations of the fortunes of
the Brotherhood over the past 85 years: from the pulpit of advocacy of
Islam, to the delving into politics, alternating between grass roots
mobilization and resort to armed violence. Finally, the Brotherhood
reached its pinnacle through the assumption of power via the ballot box.
Their mismanagement of governance led to the unseating of Morsi and the

breakup of the so-called sit-ins in mid August.

Now, self-flagellation has begun. One of their opinion-molders, Mr. Hamza Zobaa declares in the Brotherhood's daily **"Freedom and Justice": "We have fallen in the trap of excluding others from governing."** Too little too late. In the liberal weekly **"Akhbar El-Yom"** of last Saturday, Ahmed Hashem says: **"The Brotherhood's mask has fallen. That band of terrorists have committed crimes against Islam and innocent citizens."** Another liberal weekly, **"Rose El-Youssef,"** states under the by-line of its Editor-in-Chief, Issam Abdel-Aziz: **"The Brotherhood has manifested its insanity through a desperate search for re-instating their fallen regime. They have forgotten the magical love for Egypt by the average Egyptian citizen.** That average citizen could be Mustapha Ali, a warehouse worker who made his view known following the assassination attempt on the life of the Interior Minister: Referring to the Brotherhood, undoubtedly with its scorched earth practices in full view on Madinet Nassr, Mustepha Ali said: **"These people would destroy Egypt."**

An exaggeration? No!! Look at what happened early this month to a 1600-year-old Coptic monastery at Dalga, province of Minya, 160 miles south of Cairo. Speaking of that crime perpetrated by the hard-line Islamists, which engulfed the Coptic community of Dalga, Father Yoanns lamented: **"The fire in the monastery burned for three days. The looting continued for a week."** A tragic example of the Islamist scorched earth practices, which are their tool of choice.

The ouster of Morsi was not a mission for which the armed forces came to the fore on July 3. The ouster was the mission of 30 millions like Mustapha Ali who came out on June 30 to plead with the armed forces to save their beloved Egypt from the Brotherhood Then on July 26, more millions came out in the streets in response to a call by El-Sisi for public support for the Government action **"against terrorism."**

On a Collision Course with Hamas, Cairo Roars at Gaza: "Don't Mess With MISR"

Friday, September 20, 2013

Hamas is an Arabic acronym for **"The Movement of Islamic Resistance."** Misr is the Arabic word for Egypt. The incompatibility between Hamas and Egypt is multi-sided: Hamas is a renegade movement; Egypt is a historic entity. Hamas, since June 2007, is a sworn enemy of the Palestinian Authority based on the West Bank; Egypt is a unitary State since its unification 5000 years ago. Hamas is, since December 9, 1987, a branch of the Muslim Brotherhood of Egypt; Egypt has followed the Al-Azhar principle that **"Islam does not recognize a State based solely on religion."**

Let us now start by excavating the ideology gap between Hamas and Egypt with regard to peace between Israel and the Arabs.

Hamas articulates Palestinian aspirations to statehood into strictly religious, not nationalist terms. In its charter of 1988, it declares: **"In the struggle against the Jewish occupation of Palestine, the banner of Jihad must be raised."** In its leaflet of October 5, 1988, Hamas declares: **"We shall continue the uprising on the road to the liberation of our whole land from the contamination of the Jews, with the help of God."**

By contrast, Egypt has concluded a peace treaty with Israel in March 1979. At no time of its history has Egypt ever reneged on an international treaty; the examples of 1951 and 1956 notwithstanding. In 1951, Nahas Posha, as Prime Minister and Chairman of the secular Wafd Party, declared in Parliament that the 1936 treaty with Great Britain was null and void. He declared that Egypt, through him, had signed that treaty **"under duress"** - referring to the pressures of the British occupation (from 1882 to 1954).

In 1956, Nasser declared the nationalization of the Suez Canal Company in order to fund the construction of the Aswan Dam, following the withholding of western funding. Mind you that, contrary to western writings, it was **"the Company"** which was nationalized, not the Canal itself. A State cannot nationalize what it possesses as sovereign territory. And all stakeholders in the Company were compensated despite the aggression against Egypt by France, the UK and Israel in 1956.

How about the diplomatic gap between Hamas and Egypt, at both the universal level and the regional level?

Through UN Security Council resolution 242 (1967), the whole world has rendered a consensus on the way out from the Palestinian Israeli impasse. But Hamas rejects UN decision-making altogether. Ironically, it accepts UN and other charitable contributions. In its communique No. 33, of December 23, 1988, Hamas thumbs its nose at the international community. It foolishly declares: **"Do not head the UN Resolutions which try to accord the Zionist entity (meaning Israel) legitimacy over any part of the soil of Palestine ... for it is the property of the Islamic nation and not of the UN."**

The Islamic nation? Under Islamic jurisprudence, whose primary sources are the Quran and the Sunna, Muslims are referred to as **"Umma"** -meaning **"community of faith"** not **"a nation"** connoting **"a State."**

This is while Egypt, where the League of Arab States maintains its headquarters, is a supporter of that UN Security resolution (which in part resulted from unacceptable adventurism by the Nasser regime. That regime had insisted on the withdrawal of the UN peace-keepers from Sinai).

We also have the Arab initiative of King Abdullah of Saudi Arabia to which all 22 Arab States (including the yet-to-be born State of Palestine) have agreed. The core of that historic initiative is striving for mutually-agreeable territorial withdraws with the full quid pro quo of recognition of Israel by all members of the League of Arab States. Hamas is in rebellion against that consensus. But ironically it claims to have **"strategic depth"** in the Arab world -a depth which only exists in its stunted imagination.

As we look now at yet another gap among others not herein cited, between Hamas and Egypt, we cannot escape the Islamic jurisprudential gap between Gaza and Cairo. Our focus here is on the concept of **"Jihad."**

Succinctly put, Hamas, though it calls itself **"Islamic,"** does not practice what it preaches. In Sharia, jihad has dual domains: internal - fighting against one's own inner destructive urges; and external -fighting defensively and proportionally against aggression from the outside. Nowhere in the **27 Quranic verses** on jihad do I find the Hamas interpretation of that overly-used and universally-abused term. Herein exists a major legal dilemma for Hamas on that front.

In his seminal book in Arabic, entitled **"Al-Jihad,"** the late Islamic scholar, Gamal Al-Banna, a younger brother of Hassan Al-Banna, the founder of the Muslim Brotherhood (Hamas' mother) tackles that misconception. On page 7, he states:

"It is important to note the confusion between jihad and war-like combat. The danger of that confusion extends to the attempt to islamize the world... This should be regarded as a dangerous trend which opens the door to belittle the freedom of faith held by non-Muslim parties. It thrusts us Muslims into the dungeons of extremism and the raging hurricanes which attend it." (my translation)

Where is Egypt from that extremism? As far away as possible. And where would Egypt find its Coptic Church, established 200 years by its Alexandria citizen, St. Mark, hence the historic title of **"the Pope of Alexandria."** Under attack by Hamas-like marauders. In addition, where are the Christians of Palestine in the Islamic Emirate of Gaza, led by Hamas? And what is the position of Jerusalem which is revered by the Jews, Christians and Muslims? Hamas has no rational explanation. How can the Hamas extremist dogma of **"the soil of Palestine... is the property of the Islamic nation,"** be reconciled with those undeniable historical facts on the ground? Totally irreconcilable.

Well, Egypt shares no part in that Hamas iron-clad ideology. It is interesting to note that Egypt as it tries to revive its tourism industry, announces in its brochures under the title of **"Egypt Today:"** "The Egyptian people have suffered under several waves of invasions, but have never been broken. Their talent is in flexibility and thinking up novel solutions to problems."** (Booklet in English entitled **"Luxor-Egypt,"** page 50).

For Hamas to try to bring Morsi of the Brotherhood back to power is like an ant trying to move the Giza pyramids. Its resort to terrorism, either directly or indirectly, especially in Sinai, shall not be soon forgotten or forgiven by the Egyptian Second Revolution of June 30. The free ride of Hamas via the Brotherhood bus is over. End of the line!! The Egyptian backlash has begun to gradually shrink the so-called **"Islamists"** not only inside **MISR**, but also beyond it from Jordan to Gaza to Tunisia.

The **"Qassam Battalions,"** of Hamas, and its affiliate **"The Supporters of Beit Al-Maqdis,"** have been implicated in the failed attempt to assassinate Egypt's Interior Minister in late August. Faced with the huge cohesive army of Egypt, these terrorist attacks shall only work for furthering the delegitimation of that renegade movement. Denials by Hamas of its involvement in Egypt's internal affairs are nothing but transparent obfuscation.

It was Abraham Lincoln who in 1858 coined the adage **"Acts speak louder than words."** Arab poetry and prose have for hundreds of years advocated the same. A Hamas leader by the name of Dr. Salah Al-Bardaweel unthinkingly declares on September 16 that **"an eye witness has testified to Hamas that the Egyptian army has planted mines under its own checkpoints, and dug tunnels from the Egyptian Rafah side into Gaza."** For good measure, he also hallucinated by adding: **"The present Egyptian Government is trying to export Egyptian internal crisis to the besieged Gaza Strip."** Really, Doctor?!! You are not a good liar, even by the standard of that Hamas specialty.

On September 13, Ismail Haniyah, **"Prime Minister"** of a Gaza **"government"** deposed by the Palestinian Authority on the West Bank, issued a message of assurances to Egypt. In it, he opines that **"the resistance weapon is still raised in the direction of Israel.** Haniyah has also recently declared that **"Gaza is the first line of defense of Egypt,"** and that **"the Palestinian question is the most important issue for Egypt."**

Mr. Haniyah: You are far from reality on several counts: The first line of defense of Egypt is its reestablishment of its internal peace and economic viability; your side of the border has been, until recently, a conduit through hundreds of tunnels for smuggling into and from Egypt all kinds of contraband, including weapons; your jihadis have been infiltrated into Sinai to link up with other criminal elements with the objective of proclaiming **"The Sinai Islamic Caliphate;"** and the cause of legitimate Palestinian rights should be attained primarily through negotiations which you have condemned.

It is a pity that you still consider your visualization of the Palestinian future as unlinked to your reconciliation with Ramallah. So please, Mr. Haniyah, mind your own problems. But don't mess with MISR. Fighting terrorism in Egypt might take some time before it is at least contained.

The overwhelming majority of the Egyptian public shall not tire of its newly-minted refrain: "Our army: May God bless your hand!! You are the heroes of your land!!"

By an Egyptian Court Order, the Muslim

Brotherhood "BUND" is Disbanded: WHY?

Tuesday, October 1, 2013

In German, the Bund is a collective, a cabal that is secretive, exclusive and/or ideological. Within the meaning of that term, the Muslim Brotherhood has been, since its creation in 1928, a veritable Bund. After huffing and puffing, the Brotherhood has, for the third time blown its house down.. The Brotherhood's house, though based geographically in Egypt, has never been an Egyptian house. It has been a seat for a complex mix of pan-islamism cum force.

Now disbanded by an Egyptian court order, issued on September 23, the Muslim Brotherhood had reached the summit of ensconcing its agent, now deposed President Morsi, at the Presidential palace for one very long and painful year. Then came its downfall through a judicial ban, thus epitomizing the saying: **"from riches to rags."** The reasons for that ban lie within their ideology, within their actions, and within their insistence on **"my way or the highway."**

The Brotherhood ideology can be seen in their symbol: Two raised swords held aloft criss-crossed, with the holy Quran on top, and the ominous belligerent and provocative term **"Be Ready" (Aaeddou)** between the handles of the two swords. So what is wrong with that Brotherhood symbol? Many things: (1) The Quran, the primary source of Islamic law and practice, advocates peace and tolerance, not combat, except to counter aggression; (2) The term **"Muslim"** means the submission by the individual to the will of God, not to the pronouncements of the Brotherhood's Supreme Guide; and (3) **"Be Ready,"** in Islamic Law, and in the general context of the 6400 verses of the Quran, connotes readiness for coexistence, interaction, and acceptance of the other through Islam's universalistic concept of **DIVERSITY**. In the Quran, diversity is asserted in many verses including: **"If God has so willed, He would have made you a single people, but HIS plan is to test you in what He hath given you: so strive as in a race in all virtues."** (Chapter 5, verse 48).

The counter-thesis of diversity is exclusiveness. The Brotherhood's exclusivity is a doomed ideology, especially in the 21st Century. It collides head on with faith, logic and changing circumstances.

As to Brotherhood's actions which prove their rejection of diversity, the expose must perforce consist of a factual review of why those repetitive bans were imposed by the State over a period of 66 years within an 85 year period of Brotherhood existence. That expose, based on facts, demonstrates the constant tension between pan-Islamism and Egyptian nationalism with the latter coming invariably and instinctively on top.

The Muslim Brotherhood had shown itself very capable of mass organization at the village level. Their relentless process of Islamization is a cottage industry which took advantage of the natural tendency of the Egyptian people, regardless of faith, to be religious. As a kingdom until 1953 and as an authoritarian dictatorship until the fall of Mubarak in 2011, the Egyptian masses have endured repression of their freedom of speech. Politics which were expressed in opposition to the Ruler were to be avoided. But religious freedom was largely immune from such restrictions. Thus religious freedom became the only safe vehicle for freedom of speech.

The Brotherhood found in that open door its access to the organization of its adherents. And because Islam is both a faith and a way of life, the Brotherhood's bus could accommodate a broad spectrum of Islamic religious views. With demographic expansion came also a division of interpreting the Brotherhood mission: Is it Islamic advocacy combined with charity alone, or is it also advocacy combined with political action? Their mission definition was never decided upon, giving rise to **"the secret wing,"** and the diversion to the back alleys of enforcement. The two swords became a symbol in action. Advocacy combined with charity acted largely as a smoke screen for the objective of exclusive political power, with Egypt acting as a launching pad.

The ban of September 23, 2013 of the Brotherhood and all its formations and the seizure of all their assets was the direct result of a series of actions directed against a historically secular Egypt. It was the third of a series of such bans.

The first ban came about in 1947. It resulted form a confrontation between the monarchical system in Egypt and the Brotherhood under the leadership of its founder, Hassan Al-Banna. At that time, the Brotherhood, insulted by a case against one of its members, was caught red-handed in the assassination of Judge Ahmed Pasha Al-Khazendar who was assigned that case. This act of violence, especially against the judiciary, prompted Prime Minister Al-Naqrashi to declare the Brotherhood an illegal organization.

In a tit-for-tat reaction by the Brotherhood, which fancied itself as ruling the Egyptian street, the **"Secret Wing"** of the Brotherhood assassinated that Prime Minister in 1947. Not since 1910 has Egypt lost a prime minister to political assassination. That was when Prime Minister Boutros Ghali, a Copt, was fatally ambushed.

Reacting to Al-Naqrashi's assassination, and with the feud between the Brotherhood and the Royal Palace reaching its fiery zenith, government agents killed Al-Banna in 1949. That took place even after Al-Banna had distanced himself from the murder of Al-Naqrashi by saying: **"Those who killed the Prime Minister were neither Brothers nor Muslims."** By now, the battle for the soul of Egypt between the Islamists and the secularists was in full swing.

Yet secular Egypt was more forgiving than the Brotherhood. That latter saw its face on the two sides of the Egyptian coin: on one side was Islam, and on the other was Islam as the ladder to power. In the same year of 1949, the Brotherhood, under a new Guide, Mamoun Al-Hodheiby, using the Egyptian Constitution of 1923, applied to the Supreme Administration Court for lifting of the ban. The Egyptian judiciary, being one of the main pillars of modern Egypt, decreed the lifting of that ban in accordance with the constitutional **right to peaceful assembly.**

Again the Brotherhood, eager to interject itself in to Egyptian politics, caused some of its members to penetrate the proud Officers Corp of the cohesive national army. Its opening to that critical penetration was the abhorrence by the clandestinely-formed **"Free Officers"** of corruption in the Royal Palace. The **"Free Officers"** attributed the military defeat in Palestine in 1948-1949 to that corruption. Nasser, being the prime mover of that group, looked benignly upon the brotherhoodization of segments of the Free Officers ranks. He needed their fervor and their popular base. Here was a short-lived honeymoon between secularism and Islamism.

That honeymoon was doomed to ultimate failure. While Nasser recruited clandestinely officers on the basis of loyalty to Egypt, the Muslim Brotherhood officers, believing on exclusivity, had a different criterion for that strategic recruitment. Their standard was the degree of fidelity only to Islam -an early microcosm of the battle for Egypt's identity from 2011 to 2013, with the year 2012-2013 being the Morsi year.

Following the dethroning by the Naguib/Nasser coup of both King Farouk in 1952, and of his son, King Ahmed Fouad II in 1953, Egypt was declared a republic. Its Revolutionary Command Council, desiring to get rid of a parliamentary democracy based on a multi-party system, dissolved all political parties, including the popular and secular mass party of the Wafd which was led by both Muslim and Christian stalwarts. But the Muslim Brotherhood, describing itself as a society (Jamaa), not a political party, was spared dissolution.

That historic exception of the Brotherhood from dissolution did not fully accord with the Brotherhood agenda. For there was **"the national project"** of Nasser standing in the way of the **"Islamic project"** of the Brotherhood. Between the two projects, there could be no compromise. The stalemate forced the Revolutionary Command Council to issue on January 1, 1954, a ban on the Brotherhood. That second ban amounted to a new year gift from the armed forces to historically secular Egypt.

Ten months later, namely in October 1954, the Brotherhood again sought its weapon of choice - political assassination. In that month, members of that BUND attempted to assassinate Nasser as he stood in a public square in Alexandria to address the nation. The plot failed and massive arrests and prosecution of the Brothers followed.

It took the Brotherhood 20 years from 1954 to 1974 to recover, especially under the Sadat regime which in September 1970 followed that of Nasser. Under its third Guide, Omar Al-Telemsany, the Brotherhood, again in 1974 tried to have the Egyptian judiciary lift that second ban. But the case collapsed due to a provision in the Nasserite Constitution of 1964 which immunized decisions of the Revolutionary Command Council from the Courts jurisdiction. Due to that legal defect in the Brotherhood's case which had languished before the Supreme Administrative Court from 1974 till 1991, the case for lifting the ban was thrown out.

Then came the Arab Spring, resulting in the form of the Egyptian Revolution of January 25, 2011 which resulted in the fall of the Mubarak regime on February 11, 2011. That revolution was purely secular. It raised in Tahrir Square both the crescent and the cross reminding the world of Egypt's secularism, inclusiveness, and openness to the 21st century. The Brotherhood came late to that uprising. But because of its history of mass appeal to Muslims, its grass-roots organization, and its promises to be a part of the Egyptian whole, its candidate for President Morsi won.

That victory proved to be Pyrrhic -a victory gained at a great cost. It caused the Brotherhood to fall in the trap of **"Egypt was subsidiary to Islamization."** It revealed the bond between the Brotherhood and the terror elements of Hamas; it aggressed against both Al-Azhar and the Coptic church; it called the disruption of both urban and rural Egypt, through sit-ins, a **"a peaceful exercise of the right to assembly;** it declared the areas of those sit-ins **"Islamic emirates;"** it attacked the army and the police by various types of weapons from rocks to RPGs; it caused havoc in the two provinces of Sinai which became, since 1906, an integral part of Egypt; it described the Second Egyptian Revolution of June 30, 2013 and its resultant dismissal of the Islamist regime of Morsi as a coup; and it rebuffed all invitations to becoming a part of the transitional government of Hazem Al-Beblawi which it regards as devoid of legitimacy.

The Brotherhood's third ban, declared by the Court of Urgent Matters on September 23, is all inclusive of its organizations and assets. The ruling by that fast track Court amounts to a preliminary injunction which shall undoubtedly be confirmed by a higher court, the Supreme Administrative Court -the very court which had repeatedly resurrected the Brotherhood from its two previous bans.

The Egyptian proverb says: **"The third hit is the most enduring."** So it shall be with the BUND whose returned to an underground existence shall be of no avail to its attempt to subvert secular Egypt.

The reign of the Brotherhood collapsed primarily because that Bund has proved that it does not comprehend diversity within the context of Egyptian nationalism. And when the European Union asks Cairo to explain why the Brotherhood was banned, it is incumbent upon Egypt, in defense of its sovereignty, not to respond.

It seems futile to guide the Muslim Brotherhood to two pages of history for educational purposes. One page provides a contemporary lesson in diversity even in the Islamic Republic of Iran. Though Iran has only 9000 citizens of the Jewish faith, its present Parliament includes an Iranian adherent of that faith.

The other page is from the history of modern Egypt under one of my heroes, namely Muhammad Ali, its viceroy under the Ottoman Empire. The Empire collapsed for many reasons including the ignorant advice by Muslim scholars to the Sultan not to introduce European expertise for training including that of the armed forces. Muhammad Ali, a true practitioner of diversity, launched modern Egypt in 1805 supported by French technology. Within a mere 30 years, the Egyptian armies under the great General Ibrahim Pasha, his son, were at the gates of Istanbul, ready to bring the entire Empire under the poised rulership of Muhamad Ali. Europe saved

the Sultan, and the family of Muhammed Ali got under its hereditary crown until the Nasser coup in 1952.

28   OCTOBER 2013

For the Muslim Brothers, No Profit From Equating Between Themselves and the Prophets

Friday, October 4, 2013

The **Quran** in Chapter 21, verses 68, 69 and 70 relates the suffering of Abraham until saved, by the grace of God, from burning by fire. These verses depict the power of the Almighty over those of his creatures who have flung Abraham into a raging fire. Their purpose was to get rid of his persistent calls for the worship of God as one, to replace idolatry. The text reads as follows: **"They said, 'Burn him and protect your gods, if ye do anything at all. We said, "O Fire! Be thou cool and a means of safety for Abraham. Then they sought a stratagem against him: but We made them the ones that lost the most."**

How does this fit in with the campaign being waged today by Egypt's transitional government against the leadership of the now banned Muslim Brotherhood? **Plenty.** From behind its prison bars, the Brotherhood's leadership is still allowed to publish and vent its grievances against the Second Egyptian Revolution of July 3. Calling that massive popular uprising against the Morsi Islamist regime **"a coup,"** that leadership finds in the **Quran** what it fancies as parallels between the Prophets of old and themselves.

The lives of the Prophets are related throughout the **Quran** to prove God's power over those who wished in vain to defeat monotheism, for which Islam strongly stands. In their collectivity, these verses provide a message of eternal hope to all those who suffer injustice. **It is the pre-destined victory of good over evil.**

Now here is an irony: The Muslim Brotherhood, through its extensive reliance in its public campaign against the removal of Morsi as President, and the measures that followed in its wake against its leadership, is evoking the story of David and Goliath. Its extensive use of the **Quran** does not stop there. Through one of its imprisoned leaders, **Dr. Silah El-Din Sultan,** a professor of Sharia, the Muslim Brotherhood fancies its imprisoned leaders as the new Prophets. That professor expounds on this theme in the Brotherhood's newspaper: **"Freedom and Justice."**

Ibrahim (or Abraham) in the **Quran** is one such Prophet. Joseph (in the **Quran**: **"Yusuf")** is another, with the twist that Joseph, from a prisoner of Pharaoh, to Joseph becoming a Prime Minister of Egypt, ushering into it his entire family. In this connection, the Brotherhood quotes heavily from Chapter 12 entitled **"Yusuf"** with emphasis on the verse describing the historic triumph of Joseph, especially as that Prophet welcomes his whole family into Egypt by the Quranic phrase: **"Enter ye Egypt, all in safety, if it pleases God." (verse 99).**

What follows that verse is on point as regards the Brotherhood's expectation of their release from prison and resumption of power once more. Using Joseph as a parallel for their return to the governance of Egypt, their articles in **"Freedom and Justice"** quote the Quranic verse no. 100, as Joseph says: **"God hath made it come true! He was indeed good to me when he took me out of prison."**

The sad part of that scenario is that the Brotherhood manifests a desperate attempt to use the **Quran** as an instrument of their aspirations for a political come back. Ignoring the repeated injunctions in the **Quran** regarding the necessity, under Islamic jurisprudence, of the removal of injustice by all available means, as the Egyptian masses did to the Morsi's exclusivistic Islamist rule, the Brotherhood now appeals to the **Quran** as a predictor of their return to the halls of power.

Judging these utterances on their merit, how can an analyst

escape the following conclusions: (a) the Brotherhood's conviction that they have a divine mission, not at all different from "the divine right of kings;" (b) their record of one year of Islamization under Morsi has nothing in it to justify their impossible quest; (c) they see their road to power, tortuous as it might be, can only be paved by Islamic holy texts; (d) their appeal to their supporters is so narrowly tailored to the ethos of an Islamic State, indeed a Caliphate, with Egypt as a mere launching pad; and (e) the severe lessons of their populist ouster from power, in spite of their limited self-blame, have not yet sunk in.

This is a hopeless quest, a quest which is solely focused on regaining power through the Brotherhood's own interpretation of Islam. From their prison cells, the Brotherhood is, in effect, telling secular Egypt: **"We shall be back to pursue our manifest destiny: An Islamic Emirate in Egypt."**

It is not going to happen. Reasons: The Brotherhood is frozen in time. To them, nothing has changed for the past 1434 years when Islam became a community, not a State, through the Hijrah (flight) of the Prophet Muhammad from Mecca, to evade persecution, to Medina.

So, Brothers, dream on!! Islam has declared that Muhammad is the last Prophet. Your mission is foreclosed. No profit for you from equating between yourselves and the Prophets. Sorry! You are late by nearly 15 centuries. GET REAL!!

Raining on Egypt's Parade

Friday, October 11, 2013

It poured on Egypt's parade of October 6 from two cloud outbursts: One internal, that of the Muslim Brotherhood; the other external, the U.S. withholding **"some"** military aid to Egypt. In the deepest psyche of Egypt, October 6, since 1973, is celebrated as **"The Crossing Over Day."** Under President Sadat, the armed forces crossed the Suez Canal to liberate Sinai from Israeli occupation. It was a 17-day war intended to undo the humiliation of the massive defeat of the 6-day war of June 1967.

A careful study of the October war (called also the Yom Kippur War by the Israelis, and the Ramadan War by most of the Arabs) reveals interesting insights into Egypt's mind. These trends are non-changeable: the sanctity, to the average Egyptian, of Egyptian soil; the centrality of respect of the Egyptian armed forces; the ability of Egypt to disengage from regional attachment to the concept of **"One Arab Nation"** if the land of the Nile becomes its victim; and the role of transformative leadership in marshalling those trends.

The backdrop of October 6 is the failure of Arab Baathist ideology, espoused by the Nasser regime from 1952 to 1967. That is the corrupt ideology of Egyptian intervention in the affairs of other Arab States. Its primary purpose was elevating Nasserism to the level of Egyptian hegemony. Cairo's interventionism proved too costly, caused Egyptian economic and social decline, and contributed to the suffocation of an earlier Egyptian democracy at the altar of what? **The altar of nothing.**

The Sadat leadership, without disavowing Nasserism, undid that losing streak. It used the limited war of October 6 to liberate Sinai; it reminded Egypt of its solid roots in cosmopolitan Egyptianism; it freed the economy from the shackles of the negativism of the Khartoum Summit of 1967 towards peace in the Middle East; it normalized relations with the great Arab East based on the Gulf States; and it signaled to the west that friendship with the US does not mean acceptance of a Washington dictat.

For all of these historic achievements, representing a historic bivoting from ideology to practicality, Sadat was assassinated on October 6, 1981 by the Islamists. As he stood at the review stand on that fateful day to concretize the meaning of **"The Crossing Over Day,"** he was gunned down as his terrorist assassins yelled at him **"You are a dog."**

There is an Arab proverb that says **"Tonight Reminds of Last Night."** Its western equivalent is: **"The More Things Change, The More They Stay The Same."**

The similarity between October 6, 1981 and October 6, 2013, is unmistakable. The Islamists of 2013, following the ouster of Morsi of the Brotherhood are on a rampage. Their target is Egyptian secularism and inclusiveness.

On Egypt's parade, the Muslim Brotherhood rained RPGs, and other instruments of stealth killing. From Sinai to Suez; from Cairo to Alexandria; from southern Egypt to the Delta. They also exposed their adherents to assured destruction, called by them **"martyrdom."** They used

October 6 as a day of saluting, not Egypt's armed forces, but their incarcerated ousted President. To them, Egypt's armed forces, under the flag of Egypt, have become a hated militia.

To where will that rebellion lead? Not to the reinstatement of Morsi who shall be tried before the Egyptian judiciary next month. Not to the harassment of all those who do not adhere to their pan-Islamist ideology. Not to the maniacal restrictions imposed on foreign tourists, whether in dress or in food and drink. Not to the concept of a society which looks upon non-Muslims as infidels.

On Egypt's parade, also rained the withholding by the US of certain sectors of the US aid to Egypt. A puzzling interruption of observing the customary practices between allies. That suspension does not constitute **"a recalibration of Egyptian-US relationship."** Let us call acts such as these by their proper names. This is a most unfortunate **reversal.** This action promises to be neither **"modest nor temporary."**

It shall not lead to an enhancement of the democratization of the Egyptian system. Democracy is not exportable, and sovereignty is not for sale. I reckon that at no time would that act of intervention in Egypt's internal affairs will bear but a poisonous fruit for the Cairo-Washington amity. Its thrust might be weakening of the structure of peace in the new Middle East.

Yet, after all it might accelerate the pace of Egyptian self-reliance. In the early 1980's, I interviewed Frank Wisner, the then US Ambassador to Egypt. I asked him **"What does he think of the American aid to Egypt?"** His response was, **"Egypt does not need aid. It needs trade." Well said, Mr. Ambassador. The Egyptian masses are with you. They are wary of a relationship which fluctuates between hot and cold. Hot for Mubarak's dictatorship; cold for Egypt's parade moving, in spite of the Muslim Brotherhood toward a democracy born from its authentic streetocracy.**

A Novel Right To Myth-Information Carved Out By Many Egyptian Press "Opinion-Makers"

Friday, October 25, 2013

In Post-Mubarak Egypt, press freedom is translated by many Egyptian press "opinion-makers" as the right to propagate myth-information. Not only is most of the material very thin on facts and devoid of analysis and logic. It is a hodgepodge of fantasy, non-supported conclusions, name calling, and anecdotes of suspect origin. One may call it press chaos instead of press freedom.

It is a tragic phenomenon exhibited by so-called "opinion-makers" within a broad spectrum of political and ideological affiliations. It is a form of de-education through the Egyptian press. Examples abound, and events vary, but **"the bla bla bla bla"** is its main feature. Here follows are telling examples:

On the issue of whether El-Sisi intends to become a presidential candidate

Al-Ahram, the government official newspaper, supports that possibility. No problem. But one of its editorialists, **Hamdy Hassan Abul-Ainain** addresses an open letter which warns one of El-Sisi's possible competitors, Field Marshal Ahmed Shafik, not to throw his hat in the ring. Why? Here is **Abul-Ainain's** non-content advice to Shafik, who had received 49.50% of the popular vote for president in 2012 against 50.50% for Morsi:

"You have known Field Marshal El-Sisi for a long time... have determined that he was the most capable to lead this nation... Everyone knows that your decision to compete in the last presidential elections led to Morsi becoming Egypt's President. We need new faces and a new climate for a free and an enlightened choice."

Here the writer contradicts himself. He calls for a free and an enlightened choice, yet discourages competition which the essence of free choice. He reaches several faulty conclusions and makes unsupported assumptions. How could Shafik's running for the presidential office in June

2012 have aided Morsi's ascendancy to the highest office in Egypt?

On the issue of shutting down the Muslim Brotherhood and the remnants of the Mubarak regime:

Muhammad Shuman, another in **Al-Ahram** calls for the inclusion in the now Egyptian constitution of a strange provision. Here is his de-educational advocacy:

"That constitutional provision should ban those two groups (named above) from political work for 10 years. The law should also correct the meaning of leadership in all these groups... It is my conviction that the leadership of both the Muslim Brotherhood and the remnants of the Mubarak regime are appendages of the Mubarak regime. They both have contributed to the corruption of political action whereby elections became a trade in which votes are bought and sold... The main object is to attain social justice and to guarantee the process of transiting to democracy."

It is apparent that the writer ignores the historic fact that the Muslim Brotherhood was banned under the Mubarak regime. It is startling that this "opinion-maker" confused between the role of a constitution and the role of a subservient law. The present ban of the Brotherhood under the presidency of Justice Adly Mansour is by a mere law underpinned by political and security considerations. It does not extend to other groups or parties, especially **"the remnants of the Mubarak regime,"** which, under the lofty principle of transitional justice, are being integrated within the broad spectrum of political inclusiveness.

On the issue of Saudi Arabia's position on the Muslim Brotherhood and Al-Qaeda:

In the daily liberal Al-Massri Al-Yom, an editorialist by the name of Abr Nadeen Al-Budair, in her attacks against the Muslim Brotherhood, invents the following imaginary conclusions: (a) In search for a rebirth, the Brotherhood, once more, finds it in Saudi Arabia; (b) The Saudi regime is responsible for the creation of the military wing of the Brotherhood -Al Qaeda; and (c) the Brotherhood has sabotaged Saudi education and public information through making these institutions outlets for the Brotherhood.

The writer's ignorance is patently manifest. In her hallucinatory efforts to get the Saudi government to combat the Brotherhood, she is ignorant of, or chooses to ignore, the following facts: **(i)** It was the Founder of Saudi Arabia, the late King Abdel-Aziz Al-Saud, who denied the Brotherhood an institutional base in his country; **(ii)** Saudi Arabia, during the reign of King Fahd, forced Bin Laden to flee the Kingdom; and **(iii)** Saudi Arabia is leading the Gulf's financial surge to help the post-Morsi government overcome Egypt's present economic distress.

On the issue of the split in Egypt between the Islamists and the Secularists

Imad Gad asserts in the newspaper Al-Tahrir that the removal of Morsi from the Egyptian presidency has "contributed to the increased hate" between the two camps. Fair enough. But then he lurches away from that fact to the inventing of statistics, as he says: "Those who belong to the camp of political Islam do not exceed 15% to 20% of the total demographics of Egypt." The editorialist prepares us for that discovery by saying: **"The split within Egyptian society has reached a degree indicative of the existence of two peoples in Egypt whereby it is ascertainable that the split is sharp and divisive. It has reached the point where it could be said that today there are two** Egypts **in one country."**

The sad fact about Egypt and nearly all other Arab countries is that qualified social science research does not exist. The great source on Arab statistics on Arab development, published by the UN Family of Organizations was based on representative samples. I know of no census in Egypt which includes questions of party or religious affiliations. In fact there is no official census regarding the percentage of the Coptic community as regards the total population of Egypt. **Mr. Imad Gad** has clearly used his fertile imagination in two ways:

(i) the percentage of the membership of the Brotherhood within the total population of Egypt. The Brotherhood does not provide figures on anything, especially on membership and budget; and **(ii)** the conflict within Egypt is one of identity **(secular v. Islamic),** not of two Egypts, inhabiting the same territory. That opinion-maker should know that even in the case of a civil war, which is not the case of present-day Egypt, the warring factions cling tenaciously to the fact that they all belong to the same country.

On the issue of calling Dr. El-Baradei, a traitor

Several commentators have been waging a savage campaign of name-calling against that Nobel Prize Laureate, who was Director-General of the UN-related International Atomic Energy Agency. His attackers have called for his dismissal from the Egyptian Bar; one of those anti-El-Baradei campaigners, a law professor, even went to the ridiculous length of suing him. For what? For "injuring the national trust!!"

After the removal of Morsi from the presidency on July 3, 2013, Dr. El-Baradei assumed the post of Vice-President in charge of International Relations. He was one of the pillars in Morsi's removal from power. But he watched in horror, together with 35 million other Egyptians, the systemic brotherhoodization of Egypt. Yet he felt compelled to resign his high office as he believed that the forceful removal of the Brotherhood's six-week sit-ins on August 14, resulting in a thousand or more fatalities, was a mistake.

But calling him a traitor by the present secularists commentators is just as bad as the name-calling by the Islamists of their secularist adversaries as **"apostates,"** and **"enemies of God."** Criminalizing **"the other opinion"** is a slippery slope toward fascism.

On the issue of Nasser and starving scientists and maintaining illiteracy

Dr. Thabet Eid, a member of the Muslim Brotherhood affirms in one full page of the Brotherhood's daily "Freedom and Justice" that Nasser (Egypt's President from 1954 to 1970) committed the above-mentioned public sins. That voice of the Muslim Brotherhood condemns the Nasser program of "free education for all" as a plot causing the decline of public education. He accuses all those military presidents who ruled the most populous country in the Arab world of deliberately giving more importance to the number of students so educated than to the quality of their education.

That commentator ignores the historic fact that access to the freedom of education at no cost and at all levels was inaugurated by the great iconic philosopher and educator, **Dr. Taha Hussein.** Though blind, that philosopher and reformer was invited by the popular Wafd government of Nahas Pasha in 1951 to be the Minister of Education. His seminal book in Arabic, entitled **"The Future of Education in Egypt"** published in the late 1930s, which I have read twice, remains relevant to today's Egypt.

The military governments of Egypt, from 1953 **(President Naguib)** to 2011 **(President Mubarak)** maintained that system. The system was not a casualty of its openness, but of inadequate resources, both financial and teachers training. The Brotherhood editorialist directs his flashlight on the historic enmity between the Brotherhood and secular governments. As he does that, he unwittingly also shines a light on how biased commentators deceive their public through the propagation of falsehoods.

Conclusion: The Egyptian press freedom of today is practised mostly as press chaos:

Myth-information by many Egyptian press commentators has become a daily fare in the new Egypt. There exists a code of press ethics in Egypt, but it sadly lacks enforcement. Invented statistics, false accusations, and mean name-calling, non-substantiated assumptions are real hurdles in the path of Egypt towards its present goal of democratization.

The Right to Information Day was celebrated last month (September 23-28) by no less than 40 countries. That right is predicated upon several criteria. These include the right to whistle-blowing, but not the assumed right of leaking of State secrets. Nowhere in these criteria do I find the right to propagate invented facts. This is a black art. It belongs to the world of Halloween (to pretend to be what you really are not). Its only casualty is truth in reporting. Honesty in public information is the basis of an enlightened public opinion -one of the main pillars of democracy.

All freedoms are regulated in order to avoid abuse. It is a rare coin on one side of which is written "Freedom"; on the other "Responsibilities."

29 NOVEMBER 2013

The So-Called "Friends of Jerusalem" Are Friends of Neither Egypt, Nor of Islam, Nor of International Law, Nor of Peace

Friday, November 1, 2013

Like the global outlaws, called Al-Qaeda, and their franchises using Islam as a cover for their crimes against humanity, the **"Friends of Jerusalem"** have unfurled in Egypt a black flag. They call it the flag of **"jihad"** -a term in Islam which is globally misunderstood. The **"FOJ,"** to use initials in reference to that cabal, openly brag about committing numerous heinous crimes committed recently all over Egypt. They are gleeful about the mayhem they are perpetrating in the name of God.

FOJ now admits to attempting to assassinate Egypt's Minister of Interior; killing army and police personnel in Sinai; burning down Coptic (Christian) churches and private businesses; paralyzing mass transit whether by rail to upper Egypt or by cars and buses in urban areas. Further they promise more of the same, because they believe that this is their express way to paradise. Only an Islamic regime, in their image, can be legitimate. Thus, to them and to their allies in the Muslim Brotherhood, a country which is not ruled by their own fossilized interpretation of Islamic jurisprudence, is a country to be conquered, a body politic to be subdued, a rulership to be delegitimized.

Judging by an analysis of the connotations of that term, their ideological resort to jihad is totally idiotic. The Friends of Jerusalem, acting out of total ignorance of what jihad means, do not comprehend that, legally, jihad is reserved for the defense of the homeland against foreign occupation and external aggression.

In that jurisprudential context, it is a duty. But, guided by Al-Qaeda's principles, the **FOJ** extends the notion of jihad to activities categorically prohibited under Sharia. Islamic Law prohibits the coerced propagation of any faith, including Islam; it disavows Al-Qaeda's presumptions about rescuing the West from its **"ignorance" (jahiliah)**; it totally negates the terroristic attempts to call non-Muslims **"infidels."**

Islamic Law does not permit any human being to evaluate the faith of another human being. Why? Because Islam insists on the privacy and directness of relationships between man/woman and their Creator. In effect, Sharia tells any intermediary between the human being and the Creator **"Butt Out!!"**

We have seen the catastrophic consequences of 9/11. How can the wilful and criminal attacks on 3000 civilians in New York, Washington and Pennsylvania be considered justifiable? Those martyred victims did nothing offensive to merit that horrible fate. They, including hundreds of Muslims, did nothing except go on that fateful morning to earn their livelihood.

The jihad of the **Friends of Jerusalem** and like criminally-minded organizations had the disastrous effect of instilling hostility between the States so affected and mainstream Islam. The primary issue here is confusing the concept of **jihad** and the concept of **combat (Qital)**. Jihad is a non-changing legal concept of self-defense, guaranteed by natural law, customary law and conventional law. By contrast, combat (Qital) is a transitory event which arises at times out of the exigencies of the necessities an organized State. Only the State, not non-state actors such as FOJ, has the monopoly of resorting to arms.

Even the Prophet Muhammad, while in Mecca at the beginning of his mission, together with his companions, waged for 13 years **"peaceful jihad"** against his tormentors. Their jihad consisted of patience, endurance, advice, and ultimately immigration (Hijrah) to Medina. Even in Medina, which marked the beginning of the formation of the Islamic

community (in Islam **"community"** and **"State"** are two different things),
Muhammad resorted to combat (Qital) but only in self-defense.

In Islam, there is no aggressive war, and war is both defensive and
proportional. Alas, these are values lost on the criminal gangs of Al-Qaeda,
Boko Haram, AQIM (Al-Qaeda in the Islamic Maghrab), the Nusra and the
Friends of Jerusalem. The long-term danger of such criminal gangs, which
prey on the ignorance of the illiterate masses of what Islam stands for, is
this: **the adverse effects on the freedom of belief held by non-Muslims,
and the propelling of Muslims into fanaticism, including suicide (the
destruction of self -totally prohibited under Sharia).**

The great Egyptian poet, **Ahmed Shawki,** nicknamed **"The Prince of
Poets"** summed up the difference between jihad and Qital in one famous
verse:

**"War is not everday's vehicle,
and blood is not to be sanctified at every episode"** (my translation
from the classical Arabic).

That exquisite verse justifies in full measure the anti-colonial struggle in
Libya under the **Sanusis** against Italian occupation; in Algeria under **Abdel-
Qader** against French colonialism; in Morocco under **Abdel-Kareem Al-
Khattabi** also against French occupation; in the Sudan under the **Mahdi**
against Anglo-Egyptian suppression of national and tribal aspirations; and
in Egypt under the leadership of the Scholars of **Al-Azhar** against
Napoleon. This is a partial list of instances of where jihad is justifiable
under Islamic Law which clearly militates against unjust authority whether
external or internal.

The advocacy of the Friends of Jerusalem is fueled not only by common
mass ignorance. It is backed up by books like that by an Egyptian by the
name of **Magdy Ahmed Hassanain.** In historically cosmopolitan Egypt
(nicknamed **"The World's Mother"**), religious fanaticism is heading
toward one final destination called **"Station Failure."**

In his book, published in Arabic in Cairo in 2003, under the provocative
title of **"Jihad: The Nation's Vocation,"** Magdy Ahmed Hassanain, in
383 pages, totally upends the legal interpretation of jihad. In its egregious
assumptions and fanciful conclusions, Hassanain's writing evokes the spirit
of **"Mein Kampf"** (in German: **My Struggle**), authored by Hitler in the
1930's, and read by me in Arabic in the 1940s. I have little doubt that

Hassanain's advocacy shall lead to the same cataclysmic failures produced by Naziism on the world stage.

As head of the **"New Labor Party,"** Magdy Ahmed Hassanain advocates in his newspaper **"Al-Shaab Al-Jadeed"** (The New People), a unique compromise with the present secular transitional government of Egypt. That is total surrender to the Islamists!! Thus he calls for the immediate arrest and execution of Field Marshall El-Sisi, the Defense Minister and Deputy Prime Minister (who, at the urging of 35 million Egyptians led the unseating of the Islamist regime of Morsi.)

Calling El-Sisi **"a pimp,"** he forthes at the mouth when he yells across the pages of his rag that **"without El-Sisi's immediate arrest, summary trial and execution, Egyptian society shall see no peace."** Now Hassanain, this champion of false jihad and permanent war against all non-Muslims, is the subject of a subpoena issued against him by the General Prosecutor investigating Hassanain's out of sight accusations against Egypt's Military Intelligence.

There is a light at the end of the tunnel which secular Egypt is successfully traversing at present in spite of "The Friends of Jerusalem," Hassanain, and other advocates of endless conflict for no rational end.

The Muslim Brotherhood Shifts the Blame for Their Predicament of Exclusion to Higher Authority

Friday, November 8, 2013

In psychology there is a principle called **"sublimation."** It is the human capacity, positively oriented, to turn a negative into a positive. An example of sublimation is to draw a lesson for the future from a bad occurrence.

However this simple attitude of going forward after a bad fall seems to be beyond the Muslim Brotherhood in Egypt. The Second Egyptian Revolution of June 30, 2013 which put an end to their Islamist regime of Morsi as of July 3, should have been an objective lesson to the Brotherhood in how to behave in the future. This would have been both sublime and sublimation. But the Brotherhood has, since those historic reversals which chased them out of both governing and of the affection of the majority of public opinion in Egypt, shifted the blame to a higher authority.

They, through their writings, though remorseful, are not blaming themselves for those happenings. They are saying that it was **"God's will,"** meaning that their crisis has been pre-destined, that it was not their doing, but God's inflicted wounds. Why? The spokesman of the Brotherhood argue in their mouth piece, their daily newspaper **"Al-Hurriah Wa Al-Adalah" (Freedom and Justice)** that God Almighty is testing them for purposes of purification.

If this is the essential lesson which they learnt from a populist revolution staged by secular Egypt against turning the country into an Islamic Emirates, then their ability to reform themselves is severely limited. Their journey in the wilderness of being banned promises to be prolonged.

In the view of their publicists, the tragedy of the Brotherhood in Egypt resulted from **"the force of destiny."** Their educational oracle, Dr. Muhammad Wahdan, suggests that **"There is no need for either worry or anxiety. For everything is in God's hands."** This blatant shift of responsibility of the Brotherhood's downfall to the heavens above is bolstered by several of their vocal leaders and supporters.

Among those is Ahmed Al-Muhammady. He forcefully places certain verses from the **Quran** in the present mold of distancing the Brotherhood from the factors for their downfall. Truly amazing!! So from the **Quran Chapter XI,** he quotes verses 9 and 10 as follows: (Translation by Abdullah Yusuf Ali:

"If we give man a taste of mercy from ourselves, and then withdraw it from him, behold! He is in despair and (falls into) blasphemy. But if we give him a taste of (Our) favours after adversity has touched him, he is sure to say: 'All evil has departed from me. Behold! He falls into exultation and pride.'"

In a vain attempt to shore up the sagging morale of the Brotherhood the trial of several of its leadership including Morsi began on November 4, Mr. Muhammady urges patience. He looks at his fragged-up crystal ball, then sees hope of a quick Brotherhood's return to power. His words are: **"Over centuries of human history, the period of crisis was always much shorter than the period of return to empowerment."**

This mindset of defeat as a harbinger of ultimate victory is reflected in what a female supporter of the Brotherhood urges in the Brotherhood's daily. Fatima Abdulla, assuming a role of a cheerleader, says: **"Each Brotherhood member should implant in himself a feeling of dignity. He should wage jihad for the victory of what is right and for the glory of God's word. This is for God, not for the Egyptian public, the majority of whom evokes in us rage whenever we see them or hear them opposing us... The Brotherhood have opted for the path of jihad... The merciful God has chosen them to worship him and has empowered them to govern."**

Well, Ms. Fatima Abdullah: Your Islamist regime came to power through the ballot not through an act of God, and was forced out of power through streetocracy which the Morsi regime has alienated by its imposition of Islamization.

And by the way, it is one thing not to learn from one's mistakes, destructive as this could be. It is another to say that **"I do not have to learn anything because whatever mistakes were presumed to have been committed were not my doing but were ordained by God."** Unfortunately your resort to the **Quran** to justify your neutrality is not justifiable.

On this point, here, for the benefit of the Brotherhood, are two quotations from a total of eight verses which admonish owning up to one's mistakes:

"To them came their apostles with clear signs. It is not God who wrongs them, but they wrong their own souls." (Chapter IX, Verse 70). And we have provided for you. (But they rebelled). To us they did no harm, but they harmed their own souls." (Chapter X, Verse 57).

From these verses (ayas), selected from eight verses located in several chapters (suras), emerges a sacred rebuttal to the Brotherhood's artful blame-shifting away from themselves. The **Quran** assigns the blame for self-inflicted wounds to those who caused themselves that harm.

There is also **Omar,** the second Caliph after **Muhammad** who, in his appointment of a judge, issued in the appointment commission the following words which adorn most of the courtrooms in the Arab World:

"The return to the path of truth is better than going down the path of falsehood."

Teaching Islamic jurisprudence at Fordham University School of Law in New York City, I have found myself impressed by Islam's emphasis on the roles of intent and of free will in either damage avoidance or damage causation. It was not Heaven, but a deliberate Islamist coup against the January 25 Revolution, which ignited the secularists to strike back on June 30, 2013.

How can the Egyptian public regain confidence in the Muslim Brotherhood as a trusted partner in the reconstruction of the new Egypt, if, after the Brotherhood's tragic failure in governance, the Brotherhood is also manifesting its failure in understanding what inclusive Islam stands for?

The Brotherhood's epic failure resulted from misinterpreting the role of the ballot box in the democratic process. The ballot box is only a point of entry. That electoral victory does not provide the victor with a license to subvert the national Egyptian program into an **"Islamic program"** whose contents, objectives, and ideology are all alien to secular Egypt.

By excluding others in the name of Heaven, the Brotherhood is offending both Heaven and Earth.

The Idea of an US-Muslim Brotherhood Connection Has Multiple Roots -Some True, Some False

Friday, November 15, 2013

"The Americans have sold out on the Brotherhood," proclaims an Egyptian pundit, Osama Al-Ghozali Harb in the daily **Al-Ahram,** Egypt's official newspaper. On a different page of the same newspaper, another opinion-maker, Farouk Goweda states: **"Washington has no right to weep in distress for the return of Russia to Egypt."** As to the head of the Cairo Center for Human Rights, Bahi Eldin Hassan, he, in the Egyptian daily **Al-Shorook,** posits a final conclusion: **"The U.S. will ally itself with whoever is the ruler in Egypt."**

What is this all about? It is about the controversy raging in Egypt for sometime between two ideological factions. On the one hand, there are the secularists whose thesis is that that U.S. favors the Muslim Brotherhood. On the other hand, there are the Islamists whose political doctrine is that the US favors whoever rules in Egypt. Both theses have multiple roots, some of which are true, and some are false.

The basic fact is that neither the secularists nor the Islamists fully understand the making of US foreign policy. The U.S. has been overwhelmed by the sudden arrival of the Arab Spring in late 2010 and early 2011. Its anchors in Tunisia and in Egypt, President Ben Aly and Mubarak were ousted by the Arab square, and not by army coups. The sudden change of fortunes in both Tunis and Cairo, and later in Sana (Yemen), and in Tripoli (Libya) stunned the hierarchy of US decision-making. What made those changes more problematic for Washington, D.C. is that they are largely leaderless and fluid.

Those troubling characteristics were well expressed by one of the moguls of U.S. foreign policy. Richard Haass, the President of the Council on Foreign Relations stated in his recently published book, **Foreign Policy Begins At Home**, the following: **"Ousting authoritarian regimes was one thing; replacing them with something demonstratebly and enduringly better, quite another. Talk of an Arab Spring came to be replaced with the more neutral phrase 'Arab upheavals." (p.13)** Haass, who, among other important US policy posts, was Director of Policy Planning for the U.S. Department of State, knows his stuff.

The fog surrounding the present direction of U.S. foreign policy, including hugging in Egypt either the Brotherhood or the Secularists is expected to last until 2016. By that time, the Obama tenure at the White House shall be over. His presidency in general, has **"pivoted"** the U.S. foreign policy focus away from the Middle East in favor of East Asia. American democracy has been hobbled by the gridlock between Democrats and Republicans in Congress. The Republicans were able to shut down the federal government in Washington, D.C. for 16 days earlier this Fall. The civil war in Syria is expected to morph into a Sunni-Shii war over whose future America will have no role; and Afghanistan is expected to slip back into Taliban's chaos.

In the midst of all these expectations, the U.S. national interest dictates a largely hands-off policy towards the secularist-Islamist split in Egypt. America is largely becoming guarded by a U.S.-centric foreign policy.

Obama has repeatedly declared, with the present sluggish economic recovery in mind, that nation-building should be nation-building in the U.S. Richard Haass sums up Obama's case on the cover of his book above-cited. His words resonate with the majority of the U.S. public: **"The Case for Putting America's House in Order."**

Noting the shallow analysis in the Egyptian press, especially with regard to an US-Muslim Brotherhood connection, one finds the two Egyptian adversarial camps resorting either to imagery or imagination. **Al-Ahram** cites what Mr. Harb calls **"the perfect US synchronization of its policies with the Brotherhood's Islamist rule under Morsi."** Here he cites Secretary Kerry's visit to Cairo on February 28 of this year during which he asserts that Kerry tried to convince the secularists not to boycott the elections. From that alleged episode, the writer claims that ousting Morsi has angered the U.S.

It is true that Washington, D.C. bared its teeth at the ouster of Morsi. And it is true that Ambassador Patterson, formerly based in Cairo, had contacts with the Muslim Brotherhood both before and during the Morsi regime. And it is well-known that the US, in response to the Morsi ouster, imposed limited and largely symbolic sanctions against Egypt's military. A quarter of a billion dollars of military aid were withheld; advanced military equipment was denied; joint military exercises were suspended.

But to read in the these measures grimaces of affection from the U.S. to the Brotherhood is to misread the U.S. political mind. It also obscures the changing nature of US foreign policy toward Egypt which had been given by Obama a vague category. He called Egypt a **"non-ally,"** whatever this means.

There are essential facts which frame U.S. foreign policy-making. Primary among these is that Congress is a co-maker of that foreign policy. The senate votes on funding and treaty-making. Its **"advice and consent"** is required with regard to Presidential recommendations of U.S. officials appointments described by Article II, Section 2 of the U.S. Constitution as **"Ambassadors, other public Ministers and Consuls."** The Senate, when opposed to any Presidential nomination by the Executive branch, has put **"consent"** above **"advice."** Right now, Lindsey Graham, a southern senator, is blocking two important Obama nominees. There is also the power of impeachment of the President which is shared by both houses of Congress.

At present, the Democrats are ascendant in the Senate; the Republicans in the House **-a perfect recipe for frequent gridlocks.** It has never been a secret that most Republicans in Congress still regard Obama an anomaly. As a black man, Obama has become a target for frequent challenges including **"was he born in the US?"; "Is he a closet Muslim?"** -a reflection of islamaphobia.

We have also seen how brutalizing Congressional hearings of U.S. Secretary of State Hillary Clinton was. The Benghazi attack on the U.S. Consulate in 2012, which resulted in the death of the American Ambassador together with other American personnel, was used by Obama haters as an occasion for humiliating the woman who might run for President in 2016.

From the above, which is a cursory presentation of the complexity of U.S. foreign policy-making, one can discern the superficiality of defining the U.S. outlook on the Muslim Brotherhood as either amorous or hostile. National U.S. interest is the ultimate defining factor, if at times confused, in the relationship between Washington, D.C. and Cairo.

Of course there is in the U.S., in regard to any national issue including international relations, a cacophony of voices. This feature alone can account for at least some measure of confusion in Cairo as regards where the U.S. stands from various Egyptian actors including the Brotherhood.

After everything is said and done, Washington did not characterize the ouster of Morsi as **"a coup."** That would have been a true indication of **"America loves the Brotherhood."** And Secretary Kerry's brief visit to Cairo earlier this month, including calling on Field Marshal El-Sisi on the very day of opening the Morsi trial on November 4, generated a remark by Kerry that Egypt was **marching toward democracy.** An indicator which caused the shrill voices of the Brotherhood to be raised invoking God's wrath on America.

This was a strategic remark by the Secretary of State whose country is still grappling with a clearer differentiation between **"a revolution,"** and **"a coup."** That is not surprising. Each term has lots of consequences, but vague definitions. A Professor at New York University Law School, **Burt Neuborne,** who specializes in civil liberties, called democracy in the U.S. **"so dysfunctional that no rational person would choose it." (The New York Times, Sunday Review, November 10, 2013, page 2).**

Hopefully the remarks by Professor **Neuborne** in **The New York**

Times may slow down the barrage of attacks on the status of the post-Morsi transitional government by **Mr. David Kirkpatrick,** correspondent of the same newspaper in Cairo. **Kirkpatrick** invariably puts his opinions ahead of his reports.

Egypt's opinion-makers are also divided on the interpretation of the U.S.-Muslim Brotherhood connection. Those who see that connection as a permanent tilt in favor of the Brotherhood have also their detractors. In **Al-Ahram,** Farouk Gowedah claims that the U.S. has manifested animus toward Egypt as a result of the June 30 Revolution which ousted Morsi. Another opinion-maker cited-above, Osama Ghazali Harb, rebuts, also in **Al-Ahram,** the theory of enmity, though he describes the Muslim Brotherhood as **"America's historical friends."** This is while Fahmi Howedi of **Al-Shorooq,** rejects such claims by saying: **"U.S. support of the Brotherhood is a lie propagated by the enemies (secularists) of the Brotherhood."**

The cacophony of voices emanating from Washington has at least a degree of objective analysis of U.S. national interest. Unfortunately the Cairo cacophony of voices, with claims of U.S. love or U.S. hate for the Brotherhood, does not take objectivity into account. **In international relations, there is neither love nor hate. There is only national interest. It is the heart of the spirit of all times, known by the Germans in one word: "ZEITGEIST."**

One of my specialties is interpretation. It is my primary tool whereby intangible concepts are given tangible expression. Thus it is incumbent upon me to add another complicating factor in the controversy surrounding the U.S.-Brotherhood connection. **There exists a gulf of a conceptual nature between the U.S. outlook on democracy and what that outlook signals to both the Brotherhood and its opponents.**

The term **"democracy"** has never received a consensual definition across the globe. America looks upon the ballot box as a **legitimator**. But all Arab Spring uprisings regard the same box as a possible **manipulator.** To Arab Spring countries, balloting is the beginning of the process; to the U.S. political mind, it is the definitive end of the process of democratization. America looks upon opposition in a given country as a pre-ordained feature of free expression; the Arab uprisings look upon opposition largely as counter-revolutionary.

America has not broadly experienced internal opposition with a gun, except in limited cases like that of the Black Panthers; anarchists such as Timothy McVey of Colorado; and the Neo-Nazi gun-toting desperadoes. But the bulk of Egyptians see in the Brotherhood, a propagator of pan-Islamism, not and advocate of Egyptian nationalism.

The gulf between America and Egypt in regard to dealing with the Brotherhood is made more enduring because of the dearth of effective interpretation of Arabic into comprehensible American/English terms.

Under no circumstances should ideology be permitted to pose for analysis. There has never been, nor shall ever be, love between America and the Muslim Brotherhood. America is constitutionally wedded to separation between church and State. The Brotherhood sees the mosque and the Presidential Palace as interchangeable. Their motto includes the phrase: "The Quran is our Constitution" -a permanent denial of man-made legislation, which is counter to the essence of islamic jurisprudence. For one long dreary year, the Brotherhood, through Morsi, tried to put that deadender ideology into effect. But by July 3, the public in Egypt put an end to that strange Brotherhood venture.

The Most Important Priority for the New Egypt Is: "Building Egypt"

Friday, November 22, 2013

A great Egyptian educator, Lotfi El-Sayed Pasha, gave Egypt in the early 20th century a historic advice. He said: **"Raise Fences Around Egypt!!"** Because he was ahead of his time, that advice was discarded, especially by the military dictatorships from 1952 to 2011.

As if sleep-walking, Egypt plunged, at King Farouk's insistence in 1948, in a war for Palestine; lost the Sudan because of marginalization of the plebiscite of 1955 which united both countries; walked into the trap of union with chaotic Syria in 1958; and when the Baathists in Syria (the party of the Asad dynasty) destroyed that union, Nasser turned Egypt into a military ally of the Yemen republican revolution of 1962, thus alienating Saudi Arabia, and draining Egyptian resources. This charade, no parade, of events was capped by Nasser's support of Qaddafi of Libya in 1969.

From one interventionary debacle, to another interventionary debacle without heeding the great advice of **"Raise Fences Around Egypt!!"** That wisdom became concretized when smart Sadat sued for peace with Israel, signed a peace treaty with it in 1979 with US help. Of equal importance, Sadat began to dismantle the grandiose ideological and vain edifice of **"Egypt is the great sister of all Arab States."** Sadat was martyred basically for the principle of **"Egypt First."** His assassination at the hands of the so-called Islamists was due to the collision between the reality of Egypt's need for internal nation-building, and the fanciful need of the Islamists (the Muslim Brotherhood) for pan-Islamism.

Relegating the development needs of Egypt to a secondary place in terms of food production, industrialization, infra-structure advancement especially in regard to transportation and communication, descent reclamation, nuclear and solar energy, retraining of the huge workforce, reinventing the excellence of the educational system, advertising Egyptian tourism, luring back Egyptian and foreign experts to plan for Egypt of 2050, and women training -not doing much of that and more has put Egypt into a deep hole.

Egypt of today has lagged even behind the advances in Africa south of the Sahara. This most populous Arab country is today consumed by two retardant factors: **(a)** preoccupation with past glories; and **(b)** trying to solve today's problems with yesterday tools, especially in the challenging enterprise of reclamation of the Sahara, both the eastern and the western.

Decentralization has been a failure, because it does not effect devolution of decision-making from Cairo to the 27 provinces. There is a commitment to teach through lectures at the university level, instead of turning the colleges into training grounds in how to think. There is a predilection for pursuing Master's and doctoral degrees programs instead of deferring such lofty pursuits after investing into drafting graduates into public service at the village level.

Egypt's over preoccupation with the myriad of Arab problems is a poor investment into the future of Egypt. There is **"no place like home"** to begin the rejuvenation of Egypt. **"Charity starts at home,"** and planning for Egypt of 2050 is basically planning for Egypt to be the South Korea of 2013.

Today's Egypt is incapable of running safe railways; today's South Korea

313

is ready for outer space technology. The train-buses collision in Dahshour, south of Cairo on November 18, killing 27, and injuring 34, is the latest tragic chapter in the history of a railroad system of 5000 kilometers and 150 years of age. No upgrading, no proper maintenance. Only the cosmetics of firing transportation ministers and other personnel. But after the firings, the trains keep on running and colliding.

Here is but one example of the western culture of futuristic planning. In a mass circulation advertisement, **Bloomberg Business**s placed a placard in all trains of the Long Island Railroad (LIRR) whose record of being on time in eleven branches is 99.2%. The ad correctly predicts the end in a few years of the US dependency on foreign oil. It reads as follows:

"Oil fields of the future may be anchored directly to the sea floor, rather than drilling and exploring from venture floating platforms. Are you exploring new frontiers for your next future venture?"

There is also another facet of primordial importance for what I may call **"the reinvention of Egypt."** That is civic-mindedness. In essence, love of country should be manifested not merely in songs of **"I love Egypt,"** but also in serving the public beyond the call of duty.

In 1938, I sat to a written exam in Arabic composition at the end of my second year of primary education at a private school in Zagazig, Sharkia, Egypt. The question read as follows: **"What would you do for your country if you become a successful merchant?"** I wrote lots of stuff which I have learnt from highly-educated teachers at the tender age of being 10 years old.

Now in America as a teacher who keeps on learning, I learnt last week that 27 super-rich Americans, including Bill and Melinda Gates and Warren Buffet are donating half a trillion US dollars for investing in education, health and innovation. That is 500 Billion U.S. dollars including 99% of the total worth of Buffet, and 95% of the total worth of Gates. What an example in serving the public at large through private individuals!!

In the **New York Times** of November 14, 2013, **Kareem Fahim** and **Mayy El-Sheikh**, reported from Cairo that **"the public which harbors deep antipathy toward the Brotherhood...seems desperate to move on from the era of protest."** Without moving on beyond the achievement of Egypt's Second Revolution of June 30, Egypt shall be doomed to be frozen in the present victory of the secularists over the Islamists. By itself, that is not enough!!

The Brotherhood lost because of many factors, the most important of which is espousal of pan-Islamism and little or no commitment to Egyptian nationalism. They even burnt the Egyptian flag. **Next** in importance in the list of factors is the Brotherhood's lack of realization that Islam is not only a faith. It is also a civilization. **Thirdly:** the gossipy Egyptian media which live on entertaining anecdotes, non-substantiated assumptions, unrealistic conjectures, and name-calling. Journalism, which is popularly called everywhere **"the Fourth Authority"** (after the Legislature, the Executive and the Judiciary authorities), today wields neither authority nor credibility. It hardly plays any role in public education and civic awareness.

In fairness to the slow march of history in revolutionary Egypt, there are glimmers of hope enticing foreign investment to return to Egypt. The Ministry of Electricity and Energy has recently announced that the Russian energy company, **Russatom,** has offered Egypt the construction of the first nuclear energy station for the production of electricity. The Russian contractor would pay 85% of the cost, production would begin in 2020, Egypt would repay its debt 5 years beginning in 2025, and **Russatom** would involve other non-Russian companies in the project.

And from the west, General Electric of the US signed on November 18 a contract with **Carbon,** an Egyptian holding company in the amount of $500 million. The contract calls for the construction in Ain Al-Sukhnah (Red Sea area) of a petro-chemical consortium. Signed in Cairo, in the presence of **Mounir Fakhry Abdel-Noor**, Egypt's Minister for Trade and Industry, the petro-chemical complex, once in production, is expected to provide 3000 jobs and an annual return of $6 Billion. Funding will come from the Korean Import-Export Bank.

In addition, the tax system is being reformed in various ways including the imposition of a Value Added Tax (VAT). This is the difference between production cost and the sale price, and it replaces the sales tax which is difficult to account and collect.

Above all, a new Constitution is being readied for a plebiscite later this year, with parliamentary elections followed by presidential elections slated for 2014. And from various indicators, the Egyptian military does not evince an appetite for returning Egypt to military rule. Sixty years of that rule which occasioned the rise of the masses in Tahrir were enough.

What about the Nile water? It never ceases to surprise me that we seem to forget that there are two niles feeding the main Nile: The Blue Nile from Ethiopia, with which Egypt and the Sudan are trying to negotiate an amicable division of water intake, and the White Nile from the Great Lakes in Uganda which feeds the main Nile from August to March, but at a lower quantity and slower water flow.

Prior to the Sudan civil war between North and South, the Sudan (my first appointment in 1948 as a teacher was in **Jabal Awliya**, south of **Khartoum**), Egypt and France were actively removing the obstructions (**the Sudd**) from the White Nile in what is now South Sudan. The goal was to dramatically increase the water flow for the riparian States and even feed Saudi Arabia with fresh water pumped through a pipeline under the Red Sea. That great project called **"the Jonglei Canal"** has been halted by that tragic Sudanese civil war.

The three countries, South Sudan, Sudan and Egypt should go back to it. Like the ad in the LIRR says: **"Are you exploring new frontiers for your next future venture?"** If so, just look at your feet. Water wealth lies under them. Its longevity is greater and more durable and more environmental friendly than fossil wealth. The great deserts are cultivable, the human resources are plentiful, and Nile irrigation has been perfected for thousands of years.

So, Egypt, look to the future. The fences advocated by Lolfi El-Sayed Pasha did not mean isolation. He, in his wisdom as an educator, meant prioritization and well-targeted interaction with Egypt's neighbors. Mere ideology and sloganeering have never built bridges, schools, bakeries or hospitals. They built fantasies and acrimony. Egypt's next venture should have a workable motto: "Building Egypt!!" It is the most important priority for the New Egypt. It is the authentic jihad!!

Have I just mentioned Jihad? Yes!! Having done that, let me in conclusion turn to the question of Islamic jurisprudence in the context of **"Building Egypt."** Dealing with those two intertwined matters, Islamic Law and rebuilding the new Egypt, we need to revise certain terms in our dictionary. Using the question and answer method, I put the following terms under the microscope of realities.

Is it an act of jihad to assassinate 12 Egyptian soldiers in Sinai on Wednesday, November 20, 2013 by suicidal attackers as the victims were on their way to rest and recreation? No!! Jihad is self-internalization for the purpose of purification. Only in cases of external aggression against national territory does **jihad** turn to self-defense.

Can the perpetrators and their co-conspirators be called Muslims? No!! Islam is a faith which recognizes every kind of belief, especially Judaism and Christianity. The term means the submission by the individual to the will of the Creator.

If that is the case, then why, with the Muslim Brotherhood being implicated in acts of terror, is it entitled to be called "Muslim"? The Brotherhood has used the term **"Muslim"** as a **"burka"** (a veil) to legitimate its anti-Islamic acts. A real term for them is **"The Anti-Muslim Brotherhood."**

Isn't depicting them as Anti-Muslim an extreme measure? No. Their actions leave us no option but to call a spade a spade. They have made of Islam a State. **Islam is a community, not a State.** They have resorted to **TAKFIRISM** whereby they deny the faith and the existence of their opponents of all stripes whether, Muslims, Copts, Shiis, Hindus, Jews and many others. **They don't believe in the nation-State.** They believe in pan-Islamism, which limits its protective shield to Sunnis who espouse the crazy notion of paradise as the reward for **killing the innocent as happened in 9/11.**

Is Hamas in Gaza implicated in TAKFIRISM as an ideology which justifies terrorism? Absolutely. The **Anti-Muslim Brotherhood** is the womb from which Hamas was born. The proof of Hamas' idiocy is their denial that the Jews have any right over even one inch of Palestinian territory.

In view of these perceptions, ideologies and actions is Egypt's engagement in the destruction of the tunnels linking Gaza to Sinai justifiable? Of course. The Hamas Gaza tunnels represent an underground invasion of Egypt which grossly infringe upon Egyptian sovereignty in Sinai through smuggling terrorists, goods including fuel, drugs, and even items of luxury.

But what can the Gazans do when they are at present besieged by Israel from all sides? This is not Egypt's problem. It is a Palestinian problem which can be mitigated, if not resolved, by the following measures:

Hamas renunciation of terror; acceptance of the Palestinian National Authority in Ramallah as the legitimate representative of the Palestinian people; recognition of Israel's right to peaceful existence with a future sovereign State of Palestine; and ceasing to interfere in Egyptian internal affairs. *Hamas has the key to liberate Gaza from its present misery. But Hamas does not believe in reason. As an organization, it believes in the non-Islamic concept of endless conflict.*

Due to my travels in Egypt, please expect the next blog at the 2nd half of December.

30 DECEMBER 2013

Locked With the Land of the Nile in an Embrace of Reciprocal Learning

Thursday, December 19, 2013

In Egypt for 2 weeks this December, I learnt and shared my knowledge. I learnt why every Egyptian I met, in various walks of life, hated the Muslim Brotherhood. **"Liars,"** they described them; **"army-haters,"** they characterized them; **"Islam abusers,"** they lamented; **"foreign agents,"** they ridiculed them.

From the taxi driver to the university professor; from my niece, the economist, to the goat herder in our village in Sharkia; from the diplomat, to the seller of roasted corn on the cob on Kasr El-Nil bridge. Without any prompting, they see in the bearded person a menace; in the students demonstrations, the effects of brain-washing; in the killing of Egyptian soldiers and police personnel, a terrorist attack on the authentic Egyptian revolutions of January 25, 2011 and June 30, 2013.

There is the graffiti by the Muslim Brotherhood describing **"C.C."** (for the pronunciation of the name of General El-Sisi) as a **"murderer"** (Qatel). But the young and the old secularists add one letter to become

319

(Moqatel) **"a fighter."** The general public, which was my collective professor from the Delta to El-Minya, in southern Egypt, wants the General who delivered them from the Islamic grip on July 3, to run for President or to accept the premiership under an elected President. That potential president might be the same person who is now an interim President, Counsellor Adly Mansour. Those who can read English laugh at the reporting in the **New York Times** by its current correspondent, David Kirkpatrick as **"biased,"** and pro-Muslim Brotherhood.

Everyone I met, and I had no pre-arranged selected audiences, kept on asking me: **"Why does the USA support the Brotherhood?"** When I try a professorial response regarding the lop-sided interpretation in the U.S. of **"democracy in Egypt,"** my audience, while respectful, look baffled. Hearing of U.S. Congressional hearings held recently on **"human rights in Egypt,"** the average Egyptian sneers, saying:

"The U.S. has Guantanamo; a President who is daily hounded for being black; a public lurching to the right and equating between Islam and terror; and a Congressional gridlock which shut down the federal government for 16 days."

They do not hate Americans; they hate what they perceive as anti-Muslim bias and abuse of the Rule of Law in the pursuit of torture. This outlook causes them to be uncomprehending of the U.S. elevation of the Brotherhood to the level of a legitimate opposition.

The general scene in the Egyptian street which I carefully studied is one of support for the newly-amended constitution which shall be voted upon this January. The expected boycott by the Brotherhood of that plebiscite is a cause for public scorn. To the ouster of Morsi, their response is **"Maal Salamah,"** said by a hand wave of **"good riddance."** In spite of the Brotherhood's threats of disruptive violence, that constitution is expected to pass. On lamp-posts all over Egypt, the signs are hung declaring, **"Participate in constitutional-making by voting Yes,"** and **"A Yes for the constitution is a vote for the Revolutions of January 25 and June 30."** (There was a grammatical error. But so what? I was born to an Azhari father, thus a stickler for classic Arabic.)

Though trains are not running except for a few lines (the Central Station Square has the Statue of Ramses II gazing down on an empty square), all means of transport are in full swing.

Vegetables from lettuce to tomatoes, from onions to carrots, from squash to cabbage and a variety of fresh fruits, are on sale everywhere. A pound of deliciously-ripe tomatoes sell for the equivalent of ten U.S. cents. In New York City, it cost me $1.25 (125 cents).

In December 2012, my hotel in Cairo had only 20% occupancy; now it has 60% occupancy. U.S. tourists flew to Egypt by Egypt Air which I took in a direct flight from JFK to Cairo International Airport. At the Cairo International Airport, I experienced upon arrival and departure the swiftest clearance at both passport control and Customs. The country is hungry for tourism, and the Egyptian authorities are responding with alacrity.

Though university students, especially in Cairo, are still demonstrating for what they call **"The Return to legitimacy,"** I saw on two occasions near Cairo University that the numbers were few, and the spirit was less than enthusiastic. I was able to deliver my lecture on **"Egypt in Search of Allies,"** on December 9 at the University on time. Students of both genders, deans and other faculty participated enthusiastically and gave me the Faculty's shield, as a gift.

In total, I made four presentations. On December 4, at the Diplomatic Institute of the Foreign Ministry on the subject of **"politicization of the UN Security Council."** A day later, on December 5, I lectured at the magnificent British University in Egypt (BUE) on **"Behind Saudi Arabia's Refusal of UN Security Council Seat."** On December 9, my lecture on **"Egypt in Search of Allies"** was held on time and to a proactive audience at Cairo University's Faculty of Economics and Political Sciences. The students, both male and female, raised provocative questions about the need for Egypt to nation-build in Egypt as a priority. Finally, at the beautiful Province of El-Minya, which is nearly 250 miles south of Cairo, the focus was on **"The Rights of the Child."** Several senior Coptic priests were in attendance. The roads from Cairo to Aswan, both east and west of the Nile were built by the Egyptian army. The eastern branch resembles the autobahn in Germany. A clear demonstration of Cairo's attention to the development of southern Egypt.

Throughout these encounters, I witnessed the dedication of the young diplomatic attaches at the Diplomatic Institute; the spirit of public giving by **Mohamed Farid Khamis,** a philanthropist, in the mold of Warren Buffet and Bill and Melinda Gates. **Mr. Khamis** funded the establishment of the British University in Egypt (BUE) in the eastern desert as a not-for-profit institution of quality higher education. Later at Cairo University, where I continue to be adjunct professor of law, I witnessed the collaboration of the

Egyptian Council for Foreign Affairs (ECFA -an NGO) with the Faculty of Economics and Political Sciences in the co-sponsorship of my lecture on **Egypt in Search of Allies.** The lady dean, **Dr. Hala El-Said** was the moderator, and the best questions came from a student who was focused on the use by Egypt of **"soft power,"** and from **Ambassadors Mohamed Shaker, and El-Said Shalaby,** respectively ECFA's Chairman and Executive Director.

The finale of my stay in the land of the Nile was at the Province of El-Minya where several factors came together to make my visit memorable. These were: **Alaa Makady,** the dean of the Makady Clan; the well-established National Association for Human Rights (NAHR) of El-Minya; the pro-active provincial **Governor General Salah Ziadeh,** who regaled me with details of his visit to a girls high school in the town of Abu-Qirqass; Coptic priests who were eager to know more about the status of children under international law; and the faculty of El-Minya University.

As I was leaving the land of the Nile, I was introduced to the new operetta entitled: **"Blessed Be the Hands of the Army of Egypt"** (in Arabic: **"Teslam El-Ayadi"**) It is a salute to the armed forces for their support of the 35 million Egyptians who on June 30 rebelled against the Morsi Islamist one-year coup. When I asked for the words of **"Teslam El-Ayadi"** a 15 year old boy poured over my request and handed me his 9-page transcript. It was **Faisal Makady, Alaa Makady's** oldest of 3 boys. He gave enthusiastic priority to my request. It was his contribution to the rise of his secularist country. The Islamists have offensively countered by **"Cursed Be the Hands of the Army of Egypt."** Hating the armed forces is a cause of deep alienation of the Brotherhood from the majority of the populace.

How can the Brotherhood aspire to a return to power in Egypt given all the enmities they have engendered? Now I know from the Egyptian street that the Brotherhood has no future. The veneration of country, the army, Egypt and the Islam of diversity (the Islam of Al-Azhar) are deep seated. Just ask young kids like **Faisal Makady,** and you will get their non-varnished response of total distancing from the bearded hoards.

In this broad field investigation of the status of the Egyptian Sector of the Arab Spring, there is a lesson which I would like to share with my readers. The Muslim Brotherhood, having burned its bridges with the new Egypt, has the chance of a snow ball in hell to come back to power. Nor can they go forward politically as a partner in Egypt's transition to democracy. The American romantic idea of the Brotherhood's suffering a coup at the hands of Egypt's military is seen by the Egyptian street as both myopic and anti-Egyptian.

It is quite possible that secular Egypt might one day resort to the anti-terrorism convention of the League of Arab States (1998) to declare the banned Brotherhood as **"a terrorist organization."** In this, Cairo has the blood of its army and security personnel to prove it. The blood shed by the Brotherhood in mid-August, though very regrettable, was for all intents and purposes, a self-inflicted wound. For 6 weeks, the destructive sit-ins defied the pleas by the government to end peacefully that illegal occupation of public squares, weapons hoarding, and abuse of the freedom of expression.

Today at several Egyptian universities we witness the ineffectual noisy student demonstrations, in abject deviance of the newly - promulgated Egyptian law on public demonstrations. These exercises in futility shall not bring the Islamists back to power. The Brotherhood's game of victimization at the hands of both the State and the public at large, has been exposed as a ploy intended to draw in outside intervention.

That intervention shall not happen. This game is now over. The new Egypt has declared its independence from outside powers whether Arab or non-Arab. It has also cured Egypt from the myth of the Brotherhood as a democratizing vehicle. At this pivotal moment in the history and destiny of the Egyptian revolution, America should cease what is perceived as intervention in Egyptian internal affairs. Taunting Cairo by characterizing the June 30 Revolution as a coup shall only add to Cairo drifting further away from Washington. Russia is extending welcoming hands to Egypt, which is the engine that pulls behind it the entire Arab train. I visited Rebaa Square, which was the scene of the Brotherhood's armed uprising against secular Egypt. There I found it beautifully restored to its beauty through government rehabilitation.

For the new Egypt, through gradual reform policies, is rising again. The telling proof: Both the eastern and western deserts (nearly a million square kilometers) are being reclaimed for the young and restless. This is a massive renaissance which the U.S. and the rest of the world should welcome and support.

Once again, and in spite of the Islamists' disdain, the Crescent is embracing the Cross in the new Egypt. The national anthem **("Biladi, Biladi": My Country, My Country)** was played when the Constituent Committee of Fifty completed drafting the 247 Articles of the newly modified Constitution of 2013-2014.

Led by its chairman, the veteran diplomat turned politician, **Amr Musa,** they stood at attention, including a physically-handicapped member, repeating in unison **"Long Live Egypt"** (**Tahya Misr**).

By the way, that national anthem is disdained by the Muslim Brotherhood. When it is played, they remain seated gazing in the distance at a non-nationalist horizon of Pan-Islamism which is nothing more than a mirage.

When I was searching for the words of that anthem, another 15-year old Egyptian lad came to my rescue. **Aly** the son of one of my two nieces, quickly wrote the words down. As he gave me the text smilingly, he said derisively of the Brotherhood: *"They do not even salute our national anthem."*

No wonder that the new Egypt looks upon the Muslim Brotherhood as an alien group which, behind the cloak of Islam, is holding a dagger.

The Muslim Brotherhood Listed By The Egyptian Government As a Terrorist Organization

Friday, December 27, 2013

As Christmas Day was ringing to the world the famous traditional song **"Peace on Earth,"** the Egyptian Government was declaring **"The Muslim Brotherhood"** a terrorist organization. Never before has the Brotherhood been so categorized. During most of its 85 years of existence, it was banned. That was an elastic ban which was tightened or loosened depending on the Government's degree of anxiety as regards the Brotherhood's impact on politics and society. So **what has so radically changed precipitating such drastic listing?**

The tragedy of the Brotherhood in post-Mubarak Egypt began on April 1, 2012. On that date, that organization nominated its longtime strategist, Khairat El-Shater, to run for the post of President. It was a break by the

Brotherhood of its pledge not to have nominations for the highest post in Egypt.

Top US State Department officials had praised El-Shater's **"moderation, business savvy and effectiveness."** Yet in fact he was a protagonist for an explicitly Islamic government. Divisive by nature, he stood in opposition of **"the liberal wing"** of the Brotherhood. Abdel-Moneim Aboul Fotouh, Kamal El-Helbawy and Abdel-Rahman Ayyash were prominent liberal who became casualties of bulldozer El-Shater.

Elevating El-Shater to a demi-god, Badie, the Brotherhood's Supreme Guide, who is now with El-Shater in jail since July 2013, said darkly at that time: **"To all those who will slander engineer Khairat El-Shater, his prayers against those who slander him are answered."** Within a few days, demi-god El-Shater was, under Egyptian citizenship laws regarding presidential candidates, disqualified. Morsi was El-Shater replacement on the ballot for president in the summer of 2012. Morsi won the post over his military opponent, General Shafik, and thus began a year of Islamist rule in Egypt.

From the pinnacle of power in the most populous Arab country of nearly 90 millions, to the abyss of populist impeachment on June 30, 2013, the Brotherhood's journey was a series of self inflicted wounds. That self immolation, though expressed in a series of putchist moves against secularist Egypt, stemmed primarily from the Brotherhood's abuse of Islamic tenets for sordid ends of power.

In a seminal article by **Imad Al-Ghazali** in the Cairo daily **Al-Shorook,** published on December 19, 2013, this analyst lamented the continued Brotherhood attacks by word and terrorist actions against Egypt's armed forces. Quoting partially from that article which was published 6 days before the Mansoura massacre of police and civilians by Islamist Brotherhood affiliates, Al-Ghazali said: **"This is the army that sided with the Egyptian revolution of January 25. It is the army which supported the millions who rose up on June 30 refusing the rule by Morsi and the Brotherhood. It is the army which loses in Sinai every day its personnel gunned down by the bullets of treachery and terror."**

In a legal assessment of the listing by the Egyptian Government on December 25, 2013, of the Muslim Brotherhood as a terrorist organization, I posit the following in a nutshell fashion:

The declaration of "The Muslim Brotherhood" as a terrorist organization is legally sound. It is anchored in the presidential decrees of 1996, as well as in the conventions on terrorism adopted by the League of Arab States (1998) and the Organization of the Islamic Cooperation {successor of "Conference"} (1999). The perpetration of the massacre of the police personnel and civilians at Mansoura two days ago, and its adoption by Islamist units federated with the Brotherhood, fall within the parameters adopted by the UN General Assembly in the early 2000s on terrorism. The Brotherhood, having, since July 3, 2013, embarked upon a campaign of non-recognition of all actions by the transitional Government, of fomenting challenges to the law on public demonstrations, of open support of the Sinai rebellion, of generating campaigns domestically and internationally against sectarian amity, and of open collaboration with Hamas, are actions justifying defining that organization internally and externally as a terrorist organization.

Note should be taken of **Article 237** of the draft of the Egyptian Constitution which shall be the subject of plebiscite on January 14, and 15, 2014. In part, the article provides that: **"The State is committed to fight terrorism in all its forms --as a threat to the homeland and its citizens."** (my translation from the Arabic)

In addition, **Article 74,** among other things, denies the establishment of any political parties on religious basis. This accords with the document issued by **Al-Azhar,** and co-signed by the **Coptic Church** on August 11, 2011 stating that: **"Islam does not create a State based solely on religion."**

It was on December 19, 2013 that the so-called **"National Coalition For the Support of Democracy and the Opposition of the Coup"** (in reference to the present transitional government), called for public demonstrations to abort the constitutional plebiscite. That declaration called on **"The revolutionary citizens to rise up in defense of their revolution, to ignite an uprising in all public squares, and to mobilize by the millions on this Friday (Dec. 20). This shall usher a new revolutionary week under the banner proclaiming** *"The 2012 Constitution is Ours."*

Well, these millions did not respond to the Brotherhood's call. While in Cairo in early December, I heard nothing but support for the 2014 Constitution. And the dreams of the Brotherhood of establishing **"The**

Islamic Emirate of Egypt" proved to be an unreachable goal. The characterization on December 2013 by religious frauds like **Sheikh Al-Qaradawi** of the constitutional plebiscite as **"a worthless undertaking,"** caused millions to laugh at his lunacy.

The Muslim Brotherhood's advocacy of a religious uprising against a deeply-rooted secular Egypt has proven the barrenness of, and in fact, the stupidity of its manifesto. Treating stupidity charitably is to quote from a saying by Pope John Paul II who proclaimed: **"Even stupidity is a gift from God."**

Charitable interpretation of **"stupidity"** aside, Egypt is already moving in a post-Muslim Brotherhood mode. This is in spite of the Brotherhood's resort to attacking soft civilian targets. The Egyptian grade school texts have been revised to emphasize love of the homeland; the private sector, especially with regard to tourism and trade, is being energized; and the preservation of ancient Egyptian, Christian, Jewish and Islamic antiquities and edifices is once more becoming a national passion.

With a wary eye on the abuse in mosques of the Friday sermons by unqualified Muslim preachers, the Ministry of Waqfs (Entails and Trusts) has as of early December 2013, reasserted control over the pulpits. The campaign of restoration of Islam to its traditional advocacy of tolerance and moderation, is in vogue. **Waqf Minister Muhammad Mokhtar Gomaa** ascended the pulpit at Al-Azhar mosque on December 6, 2013. His message was an official declaration of the start of purification of the pulpits in Egyptian mosques of the venom of fanaticism.

No less than 527 non-qualified and non -Azharite religious pulpit-mongers were forbidden from delivering Friday sermons. The Minister of Waqfs also called for the dissolution of the Egyptian branch of the Union of Islamic Scholars. This prompted Sheikh Al-Qaradawi to resign from the union's membership. *His pet sermons called on the Egyptian army to mutiny against its commanders. That call for insurrection went nowhere eve prior to declaring the Brotherhood, whose spiritual leader is Al-Qaradawi himself, a terrorist cabal.*

Oh, and one more thing **Sheikh Qaradawi:** Your accumulated wealth as a Qatari citizen is no passport to your ill-conceived fatwas, especially regarding the Shiis being non-Muslims. Your dialogue with the Iranian reformist, former President Hashem Rafsanjani, was nothing but a dark episode in the recent history of Sunni-Shii dialogues.

Here is an adage for you, **Sheikh Qaradawi.** It applies to your urging mutiny upon Egyptian armed forces recruits. *The source of this adage is the late great novelist, Tom Clancy who said: "If you want to kick the tiger in his a.., you'd better have a plan for dealing with his teeth."*

31 JANUARY 2014

Regarding the New Egypt, The New York Times, Like Other US Media, Gets It Wrong Most of the Time!!

Friday, January 3, 2014

Happy 2014 to our Readers. Apologize for starting the New Year negatively about US media reporting on Egypt's transition to democracy.

The respectable **CBS** program **"60 Minutes"** of Sunday evenings led off last week with **Reporter Leslie Stahl's**interview with Obama's National Security Adviser. Stahl described events in Egypt after June 30 as **"a fiasco."** Fiasco, or-ignominious results, for whom? Certainly not for the 35 million Egyptians who rose up that day and brought the brutalizing Islamist regime of Morsi down. The **New York Public Radio (NYPR),** which draws its credibility largely from it being funded by its public, features its Cairo correspondent on December 22, 2013 at 9:00 AM. The correspondent decries what she perceives to be the collapse of the Revolution of January 25, 2011. Why? She sees in the Egyptian public urging of General El-Sisi to run for President a hypothetical link to declaring the **Muslim Brotherhood "a terrorist organization."**

But the Cairo correspondents of the New York Times take the cake in their spinning off the impact of events in transitional Egypt into systematic negativity. They are **David Kirkpatrick, Kareem Fahim and Mayy El-Sheikh.** Content analysis over only a 4-day period from December 26 to December 30, 2013 vouches for the accuracy of my criticism.

All references to the present transitional presidency of Counsellor Adly Mansour are prefaced by the term **"military-backed."**

Objection: The army did not force 35 million Egyptians to go out screaming at Morsi on June 30 to leave the Presidential Palace. It stood guard on the multitude, as they stood guard on the Islamic march of the Brotherhood through Morsi's move to that palace in June 2012.

Since July 3, which signaled the end of Islamic colonialism of secular Egypt, the pet terms of these correspondents, one at a time, have been **"a society already riven by violence and suspicion in the months since the military."**

Objection: You must be kidding me!! You mean to characterize the reign of Morsi and the Brotherhood as one which was free of violence and suspicion? Have you heard of the so-called **"peaceful sit-ins"** at Rabaa, Nahdha and Orman which were battle zones and trench warfare? You must have heard of the Sinai war against the Egyptian army and police, fueled by out-of-control Hamas and their jihadist cohorts!!

Did you consider Morsi's incessant verbal attacks on the judiciary, Al-Azhar, the Coptic Church and Shiism? Surely you must have known of the appointment by Morsi of 13 Provincial Governors (Egypt has 27 provinces) who were **Ikhwanis** (adherents of the **Brotherhood**)!! How about the avalanche of amnesties granted by **Morsi** to persons already adjudged as terrorists?

Your unfounded claims that the Brotherhood is **"deeply rooted in Egyptian social and civic life."**

Objection: Prove it!! Is the mere existence of the Brotherhood for nearly 8 decades a qualification of **"deep rootedness?"** The **Brotherhood** itself has no statistics on its numerical strength. There is hardly any social science surveys in Egypt. That is not to mention the **Brotherhood's** commitment to secrecy in all matters, including its sources of funding. And is it permissible for a group like the **Brotherhood** to be given a green light to use Islam as a cover for a power grab as a reward for its assistance to the poor? The Egyptian **Ministry of Waqfs** (Charitable Trusts) has been, for the entire history of modern Egypt, the purveyor of goods and services for the needy in Egypt and beyond.

Your attack on the Egyptian Government, following its listing of the Brotherhood as a **"terrorist organization,"** for **"seeking to deny the group foreign help or shelter,"** and for **"urging other Arab governments to honor an anti terrorism agreement and shun the organization."**

Objection: How imbecile can you get? The international conventions against terrorism adopted by the **League of Arab States** and the **organization of Islamic Cooperation** call for such collective action. Actions in that regard by the Egyptian Government fall within the international law doctrine called **"Acts of State."** The doctrine confines itself to acting internally within its sovereign domain, while advising other governments of such actions for their own consideration. Unlike the **Bush** administration, Cairo has never tried to impose on the outside world the imperial doctrine of **"You are either with us or with the terrorists."**

Your assertion that **"State forces have killed hundreds of the group supporters during protests against Mr. Morsi's removal."**

Objection: How one-sided can you get? This is a typical half-truth!! All human casualties, be they pro-Morsi or anti-Morsi supporters, are to be regretted. But you, through your biased reporting, deal with the consequences and ignore the root causes. For six very long weeks (from July 3 to August 14, 2013), the Government appealed to the marauding hordes at Rabaa and elsewhere to disband peacefully. But their commitment to victimhood as a means of internationalizing a purely internal Egyptian matter prevailed.

Those encampments had quickly turned into armed garrisons, with pre-arranged armament storage. Declaring them peaceful sit-ins defies imagination. They besieged the HQ of the Presidential Guards (a military outpost) and conducted massive security and civil disruptions in their bivouacs. It finally came down to this: either the integrity of the State or the chaos perpetrated by the **Brotherhood**. Many army and police officers, not to mention peaceful civilians, were gunned down. In your casualties count, have you included those also? Or is your definition of casualties confined only to the **Muslim Brotherhood** whose affiliate **Hamas** has been listed by the US as a terrorist organization?

By December 25, Mr. Kareem Fahim, one of the three New York Times musketeers based in Cairo, has made yet another false discovery within the ranks of the Egyptian administration. His report was headlined **"Crackdown on Islamists stirs unrest across Egypt."** Then came his statistical attempt to explain **"unrest across Egypt."** These are his words **"At least three people were killed in Cairo, Damietta and Minya on Friday as officers fired tear gas and birdshot at protesters who threw rocks, burned tires and set fire to police vehicles."**

Objection: Need I say more, except that violating the newly-promulgated law regulating demonstrations needs to be upheld by the Government. That is a government which is faced with threats by the **Brotherhood** in its futile attempt to disrupt the mid-January plebiscite on the new Constitution.

Spinmeisters, **Fahim and El-Sheikh** were at it again. For their slanted report dated December 30, **The New York Times**, headlined: **"Egypt Detains Journalists It Says Aired False News."** That is in spite of the fact that those two New York Times reporters engaged in the same unethical support. The peg on which **Fahim and El-Sheikh** hung their poisonous New Year gift was the announcement by interim **President Adly Mansour** that Egypt could hold a presidential election before electing a new Parliament.

Now comes the reporters' main spin: They raised **"the possibility that the military-backed government was preparing to deviate from the transition plan it unveiled after the ouster of the former president - Mohamed Morsi, a Brotherhood leader -in early July. The government has said it would follow that plan, citing it as evidence of its commitment to democracy."**

Then more spin: **"Analysts have said that switching the order of the elections could allow Egypt's leaders to maintain tighter control over their outcome, by allowing the newly elected president to influence the makeup of Parliament."**

Objection: (1) Who are your **"analysts,"** and what kind of strong weed are they smoking? (2) You cite **Michael Wahid Hanna** **"**a fellow at the **Century Foundation in New York.** Having followed his **"analyses"** over a long time, your conclusions, Mr. Hanna have proved to be **"fiction confirmers."** You, supporters, have gone to him repeatedly to vouch for the authenticity of your fictions; **(3)** The announcement by **Counsellor Mansour** has no conspiracy behind it. It has behind it the provisions of the newly-drafted Constitution which left the sequencing of the elections to the President; **(4)** That Constitution shall replace the Islamic Constitution of 2012 which was heavily manipulated by your darlings -the **Muslim Brotherhood.**

Egypt keeps its nose largely in its own business. I don't see its officials offering unwanted advice to American policy-makers regarding America's pitfalls in the practice of democracy. No Egyptian attacks on State measures to make it harder for Blacks and Latinos to vote. No Egyptian formal declarations addressed to America about Republican defiance of science or the stigmatization of aliens. No Egyptian Minister of Foreign Affairs has ever issued condemnations of the rise of racism or of State legislation against the use of Islamic law in the courts of 18 States. No Egyptian human rights group has ever attacked the Republicans in Pennsylvania, thanks to gerrymandering, winning only 47 percent of the votes but walking away with 72 percent of the seats.

Nor have the Egyptian sneered at the Republican Party shutting down the federal government for 16 days last year. So why doesn't America mind its own business and stay away from being the Big Brother who is voluble with uninvited course corrections?

Yet America, as policy-makers, media outlets, or even civic groups based in Egypt and allied with either the democrats or the republicans find it fair game to attack the course of Egyptian transitioning to democracy. Describing the situation in Egypt as **"a mess"** has become daily media-speak.

I found not one official world coming out of Cairo in condemnation of the US policy of detention, fully expounded in 2013 in the 560 page report issued by the**Constitution Project's Task Force** covering Guantanamo, rendition, black sites and the efficacy of torture and brutal interrogations. No Egyptian official voice was raised calling on Washington, D.C. to go easy on its citizens and allies by reigning in its **National Security Agency's** global infringement of privacy through mass surveillance.

As a lawyer and academic belonging, through nationality, to both the U.S. and Egypt, and loyal to whatever is good in either culture, I find in the negative characterization of the teething pains of the present Egyptian transition to democracy, the fowl air of cultural and political arrogance. And by the way, I get no financial benefit from any government. I am self-employed and not a mouth-piece for any government.

Your biased reporting does not help the US maintain workable relationships with the new Egypt. More importantly, your drum beat of misstatements shall not stop the new Egypt from seeking broader alliances away from the U.S. As of January 25, the period of Egypt being a client State has ended.

The rational of the basic doctrine of freedom of expression embodied in the First Amendment of the U.S. Constitution does not protect a person in falsely shouting fire in a theater and causing panic. Its object is a citizenry of intelligent decision-makers seeking and empowered to govern a free society. (see Barron and Dienes, **Constitutional Law in a Nutshell**).

If you were capable of putting matters in Egypt in their global perspective, how would you rate the security in Egypt in comparison with the internal security in Putin's Russia (the Volgograd explosions) or the rebellions in China?

In order to be a credible spokesman or a reliable reporter, you must stick to professional ethics, and take to heart this advice from **Sherlock Homes.** Nearly 130 years ago, he said: **"Do not theorize before you have the facts!!"** He truly was the purveyor of deductive reasoning which is based upon using the evidence to reach reasonable conclusions.

The New York Times reporters based in Cairo, David Kirkpatrick, Kareem Fahim and Mayy El-Sheikh keep on crowing doom and gloom. *Just try for even once to describe the Egyptian Government as "people-backed." In this connection, an Arab proverb is on point: "The caravan moves forward, as the dogs keep on barking."*

If You Expect the Egyptian Press to Be An Educational Vehicle, You Shall Be Disappointed

Friday, January 17, 2014

The opinion-makers in most of the Egyptian press have opinions. But they lack the ability in how to make them. Their topics are important to the Egyptians and other readers. However their writings do not have the backing of evidence, objective analysis, or measured quotations from statistics and expert opinion. Their launches are promising, but the launched essay, if you call it that, quickly disintegrate into guess-work, non-supported expectations, and reliance on either personal attacks or praise. That press seems to function on the premise that words have the capacity to prove the truth of their own assertions.

Examples abound.

In **"Al-Massrioun"** newspaper, with its Islamist orientation, we read a non-substantiated attack by its Chief Editor, **Gamal Sultan,** on the transitional Government whose Prime Minister is the economist **Hazem Al-Biblawi.** The topic is of national importance as it deals with the development of the Suez Canal Zone. The Prime Minister had gone to that strategic zone to launch a national scheme.

But **Gamal Sultan** objects. His reasoning is that: **"How can a transitional Government have the audacity of launching such a vital project which shall impact the country's economy at least till the year 2040?"** He takes the term of **"transitional Government"** as an inert mechanism sitting in a parking lot without the right to take actions promoting the country's economy or security. That Editor-in-Chief does not realize that the term **"transitional"** is applicable to a government which has come to power pending the adoption of constituent instruments (e.g. the Constitution) which bestow durability.

In **Al-Ahram** newspaper, the official mouthpiece of the Government, **Makram Muhammad Ahmed,** a veteran writer in that newspaper, writes about the Nile water issue between Egypt, the Sudan and Ethiopia.

Negotiations with Ethiopia regarding the construction of the Ethiopian dam called **"Al-Nahda"** have run into difficulties. Egypt, afraid of the dam's effect on its intake from the Nile waters, is standing by its water quota determined in a 1929 treaty. This is although that treaty was concluded prior to Ethiopian exercise of its independence and its developmental needs for a bigger share of those life-giving waters.

Makram Muhammad Ahmed looks upon the present failure of those negotiations as a casus belli (reason for war between Egypt and Ethiopia). Acting as a mind reader, he justifies such radical measures for which Egypt is unprepared, on: **"Ethiopia's prevarication has now reached its ultimate limit. This should force Egypt to be ready for other alternatives to protect its national interests."**

In the same daily of **Al-Ahram,** another opinion-maker by the name of **Morsi Attallah** creates an out of sight reason for the popularity of**General El-Sisi** whose popularity does not need Attallah non-reasoning. The writer attributes **El-Sisi's** high standing in the minds of millions of Egyptians to the problems faced by Turkey's Prime Minister, Ordoghan. But every myth needs a few grains of sand of facts to build something on their shaky base.

It is true that **Ordoghan** has interfered in Egypt's internal affairs by siding with the **Muslim Brotherhood** when it was kicked out of its power perch on July 3. But coincidentally he was also facing a sharp downturn in his popularity on the Turkish street. But there is absolutely no cause and effect between what is happening on the Turkish street and the events on the Egyptian street. The bridge which **Attallah** builds between Ankara and Cairo is constructed from the writer's own mental girders.

Two quotations from his pipe-dream would suffice: **(1) "The book of instructions used by the Turkish party of "Justice and Development" is the same book which instructs the Muslim Brotherhood's party of "Freedom and Justice." (2) "In Egypt, the public adores Field Marshal El-Sisi while in Turkey, the anti-Ordoghan demonstrations raise the pictures of El-Sisi aloft."** I hope that **Attallah** realizes that Cairo, after July 3, in reprisal against **Ordoghan's** interventionism recalled its Ambassador from Ankara. And **El-Sisi** has enough ascertainable popularity that I doubt it than he needs **Attallah's**imaginary boost.

On the issue of the Government's response to the **Muslim Brotherhood's** declaration of resistance to the law regulating public demonstrations:

An Islamist leader and writer in the newspaper **"Al-Watan,"** by the name of **Dr. Nageh Ibrahim** declares the following: **"The Government has manifested total incomprehension of politics, wisdom, and aforethought...The conflict with the Brotherhood began as a small matter, but became bigger. That conflict could have been avoided had the disbanding of the sit-in at Rabaa been done with more sagacity and professionalism."**

How detached from reality could **Dr. Nageh Ibrahim** get? And how much obfuscation of the realities of August 14, 2013 on which the army and the police broke up that sit-in? For six weeks, from July 3 to August 14, the authorities have pleaded with those Islamist insurrectionists to leave peacefully.

Evidence shows that that sit-in, like others of its type, has turned in trench warfare in the heart of the Egyptian capital. Arms were smuggled; snipers were posted; declarations of support for terrorism in Sinai were made; and acts of torture were committed. The road to democracy should be safeguarded by stability, participation in the political process, and respect for the Rule of Law. This is the broad framework by which the term **"legitimate opposition"** can be defined. Lawlessness does not confer on its practitioner the badge of honorable opposition.

On the U.S. role in the unseating of former President Morsi: A writer in the newspaper **"Al-Shaab,"** by the name of **Magdi Qarqar** of the **"Labor"** party, asserts that: **"The military coup of July 3 was supported by the CIA. We all know that and we know who is in daily contact with the U.S. administration and its intelligence institutions."** Incredible!!

The writer seems to be more busy reflecting his pure fantasies through writing than having the capacity to simply read, in order to get a hold on well-known facts. **Mr. Qarqar** (the name is also the sound of inhaling on a water pipe or shisha) must know that: **(a)** the U.S. imposed some sanctions on Egypt following the ouster of Morsi; **(b)** the millions who rose up on June 30 demanding an end to the **Brotherhood's** hijacking of the Revolution of January 25 attributed those U.S. sanctions to an American tilt towards the **Brotherhood;** and **(c) Secretary of State Kerry** visited Egypt after July 3 on his way to Saudi Arabia to advocate a **"go easy"** policy on the Muslim Brotherhood.

On admission that no-evidence exists to back up the assertions of another editorialist.

In the newspaper **"Al-Shorooq"** we finally discover that the maximum of the level of honesty in reporting exists only in the admission of **"although I have no evidence."** That writer is **Mahmoud Al-Kardousi** who claims that **"the activists who ignited the January 25 Revolution are "an essential factor in all the scenes of chaos and**

destruction which followed." He backs this up by declaring: **"Of course I have no evidence!!"** Well!! If you have no evidence. Why don't you just shut up?

It is truly amazing that in the midst of the Brotherhood's acts of defiance of the presidency of **Adly Mansour,** there exists no elucidation in the Egyptian Press of what constitutes recognition of governments. Those who are for it, praise it in general terms, and those who are opposed to it denounce it also in general terms. Not one iota of public enlightenment for any cause, through the use of credible information, logic, analysis, examples or history. Nearly everything is **blah blah blah.**

As a concrete example, there is no word on the general parameters for recognition of governments. There is no education on the concepts of control, acceptance by the general public, or on the ability of the government to comply with international agreements and standards. **This is the tripod of the 3 Cs (control, consent and conduct). Sad!!**

What is the moral of all the above? It is that a good part of the Egyptian press has nothing to contribute to public enlightenment. Absolutely nothing!!

Searching For a New Adversary, The U.S. Seems to Declare Cold War on the New Egypt

Friday, January 24, 2014

Why doesn't Secretary Kerry take care of the U.S. business and let the New Egypt mind its own business? Where are the fault lines in official U.S. foreign policy toward post-constitutional referendum Egypt? And whose interest would waging this Cold war on the most populous Arab country serve?

This is not rhetoric!! This is a reality which can be defined by a succinct presentation of the primary elements of this futile interventionism in the internal affairs of Egypt.

Element One: Attacking the legitimacy of the Egyptian vote earlier this month approving the post-Morsi Constitution of 2014. The U.S. claims that that referendum was **"unfair"** as it was **"one-sided."** **Rebuttal:** The Muslim Brotherhood had taken itself out of the political process by declaring a boycott of that referendum and by waging a campaign intended to disrupt it.

Element Two: Approval of the Constitution of the post-Islamist regime was declared by the **Supreme Elections Committee** to be 98.1% of the vote. Yet Secretary Kerry expresses **"the concerns of international monitors."**

Rebuttal: The plebiscite wasconducted under the scrutiny of the Egyptian judiciary. Egypt's judges are likely to be more trustworthy than **"international monitors"** because they are an integral part of the structure of every polling station, speak Arabic, and are sworn to neutrality. Those monitors may be credible if they publicize specific concerns, document them, and assert fraud in the vote through credible findings.

Element Three: Secretary Kerry bemoans what he described as Egypt's**"polarized political environment."**

Rebuttal: True, but: How can that environment be but **"polarized"** when you have the Muslim Brotherhood in open rebellion against the second Egyptian Revolution of June 30, 2013? Elections in countries in transition to democracy produce polarization which by its mere existence does not deprive the electoral process of its legitimacy. The production of winners and losers does not lead to a conclusion of electoral malfeasance.

Element Four: Official U.S. utterances claim **"the absence of an inclusive drafting process or public debate before the vote."** **Rebuttal:** During the formation of the Egyptian transitional government, the interim president, Adly Mansour, the Prime Minister, Dr. Hazem Al-Beblawi, Field Marshal El-Sisi, and Foreign Minister Nabil Fahmi pleaded with the**Brotherhood** to join the political process produced by the Egyptian masses of June 30. They utterly refused. It was a repeat performance of the**Brotherhood's** recusal from participation in the drafting of the Constitution. No government on earth can force an opposition group to enter the political arena. The adamancy of the **Brotherhood** to stay out of the political game was due to their mistaken belief that the majority of Egyptians would heed their obstructionist call for sabotaging the Constitutional referendum. They failed miserably.

Element Five: The U.S. claims that **"the near unanimity of the vote was plausible because the government thoroughly suppressed any**

opposition to the new charter.

Rebuttal: The urban guerrilla warfare pursued by the Brotherhood through its prolonged sit-ins lasting for six weeks (July 3 to August 14, 2013), its waging of terrorism including attempting to assassinate Egypt's Minister of Interior, and its solidarity with Hamas in warring on Sinai, left no option for the established order to declare it as a terrorist organization. The suppression of terrorism on Egyptian soil is a sovereign right of survival of the State. The State's life support system depends on sectarian harmony, the State's secularity, and the re-establishment of law and order.

Element Six: The U.S., since July 3, 2013, has placed Egypt under economic sanctions because of the removal of Morsi as **"the first democratically elected president"** of Egypt

Rebuttal: It is short-sighted for the U.S. to politicize some of the terms of the Egyptian-Israel Peace Treaty of 1979 whose protocols provide for $1.3 billion as assistance to Egypt. Picking selectively at that Treaty is destructive as it sends a message that Egyptian sovereignty was a matter for bargaining at a time when Cairo has begun to assert its independence from U.S. foreign policy objectives in the Middle East.

Being of dual nationalities (Egyptian and U.S.), and beholden only and freely to the common interest of both countries, the main question which arises in my mind is: **What does the U.S. gain by this intrusion? Nothing, except that:**

It shall not change the facts on the Egyptian ground;

It shall evoke in secular Egypt revulsion at Washington and a stronger desire to look east for alliances and friends -a good move for Egyptian reborn nationalism, but with possible negative consequences for cooperation in matters of peace in the Middle East;

It shall embolden the **Muslim Brotherhood** to keep on defying secular Egypt, thus using such self-inflicted victimization as a means for internationalizing its hopeless cause;

It shall cause the Coptic community to wonder why whether the U.S. is standing by minority rights or by the fiction of looking upon **the Brotherhood as bona fide opposition;**

It shall fragment, and perhaps destroy any future chances for Cairo's cooperation in the broader war on terror in Gaza, Syria, Lebanon and Iraq;

It shall weaken the cooperative relationships between the U.S. and the Egyptian military; and

It would move Egypt toward more neutrality in the spreading Sunni-Shii conflict east of Suez.

Returning to my pet subject of definitions, my wonderment bifurcates into two issues:

The role of the so-called human rights organizations in Egypt, and

The legitimacy of General El-Sisi's possible quest for running for president.

On the issue of human rights organizations, I am critical of their wooden, non-changing, and inflexible reliance on the definition of democracy as measured by non-Egyptian standards. As regards the U.S., the democratic model is so infested with the power of special interests. There exists a tragic tilt toward what President Wilson warned against - **Congressional Government**.

In its present transitional phase, and in view of the lack of any universally-agreed definition of the term **"democracy,"** I find it comforting that 40% of the Egyptian electorate has voted for a post-Islamic Constitution. That is double the figure of 20% who, including me, voted for Morsi in the mistaken belief that he and the **Brotherhood** are antidote to the return to military rule.

Danielle Pletka's article of January 14 entitled **"The End of Egypt's Democratic Experiment"** is based on sheer conjecture. **Pletka's** writing does not provide evidence of a breach by a supposedly military rule in Egypt. That is even before **El-Sisi** throws his military cap in the ring of presidential elections.

If **Field Marshal El-Sisi** does run for president, what might be the basis for the legitimacy of that move?

Under the Constitution of 2014, every qualified Egyptian citizen has the privilege of running for the highest post in the land;

The final choice of the winner belongs to the Egyptian electorate of 53 millions. It does not belong to army tanks besieging the presidential palace and the means of mass communication;

A choice of **El-Sisi** as president does not qualify his rule as **"military,"** only because he had a military career;

When Morsi came to be president of Egypt (June 2012-July 2013), his opponent was **General Shafik** who was also a member of the defunct Mubarak government. At that time, even the **Brotherhood** did not raise any objection to the supposed danger of the return to military rule had Shafik not missed that post by only 1%;

Both the Islamist Constitution of 2012 and the Secular Constitution of 2014 provide for the right of members of the armed forces to vote and participate in national elections;

At the present period of the Brotherhood's rebellion posing the threat of civil war, Egypt needs a strong hand at the helm. **Witness the multiple explosions in Cairo on the eve of the 3rd anniversary of the January 25 Revolution; and**

El-Sisi gained his popularity not because he was only a military person, but because the armed forces of Egypt have protected the sovereign right of the people to bring down autocratic governments (Mubarak's in February 2011, and Morsi's in July 2013).

In conclusion, **Secretary Kerry** should first and foremost care for the myriad of problems forcing the U.S. in the world. Let the Egyptians mind their own transition to whatever follows after the coming presidential elections. **Today, Al-Qaeda is in Sinai, Beirut, Damascus, Baghdad and Gaza,** to cite a few locations. Under these exceptional circumstances, there is a clearly perceived need for ceasing political fire in the new cold war against the New Egypt. Though Egypt is regarded by Obama as **"a non-ally,"** it is nonetheless a **sovereign entity which is trying to reclaim its full independence from outside powers.**

In regard to the New Egypt, the U.S. should not be behind the curve of history. Secretary Kerry, together with U.S. and other human rights organizations, should not listen but to the voice of the Egyptian majority. Good communication begins with good listening. Or to quote from the Chinese, whose economy has now forged ahead of the U.S. economy to become No. 1 in the world, their adage is "One learns not from the mouth, but from the ears!!"

What a puzzling anomaly for a country like the U.S. whose Constitution separates between Church and State to appear or to act as supportive of the Muslim Brotherhood which proclaims no such separation? In the process, the Brotherhood is at present looking for a civil war conflagration in Egypt using the deceptive veil of a persecuted opposition.

I Had a Dream - A Long Conversation With Morsi!!

Friday, January 31, 2014

On the third anniversary of the Egyptian Revolution of January 25, 2011, 49 Egyptians died, 247 were injured, 1079 were detained, and a military helicopter was shot down over Sinai by a missile killing 5 armed forces personnel. The celebrations turned bloody as supporters of the Government and those of the defunct Morsi regime clashed. The series of terror killings began with 4 explosions aimed at the police in Cairo. The **"Friends of Jerusalem" (Ansar Beit Al-Maqdis)** claimed responsibility. Morsi's trial has now resumed with 4 charges listed on his arraignment.

Let us frame the conflict between the **Adly Mansour** Government and the Islamists of the **Brotherhood** and its affiliates like **Ansar Beit Al-Maqdis** in an imaginary Question and Answer period. The session shall be with **Morsi** himself. Let us imagine that he had agreed to see me before he was flown to a sound proof defendant's cage to appear in his resumed trial in Cairo.

Einstein had said: **"Imagination is Better Than Intelligence."** I started my professional career in Cairo at the age of 19 as a novelist based on imagination. The title of my novel is **"An Impostor in the Village."** It was first published in 1948, and has now been republished by **Aalam Al-Kotab (The World of Books)** in Cairo. Its theme is **the manipulation of faith for sordid power ends.** Even after 66 years of its publication, it applies to the present deadly conflict between the Islamists and the

Secularists.

Morsi is here imagined to have granted me this rare interview with the approval of the authorities for several reasons. He and I hail from the same Egyptian Province of **Sharkia (the Oriental);** both of us have lectured at the**University of Zargazig,** the capital of the province; both of us are interested in letting his views known to the world. With this in mind, I, in my dream, entered his cell before he was flown to Cairo for his resumed trial.

El-Ayouty (E): Al-Salam Alaikon Mr. Morsi. Thanks for granting me the privilege of this conversation.

Morsi (M): Alaikon Al-Salam!! But you must address me not as **Mr. Morsi**but as **President Morsi.**

E: Well, Sir, but you were removed from the presidency on July 3, 2013!!

M: By whom? It was a military coup staged by **El-Sisi** against me as the first democratically-elected president in the history of Egypt!!

E: But before those actions by the military, two events had taken place: 35 million Egyptians voluntarily assembled in Tahrir and other Egyptian public squares demanding your ouster. In addition, there were appeals addressed to you by the military to save Egypt from conflagration by agreeing to a compromise with the secular opposition. You refused.

M: El-Sisi was appointed by me as Minister of Defense. He took an oath of loyalty to the regime and was thus in no position to go over the head of that regime, namely me.

We had a Constitution in place since December 2012, and parliamentary elections were scheduled to take place in the course of 2013. Until then, I held both legislative and executive powers. The so-called millions who assembled against me on June 30 were paid thugs (baltagiah) and had no power to end my presidency.

E: You raise interesting points. **El-Sisi** was sworn before you as Defense Minister of Egypt, not Defense Minister of the Morsi regime. And the December 2012 Constitution was regarded as an Islamist document from the drafting of which the secular opposition withdrew. And I was in Cairo before the vote on it in 2012. People on the street told me that they were given no time to debate it. Even before it was put to a vote, your Constitutional Declaration of November 22, 2012 was alarming to the secular opposition and the judiciary. You put yourself above the law.

M: You seem to forget that I had cancelled that Declaration within a few days.

E: True, but public trust in the regime had already shattered and that lack of trust transitioned to the post-2012 Constitution period. You refer to the multitudes of Egyptians who rose up against you on June 30 screaming**"IRHAL" (Leave)** as paid thugs **(baltagiah).**

M: If you disagree with the term **"paid thugs."** how else could you describe them, and what power do they have to unseat me using the armed forces to engineer that coup?

E: It is impossible to regard more than one-third of the population of Egypt as**"paid thugs."** Their cause could be legitimated on the basis that in the 2012 Constitution there was no recall clause and no impeachment provision. The only mechanism was the street which spoke loudly and clearly against the regime.

M: Why would I be impeached, even if there was such a constitutional clause?

E: I shall not refer to that charges on which you had been arraigned, as I am not privy to the evidence. So as regards your actions in the public domain, you have resigned your membership of the Muslim Brotherhood following your election to the presidency. But you continued to regard the **Guidance Bureau** of that organization as your point of political reference. Thus began the process of brotherhoodization of the country.

You prevented the armed forces in Sinai from standing up effectively against **Hamas** and its affiliates as they proceeded to detach Sinai from Egyptian sovereignty. You have humiliated **Al-Azhar,** frightened the **Coptic** community, denigrated the judiciary, especially the **Supreme Constitutional Court,** and have allied yourself with **Qatar** whose funds are said to flow even until now to the **Brotherhood.** This is not to mention your encouragement of sectarian violence against the **Shiis.** And **Sharia** was being interpreted as if legislated law was at odds with it.

M: The **Freedom and Justice Party** of the **Muslim Brotherhood**

nominated me for the presidency which I won in June 2012. My relations with them paralleled the relationship of any political personality with his base. True, I chose **13** Governors out of a total of **27** from the Brotherhood. But these were capable persons who had my full trust.

Hamas is under siege by **Israel,** a siege that had to be broken through tunnels into our territory. The Palestinian question is Egypt's primary cause. The armed forces had to understand that they function under civilian control as represented by me. Let us remember that between Arab countries there should not be national boundaries.

As to **Al-Azhar** and the **Coptic Church,** these are institutions that, with the approval of the 2012 Constitution, there can be no State within the State -no autonomy for such establishments. The judiciary has exceeded its authority, as, for example, in disbanding the Egyptian lower chamber of Parliament. Who gave them that authority? We did not support sectarian violence. We simply responded to actions by minority sects by enforcing majority rule.

E: Sir, do you regard Egypt as the center of loyalty by you and the **Brotherhood?**

M: Well, **Egypt** is an integral part of the Arab and Muslim worlds and our focus is on an ever expanding Islamic State.

E: What you are in effect saying is that pan-Islamism should be the national identity of Egypt?

M: In a way, yes!! **Islam is the solution.**

E: But Al-Azhar in its document of August 2011, which was supported by the Coptic Church and women organizations, declared that the **"Islam does not recognize a State which is solely based on religion."** And **Al-Azhar** is the only point of reference for the issuance of **Fatwas.**

M: This is why Al-Azhar's Rector has to be removed because we see no separation between State and Religion.

E: I am concluding from your response that the confrontation between the Islamists and the Secularists shall last for a long time.

M: You may say so, until legitimacy as represented by me is restored, **El-Sisi**and his supporters are disciplined, and the course of the Egyptian Revolution is corrected. **Even if this process takes decades.**

E: Did you say **"decades?"**

M: It shall be a long conflict!!

E: If your aim is an **Islamic State,** your aim is doomed by the historical realities of Egypt. Just look at where the **Muslim Brotherhood** is now.

M: We are every where!! Thousands are marching all over Egypt in support of my return.

E: You may be every where yet no where. Your thousands have failed to translate into the millions. The movement is decapitated. The massacre of the police at **Mansoura** resulted in declaring the **Brotherhood** a terrorist organization. Seizing your assets is easier than tracking Mubarak's assets. Attacking the armed forces is further alienating you from the masses. Since 1814, the armed forces have been a part of the DNA Egyptian nationalism. Except for media snipers from the outside, the charge of militarization of Egyptian rule sounds very hollow to Egyptian ears. **"Teslam El-Ayadi" (God Bless the Army's Hands)** is not only a song; it reflects a historical creed. The quest for stability has outsized the quest for a defective democracy.

Throughout world history, terrorism has never unseated an established order. Not only was the **Muslim Brotherhood** a **"Johnny Come Lately"** to the January 25 Revolution. The **Brotherhood** had, at the start, declared that opposing **Mubarak** was **un-Islamic.** Your outside allies, from Qatar to Turkey, are on the run. **Lavrov,** the Foreign Minister of Russia has recently rebuked the **Qatar** Foreign Minister, saying: **"Sir!! I cannot find your country on the map!!"** And **Ordoghan** of Turkey, in spite of his **Rabaa**salute, is fighting for his political life.

Internationally, the plight of the **Brotherhood** is impossible to translate into an unambiguous cause of human rights violations. For historic Egypt has always regarded seeking such foreign support as a form of high treason. The **"Friends of Jerusalem"** has no friends in Jerusalem, whether **Jewish, Christian, or Muslim.** And the **Brotherhood Inc.** has refused to join the new wave of July 3.

M: I do not succumb to pessimism. I trust in **God** and in our cause.

E: I think that this conversation has become circular. We are ending where we have started. **Islam,** under its own jurisprudence **(Sharia)** creates a **community, not a State.** The quest for an **Islamic** State reminds me of **Don Quixote's** hopeless quest. He and **Sancho Panza** saw windmills as attacking knights. May I, with your permission, call **Mohammed Badie,** the jailed Supreme Guide of the Brotherhood your **Sancho Panza?** Or does this honor go to **Khairat El-Shalter?!**

To be secular does not contradict being also Islamic. For Islam is based on **"Ma Yanfoo El-Nas" (Whatever is good for society).** Not on what ever is good for the Brotherhood!!

As to Egypt, the late Pope Shenouda, that historic church leader and scholar, described to me in New York his belief in Egypt. He repeated what he had always advocated: "Egypt is not only a country in which we live. Egypt is also a country which lives in us!!"

Time to wake up, Mr. ex-President!! Field Marshal El-Sisi is at the door!!

32 FEBRUARY 2014

Destruction of Egypt's Artistic Patrimony Is a Form of Genocide

Friday, February 7, 2014

In the mid 1950's, I had the good fortune of assisting the late Professor Lemkin of Yale University. He was lobbying for increasing the number of UN Member States acceding to the Genocide Convention. From Lemkin I learnt a great deal about various forms of genocide. These included the destruction of museums, antiquities, artistic relics, and historical sites. He described the destruction of cultural heritage as genocide because it eliminates the ID of the nation affected -a war crime.

The truck bomb blast of January 24, 2014 in Cairo, though in principle aimed at Cairo's police headquarters, wrecked also the Museum of Islamic Art. Centuries of art from all corners of the vast Islamic world were largely obliterated. Exquisite medieval lamps, among other countless artifacts representing Islamic history from the seventh to the 19th centuries were reduced to rubble. The Antiquities Ministry lamented the catastrophic loss while the **Friends of Jerusalem, (Ansar Beit Al-Maqdis)** gloated over its heinous act of destruction. It called it revenge for the ousting of the

Islamist rule of Mohamed Morsi while the consequences of its war crime were a devastation of a critical part of Islamic ID.

To **Ansar,** power has priority over art and monuments. It thus shares the Taliban ideology which led to the destruction of the Buddhist Temples of Bamian in Afghanistan. Here **Ansar** also takes a bow of approval of the **Muslim Brotherhood's** description of the monuments of ancient Egypt as idols worthy of destruction. The form and contents of their opposition to secular rule have the sword's other edge of cultural obliteration. To them, Islam is a non-evolving faith which cannot co-exist except in forms of practice which they claim to be the right path to salvation -to paradise. **How misguided can one be?!**

At the age of 8, my late father, Sheikh El-Sayed Muhammad El-Ayouty, a graduate of Al-Azhar and a teacher of Islamic history, took me from our village in eastern Egypt to Cairo to introduce me to the country's cultural centers. Starting with Egypt of the pharaohs, where the pyramids and the sphinx stood guard, for millenia, he took me to **"old Cairo"** to visit the Coptic **"Hanging Church"**where he pointed out: **"This is where Jesus, Mary and Joseph came from the east to take refuge from Roman persecution."** Then it was the turn of Islamic Cairo, with its great mosques and lofty minarets and its wondrous Museum of Islamic Art.

Even as a child, I felt proud to be born in such a country with deep historic and diverse roots. This is when my turn towards universalism began. I became a part of all humanity!! Thanks Dad!!

Reports about the criminal devastation at the Museum of Islamic Art state that it had nearly **1471 artifacts** on display in **25 galleries** and **96,000 objects** in storage. Its second floor also houses Egypt's National Library. There are several rare manuscripts and papyri that suffered damage at the hands of those cultural terrorists.

The country's ID destruction had also been visited upon at the **Mallawi museum in El-Minya Province** which lies about 200 miles south of Cairo. Mob attacks last August, one month after the ousting of Morsi, resulted in the theft of **1050** of the **1089 artifacts.** These included pharaonic statues, jewelry and Greco-Roman coins.

Coptic places of worship have also come under wanton attacks in convulsive sectarian violence of **Brotherhood vs. Copts.** These churches are the repositories of what Orthodox Christianity had, since 200 years after Christ, bequeathed to Egypt and the world in terms of icons, bibles, manuscripts and all artistic representations of the Coptic cross.

In addition to funds flowing to the Egyptian Ministry of Antiquities from UNESCO, the U.S. and other international donors, secular Egypt is also responding. Included in the counter-attack against that cultural barbarism are the creation of an Egyptian non-profit by the name of the **Egyptian Heritage Rescue,** founded by **Abdel-Hamid El-Sharif,** and a magazine devoted to Egypt's heritage and history by the name of **Al-Rawi,** whose publisher is **Yasmine El-Dorghamy,** a woman at the front line of heritage defense.

In the aftermath of those attacks, a banker in Cairo summed up the feelings in Egypt against the **Brotherhood. "Who else but the Muslim Brotherhood has an interest in this kind of attack?,"** he asked. And on behalf of the government, the Interior Minister, **Mohamad Ibrahim,** declared: **"These attacks would not deter the Egyptians in their fight against black terrorism."** That is the same cabinet member whom the terrorists tried to kill last August.

Such determination to confront terrorism also has Egypt's economic interest in view. The country depends upon 20% of its foreign earnings from tourism. And whenever terrorism enters, tourism exists!!

On CNN, Fareed Zakaria Keeps on Claiming that "Egypt is a Mess"!! As Compared to What?

Friday, February 14, 2014

So I ask him in this posting: **"A mess as compared to what?"**

To Tunisia, where the Islamic party **"Al-Nahda"** gave up power to enhance democracy?. In Egypt, the **Muslim Brotherhood** clung to power, refusing to compromise with the secularists;

To Turkey, where Prime Minister Ordogan, skipping over his primary concern for civil peace in Turkey, preferring to interfere in Egypt's internal affairs?. In Egypt, the two revolutions resulted into a gush of nationalism that refused outside intervention.

To the Ukraine or to Thailand, where mobs have overwhelmed their presidencies demanding regime change?. Egypt has already passed this hurdle except for the so-called Islamists challenge.

To the U.K., where the country may break asunder if Scotland does not heed the pleading of **Prime Minister Cameron** not to secede?. Egypt's unity between North and South was already enshrined since the rule of Pharaoh Narmer 5000 years ago.

To the U.S., where the great Jeffersonian democracy under the U.S. Constitution is daily threatened during the Obama administration with the unending stalemate between the Democrats and the Republicans?. In Egypt, it would be impossible to imagine a government shutdown for 16 days as happened in the U.S. in late 2012.

To Russia, where four rebellions in its four corners are using terrorism as a means of gaining at least an autonomous special status within the Russian federation?. In Egypt, there are no such rebellions, except for random attacks on the transitional government which is fast learning how to employ counter-terrorism measures. As to **Syria,** or to **Libya**, or to **Yemen** - just forget it!!

How does **Fareed Zakaria** define the word **"mess?"** If **Zakaria** employs that term as applicable to Egypt because of the rising level of terrorism in the country, it has been common wisdom since Lockerbie of 1981 that terrorism cannot be ended, but can be contained. Let us now look at the new phenomenon of so-called **"jihadism"** on the Egyptian front.

Is there anything new in that alarmist reporting about so called **jihadists**returning to Egypt to fight for the restoration of the Morsi regime? None whatsoever!! A researcher at the **New America Foundation** opines from the comfort of his office in Washington, D.C. that **"Egypt is again an open front for jihad!!"** On the basis of that faulty premise, the **New York Times** on February 6, 2014, goes on to describe Egypt as **"the birthplace of political Islam,"** and as such **"has sent fighters to battle zones from Kandahar to the Caucasus for decades."**

The facts are: the **Muslim Brotherhood,** from 1928 to 1954, had no record of mass violence. Calling Egypt, where the **Brotherhood** was founded, **"the birthplace of political Islam,"** is sheer ignorance. And sending fighters to battle zones, as if terrorism is stamped with a **"made in Egypt"** label, has no demonstrable evidence. Above all, there is no terror ideology that has its roots in any faith, **Islam** included.

An entire dictionary of terms defining terrorism has grown like poison ivy on the walls of Islam. It has become the source for faulty labels, including the term **"jihadism."** In Islamic law **(Sharia),** there is no aggressive war, only defensive war, and there is no principle which calls for killing the innocent. The only explanation which I find admissible in the media jargon about the so-called **"political Islam,"** **"jihadism,"** and **"Islamic terrorism"** is the thread of **Islamophobia.** Terrorism has no religion.

It is interesting to note that U.S. media, including **Zakaria's CNN weekly** program, has scoured the entire map of the Muslim World to select **"a birthplace"** for terrorism. Their faulty GPS pointed first to Tehran, then to Riyadh, then to Islamabad, then to north-east Afghanistan. Each one of these locations had its place in the hot sun of adverse publicity. The fact of the matter is that terrorism travels, and its spread from southeast Asia to the Caucasus, and from Kandahar to Timbuktu is an aspect of its morphing into a franchise. And Islam, as a cover, is readily available. Why? Because any Muslim can claim the right to render a **fatwa** (a non-enforceable legal opinion), under the guise of **jihad.**

As the pendulum of approbation/disapprobation swings now in media thinking, and is now disfavoring post-Mubarak/post-Morsi Egypt, the history of U.S./Egyptian relationship has kept up with its gyrations. During the dictatorial **Mubarak** regime, Egypt was one of **"the black holes"** to which America's **"enforced rendition"** of suspected terrorists for the purpose of torture was a common practice. When the dictatorship of **Mubarak** was ended by the millions in Tahrir, and was followed by electing **Morsi** as President, one of the primary supporters of his **Brotherhoodization** of Egypt was **Ann Patterson,** former U.S. Ambassador to Cairo. That support remained undiminished even after the Egyptians by the millions, protected by the military, caused **Morsi's** ouster.

It was therefore not surprising to hear **Michael McFaul,** the present U.S. Ambassador to Moscow who is leaving his post to academia at Stanford define Russia's attitude toward the U.S. On **Zakaria's CNN program** he stated:**"Most Russians believe that the U.S. is fomenting**

regime change around the world." It was a shrewd move by **Putin** to send **"good luck"**greetings early this week to **Field Marshal El-Sisi.**

Within a few days of that revealing statement by **McFaul** came another revelation to confirm that notion. It was in a taped conversation between a U.S. Assistant Secretary of State, **Victoria Nuland** and the American Ambassador to the **Ukraine.** That exchange, which included an expletive against the**European Union** by that senior lady diplomat, evidenced Washington's activism in the internal affairs of the **Ukraine,** the birthplace of pre-communist Russian nationalism.

All of the above makes the present reading of the works of the late Robert A. Dahl a must. Dahl defined American politics and power in a very refreshing and authentic way. He said: "Instead of single center of sovereign power, there must be multiple centers of power, none of which is or can be wholly sovereign."

Mr. Fareed Zakaria: If Egypt, in your oscillating judgements is now **"a mess,"** then how would you impartially describe the inability of **President Obama** to get his important reformist agenda legislated except by resorting to bypassing Congress through executive orders as per his constitutional right? Until today, one-hundred sixty-eight executive orders have been issued by President Obama to get the U.S. moving ahead in spite of the insane politics of the **Tea Party, Senator Ted Cruz,** and the political hordes of the American political right.

Fareed: You have a pulpit, **CNN,** which is huge by comparison to mine, this weekly blog. You get paid for using **CNN** as a medium; I don't get paid for writing this blog. Your is for what goes for public information; mine is for public education. In spite of these differences, there should be similarities -sticking to credible facts, and making judicious conclusions based on them. Though we share in being both U.S. naturalized citizens, we do not share in many outlooks, especially when it comes to the role of the military in national crises.

For example, I see no stigma attached to Egypt's difficult transition to democracy, even if **El-Sisi,** through the coming presidential elections, becomes the third Egyptian president in the post-Mubarak era, succeeding **Morsi,** then**Mansour.** From your recent interview with **Prime Minister Hazem El-Beblawi** of Egypt at **Davos,** your questions were laced with negativity about this prospect.

Personally, I look upon it this way: There is a qualitative difference between a military man becoming, through democratic means, the ruler of Egypt, and an America which practices democracy at home, but uses military rule off shore **-Guantanamo!!**

This, to me as a law professor, is a form of political/military laundering using the tactics of money laundering in the Caribbean. The same American tactic has been perfected in **"forced rendition"** to other countries, in the prisons in **Abu Ghraib** (Iraq) and in Pagram (Afghanistan).

Then that tactic was elevated to a new science: shifting parts of the U.S. military power abroad to private security companies, like the infamous **Black Water** of **Erik Prinz. Black Water** was even given diplomatic immunity by the U.S. State Department as if it was a sovereign entity.

So when **Black Water** killed 17 innocent civilians in **Iraq** in 2007 in **Al-Nesoor Square, Baghdad,** immunity sheltered it from prosecution. When later I visited the scene of that war crime in Baghdad, I knew that I was standing on the ground of a real American mess!!

So, Fareed (your name in Arabic is translated into "unique"): The mess exists only through your process of subjective selection!! Unfortunately, this has become your unique fare which on your weekly CNN program, you preface it by : "I have today for you a great show!!"

Egypt's War on Terror is Winnable: The Terrorists are Largely Non-Egyptians Fighting in a Highly Security State!!

Wednesday, February 19, 2014

The attack by terrorists on February 16, 2014 on a tour bus in Taba, Sinai, killing **three** and wounding **17** South Koreans is a mirror incident. Tragic as it is, it sums up the contours of Egypt's war on terror in the **post-Morsi** period.

Is that war winnable, and why?

It definitely is winnable, and here is why: Since 1952, Egypt, under military rule until the Revolutions of January 25, 2011, and June 30, 2013, has become a highly security State. Calling it a security State is not to praise it, but to describe it. The security apparatus, during the Arab Spring in Egypt, was not dismantled. It simply became invisible.

When the **Muslim Brotherhood** became ascendant, its one-year in power was denied the cooperation of that deeply rooted apparatus. The security forces (police, intelligence, special forces, and the army) saw in the **Morsi** regime the face of an old adversary wearing a transparent Islamist veil.

So when that regime denied the secularists their fair share of the power pie, both the army and the police knew exactly where to go to kick the **Brotherhood** out from the presidential palace. They appealed to the masses, and the response to that appeal on June 30, 2013 was massive. Egypt was not going to be a turbaned theocracy.

As the old security apparatus once again finds its footing in the Egypt of interim President **Adly Mansour,** it is coming back to the front lines of the battle for a historic and secular Egypt.

Let us have a quick look into the nature of Egypt as a State. **Dr. Gamal Hamdan** has published a 4-volume book in Arabic entitled **The Personality of Egypt.** In the last volume, he points out the Egyptians inner pride in what the author describes as **"the genius of location"** in these words: **"Since long time ago, Egypt has given the Arabs their first city of one million inhabitants." (p.664).**

Pride in demography as well as in location and history, has caused the national flag in Tahrir to be raised on January 25, 2011, with the inscription **"I love Egypt."** No Islamist flags, with their two raised swords, and definitely no black flags of **Al-Qaeda** and its terrorist affiliates like **Ansar Beit Al-Maqdis**(Friends of Jerusalem) were to be seen at that time.

Now **Ansar** has been claiming responsibility for its terror in Sinai. Aside from the daily mopping up by the army and the police of these groups, Egypt, in a bold challenge to terrorism, is putting **Morsi** and **35** other **Brotherhood** leaders on trial. The charges of espionage and conspiracy with foreign powers (i.e. **Hamas, Qatar,** etc.) carry the death penalty.

On the media front, foreign journalists saw in the **Taba** attacks on the **South Korean** tourists **"worrying new evidence that militants...were broadening their campaign against civilians."** In a worthy rebuttal,**Counsellor Adly Mansour,** Egypt's President, called it **"a despicable act of cowardice directed at innocent tourists."** The **South Korean** were in Sinai visiting the **Orthodox Monastery of St. Catherine.**

In its own way, the terrorist attack on tourism in Egypt, an industry which provides millions of jobs and a big chunk of badly-needed foreign currency, has sharpened the lines of battle on terrorism in Egypt. In a meaningful lament, Egypt's Tourism Minister, **Hisham Zaazou,** said, **"I am very sorry this happened."**

Gone by the wind any residual sympathy in Egypt for **Hamas** or the **Muslim Brotherhood**; so has any limits on the use of power within national territory against terrorist acts; so has the humanitarian practice of easy admission into Egypt of refugees from whatever Arab origin.

So has any softening of security measures against dissent; so has any receptive ears for various human rights groups a strict application of the standards of civil society during civil strife. **The outlook in Cairo today is that the country is at war with an elusive enemy which national security requires its pursuit to the bitter end.**

Consequently, Egyptian chauvinism is definitely on the rise; the diversity of Egyptian public opinion on the eve of presidential elections is behind ever-tougher measures against any hint of sympathy for terroristic Islamism; a land slide for **Field Marshal Abdel-Fattah El-Sisi** as the next president of Egypt is now a near certainty.

The old call by former **President Nasser** that **"security trumps development"** is once again in vogue. Egypt's Prime Minister Al-Biblawi called on all tourists **"to evacuate Sinai;"** His Minister of Tourism, on his way to visit the injured **South Korean** passengers in Sinai declared: **"This will not recur."** **The Egyptian security empire is getting ready to strike back in full force!!**

David Cole, in an article in the **New York Review of Books** dated November 7, 2013, asked the perennial question: **"The End of the War**

on Terror?" He answered his own question by saying, **"Some have suggested that this is a permanent state of affairs, and we might as well get used to it!!"**

I wager that Egypt's response shall be quite different. For it is not fighting terror beyond its frontiers. Its forces are not over-extended. Egypt has boots on the ground, an inflamed public opinion, thousands of agents who can blend, alliances within Sinai bedouin structures, and a determination to see its internal war on terror winnable.

In his speech on the subject of fighting terrorism at the National Defense University in Washington, D.C., on May 23, 2013, **President Obama** quoted**President James Madison's** warning to the newly created United States of America: **"No nation could preserve its freedom in the midst of continual warfare."** Well, in today's Egypt, this may be read in a different arrangement: **"Continual warfare (against terrorism) might by the price of preserving Egypt's freedom."**

No compromise is attainable with the agents of death and destruction.

That is especially so with Ansar (The Friends of Jerusalem), an affiliate of Al-Qaeda in Sinai, which is fighting the wrong war, with the wrong tools, for the wrong cause, in the wrong place, with a contrived adversary, with a predictable result -publicized conflict for fundraising with no hope for an Ansar victory.

It is time for **Egypt** to try to puncture this balloon of vaunted anti-Islamic myth which goes falsely by the name of **"jihad."** Theirs is a nihilistic ideology which reached the zenith of idiocy when it glorified **Osama Bin Laden,** a world class faithless fanatic, by calling him **"Sheikh Bin Laden," "a martyr,"** and a source of religious Islamic opinions called **"Fatwas."**

There is nothing on record that indicates that Bin Laden had ever sat for a class on Sharia or Islamic jurisprudence. His issuance of Fatwas was nothing more and nothing less than a means for the usurpation of power. And his ideological descendants, whether in Sinai or elsewhere, do not possess the capacity to comprehend that ultimately they are doomed, because terrorism is a dead-end street.

33 MARCH 2014

To American Critics of Egypt's Handling of Its War on Terror, I Would Retort: Where Were You When John Yu Falsely Claimed "The Geneva Conventions Are Obsolete?"

Monday, March 10, 2014

Or is it a double standard?! Is America's war on terror to be set apart from Egypt's ware on terror? Does terrorizing Americans call for a robust response, but terrorizing Egyptians in Egypt calls for velvet handling? Is trying to explode an aircraft on its way to Detroit terrorism, but the downing of an Egyptian military helicopter in Sinai a form of dissent?

Is water boarding of suspected Taliban operatives in Afghanistan an accepted form of interrogation, as former U.S. Vice President Cheney opined, but detention of collaborators with the banned Muslim Brotherhood in Egypt a violation of basic human rights?

Whatever the answers to the above list of questions might be, sovereign Egypt does not answer to Amnesty International or to the talking heads on **Al-Jazeera of Qatar.** It answers only to its public which is clamoring

359

today for resolutely confronting the so-called jihadists. Today secular Egypt is in an active armed confrontation with those who wish it ill including through the return to Brotherhood's hegemony. The battle might be long. But its outcome might determine the future shape of the new Middle East.

What did John Yu advocate? Upending the norms of international law developed as of 1942, this former legal counsel essentially advised both the U.S. Department of Justice and the White House of the Bush/Cheney era that warring against terrorism called for ignoring the Geneva Conventions of 1949. His take was that terrorists were not legal combatants; that, with terrorism, the world has entered the era of war without end; that new rules of engagement had to be developed; that due process, whether substantive or procedural, was inapplicable; that "enhanced interrogation" (i.e. torture) was not illegal in dealing with terror suspects; that military commissions were appropriate replacements for a criminal court adjudication; and that sovereign borders should not impede finding and **"bringing to justice"** any terror suspects.

The John Yu's approach was an open invitation for the use of draconian measures which in his opinion were the new tools needed for the security of the U.S. Thus Counselor Yu may be regarded as one of the main propagandists for what might be described as an American imperial security system. In 2009, the new Obama administration signaled the end of that system which, in effect, caused the membership of terror organizations to soar. But that administration did not dismantle it. It largely recast it in a new garb, new terminology, and new rationales.

In the midst of those transformative events, the voice of civil society organizations was muted. But with the Arab Spring, unleashed as of 2010 in Tunisia, and sweeping into Egypt in 2011, Arab masses rediscovered the power of the street. And soon the presidents of Tunisia, Egypt, and Libya, were respectively, either on the run, or in jail, or massacred. With these Arab voices clamoring for dignity, democracy and development, NGOs and other civil society organizations, most of which were being funded from abroad including from the U.S., discovered a new role for them in Tahrir and its equivalents across the Middle East.

That new role was wrongly anchored. Their index for the progress of democracy in a country like Egypt was measuring democratization by a western yardstick even after the Muslim Brotherhood had demonstrated its penchant for violence for the sake of naked power. And with the Brotherhood's resort to terrorism to avenge the popular uprising which unseated Morsi in July 2013, these civil society groups, in their attacks on

Egypt's actions against that "jihadist" mayhem, seemed to forget the John Yu rules.

This is not to applaud the John Yu rules. This is to remind that Egypt, as it fights for its secular existence as it confronts terrorism on its soil, must at least be measured by the standards afforded to the U.S. in its war on terror inside and outside the U.S. during the reign of the administration of Bush II.

This is not only a media matter. It is a situation of vast geo-strategic importance. U.S. uninvited intervention in Egypt's internal affairs, especially during this phase of **Egypt versus Jihadi Terrorism,** is probably destined to dismal failure.

The U.S., though refraining so far from calling Egypt's Second Revolution of June 30, 2013 **"a military coup,"** has basically looked upon Egypt's difficult transition to democracy, with ambiguous and doubtful reserve. The **Christian Science Monitor Weekly** of February 26, 2014 reflected this state of affairs in a lengthy commentary headlined **"Democracy's Dangerous Decline in Egypt and Turkey."**

The substance of the entire article is summed up in the following paragraph:

The U.S. can no longer afford to remain mute in the face of assaults on democratic norms in countries as vital to regional and global security as Egypt and Turkey. While certain strategic interests -such as military partnership with Egypt and its peace treaty with Israel -may encourage Washington to emphasize stability over democracy, this is a mistake. "

Then the two authors go on to emphasize their thesis in these words: *"A failure to speak out against the erosion of liberty in Egypt and Turkey, which seem to be following in Russia's authoritarian footsteps, not only damages America's ideals and image, but it harms long-term strategic U.S. interests. "*

Through writings like those paragraphs quoted above, I see an imperialist approach to domestic happenings which have no impact on **"long-term strategic U.S. interests."** This is not to mention its reflection of the double standard syndrome which has plagued the preaching of those who talk about**"assaults on democratic**

norms" and **"America's ideals and image."**

Such expressions of concern might be taken seriously by the new Egypt providing that account is also taken of the embarrassing facts surrounding John Yu's rules, or National Security Agency surveillance of telephone calls, Guantanamo, or surveillance by the police in New York and New Jersey of mosques. On the latter, a U.S. District Court Judge in Newark dismissed, on February 20, 2014 a civil rights lawsuit brought in 2012 by eight Muslims. The Muslim plaintiffs said the New York Police Department's surveillance was unconstitutional.

The plaintiffs in the Newark, New Jersey case claimed that that program focused on religion, national origins and race. The federal judge disagreed. In his ruling dismissing the case, he said: **"The motive for the program was not solely to discriminate against Muslims, but to find Muslim terrorists hiding among the ordinary law-abiding Muslims."** In response, the **Center for Constitutional Rights** which represented the plaintiffs declared:

"By upholding the New York Police Department's Muslim Surveillance practices, the court's decision give legal sanction to the targeted discrimination of Muslims."

Therefore, I say to the American critics of Egypt's handling of its war on terror: look at your own backyard. Clear it from its overgrowth before you cast your critical gaze seven thousand miles east toward Egypt.

What is wrong with us, Americans, minding our own business and lending credibility to our ideas? Let Egypt solve its problem with its national security, even by borrowing a page from America's handling of its own security. **Egypt is not an American protectorate!!**

The Egyptian street, to which this blog has been dedicated since its inception in April , 2011 is clamoring for a decent living. In accepting the resignation of the**Beblawi** cabinet on February 24, **President Mansour** described **"the burden of the nation's problems"** as **"immense, both in terms of economic deterioration and marginalization of a number of different segments of society."**

Pretending that Egypt's first need is democratization and total freedom of expression is a false pretense. It ignores the realities on the ground, and the hierarchy of values brought to prominence by the Arab Spring. The pragmatic sequence seems to be stability leading to development leading to democratic structures which stress, among other things, freedom of expression.

A forthcoming book by **Paul Brinkley** entitled **War Front to Store Front** brings this point home.

Speaking of Iraq and Afghanistan, Brinkley who had worked for the Pentagon to build companies came to an unavoidable conclusion: **The single most important task in both countries was to create a self-sustaining economy to which the U.S. paid little attention.** As reported by **Fareed Zakaria** in **Time magazine** of February 17, **Brinkley** told him:

"**Our focus in Iraq and Afghanistan was to get the politics right - have elections -and somehow economics will flow naturally. But that's not actually how it works. We need to get the economics right first, create a self-sustaining market economy, and then the politics will get much better...In the West, trade and markets led to individual liberty and political freedom, not the other way around.**"

That important sequence seems to have been understood by jihadi terrorism in Egypt when in February they attacked South Korean tourists in **Taba, Sinai.** Tourism is a huge asset for Egypt's economic recovery. Egypt, in striking back at those criminals, has to place its economic recovery ahead of the uninvited advice of the so-called civil society organizations and Washington, D.C. talking heads!!

The Dangerous Sport of Pre-Judging an El-Sisi Presidency

Monday, March 10, 2014

Thomas Friedman, in an article in the New York Times of March 2, 2014 says "Putin and El-Sisi both rose to power on that longing for stability after so much revolutionary ferment." I could not see the face of a factual comparison between the two personalities, except for Friedman's anticipation of rulership with a strong hand by El-Sisi in Egypt.

Pre-judging of events in an Egypt presided over by **El-Sisi** is a dangerous sport. In effect it harbors triple anticipations: that **El-Sisi** shall be a presidential candidate; that he will win; and that he shall rule democratically. To my mind, this is a reflection of either panic or deception. It could be both even if we overlook the awkwardness of a journalist whistling in the wind like Mr. Friedman.

I do not expect media presentations to be akin to a classroom lecture. The reason is that in a classroom, a well trained instructor is supposed to train his or her charges not in what to think, but in how to think. A classroom should not be a pulpit for the propagation of the private thoughts and convictions of the professor. I personally have not tried it even once since I began my teaching career in Cairo in 1948. Not even when I taught a graduate course on the Arab/Israeli question, from 1966 to 1972 at **St. John's University, New York City,** then from 1972 to 1997 at the **State University of New York at Stony Brook.**

It is of course naive to expect media opinion-makers to sanitize their material from their preconceived ideas. But at least in the case of a Mr. Friedman, the distinguished author of **Beirut to Jerusalem,** one expects a measure of healthy detachment. Even at the pragmatic level, his abhorrence of a predictable**El-Sisi** presiding in Egypt shall not change the situation on the ground. It is nothing more than a ventilation of personal preferences.

The naysayers say that the Revolution of June 30, 2014 resulting in the ouster of **Morsi** was a coup. We say it was a revolution ignited by 35 millions citizens against the Brotherhoodization of Egypt. The naysayers say that **Field Marshal Abdel-Fattah El-Sisi** ended the Islamic rule of one year using military muscle. We say the armed forces led by **El-Sisi** acted on the basis of the popular will in the absence of any other institutional mechanism to have **Morsi** recalled. The naysayers say that Islamic rule from June 30, 2012 to July 3, 2013 came through the ballot box. We say that this a half truth as the ballot box produced a Brotherhood iron-fisted rule which threatened to tear Egypt apart.

The primary issue here is what shape and content would the Egyptian revolutions of 2011 and 2013 produce? The majority of Egyptians as attested to by the millions in the street respond: **"A secular not a religious State."** This has been the rock bottom position adopted by the January 25, 2011 Revolution in which the **Muslim Brotherhood** participated, though belatedly. From January 25, 2011 to the presidential elections of June 2012, Egypt reflected inclusiveness of all currents of opinion, and covered both Muslims and Christmas. So it was no wonder that **Al-Azhar** reflected that broad national consensus which carried the stamp of approval of the great Coptic Church and community, in its Declaration of August 19, 2011.

The first of those 11 principles of that Declaration entitled **"Al-Azhar Document on Egypt's Future,"** provided as follows:

"Egypt as a State is based upon a constitutional democracy with separation of powers, of which the legislative power is to be exercised by the people's representatives. Islam, in its legislation, civilization, and history does not recognize a "religiously-based" State. The overall arching principle of Islam (Sharia) are the primary source of legislation, providing that the adherents of other religions are guaranteed, in their personal status cases, resort to their own religious laws."

The reaction to that declaration on the part of the **Egyptian Supreme Council of the Armed Forces** (SCAF), which ruled the country prior to the election of Morsi to the presidency in June 2012, was confirmatory. **SCAF's Deputy Chairman, General Sami Anan** who was Egypt's point man in US-Egyptian military relationship stated: **"The secularity of the State is a matter of national security which is non-negotiable."** The nexus placed by Egypt's military between secularity and security could not be more organically emphasized.

With the rise of terrorism within Egyptian borders, security has become the number one issue. It has become the national portal to secularity. And the more police and army officers and innocent civilians including tourists are killed or injured by the acts of the so-called jihadis, the more attachment to the army and security forces is manifested by the public. Thus the new **Prime Minister, Ibrahim Mihleb,** at his first press conference held on February 25 summed up his cabinet's priorities in these few words: **"Restoration of security and defeat of terrorism."**

In a phone conversation I had earlier today with one of my nieces who resides in Cairo, I asked her about her expectations for the forthcoming presidential elections to be held later this Spring. I asked her: **"For whom would you vote?"** Her immediate and non-varnished response was: **"For El-Sisi, if he runs."** My follow-up question was: **"Why?"** Her long response included the following: **"Where in Egypt of today do we find the most stable, the most inclusive, the most nationalistic, and the most cohesive institution outside of our armed forces?!"**

Theoreticians like **Tom Friedman** and **Fareed Zakaria** can keep on attempting to create the myth of an Egyptian Revolution hijacked by the military. It is the Egyptian Revolution which is being hoisted aloft by the military, regardless of whether or not **El-Sisi** becomes the next president of Egypt. Such voices are reading Tahrir from the narrow windows of faulty measurements applied from a distance of 7000 miles. This is the distance between the Nile river to the east, and the Hudson river to the west.

What is There In Common Between a Reality Called Egypt, a Fantasy Called Hamas, and a Mouse That Roars Called Qatar!!

Monday, March 10, 2014

Cairo has had enough!! Hamas, the so-called **Islamic Resistance Movement,** encircled by Israel in Gaza, has crossed more than one red line in regard to Egyptian national security. From smuggling of weapons and jihadists into Sinai through illegally-dug tunnels, to consorting with the **Muslim Brotherhood** which has recently been declared a terror organization by Cairo. From espousing **Al-Qaeda** affiliates like **Ansar Beit Al-Maqdis** (Friends of Jerusalem), to becoming hostage to Qatar's manipulation through petro-dollars. From declaring repeatedly non-recognition of the Israeli-Palestinian peace process, to declaring the overthrow of **Morsi** in July 2013 a military coup.

With such accumulated grievances, made even more grievous by a series of hit and run terrorist attacks on Egyptian security personnel and army officers and soldiers, Egypt at long last has banned **Hamas** and frozen its assets in Egypt. This is a prelude to the tightening of the movement of persons, goods and services between Egypt and Gaza. Now the only available land connection between Hamas and any Arab territory has been sealed. The dark fantasy of Hamas, an offshoot of the Muslim Brotherhood, now has to face on a daily basis the bright reality called Egypt.

From 1949 to 1967, Egypt has administered Gaza, but for good measure, has refrained from annexing it. Cairo has done that out of its hope that one day, a State of Palestine would rise up on territories allocated by the UN partition resolution of 1947. That hope, which has been repeatedly dashed by extremism on the two sides of the green line, has cost Egypt lots of blood and treasure. The Egyptian/Israeli war was the longest war in the annals of the Egyptian military -a 30 years war from 1947-1977.

That 30 year long war was bought to a sudden end by a great visionary - the late Egyptian President Anwar Sadat. In 1977, he journeyed to the Kennest, sued for peace, concluded with Prime Minister Begin the Camp David Agreements of 1978, and finally signed the first Arab-Israeli peace treaty in Washington, D.C., in March 1979, with former President Jimmy Carter smiling broadly. For that act of unbelievable courage, both **Sadat and Begin** received the Nobel Prize for Peace, and Cairo, once again, became a tourist Mecca for thousands of Israeli tourists. But the price of that historic peace, which is still in place, was high. Sadat was assassinated in his own capital on October 6, 1981, at the hands of so-called Islamists.

The first Arab reaction to the Sadat assassination came from the PLO in a short unbelievably cruel statement: **"May God Bless the hand which pulled the trigger!!"** Arafat was in charge, and he bore the responsibility for that betrayal. It should be here noted that **"betrayal"** has been a modus operandi for the Arafat regime: In 1970, the PLO tried but failed to replace the benign Hashemite Kingdom of Jordan; in 1981, the first advocates for isolating Egypt for having entered into a peace treaty with Israel, were the Arafat conclave; in 1983, the PLO tried but failed to subvert Lebanon through reneging on the Cairo Agreement of 1969 concluded by Nasser between PLO and Lebanon; in 1990,**Arafat** flew to Baghdad to hug **Saddam Hussein** for having invaded the State of Kuwait, thus precipitating an en masse expulsion of Palestinians from Kuwait and Saudi Arabia.

Finally, as the corruption within the Palestinian leadership shot up (**Forbes magazine** has estimated Arafat's net worth upon his death at **$5 Billion**), Hamas' appeal to Gaza voters in 2006 increased. The notion there, as in Egypt toward the Brotherhood, that the Islamists were **"pure"** (above corruption). Not so!!

By 2008 Hamas rode rough shed on Fatah/PLO in Gaza, and through a mini-civil war, Hamas, under **Haniya** became **"the Gaza government."** Thus, as of 2008, we have two Palestines: One in **Ramallah** headed by **Abbas;** the other in **Gaza** strip, ruled by a rebellious splinterist **Hamas.** Ramallah sought peace with Israel; Hamas sought war through rocketing Israel. **Egypt's Mubarak,**with the help of **Omar**

Soliman, the then head of Egypt's State Security, spent years trying to unite the Palestinians, and to stave off Israel's might against Hamas. These were wasted Egyptian diplomatic efforts.

With the Arab Spring, **Mubarak** and **Soliman** were gone. The **Muslim Brotherhood,** having won in 3 successive elections, closed ranks with **Hamas,**its offshoot; sectarianism, a la Gaza, became the daily formula with the **Copts**and the **Shiites** its cannon fodder; and the peace treaty with Israel was targeted by Hamas through attacks on Israel from Sinai. **Morsi,** in response, tied the hands of Egypt's armed forces which were eager to end Hamas' rampage in Sinai.

Studying the Islamist rule in Egypt under Morsi (June 2012-July 2013), one is surprised at how Egypt began to look as a colony of Hamas, aided and abetted by Qatari financial infusion. Egyptian secular anger at that situation was misread as reactionary pressure against Egypt's Islamist march toward democracy. And the U.S. swallowed the poisonous bait. Then came the Second Egyptian Revolution of June 30, 2013 (shamelessly called a coup by its opponents), to put an end to Islamism in Egypt, especially in Sinai. The Hamas invasion of Egypt through tunnels was halted, causing Hamas to lose $250 million annually.

One can safely say that Egypt's political liberation from the Mubarak autocracy in 2011, was soon followed by Egypt's liberation from a rule by false turbans and deceptive beards in 2013. The dependency of terrorism by **Ansar Beit Al-Maqdis** and **Ansar El-Sharia** and other similar lunatic fringes of **Al-Qaeda**on the Muslim Brotherhood and Hamas and Qatar came abruptly to a screeching halt. The declaration by Cairo of the Brotherhood to be a terror organization, followed by the banning of Hamas was in effect a declaration of the primacy of security over other considerations. The bright reality called Egypt has won over the dark fantasy of Islamic rule. That fantasy has been made even darker in Gaza. Pity the Palestinian cause which had no leadership dedicated to its cause. That cause has never benefited in terms of leadership from the equivalents of a **Ghandi** or a **Mandela.**

As a result it had turned into an endless political game with an eye on empty sloganeering and on continuous search for a **"sugar daddy"** like Qatar whose ambassadors were kicked out on March 5, from Saudi Arabia, the United Arab Emirates, Bahrain, and Egypt.

In a joint statement, those countries accused Qatar of engaging in espionage against them by supporting the **Brotherhood** and providing a media platform for its allies. That media platform is **Al-Jazeera** which is now banned in Egypt, having been accused of fabricating news instead of reporting the news.

Commenting on his country's isolation, a former Qatari ambassador to Washington told Al-Jazeera: **"The whole issue is really about Sisi. These countries are supporting a coup d'etat...We are not going to support dictators."** Compounding Qatar's confusion, the Qatari foreign minister declared that that expulsion had **"nothing to do with security or stability."** For all intents and purposes, Qatar's petrowealth could not save it from becoming a pariah State.

In a recent diplomatic confrontation between Russia's foreign minister, Lavrov, and Qatar's foreign minister, the former, in exasperation, is said to have told his Qatari counterpart: **"Sir!! I cannot find your country on the map!!"** But the mouse that keeps on roaring (Qatar), artificially elevated by a mountain of oil money, by Al-Jazeera TV channel, and by a US huge naval base, sees its reality in pursuing impossible causes. Political Islamism and Hamas are such causes. There is nothing in common between the mouse (Qatar), the fiction (Hamas), and the reality of Egypt whose recorded history goes back to 10,000 years!!

On March 7, a great anchor on MSNBC TV Channel, **Chris Matthews,** recently described Egypt succinctly in a few words: **"A real country with a real history!!**

No wonder that Qatar and Hamas are ideologically suited to one another: a roaring mouse and a stealthy scorpion!! While Qatar is busy trying to subvert other Arab regimes through illicit financial subventions, Hamas is busy trying to use these subventions to subvert those regimes including the Palestinian Authority in Ramallah.

Who are the World's Number One Enemies of Islam? The Jihadists!!

Friday, March 14, 2014

They go by different names: Al-Qaeda; Al-Nussrah; Ansar Beit Al-Maqdis, the Islamic State of Iraq and Syria (ISIS), Boko Haram, Jihad in Gaza, Ansar Al-Sharia, Al-Qaeda in Arabia, and the like. They use Islam as a cover for killing the innocent and destabilizing regimes and societies. Their faith is in power, their recruits are mostly the ignorant and the unemployed, their environment is one of intrigue, and their fallen are undeservedly glorified as "Shaheed" (martyr).

They burst on the international scene by perpetrating **the criminal act of 9/11.** In a way, **Islamophobia** is their unintended ally as it generates for them funds and recruits. The more they kill, the more Islamophobia, the greater justification for more killings by jihadists. Hatred is their oxygen. Even in deaths, **Osama Bin Laden,** a global crook, remains their prophet, and **El-Zawahiri,** his successor, a physician whose prescription is brutal killing, preferably by beheading, is their Calipha.

Where does **Islam** stand from them? And why are they Islam's number one enemy? Here follows a crash course in **Sharia or Islamic law** (a mini presentation of the course I teach at **Fordham University School of Law**).

The two primary sources of Islamic law are the **Quran and the Sunna** (The words and conduct of the Prophet Muhammad). However, if there is no textual reference to a specific issue, **ijtihad** (application of reason and common sense to the text) fills in those gaps. In general, **ijtihad,** though allegedly ended to avoid subjective controversies and divisiveness, has remained available. Changing circumstances over **1435** years have made ijtihad and indispensable tool for the judiciary in Muslim societies.

In appointing judges, **Muhammad** made the resort to competent ijtihad in matters where the Quran and his own authentic utterances offer no clear guidance, a condition of appointment. This is particularly so because the concept of **"justice"** (Al-Adl) is so highly regarded in Sharia that, in Islamic tradition, it is one of the **99** names used in reference to **God (Allah, in Arabic).**

A corollary of the concept of justice in Islamic jurisprudence is **"the free will."** Coercion is abhorrent to the point that for centuries, that principle has become a sanctified adage: **"No Coercion in faith."** The dogmatic justification for that principle is that faith is a matter of the heart, that it cannot be negotiated. The reason is simple: the relation **between God and man** (i.e. male and female) is direct -no intercession and no middle man!!

In Islamic law and practice, this is the main gate to diversity of all kinds, especially in religious matters. Thus from a legal perspective, this means that a Jew, a Christian, a Muslim, a Hindu...etc stands in equal position, proximity and status before their Creator. Muslim jurists have even issued **fatwas** (a non-enforceable legal opinion **-opinio juris**, to the effect that Islam accepts agnosticism. That is holding that nothing is known, or likely to be known, of the existence of **God** or of anything beyond material phenomena. Is that extreme? **No!!**

The premise here is that no human being has the right to judge another as a believer or a non-believer. It is **God** who is regarded as the only evaluator, the only assessor. Hence the Quranic verse: **"The truth is from your Lord: let him who will believe, and let him who will reject" (Chapter 18/Verse 29)**. The flip side of this total acceptance of diversity is that in Islam, the Prophet Muhammad is a messenger of God, and as a messenger, he is not a controller, a dictator, a thought oppressor, a deputy God.

What flows from these textual and ijtihad premises is a whole panoply of legal premises: **(a)** gender equality; **(b)** judicial discretion in sentencing, due regard being given to the accused. Such discretion dictates that the treatment of sentencing stated in the **Quran,** as in the cases of theft (cutting of hands or legs) or of adultery (stoning) as parables. Consequently **Omar,** the second caliph after Muhammad, acted accordingly in dismissing cases even where the accused of theft offered his hand to be severed. Omar's rationale: **the accused has been victimized by society which did not afford him the means for a decent living; (c)**freedom of expression and of assembly; **(d)** the right of the governed to remove an oppressive ruler; and **(e)** good government is based on justice which is premised upon the protection of minorities which might be vulnerable to the dictates of the majority.

From the above, one could see the huge distance between **Sharia (Islamic law)** and **jihadism.** In fact the solid interpretation of the term **"jihad"** is the inner fight within the person to overcome his/her base urges, and the resort to self-defence in cases of outside territorial aggression. **In Islamic law, there is no offensive war, no proselytizing, no infidels, no difference between Sunni and Shii, and no terrorism.**

Taking into account the aforementioned Sharia framework as an indispensable yardstick to measure the islamism of the terrorist jihadi organizations which sport the deceiving label of **"Islamic,"** we find them lacking in every respect.

The Jihadist primary tool is terror. Terror is anti-thetical to the exercise of the free will which is regarded by **Sharia** as an inalienable right for every human being. Through the unislamic process of **TAKFEER** (declaring an individual an apostate), the jihadis nullify the twin concepts of the individual's direct relationship with God, and of diversity. Those twin concepts have been at the heart of the vibrant Abbasid dynasty which had Baghdad as its capital, and which had fully absorbed the great experiences of the Byzantine empire, the Persian empire, and of Coptic Egypt.

Under the black banner of **Al-Qaeda** and like-minded retrograde murderous groups, gender equality does not exist. Women liberation under Islamic Law had been obliterated. The brutal resort to inhumane sentencing for illegal acts by reading the Quran's parables about the cutting of hands, legs (not to mention decapitation), as an external sentencing guide, attest to their total ignorance of what Islam is all about.

As to freedoms of expression and of assembly, these are the first casualties of jihadism where the right to rebel against injustice is regarded as a rebellion against God. For them, sectarianism and endless war are to be waged for the glory of the Almighty God -for a quick ride to paradise!! **By the way, the fiction of 70+ virgins in paradise is a sample. It is a reflection of a jihadi freedom from sanity zone of jihadi hallucination.**

The abdication by the jihadis of this frame of Islamic Law and jurisprudence has made **them Islam's enemy No. 1.** Their malicious call for the return of Islam to its pristine origin rings hollow: They are returning to a red dawn of their own making, as a means to sinister ends.

Where in Islam is the justification for terrorizing the innocent? Where in the**Quran, the Suma, or in ijtihad,** is a license to attack the Copts in Egypt, the Shiis in Iraq, the Americans in New York, the Spaniards in Madrid, or the Christians in Nigeria or in the Central African Republic!

Their criminal and insane acts in Egypt of attacking the army, the police, and innocent civilians, are solely intended for destabilization of the emerging new order in the vain hope of stopping it to fill the vacuum. Robbing them of the description of **"Islamic"** this or that, is a priority in warring against the mayhem which they are trying to spread from various locations thus giving the false impression of their **"wide reach."**

The only hope they cling to is to stay alive, and for them staying alive requires suicidal acts by their misguided cohorts which their leadership adopts for both fund-raising and more recruitment.

Their use of the pulpit in small mosques scattered throughout rural villages for spreading their venomous hate against moderate Muslims and all non-Muslims is being curtailed. As an example, the Government in Egypt has recently announced the sequestration by the State of all such places of worship. The purpose: Teaching of Islam to Muslims must be taken away from uneducated free lancers who, at times, are jihadi conduits. The jihadis are in fact the propagators of world-wide resentment toward and suspicion of Islam. **In their attacks against U.S. President Obama, the American right keeps on calling him "a closet Muslim," and citing his middle name "Hussein."**

In support of this process of preempting jihadism within its borders, and as an example to other Arab Spring States, the new **Egyptian Constitution of 2014** contained various articles providing as follow: **Article 7: Al-Azhar** is an independent Islamic entity ... and is the main recourse in matters of religion and Islamic affairs; **Article 74:** It is not permissible to undertake political activity or to organize political parties based on religion or on discrimination based on gender, national origin, sectarian or geographic differentiation; **Article 237:** The State is committed to combat terrorism in all its forms.

In the **Quran,** we read: **"We ordained for the Children of Israel that if anyone slew a person -unless it be for murder or for spreading mischief in the land -it would be as if he slew the whole people..."** (Chapter V/Verse 32).

You, **"Jihadists,"** have the blood of thousands upon thousands of innocents on your hands. You continue to spread **"mischief"** (FITNAH) every where. You psyche up yourselves to dream of the unattainable and unwanted resurrection of an **"Islamic Caliphate."** Your advocacy of **"freedom to hate"** is not a human right. You have even created a fiction of **"the jihad of fornication"**whereby your operatives justify prostituting young Muslim woman as a religious offering for satisfying them while waging **"jihad."**

You have recreated the medieval tradition of assassination. In spite of all your acts of aggression against Islam and civilization, the real jihadis are those who are hunting you down worldwide in order to close down your "Murderers Without Borders!!"

My Vote for Morsi Was a Big Error; My Vote for El-Sisi Shall Redeem It

Friday, March 28, 2014

In 2012, I voted for the wrong President. Now comes my chance for course correction. A vote for El-Sisi shall be a vote for a resurgent Egypt, in spite of the naysayers.

When Morsi ran, his opponent was Shafik, a General. My friends, especially my Coptic brothers and sisters, urged me to join them in voting for Shafik. They reasoned that Egypt needed security and stability which can only be guaranteed by a strong military hand. I rebutted their counsel with a ready-made argument:**"How can I vote for the continuation of yet another military regime after 60 years of the same?"**

They were right; I was wrong. This had nothing to do with my being a Muslim by faith, with Morsi being my co-resident in the eastern province of**Sharkia,** or even with Morsi being on the faculty of my home **University of Zagazig,** the provincial capital. It had to do with giving the Muslim Brotherhood, suppressed for 80 years, a chance at governance.

Morsi won; so did chaos!! That one year of Islamic rule was a true calamity: the liberals were on the run; the new Constitution was rigged in favor of islamization; the Copts were persecuted; non-veiled women were harassed;**Hamas** in Gaza threatened to undo the Egyptian-Israeli peace treaty of 1979.

Under Morsi, Egypt itself was marginalized. **"To Hell With Egypt"** was uttered by a Supreme Guide of the Brotherhood who believed in pan-Islamism; tourism dried up; the army's hand in dealing with terrorism in Sinai was stayed; the Shiis were called apostates; Al-Azhar's independence and its message of moderate Islam was curtailed; the police disappeared from the streets in an attempt to curtail the Brotherhood's influence; **Qatar** and **Turkey** seemed to regard Egypt as their protectorate with **Al-Jazeera TV Channel** as its official voice; the Egyptian judiciary was besieged.

The great armed forces of Egypt were looked upon as the protectors of the Brotherhood and the presidency, not of sovereign Egypt; the great monuments of Egypt, which belong to the whole world though located in Egypt, were regarded as idols insulting Islam; music, dance, songs, the arts, and the great museums became suspicious cultural aberrations.

The list of examples of the **Brotherhoodization** of Egypt can go on and on. In essence, my vote for Morsi has contributed to the enfeeblement of that historic country of my birth. The revolution of January 25, 2011, against which the Muslim Brotherhood issued fatwas, was being hijacked under the cover of the ballot box and the so-called democracy. Secular Egypt had to strike back.

And it struck back on June 30, 2013 with 35 million Egyptians in Tahrir and in every public square in Egypt of 90 million people, saying **"KEFAYA" (ENOUGH)!!** As they protested the Islamist regime, the army and other security forces protected the popular uprising. Refusing to be inclusive through reaching a compromise with the opposition, Morsi ridiculed an ultimatum issued by the **SCAF (the Supreme Council of the Armed Forces)**, headed by **El-Sisi.** The unavoidable result was Morsi's ouster on July 3, 2013, and his replacement by **Judge Adly Mansour,** of the **Supreme Constitutional Court.** The irony here was that the judiciary, which had been the nemesis of the Brotherhood, was now, through Mansour, its successor.

At that point, it was time for the Brotherhood to resort to what it has practiced for 80 years: sloganeering, intimidation; strong arm tactics, and a call to arms to its thugs inside Egypt, in Gaza, and elsewhere through its international network which propagates the re-establishment of a **pan-Islamic caliphate.**

In response to these calls which use Islam as a ready-made cover, mini-emirates were formed in Cairo: one in **Rabaa Square;** the other at **Al-Nahda.** For six weeks these two locations fell outside the control of the interim regime brought about by, not by the military, but by populism. Barricades were constructed; arms were smuggled; bakeries, barber shops, mini-commerce flourished, weddings were celebrated; hostages were tortured. At the same time, opponents were abducted and tortured; through-traffic was halted, taunting the authorities was the daily practice.

The false calls from **Rabaa** and **El-Nahda** were for the return of the Islamic reign of terror. For six weeks, the Government of **Prime Minister Dr. Hazem El-Beblawi** appealed to the **"sit-ins"** to disperse. These appeals were laughed at by the Brotherhood which manned the ramparts. Finally on August 14, 2013, the police and the army struck, leaving exits for those who wished to extricate themselves. Hundreds, mainly dead-enders, fell, including a limited number of security and army personnel; more were injured. Human rights organizations cried foul, but the millions of June 30, 2013 celebrated the Brotherhood's containment.

El-Sisi announcement of March 26 that he intended to resign his army service in order to run for the post of president of Egypt was in essence denounced by the **New York Times** of March 27. Its principal reporter in Cairo, **David Kirkpatrick,** using his worn-out, script reported the news under the heading of **"Commander of Egyptian Takeover Leaving Army to Run for President."** The Kirkpatrick problem is anchored in a non-workable formula based upon measuring the events in Egypt by the yardstick of the last century. **How?:**

It was the **Muslim Brotherhood** which **upended the vote for Morsi** through interpreting the vote for him as a vote for an exclusive Brotherhoodization of the country;

The Brotherhood's coup of June 2012 was ended by the Second Egyptian Revolution of June 30, 2013 which, in the absence of **"a recall"** provision in the Islamist Constitution of 2012, effected Morsi's removal;

The bloody confrontations of August 14, 2013 between Morsi's supporters and the forces of law and order were precipitated by the rebellious refusal to abide by the newly-minted law regulating public demonstrations. That law is a replica of all such laws in democratic societies, including the U.S. where **"Time, Place, and Manner"** govern the expression of popular feelings through demonstrations.

August 14, 2013 shall forever go into history books, especially in Egypt, as the day which unleashed Brotherhood's terror on the Coptic community everywhere in Egypt. Churches were burnt; bible schools torched; Coptic icons and religious symbols desecrated; private businesses looted; Coptic citizens massacred; peaceful citizens fled their historic family houses. The Brotherhood was doing what it knows best: Shift the blame for their removal from power on others. The Brotherhood is **"infallible"** (incapable of erring). **Insane!!**

Terror affected the length and breadth of Egypt, from Sinai to the Libyan border, and from the Mediterranean to Lake Nasser at the Sudanese border. Hit and run attacks on the army, the police, tourists, cabinet members, museums and highways became common events. **Al-Qaeda** affiliates, such as **Jihad** of Gaza, and the**"Friends of Jerusalem,"** in search of the unattainable return of Morsi to power, enjoyed the unmerited publicity of **"popular opposition to the coup of July 3, 2013."**

With terror rampant, the economy in tatters, illegal funding of terrorism flowing from abroad, and faith being manipulated for the Brotherhood's sordid ends of power through the barrel of a gun, Egypt had to react in self-defense.

The Brotherhood was declared a terror organization. Egypt, a traditionally security State, marshaled its resources of pre-Mubarak days, with the armed forces, and intelligence apparatus in the forefront. A strong hand was needed to navigate the ship of secular Egypt to a safe harbor.

Ignoring the realities on the ground in Egypt by a powerful medium like the **New York Times** can not change those realities. The country is at war with terror. Its success in these efforts shall undoubtedly rebound to the benefit of global security. Regardless of what **David Kirkpatrick** might devine in the service of worn-out formulas about **"a coup"** and a **"revolution,"** his advocacy does not see in the Brotherhood's two raised swords another depiction of the Nazi's swastika. **The latter made of exclusive nationalism a new religion; the former made of exclusive religion (Islam) not only a new nationalism, but an imaginary pan-Islamism.**

That is why I shall vote for El-Sisi to atone for my mistake of voting for Morsi in June 2012 (I am a dual citizen: an Egyptian American). **El-Sisi** did not remove Morsi. He protected those who removed Morsi. The right of a president (in this case Morsi) to the honor of being described repeatedly by Kirkpatrick as **"freely elected,"** is inferior to the right of his **"free electors,"** of whom I was one.

Reading El-Sisi's declaration of March 26 in Arabic (which I assume is not the native language of **David Kirkpatrick**), I shall construct what the former general is advocating in broad terms:

Egypt is facing security challenges which must be confronted. Moreover the economy is in a free fall, and millions of Egyptian youth are unemployed. The country is threatened by terrorists who are bent on destroying Egypt's peace and security.

Running for the presidency has been demanded by the rank and file of Egyptians; nobody who has not offended Egyptian laws can be excluded from the political process.

Egypt, a country which has abundant natural resources, should not remain reliant on foreign assistance and donations.

As potential president of Egypt, El-Sisi does not promise miracles; only hard work and selfless efforts intended to revive an Egypt. The country should assume its natural place within the community of nations, free form fear, from poverty, from need, and from national doubt.

The new Egypt shall not brook any outside interference in its internal affairs.

Well!! If that is the Egypt of the future, why should I not favor the guiding strong leadership of El-Sisi under the post-Islamic Constitution of 2014 which has been adopted by a broad national consensus? I, like many others have limitless aspirations in a rejuvenated secular Egypt to be ushered in by El-Sisi who is favored to be Egypt's 8th president after the collapse of the monarch in 1952.

34 APRIL 2014

The Coptic Question: Protecting Minorities During Periods of Upheavals

Friday, April 11, 2014

In my view, the most effective presentation of a case, is one that begins with the conclusions. Most education in U.S. law schools, especially in Year One, the horrible year, begins by briefing cases, not by study guides. Invariably I do the opposite. Begin by defining the terms and the issues, then go to the 60-page case and you will quickly find the holding.

The same here tonight in studying "the Coptic Question" in Egypt. It is vastly complex, and I hope that, through the principle of "start with the conclusions," the details, which follow, shall be made clearer.

When I began my research on this question, I was fortunate to have among the resources brought to me by my friends from Cairo in Arabic, especially Mr. Wagdy Rizk of the U.N., a seminal report dated November 1972. The significance of that report is that it was drafted by a blue-ribbon committee called **Al-Etaiffi Committee.** It was made up of members of the Egyptian House of Representatives, Muslims and Copts. The

379

Committee was instructed by Parliament, and guided by a decree issued by the **late President Anwar Sadat,** to investigate terrible events of communal clashes in a town called **El-Khankah** in the **Province** of **Qalyubiyah** north of **Cairo.**

The central event was an attack by Muslims on Nov. 6, 1972 against the Headquarters of the **Holy Bible Society,** a Coptic organization, which was used as a Church without a government license. The building was torched by a group which started from a mosque called **Al-Ashraf mosque.** Six days later, in a show of coptic solidarity, a large group of Coptic Clergy and Coptic civilians, travelled from various places to **El-Khankah** and held prayers at the attacked site. Counter Muslim demonstrations approached the site; a Copt is said to have fired a weapon in the air to ward off the approaching angry mob. The result was torching his and his neighbor's homes. There were no human casualties. End of **El-Khankah** episode of 42 years ago.

Studying this incident of communal clashes, one finds in it a typical example of the Coptic question which reveals, in a repetitive though more severe fashion, conclusions which I am now able to present:

The two issues involved in the Coptic Question are: Licensing to build churches, and the right to advocate and teach Christian orthodoxy;

The Muslim/Coptic confrontation incidents are usually described by the authorities, not as a "sectarian conflict," but as threats to "national unity;"

Institutional responses to these incidents, from 1970s till the present, aim at containment, not at eradication of root causes;

These responses, whether effectual or ineffectual, involve the entirety of institutional Egypt. This means from the top of the pyramid, Presidential decrees, through parliamentary committees of investigations, through the provincial levels (Governors, rural leaderships...etc), all the while guided by an advisory and reconciliation combination of **Al-Azhar,** the citadel of mainstream Islamic learning, and the **Coptic Church;**

The legal systems which impact upon the Coptic Question have their roots in the **Ottoman system** since 1517. It is called the **Millet system:** namely each religious community, in matters of marriage, divorce, wills and charitable contributions, is governed by its own internal **Canon Law** and **Sharia Law** and **Mosaic Law** based on the Old Testament;

After the collapse of the old Parliamentary system, the rise of dictatorship in Egypt caused the concomitant rise of sectarianism. The monolithic ruler, from **Nasser** in 1952 to the fall of **Mubarak** in 2011, tried at to govern through "Divide and Rule;"

Islamism in Egypt, a country which historically is secular, was bolstered unofficially by **Wahhabi** extremism, the radicalization of the **Muslim Brotherhood,** the rise of the religious state in the Middle East such as **Saudi Arabia** in 1932; **Pakistan** in 1947, **Israel** in 1948, and the **post-Shah** Iran in 1979;

The aggression against Coptic churches and establishments was met by laws which were unenforced, especially as regards the principle of equality before the law;

There is hope that Egypt, which got rid of Mubarak through a direct and solid amalgam of Muslims and Copts, promises to deal with the transgressions against the Copts through a robust legal and security system. This is the dividend accruing from the victory in **June 30, 2013** of secular Egypt over the **Muslim Brotherhood** which had promised a reign of anti-Coptic terror because of Coptic support of the ouster of Morsi; and

The term Egypt means **"the land of the Copts."** The roots of the Copts in Egypt could be traced religiously to the establishment of the first Christian Church only 200 years after **Christ.** However, civilizationally, these roots go back 5000 years to Ancient Egypt where the **ankh,** the key-like cross symbolizing enduring life, was described by the great Chicago University historian, **Breasted,** as the direct predecessor of the **Cross.** The Arab roots go back to the year 640 A.D. when Egypt came under Muslim control. That was during the reign of Omar, the 2nd Caliph after Muhammad.

These are 10 basic conclusions of my presentation which now goes into the area of forensic analysis of the on-again, off-again eruptions of the Coptic crisis in the largest demographically Arab country Egypt whose best description was offered by the **great late Shenouda,** the **Pope** of **Alexandria.** In a dialogue, two years before his death, that highly learned leader told me that **"Egypt is not a country in which we live. It is a country that lives in us."** Now let us see how this country, whose map I am now holding in my hand, lives in the heart of all Egyptians, both Christians and Muslims.

There are five areas that are worthy of probing. These are: **(a)** The demographics and the geography; **(b)** The anti-Coptic ideology; **(c)** The broad expanse of the anti-coptic attacks; **(d)** Containment: the historic, legal, and religious frameworks; and **(e)** What can be done?

(A) The Demographics and the Geography:

As in the case of Lebanon, there has not been a census determining the exact percentage of the number of Christians in egypt. We say "Christians," because, in Egypt, there are Copts (orthodox); Catholics; and Anglicans. The rank and file of Egyptian Muslims lump all of those denominations together as "Copts." In my case, having been raised in a Coptic neighborhood in eastern Egypt, and belonging to a family which historically has been the administrative link between minorities and the seats of powers, I have always been interested in, let us say for ease of reference, "the Coptic Question."

The percentage of Christians is generally considered to be anywhere from 10% to 15% of a population which now numbers approximately 90 million.

The geography of Coptic residence is not limited to one area of this country of nearly one million square kilometers. The Christian population lives all over Egypt with the villages, especially in southern Egypt, housing Copts and Muslims side by side. This factor is important in two ways: The absence of a Coptic region makes security a very local issue, but with national repercussions; and the Copts, being generally better educated, have a better understanding of the outside world than most of their Muslim neighbors. In the job market, in a country with 40% illiteracy, the recruiter, if a Muslim, would generally be inclined to favor a Muslim applicant, especially that no Copt is called Muhammad, and no Muslim is called Guirgis (George).

In this regard, we exclude the composition of the Egyptian Cabinet, which invariably and by tradition, has included 2 Copts, neither of them occupies **"sovereign portfolios"** such as Defense, Foreign Affairs or Justice. No Copt has ever been a President of Egypt. This is although Copts have always been in the forefront of national movements for independence and national defense.

When the British granted Egypt self-rule in 1922, the Declaration of that status contained 4 reservations, including the right of Great Britain to intervene for the protection of minorities (i.e. largely the Copts).

(B) The Anti-Coptic Ideology:

Never in the history of Egypt has there been a horrific scene of what nowadays is called ethnic/religious cleansing, or generalized inter-communal hatred like what we see between Muslims and Christians in **Nigeria** or in the **Central African Republic.** Or what we have witnessed in the case of **Serbia vs. Bosnia Herzegovina,** or are witnessing now in **Syria, Iraq and Pakistan** between **Sunnis and Shiis.**

Nonetheless, since the 1970s, after the death of Nasser, an anti-Coptic ideology has been fueled by several factors. Foremost amongst these is the transformation of the **Muslim Brotherhood** from religious advocacy **(DAWA)** to the politics of power through force and coercion. The Coptic issue was a ready-made Islamist instrument for recruitment and mass appeal. The veil of moderation fell with the Islamists ascending to power in 2012, after the fall of Mubarak. That ascendancy was through the defective mechanism of the Ballot Box, and the **"hate -the Copts"** ideology became structured, propagandizing the following mythology:

The Copts are the enemies of an Islamic State, not only in Egypt, but anywhere. Their opposition to a **Caliphate** is fueled by their desire to oppose **Sharia,** especially as a principal source of legislation;

The Copts, in their quest for a secular Egypt see in the gradual and surreptitious conversion of the young Muslims, a path towards arresting that islamization;

Copts converting to Islam are only seeking to benefit from the liberal divorce practices of the Muslims because the Coptic Church does not permit religious sanctification of divorce of Coptic spouses;

The Copts, especially those who have immigrated from Egypt, are actively seeking to invite foreign intervention in Egypt through raising the cry of human rights violations, thus weakening the State and, with it, the right of the majority, namely the Muslims, to exercise a dominant nationalistic role.

There are other aspects of that anti-Coptic mythology beyond the enumeration herein presented. Ironically, each one of the enumerated four aspects has a small kernel of factual validity. The ideology of the recently assertive Muslim Brotherhood, and its more virulent allies, like the **Salafis,** became the oxygen keeping that anti-Coptism, not only alive, but entrenched. Translation: **Attack the Copts!!**

383

Although January 7, the Orthodox Christmas was made a national holiday by Mubarak, and although the Arab Spring in Egypt was a Muslim/Coptic product, yet the national upheaval was later hijacked by a Muslim Brotherhood who at first condemned the rebellion then belatedly joined it and unsuccessfully tried to co-opt it.

Protecting the Copts became difficult for the new Egypt to maintain. As of June 2012, **Shafik,** the military general, though supported by the Copts, lost his presidential bid to **Morsi,** the candidate of the **Muslim Brotherhood.** During the turbulence from November 2012 to June 2013, the security of the Egyptian street became a thing of the past.

The Ministry of Interior which controls the Police became the enemy, due to the killing of nearly 900 Egyptian demonstrators and to a prior record of torture. The only institutions which remained standing in a bureaucratic Egypt of 5000 years were: **the army and the judiciary.** To the Copts, the Islamist rule by Morsi from June 2012 to July 2013, was a year of terror. Its gradual evaporation caused by the armed forces, which are based on compulsory draft of both Muslims and Copts, (Coptic generals were in the forefront of the leadership of the war of 1973 under **Sadat**), gave the Copts the hope of a light at the end of the tunnel. Their support for **General El-Sisi,** and of the post-Islamic **Constitution of 2014,** was a natural. Yet a structural damage to Egypt's national unity had already occurred: Brotherhood versus the State; Brotherhood versus the Copts; moderate Islam, the bedrock of Coptic security, versus terrorism. Too many splits; precious little cures. An **El-Sisi** presidency in Egypt, a near certainty, shall be an early Christmas for the Christians in historic Egypt. It shall represent security wedded to, secularity.

(C) The Broad Expanse of Anti-Coptic Attacks

Translating the above into a saga of anti-Coptic attacks has been lucidly expressed by the large volume of official Coptic material provided to me by the **Secretary-General of the Council of Egyptian Churches.** I was also provided by a large amount of photos to document those sad events which are available for the audience to review, but not to take away after this formal event.

Pastor Dr. Bishoy Hilmy, has provided us with an important document dated **September 5, 2013,** two months after unseating **Morsi** who is now on trial, but three months before the present Government declaring the Brotherhood in December 2013 a terrorist organization. It is an official letter signed by **Pastor Al-Biady**, the **Head of the Anglican Church; Patriarch Ishak,** the leader of the **Catholic Copts;** and above all, by the **Pope of Alexandria, His Eminence Pope Tawadros the Second,** who presides over the Coptic Orthodox community.

The letter is addressed to **Field Marshall El-Sisi** and copied to **General Taher Abdullah,** who leads the Corps of Engineers of the nearly one-million armed forces. This Corps has been active in rebuilding, at the cost of the State, Christian establishments damaged by the marauding hooligans affiliated with, or paid by, or Islamically misled by the Brotherhood in Egypt, and by **Hamas and Qatar** outside of Egypt.

The document reminds El-Sisi of an agreement reached with **El-Sisi** at a meeting in which El-Sisi asked for a comprehensive list of Coptic establishments damaged on August 14, 2013. On that date, the army and the resurrected security forces stormed the militarized sit-ins by the Brotherhood at two locations, **Rabaa** and **Al-Nahda.** After 6 weeks of appealing to the occupants of those armed enclaves to peacefully disband, official Egypt was striking back to assert the legitimacy of its Second Revolution of July 3, 2013 which the Brotherhood and most of the West, together with Turkey and Qatar and Gaza, dubbed as **"a coup."**

The letter covered Churches, schools and other Christian facilities either burnt or damaged in whole or in part after August 14, 2013 by arson, molotov cocktails, and firing of various types of armaments. It also documented theft, pillage and desecration in whole or in part. The high-level signatories of this document requested action on El-Sisi's resolute decision to rebuild and or compensate the Christian Churches and citizens.

It ended with the following phrase: **"We pray for you to be blessed and to attain full success. We ask the same for our beloved Egypt to enjoy security and prosperity. We cherish you and our brave armed forces which constitute Egypt's shield."**

We note here that that language by the Christian religious hierarchy reflects both anguish and resilience. It reflects the historic official line which proclaims that **"Egypt is not Iraq. The Egyptian Society has different characteristics. It is unified in the sense that there are no minorities. The Egyptian people, by its own nature, is integrated. Its Muslims and Christians occupy the same neighborhoods everywhere."**

But official lines and the facts on the ground in post-Mubarak Egypt suffer from a disconnect. The reports which I have from the **St. Mark Cathedral, thanks to the help of several Coptic friends,** both clerical and laity, shows that in nearly all the Egyptian provinces which number 27, destructive attacks and desecration and theft, were perpetrated. By comparison with Revolutionary Egypt, the reign of Mubarak looked in the rear view mirror to the Copts who brought it down, to have been a relatively golden age in regard to security which in this context trumps other values.

(D) Containment: The Historic, Legal and Religious Frameworks:
It is axiomatic to say that we live in an age of rage. Law in Egypt suffers at present from an enforcement deficit, has nearly ceased to be a solution. Obviously this affects not only the Copts, but also other important sectors of life in Egypt. It also suffers nearly everywhere from erroneous re-interpretation. Even in an iconic democratic system such as in the U.S., America has refused to apply an important international convention, such as the U.N. Convention on Civil and Political Rights, to situations outside U.S. borders. Prior to this, there was even greater anomalies: discarding the Geneva Conventions of 1949 by the Bush Jr. administration as obsolete in the context of the war on terror, and the abstaining thus far from acceding to the Rome Convention of 1998 which created the International Criminal Court.

In the specific case of Egypt, there is a legal framework in existence since Ottoman times, which should have prevented anti-Coptic aggression. During the reign of **Sultan Abdel-Meguid the First,** an important Ottoman decree was promulgated in February 1856 which regulated the issue of construction of places of worship for all faiths throughout the Empire including Egypt. It went by the name of **"The Hamayooni Line."** And during the great age of **Muhammad Ali,** the founder of modern Egypt, from **1805 to 1849,** all Ottoman decrees issued with adverse effects on the Copts were rescinded. The Copts were allowed to build new churches, to carry arms, to join the armed forces, and to attain Cabinet ministerial ranks. More importantly, during the reign of **Said,** one of **Muhammad Ali's** sons (1854-1863), the tax imposed on the Copts, known by its Islamic term as **"geziah"** which was in force since the year 640, was eliminated and replaced by military service. Therefore we have here a solid legal and historical foundation on which security for Egyptian minorities, whether Copts or Shiis can be rejuvenated.

We also have in Islamic jurisprudence, a non-recognition of the term

"infidel," total equality between Muslims and non-Muslims, and the co-existence between Sharia and legislated law. **Muhammad** had married a **Coptic** woman, **Mary,** and the second Caliph after Muhammad, **Omar** had ordered the whipping of the son of his General Amre who conquered Egypt who had whipped a Coptic lad. In this regard, Omar famously said: **"Since when have you enslaved human beings whose mothers have given them freedom through birth."** The Quran glorifies Mary and the immaculate conception 43 times, the only woman so mentioned by name in the **Quran,** and glorified **Jesus** as the word of God more than 30 times. This is not all for that solid Islamic foundation in cosmopolitan Egypt for the protection of minorities during periods of upheavals.

The great declaration of **Al-Azhar** dated **August 19, 2011,** and endorsed by the **Coptic Church** states the following in its 4th, from among eleven principles:

"Full respect to the view of the others, which implicates the necessity of avoiding declaring others to be apostates and traitors; and the abuse of religion for the purposes of sowing divisiveness and hatred among the citizens. Sectarian conflict and racist advocacy are criminally injurious to the homeland."

Moreover, the preamble of the post-Islamic Constitution of 2014 states that "Egypt is the birthplace of faith -all faith- and that the Egyptians have embraced the Virgin Mary and her son and offered thousands of martyrs in defense of the Church of Christ"

Its **94th Article** proclaims that **"the Rule of Law is the Basis of Governing the State."**

The first lines of the great history book on **"The Flight of the Holy Family to Egypt,"** is introduced by **Egyptian Bishop Mataous**. It starts by this phrase: **"The flight to Egypt is one of the most important historic events which took place over the soil of our dear Egypt over its long history."**

One of today's great Coptic scholars in the U.S., **Francis Basili,** the son of a luminary from among the clergymen of the Coptic Church, states the following in **"Sawt Biladi" (The Voice of my Homeland)**, the issue of February 2014:

"The conflict between the brethren of Egypt, Muslims and Copts developed only when the Muslim Brotherhood and their affiliations ignited the powder keg of religious militancy as of the 1970s."

(E) What Can Be Done?

Now is the time to start anew in the new Egypt. The upheavals of the Arab Spring should be followed by the return to Egypt's roots, especially as regards the Coptic question. I believe that we now have a clean slate in the country which is the engine which pulls the entire Arab train behind it.

Let us start with the process of re-education, to remind Egypt of its true identity. In doing so, we do not need new laws, we need enforcement. We have enough laws except for strengthening the judiciary and its independence, and of teaching the cops that the age of torturing suspects is over.

Both **Al-Azhar** and the **Church** in Egypt have a history of mutual respect, collaboration, and the compulsive need for containment, especially in the area of tormenting the Christians in other Arab Spring countries such as **Libya and Syria.**

By education, the teaching of Islamic law should be cleansed from the aberrations of archaic interpretations of how Islam should deal with non-Muslims. Militant Islam at least in Egypt, I believe, is on the ropes. I do not expect the **Muslim Brotherhood** will have the chance of a comeback. The mosques are now being sequestered by the Government to prevent the pulpit from again becoming a free zone for hate speech. Inter-faith events should be institutionalized. Trials of religious malfeasants should be televised. Compensation for the Copts should be legislated. University education and curricula should stress what the Egyptians so far mouth, but do not practice: **"Faith is for God; the homeland is for all."**

A final word about what not to do, and then what also should be done: First: any foreign intervention or internationalization of the Coptic question is immensely counter-productive. The ethos of the Arab Spring is that reform and restoration are a home industry. We must look upon these restorative values, especially in the critical area of education, as a cottage industry. The rural areas must become the center; the capital is the periphery. The individual and the local communities are the main actors.

Since we are dealing with faith, an area which is not negotiable, let Egypt, with its unique history of Muslim/Coptic co-existence, show other Arab and Muslim countries the way. **Al-Azhar** which gave my father the way of culturally rearing me, is the focus of teaching Islamic moderation. This is why Al-Azhar is in the cross-hairs of the **Muslim Brotherhood.** Its influence in Sunni and Shii learning is phenomenal It was established in the year 975 A.D., together with Cairo, by Shiis. Under **Article 7 of the 2014** post-Islamic Constitution, Al Azhar's independence was restored. Al-Azhar/Cathedral intertwining, through joint educational programs, is a must.

The issues of the laws governing church construction without too much red-tape should be reviewed. The public and private information systems should not muzzle up the events affecting communal relationships. The Coptic community should feel that its impact on legislation, diplomacy, education, social services is assured. Interfaith events should be multiplied and the basics of interpretation of Islamic law **(ijtihad)** should find their way to the textbooks as of the primary school.

The State, all over the world, has been overstretched, thus weakened. Now, individual and communal action have their chance. In that spirit, I am launching this summer in southern Egypt, where Muslims and Copts live together, a pilot project to uplift the level of University education.

Do Not Fool Yourself: In Its Entirety, The Brotherhood Is an International Organization!!

Friday, April 11, 2014

When a Supreme Guide of the Brotherhood **(Al-Ikhwan)** said **"To Hell with Egypt" (Tozz Fi Masr)**, he was confessing an ideology. The Brotherhood is concerned with pan-Islamism as an identity and as a program. To it, Egypt is only a location where they were born 86 years ago, and where they will be reduced to a past nightmare in a much shorter time. There exists no Brotherhood department or a section called **"the International Organization Department."** Only the inept Egyptian media, and the ideologically-oriented foreign media espouse that huge fiction -a total falsehood.

Their funding is largely global; their affiliates, like **Jihad** and the **Friends of Jerusalem** in Gaza, are like commercial outlets in an international franchise akin to **Walmart;** their allies, like **Turkey and Qatar,** see in secular Egypt a field for destabilization; and their propaganda sites are in Europe spreading a message of victimization whenever they are the mischief makers; their way to exclusive power seems to have been copied from the Nazis and the Communists: use the openness of democracy and, once you are in, subvert it.

Their year in power in Egypt (June 2012 - July 2013), which was ushered in through democratic elections, witnessed the closure of the window to that nascent democracy. Pushed out by 35 million demonstrators in June 2013 who were backed by the army, they cried **"foul."** Under the guise of lamenting **"a coup,"** they declared utter defiance of the transitional government, began an armed rebellion through **"sit-ins,"** and for full six-weeks openly called for army defections.

They blamed their ouster on the Copts for supporting the forces of law and order, and turned deaf ears and throaty hooliganism on the government appeals for a peaceful end to that clear and present danger of urban warfare.

Arrayed against them were: the new laws regulating public demonstrations; Al-Azhar's declaration that **"Islam, in its legislation, civilization, and history does not recognize a religiously-based"** State; the long history of Egyptian cosmopolitanism; and the dedication of the judiciary, the armed forces, the police, and the overwhelming majority of public opinion, to maintain Egypt as a secular State.

Determination was winning over the Brotherhood's intimidation. The man of the hour, **Field Marshal El-Sisi,** whose ultimatum to Morsi of July 2, 2013 which culminated in the replacement of **Morsi** by **Judge Mansour,** spoke for the nation. He publicly put it this way to the Brotherhood: **"Is it your choice either to rule us or kill us?"**

In essence, Egypt was not going to be **"an Islamic Republic of fear."** The Brotherhood's calls for a popular uprising against the Revolution of June 3, 2013 failed miserably, and with them, the dream of return to the Presidential palace.

The Brotherhood's shallow roots in Egyptian soil doomed it to a life outside the newly-emerging political system in Egypt. That unhappy status became a solid reality between **July 2013 and December 2013.** During those fateful six-months which culminated in declaring it a terrorist organization saw the true face of the Brotherhood. Bombings in Sinai and in Cairo and other provinces; Brotherhood exaltation of **Hamas** for it shifting the battleground of conflict with Israel from **Gaza** to northern and southern **Sinai;** regular fatal attacks on the army and the police; the inception of an **Al-Qaeda** presence in Sinai; murder of Coptic workers in Libya; downing of a military helicopter in Sinai, and incessant propaganda against the new Egyptian system from **Al-Jazeerah TV channel of Qatar,** from Turkish controlled news outlets, and from London.

While Egyptian diplomatic relations with **Qatar and Turkey** were severed, diplomatic demarches in London led in April 2014 to **Prime Minister David Cameron** ordering an inquiry into the activities of the Brotherhood in London.

The objective was to determine whether the **Brotherhood** (calling them**"Muslims"** is an error) was using London as a base for planning extremist attacks in Egypt. A specific aim of the British inquiry was to have the British intelligence service **M16** report on any involvement by the Brotherhood in attacks in Egypt like the **February 2014** attack on a busload of **South Korean**tourists in **Sinai.** The leader of that investigation is **Sir John Jenkins,**Britain's Ambassador to Saudi Arabia, a country which also branded the Brotherhood a terrorist organization in March 2014.

In Egypt, a provision in the **2014 Constitution** closed the backdoor to a possible Brotherhood return to power. **Article 74** provided that **"it is not permissible to undertake any political activity or to form any political party on a religious basis...or to engage in any activity which may be contrary to the democratic principles, to clandestine, or has a military or a para-military characteristic."**

But that **Brotherhood International** finds in these provisions an anti-thesis of their core beliefs. Events and revelations by **Egypt's Minister of Interior,General Muhammad Ibrahim,** strongly point to the Brotherhood's link to Qatari intelligence and petro-dollars. **Amin El-Sirafi** an aide to former President Morsi has been detained on charges of spiriting documents on army deployments and arming the Egyptian armed forces to **Qatar.**

The **Qatar/Brotherhood** connection is also evidenced by Qatar's granting, not only asylum, but also Qatari citizenship to Brotherhood members who are considered fugitives from Egyptian justice. Among these are **Assem Abdel-Majid** and **Salah Abdel-Maqsood.**

Mindful of the danger posed by that threat of a budding alliance between the**Brotherhood and Al-Qaeda,** through **Muhammad El-Zawahiri,** brother of the successor to **Bin Laden,** the Interim President of Egypt, Judge Adly Mansour, said recently in a televised interview that he **"would take any measure necessary to safeguard Egyptian lives."** This is a code language for the possibility of returning to emergency laws in Egypt. That declaration by the interim President came on the heels of an escalation of terrorist activity by**Ansar Beit Al-Maqdis,** a Brotherhood ally and Hamas-inspired group of so-called jihadis.

Army operations against terrorism in **north eastern** Sinai, especially in the areas of **Al-Toma** and **Al-Mahdiya,** leading to the death an Ansar field commander, **Tawfik Mohamed Freij (Abu Abdullah),** were a punitive response to **Ansar. Ansar** had struck in late March at the army. One of their attacks took place in Al-Zeitoun, and the second in **Mustorod,** both near Cairo. Six soldiers were killed largely by non-Egyptian terrorists.

For the first time, a military spokesman, **Ahmed Ali,** openly made a direct link between the **Brotherhood and Ansar.** That shift is consistent with security expert opinion which makes a strong connection between the **Brotherhood and Ansar Beit Al-Maqdis. Nageh Ibrahim**, a former leader of **Al-Gamaa Al-Islamiyah** group asserts that **"January 25, 2011 gave the kiss of life to Al-Qaeda which created a branch for itself in Egypt."**

So call it what you wish: an alliance; a rapprochement, or even a convergence of interest between the **Brotherhood and Al-Qaeda.** Semantics are no cure for the perception in the Egyptian mind of a **Brotherhood** which is knee-deep in terrorism, in anti-Egyptian internationalism, and in amity with foreign actors who are in the business of using the term **"islamic"** to cover their failing attempts to replace a secular Egypt with an **Egyptian province of an Islamic trans-continental emirate**. **NUTS!!**

No wonder that secular Egypt, in its hour of self assertion, is reaching out for a strong hand to lead its fight against the Brotherhood International. Egypt of today sees in El-Sisi that strong hand. Delegations from Sinai all the way across the country to the Libyan border are flocking to his door to pledge their votes in the mid-May presidential elections.

This is a natural phenomenon in societies whenever they are in danger of having their identities submerged in an international

avalanche of a destructive nature. The prospective ascendary of El-Sisi to the Egyptian presidency shall represent the expression of a popular indigenous will that shall be immune from any distortion from beyond its national boundaries. It is a transformative period for the new Egypt which is determined to leave the Brotherhood International in the dust of their murderous illusion of a pan-Islamic caliphate!!

The Remaking of an Egypt Worthy of the 21st Century

Friday, April 18, 2014

"Only God knows the future!!" Now my late father, an Azhari ended his lectures on Islamic philosophy. Thus I am left with predictions regarding an Egypt under the expected presidency of **El-Sisi.** As I do so, a line from the great song about Don Quixote **"The Quest"** rings in my non-musical brain: **"To reach for the unreachable star."** The only candidate for the Egyptian presidency, which is predicted (a safe prediction) to begin before this June, is that military gentleman, **El-Sisi,** turned civilian. My vote for him is a vote for Egypt reaching **"the unreachable star."**

I am not in his pay. He does not know me. I have never met him. But I carefully followed his trajectory from Chief of the Egyptian Air Force; to a successor to that good man, **General Tantawi,** as Field Marshal; to his submission of his name as of April 16 as a presidential candidate. I also know his Cairo neighborhood of **Al Gammaliyah** which includes the tourist Mecca of the historic bazaar called **"Khan El-Khalili."** That is where ancient Egyptian art embraces Coptic and Islamic Egyptian art. And that is where my wife of 44 years, an American by the name of Grace to whom I was married at **Al-Shahr**Al-Aqari (Egypt's Notary Public Office) spent most of our vacation money. More importantly, I followed his public meetings and utterances from July 3, 2013 when he endorsed the public outcry against **Morsi** and the **Brotherhood** till this date.

The objectives of reaching the unreachable star of an El-Sisi presidency (or to copy the Egyptian graffiti: an CC presidency) parallel those of the UN objectives. These are: **peace and prosperity.** Let us transpose these on the Egyptian scene.

In Egypt, **"peace"** starts with the safety of the Egyptian street. The resurrected security apparatus, in terms of a re-trained police force, is now at work. Their nearly daily attacks on its personnel, especially in **Sinai** and rural areas perpetrated by the Brotherhood and affiliates within its franchise, since the legitimate ouster of Morsi's islamist regime in July 2013, are acts of desperadoes dead-enders. The role of the armed forces in these terrorist confrontations by the outlawed **Brotherhood** has made it necessary to have these forces act as **"police auxiliaries."**

Feeling the pain of the knock-out punches of the police and the army, the **Brotherhood International** has reached for its lowest ranks -university students. Their demonstrations throughout the nearly 20 universities in Egypt (where tuition is free) are akin to other terrorist organizations using unthinking human shields. To think that those infantile demonstrations are going to bring down the transitional government of **Judge Adly Mansour** is truly laughable. More comic in their ineffectiveness is the Brotherhood's aim of giving to the outside world the false impression that they are a **mass movement.** In reality, these outbursts on Egyptian university campuses prove daily that the Brotherhood is a **"mess movement."** The Egyptian judiciary is now in an overdrive to bring the law-breakers to justice.

The peace objective which an **El-Sisi** presidency is expected to pursue shall be sought relentlessly also beyond Egypt. A ring of steel around **Hamas** and **Ansar Beit Al-Maqdis** and **Islamic** jihad shall be perfected. Their 1500 tunnels from Gaza into Sinai are mostly gone; **Hamas** coffers are losing now from $250 million to $400 million of annual revenue from tunnel smuggling; the banning of the Brotherhood branches in the Gulf, with the exception of **Qatar,** is in effect together with their criminalization as terrorist outfits, a la Egyptian model; and the British investigations in **Brotherhood International** activities are being assisted.

In his meeting of April 15 with the representation of Arab/Egyptian tribes, numbering 240, whose leaders hailed from **Sinai,** the **Delta,** southern Egypt, the western desert, and the eastern desert, El-Sisi uttered as follows: **"Your role in bolstering Egypt's stability, and the aid you provide the State in restoring the country's peace and security, are crucial."**

Branching out beyond the country's primordial need for security, an **El-Sisi** presidency shall undoubtedly pursue in foreign policy a new mode: non-interference in Egypt's internal affairs. This is one area where the**Brotherhood** contributed to its own demise: the anti-Egyptian search for internationalizing the call for the return of Morsi to power. Egypt, especially after the imposition of American limited sanctions on it, has pivoted eastward. **Russia** for armament, **China** for trade, **India** for technology, the **Gulf** for investment in desert reclamation.

And in pursuit of the resurrected policy principle of **"focus on Egypt,"** the new Egypt has distanced itself from husbanding **"the Palestine Question."** With that in mind, the following questions have assumed a new urgency: **"the Coptic question," "The Nuban question," "the African question in the context of the water issue."** No more Egyptian military footprint outside of Egypt, and all international agreements, including the 1979 peace treaty with Israel, shall be observed.

With that focus on **"Egypt First and Always,"** the daily manifestations of the search for Egypt's development and prosperity have been publicized by **El-Sisi**campaign whose **"General Coordinator"** is the highly qualified **Ambassador Mahmous Karem,** a valued friend of nearly 40 years. Reporting on a visit to El-Sisi on April 17 by the Middle East envoy of the Government of Japan, the campaign highlighted El-Sisi's statement of welcome. In it he said: **"The Middle East is a region which faces great dangers and is in need of substantial and speedy aid in order not to fall prey to extremist influences... The Egyptian public has, throughout the past period, waited patiently. The coming phase calls for hard work to fulfill its expectations, and to solve its long-neglected developmental problems."**

In that context, I recall an interview in the early 1980s with **Frank Wisner,** the then-U.S. Ambassador to Cairo. Reporting on that interview for **Forbes Magazine,** I quoted **Wisner's** response to one of my questions regarding U.S. aid to Egypt. The Ambassador responded succinctly: **"Egypt does not need aid. It needs trade."** An aspect of the new Egypt's search for dignity is its grudging acceptance of U.S. aid. In fact, the Egyptian lower house of Parliament, before its dissolution by a court decree in 2012 had passed a non-binding resolution calling for refusal of U.S. aid. It is axiomatic to say that foreign aid is generally the other side of the coin of outside intervention -an anathema to the now rising Egypt.

It is common knowledge that Egypt's considerable natural resources have so far remained untapped. However, the real and durable resource is the huge untrained human resources whose skills are not up to the challenges of the 21st century, especially as regards to science and technology.

The unreachable star may yet be reached under this new presidency of **El-Sisi**which puts security first, and democracy and development as assured consequences of that security next. From these premises, begins the remaking of an Egypt worthy of the 21st century.

An Arab poet has once said: "The strong will to succeed exacts a price; that price is the exhaustion of the body to achieve its quest." Lost in this translation is the beauty of the cadence of Arabic poetry!!

35 MAY 2014

Inventing Non-Existing Facts About Egypt Has Become An Industry of The New York Times

Friday, May 2, 2014

In his op-ed column in New York Times of April 23, 2014, Thomas Friedman writes about Ukraine. Being a word-smith, he says: "Indeed, Ukraine has some Tahrir Square disease. The Kiev revolutionaries have been incredibly brave. But, like in Egypt, they have not yet translated their aspirations for an inclusive, non-corrupt, pro-E.U. future." A faulty comparison, and a conclusion about Egypt which reads the future about an Egyptian government which shall come into existence only several weeks from now. How prescient!!

Add to these inventions of facts, which undermine the credibility of the motto of **The New York Times,** at least when it comes to the new Egypt - **"All the News That's Fit to Print,"** is the paper's editorial page. In the issue of April 25, 2014, the relevant editorial entry is titled: **"A Questionable Decision on Egypt."**

That item, being by the paper's editors reflecting its programmed bias towards the new Egypt, begins by: **"American policy toward Egypt continued on its tortured, confusing path this week when the Obama administration resumed some aid to what has become an increasingly repressive State."**

And in his reporting from Cairo, on the front page of the **New York Times** of April 25, **David Kirkpatrick,** was true to form. His advocacy tarnishing the developments in Egypt is his mainstay. The headline in that report is subtitled:**"New Leaders Targeting Christians, Shiites and Atheists."** The third paragraph sums it all, as he asserts: **"Prosecutors continue to jail Coptic Christians, Shiite Muslims and atheists on charges of contempt of religion."**

Ironically, his last paragraph debunks his selective evidentiary statements, at least with regard to the Christians. That paragraph, which must have escaped his blue pencil of redaction. It reads: **"But Yousef Sidhoum, the editor of a Coptic newspaper, said it was natural that church leaders felt both sympathy and gratitude for Mr. Sisi. So do most Egyptians, Mr. Sidhoum said."**

Thanks God, **The New York Times,** even with being nearly daily **(April 23, 25, and 26)** deflating revolutionary Egypt, cannot dictate to a sovereign State its course of development. Yet such unrelenting ideological reporting by a paper of the status of the **N.Y.T.** has a provable effect on both the American and the Egyptian readers. I say **"provable effect"** on the basis of what I receive by the way of comments and questions from my readers and interlocutors. From the American side, I get questions such as **"why did the Revolution miss its mark?"** And from the Egyptian side, the questions usually revolve around**"Why are the Americans siding with the Muslim Brotherhood?"**

Legitimate questions, based on a barrage of falsehoods, propagandized by boastful and self-promoting ads in **The New York Times** such as **"Behind-the-scenes accounts of how our journalists capture the big stories of the day."** (April 25, 2014; page A.21).

But here are the veritable **"big stories of the day"** that **The New York Times** does not consider them **"Fit to Print":**

The Egyptian masses gave the **Brotherhood** its chance at the helm for one year (2012 to 2013). To their amazement, they discovered that the Brotherhood had used the legal means of the ballot box to achieve the illegal means of excluding all stripes of public opinion which do not subscribe to their quest for a **pan-Islamic Caliphate.**

The Revolution of June 30, 2013, far from being **"a coup,"** was the only available avenue to get rid of an Islamist reign of terror. That horrible experience had nothing to do with faith, any faith, nor with the historic tradition of a secular Egypt where Islamic Law and legislated law worked in harmony for the good of both the majority and all minorities.

The support of the national armed forces, under **El-Sisi,** protected the mass movement of **June 30, 2013.** Under **Field Marshal Tantawi,** those forces, being non-ideological, had also protected the January 25, 2011 Revolution which the Brotherhood saw fit to belatedly join.

All governments in the world, and here Egypt is no exception, are backed by their armed forces for security purposes, provided that they do not take over from the elected representatives the reigns of governance.

As in any revolution anywhere in the world, Egypt's two revolutions are a process. It does take time to mature, and to solidify. To prejudge this process as a failure is not and cannot be a rational judgement. Such irrationality casts aspersions not on Tahrir, but on**The New York Times** as a propagator of non-content news. Undoubtedly there have been errors committed in the course of Egypt's revolutions (January 25 and June 30). Sadly such errors have been recently committed, not by the Armed Forces, but by a member of the judiciary.

It was an unhinged judge who on April 28, 2014 at a court in **El-Minya** sentenced to death more than 680 members of the Muslim Brotherhood, including Mohamad Badie, the Brotherhood's Supreme Guide. That heinous ruling was in connection with the killing of a single police officer during riots at that provincial capital in southern Egypt last summer.

In a similar view of what may be described as **"judicial revanchism"** against the opponents of the present transitional government, another court in Cairo banned the activities of the April 6 movement, a liberal group which, in Tahrir on January 25, 2011, contributed to Mubarak's fall.

In these two instances, **The New York Times,** in its issue of **April 29** was correct in condemning the capital punishment, en masse, as**"political execution,"** and the banning of that liberal movement as**"a**

crackdown on dissent." In fact the **El-Minya** crazed judge is now besieged by an investigation by the **Judicial Inspection Department of the Justice Ministry.**

Yet, here again, the paper, with a broad brush, lays the blame on the entire post-Morsi government of which the judiciary is but one branch.

Without excusing such aberrations on the part of one Government branch which has been recently restored by the 2014 Constitution to its independence, that across the broad condemnation misses an essential fact: the post-Islamist Egyptian Government, which El-Sisi, in spite of his popularity, does not yet run, is ongoing through the teething errors of hit and miss. Fairness in reporting is the bedrock of educating public opinion as regards the realities of the yet unfinished Arab Spring/the Egyptian sector.

Egypt's present struggle against terrorism perpetrated by the**Brotherhood International,** directly or through proxies like**Ansar Beit Al-Maqdis** and **Al-Qaeda,** constitutes a huge boost to the global war on terror.

Among other salutary effects, it forced Hamas, now declared a terrorist organization by Egypt, Saudi Arabia and other Gulf States, into reconciling, at least for now, with the Palestinian National Authority.

It also propelled a meeting in late April between U.S. Secretary of State, **John Kerry,** and the Chief of Intelligence of Egypt, **General Muhammad Farid Al-Tohamy** in Washington, D.C. The obvious purpose: to coordinate the measures relating to the war on terror between Egypt and the U.S. This was followed by a meeting between**Kerry** and **Nabil Fahmy,** Egypt's able foreign minister.

Towards the same goals, President Obama has recently approved the release to Egypt of 10 Apache helicopters to bolster Egypt's warring on terrorism in Sinai, where as recently as yesterday, 2 security personnel were eliminated at the criminal hands of Sinai terrorists.

As the U.S. s gradually turning inward, for the sake of better serving American development priorities, so is the case with Egypt. Gone are the go-go years of Egypt's disastrous interventions in the affairs of other Arab States.

A simple reading of a statement made by El-Sisi on April 26, 2014, to a delegation representing sports in Egypt, reveals this trend -not one word about Arab issues outside Egypt. That solitary emphasis on the age-old principle of **"charity begins at home"** is galvanizing not only Egyptian and other efforts, including Gulf States support. It is leading the Davos economic organization to consider holding that prestigious conference in Egypt after the elections.

These are but some of the news which this blogger sees as **"fit to print."** The two Egyptian revolutions do not deserve the myopic view of **The New York Times** of being constantly seen only through the prism of **"the glass is half empty."**

Such faulty judgments remind me somehow of the irrationality manifested by some top Republican senators in the U.S. Congress who are rooting for new wars.

But **The New York Times** is not the only voice of doom crying foul for every misstep which the Egyptian Revolution might take, even before these steps are taken.

In an article in the prestigious **Foreign Affairs** of May/June 2014, entitled**"Near Eastern Promises,"** its two authors indulge in an imaginary hypothesis. They fancifully claim the following:

"Although it is impossible to prove a hypothetical, had the United States been willing to come forth quickly with $5-$10 billion in additional aid for Egypt (on top of the roughly $1.5 billion that Egypt already receives annually), it probably would have bought Washington enormous leverage -perhaps enough to prevent the worst excesses of Mohamed Morsi, the Islamist president who came to power after the revolution, and thus forestall Morsi's overthrow by generals who seem determined to return Egypt to its pre-revolutionary torpor."(p. 100)

Are you guys for real? So you think that throwing a bunch of $$ at **The Muslim Brotherhood International** would have placated it and saved Egypt form its internal confrontation with terrorism?

The **Brotherhood**, with continuous infusion of money from **Qatar** and its foreign franchises, not to mention Mr. Money Bags, a.k.a. (also known as) **Khairat El-Shater,** its Deputy Supreme Guide, has always been awash with money. Its fatal deficiency has not been **lack of funding** -but **lack of founding** on Egyptian soil which it had regarded as a mere staging ground for **pan-Islamism.**

You seem to advocate to America and the world that an Islamist Egypt would have been more preferable to a secular Egypt led by El-Sisi. Please, get your facts straight from the Egyptian multitudes. That would be more lasting than inventing hypotheses which has no shelf life!!

From The Great Hall of St. Mark's Cathedral, a New Chant Arose: "El-Sisi Raiisi"

Friday, May 16, 2014

It was the holiest of the Holy Days in the Egyptian Coptic calendar: **April 20,**when **Easter of the West and Easter of the East** happened to coincide. **Pope Tawadrous II,** the Pope of Alexandria, had on April 19 received Field Marshal **Abdel-Fattah El-Sisi,** who had come to the Cathedral, named after an Alexandrian, St. Mark (one of the Gospel writers), to pay his respects. As the Pope began on April 20 to celebrate the holy mass, he, out of courtesy, expressed thanks for the visit of El-Sisi, that iconic presidential candidate.

At the mere mention of the word **"El-Sisi,"** it was as if **His Holiness the Pope**had pushed a **"Go"** button. The congregation of thousands of worshipers rose up as **"one man"** in a new chant: **"El-Sisi Raiisi"** (El-Sisi is my President). It was a new chant lasting for several minutes; a rhythmically vocal celebration of an El-Sisi presidency; a unanimous vote of confidence in the way Egypt was being transformed.

The **Copts,** being a minority of about 10% of a population of 93 millions, of which the Muslims are an overwhelming majority, were hailing the rebirth of a secular Egypt. The dark era of Brotherhood rule of one year **(June 2012 to July 2013)** was over. A secular rebirth has taken place, lending more joy to the coptic 50 days of post-Easter greeting in the Coptic language: **"Ekhrestos Anesty"** to which the response is **"alisos Anesty!!"** **(Christ Has Risen - He Has Truly Risen).**

The **Easter episode is more about the revolutionary transformation of Egypt from 2011 to 2014, than about El-Sisi presidency.** That in spite of the fact that that presidency is to be regarded a high point in that transformation. The battle for the soul of Egypt between the **Islamists** and the**Secularists** has been decided in favor of the secularists, with vast implications for the whole region. This is regardless of the results of the expected determined efforts of an El-Sisi team to tackle the huge heap of issues in all fields which have dragged Egypt down the steep hill of development in the digital age.

First and foremost, the war on terror inside Egyptian borders has now pitted a whole nation behind it, battling the enemies of its security and development. Declaring the **Brotherhood** a terror organization under Egyptian laws has finally put an end to the zig-zagging relationships between successive Egyptian Governments and the Brotherhood since 1928, the Brotherhood's birth date. The abuse of Islam by the Brotherhood for an ultimate political grab is now getting its oxygen tube cut off. Now all the **Brotherhood International**franchises from South East Asia to Africa and on to Europe and the Americas shall undoubtedly be impacted by the deterioration of its poisonous root in Egypt.

These historic developments cannot but have a salutatory effect on mainstream Islam which for a long dreadful period, especially after 9/11, has suffered the indignities of **Islamophobia** nearly world-wide. Muslims, whether traveling by air or running for public office in non-Muslim areas, have largely been presumed guilty till proven innocent. Even **President Obama** is periodically harassed by his political adversaries as **"a closet Muslim."** His middle name**"Hussein"** has become a political liability. Mosques in the **U.S., the U.K., France and Germany** are looked upon as if they were terrorist recruiting establishments.

The wars in both **Iraq** and **Afghanistan** furthered the gulf of hatred between the Muslim and non-Muslim worlds. Torture became the tool of enhanced interrogations. And the criminality of **Boko Haran** in **Nigeria** together with the rise of sectarianism throughout the vast Muslim region of 1.5 billion inhabitants are now the topics of daily news reports and the justification for wars and repression in Muslim areas in both **Russia** and **China.** And now there is in**India** a **BJP Modi** administration sending shivers of fear up the spines of a 100 million Muslims, both **Sunnis and Shiis.**

Faced with these inter-faith calamities, neither the **Organization of Islamic Cooperation** consisting of 57 U.N. Member States, nor the Iranian-induced inter-faith dialogue at the U.N., could stem the anti-Islamic tide. The crescent on Muslim flags began to cause non-Muslim societies unspoken unease.

Is the **Brotherhood** responsible for all these calamities which have befallen Islam whose primary emphasis is on **"No Compulsion in Faith Adoption?"** Not entirely.

But its advocacy of returning Islam to what it perceived as its puritanical origin caused its offshoots in various parts of the world to magnify that advocacy. Its resort to force, especially assassinations and oppression of non-Muslim minorities, catapulted its offspring organizations into the formation of the dreaded and dreadful **Al-Qaeda. Bin Laden's** top lieutenant is **Ayman Zawahri,** an Egyptian physician whose brother, **Muhammad Zawahri,** remained in Egypt and helped bring the Morsi regime closer to Hamas in Gaza.

The **Brotherhood** hubbub nearly drowned the historic message of non-political Islam announced by **Al-Azhar** on **August 17, 2011,** 6 months after the fall of Mubarak. Entitled **"Al-Azhar Document on Egypt's Future,"** it encapsulated eleven principles, the first of which included **"Islam, in its legislation, civilization, and history does not recognize a religiously-based State."** No wonder that the **Coptic Church** enthusiastically endorsed that document, while the **Brotherhood** denounced it because the Islamists saw in it the torpedoing of their advocacy for pan-Islamism within a mythical Caliphate.

And when the Islamic governance of one year was ended by the many millions gathered in Tahrir on **June 30, 2013,** millions whose chants of anguish had the backing of the military under the leadership of **El-Sisi,** the Brotherhood went on a rampage in Cairo, through the 6-week sit-ins, and in Sinai, through the activation of its terrorist comrades in Sinai where army and police personnel were the targets of a mini-war.

With all their bravado about mass support and the possibility of army and police defections from **"the un-Islamic regime,"** their propaganda resulted in no more than a few demonstrations by a limited number of university students who clamored for the release of **Morsi** from jail and his **"second coming"** to the presidential palace. **Pipe dreams!!** The more the Brotherhood gunned down both security and civilian personnel, the brighter **El-Sisi** image shined, and the greater his march to the presidency, as the symbol of the re-normalization of Egypt, was welcomed. In spite of another presidential candidacy, that of **Hamdain Sabbahi,** El-Sis's march to the helm became hugely unstoppable.

Evidence indicates that the rise of **El-Sisi** to the position of largely uncontested presidential candidate, following the national elections later this May, is largely due to the masses' burning desire for security and development.

In Egypt, the Arab spring has caused major dislocations of these twin areas of national priorities. Examining those popular demands from the perspective of Egypt as a republic since July 1952, one finds them to have become a constant throughout the reigns of the previous 7 presidents: **Naguib, Nasser, Sadat, Mubarak, Tantantawi, Morsi, and Mansour.** It was only during the Morsi regime that neither security nor development was the major concern. The emphasis of Morsi and his parent organization, **The Brotherhood, has been on Islamization through Brotherhoodization.**

Against this unsettling background, the **El-Sisi** campaign has remained focused on translating the huge popularity of El-Sisi into a clear national program: **security and development.** Throughout the many group meetings which El-Sisi held with a large variety of Egyptian organizations, the emphasis on those national needs has been unremitting.

As a presidential candidate, his symbol, **a five-points star** on ads in the Egyptian street and on the ballots, symbolized the hope of a new dawn. That dawn brought with it over the national horizon, **the concept of Egyptianness.** It resonated dramatically with a public that has grown not only weary, but in fact disgusted, with the failed policies of interventionism in the affairs of other Arab countries. The average Egyptian citizen, as produced by the Arab Spring in Tahrir, saw in that over the borders outreach the root cause for Egypt's retardation.

The groups which heard El-Sisi's message from El-Sisi himself did not only represent a source of added legitimization to El-Sisi's candidature. They also reflected broad concern for the previously marginalized groups as well as under-utilized professional constellations.

They included Arab tribes from Sinai and the western desert; the sports community; the peasants from the south; the small business and commerce communities, the media community, youth organizations; women syndicates; representatives of the science and technology communities; the leadership of the various branches of the armed forces and police recruits; the film and arts unions; and the diplomatic and foreign policy communities and the judiciary. **An overwhelming amalgam of various sectors of Egyptian society, flocking to vote by their feet for El-Sisi before giving him a landslide victory which is expected to bury the question of "an El-Sisi coup" as propagated by the Brotherhood and its foreign allies.**

They chanted with him **"Tahia Misr" (Long Live Egypt).** The vision presented through these meetings was to have Egypt, in the long run, rise up gradually to the levels of the newly-developed societies of **India and Brazil.** This was an El-Sisi version of **"Yes We Can."**

As to the form of democracy emerging under an El-Sis presidency, the candidate did not shrink from explaining that each society has the right to fashion its own brand of democracy in accordance with its societal norms. In his meeting with the Editors-in-Chief of the Egyptian press, held on May 7, El-Sisi said: **"We face a problem of evoking the prototype of democracies as practiced in settled States. Applying at this stage the standards of western democracies does injustice to the Egyptian reality of today. Then in a lengthy interview with two Egyptian talk show hosts, he urged the U.S. to "Look at us with Egyptian eyes."**

These stances lend more credibility to the Coptic chants during the celebration of the Orthodox Easter: **"El-Sisi Raiisi."** For they now feel safe in a secularly-reborn Egypt, which is inclusive and respectful of the rights of minorities.

The chant of **"El-Sisi Raiisi"** goes on, in spite of the ill-informed characterization of the U.S. media of an El-Sisi presidency as a return to military rule -an abortion of the march towards civilian rule and democracy. Our last blog posting dealt with the selective reporting of **New York Times** in that direction, contrary to the paper's motto **"All the News That is Fit to Print."**

It was therefore with satisfaction that I received from a friend a comment on my blog posting disparaging that motto. In his email, the commentator, a graduate of Columbia University, quoted from an article on **The New York Times,** published in the 1960s by a University newspaper by the name of **"The Columbia Jester."** The article reversed the motto of the New York Times to read: "All the News That Fits, We Print."

At a meeting with the representatives of southern Egypt, on May 14, a speaker,**Judge Ihab Ramzi,** a prominent copt, addressed El-Sisi in these

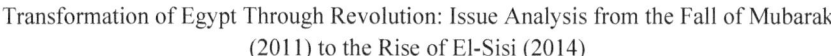

words: **"It was love for country and concern about its destiny which united the Egyptians in their second revolution of June 30, 2013. When these millions took to the streets, they were aware of the great role which you would play in rescuing Egypt from the dark tunnel in which it lived for one year of Brotherhood rule."**

Ramzi's words found tangible expression by the throngs of Egyptian Americans voting for their hero at the Egyptian Consulate-General in New York on May 15. Braving the rain, they turned that event, under my own eyes, into an impromptu festival -a wedding.

Unfurling the Egyptian flag, holding up laminated photos of El-Sisi, they chanted while swaying with their pastors and their children: "El-Sisi Raiisi." You cannot make that historic scene up, even if you tried!! I was there witnessing it.

36 JUNE 2014

By His Farewell Speech to Egypt As Its Outgoing Interim President, Judge Adly Mansour Redefined His Homeland

Friday, June 6, 2014

How did **Justice Adly Mansour,** Egypt's interim President bid the public **"farewell"** on June 3, 2014 so that **El-Sisi** assumes his rightful post as the legitimate successor? Here follows an analysis from the original highly articulated Arabic, translated by this blogger in the form of highlights:

The great Egyptian public, through exercising their right to vote in that presidential election in May, have manifested a keen political sense. They proved that they were truly worthy of their great Egypt;

The Egyptians observance of discipline as they voted for their choice of the next President (**El-Sisi** won by a landslide against **Sabbahi**) has made **Mansour** proud to be an Egyptian;

The greatness of the homeland is anchored in its historically being the world's crossroads, the Locus of revealed religions, the cradle of civilization, the fount of arts, the locus of distinctive architecture, and the bridge between 3 of the world's continents;

Egypt is the beacon of Africa's freedom, the gift of the Nile, the owner of the Suez Canal, the host of **Al-Azhar** and the great **Coptic Church.** Egypt is defined in four ways: An Arab, an African, an Islamic, and a Mediterranean State;

After evoking **"the genius of it's geographic location,"** he turned to the low ebb at present in the fortunes of revolutionary Egypt, by affirming that after darkness there shall be light. The country's youth are its vanguard and its pulsing heart. **June 30** was a date not to be forgotten in the turnaround of Egyptian fortunes. That **Second Revolution,** sparked by popular will, would not have succeeded without the backing of the military and the police.

"At that critical juncture, it was the Egyptian people who brought me to be their interim president. History shall register that it was the citizens who had kept the oldest State in recorded history from collapse. Since the Pharaoh Narmer (Mena), southern Egypt and northern Egypt had been forever united, not to be split asunder by those who had been forced out of power in July 2013." No mention by name of the **Muslim Brotherhood.** There was no need to include their name in **Mansour's** farewell speech.

Looking at the security and economic bottomless chasm which **Adly Mansour** peered at upon assuming his one year of transitional presidency, he said: **"Egypt is a body which has been for decades exhausted by political confusion."** Yet within three years, its public rose against two failed regimes (again without naming either **Mubarak** or **Morsi**). **A period of decay during which both faith and country became the preserve of monopolists who led it into political and economic deadends followed by blind terrorism** determined to impose its distorted vision on both Muslim and Coptic Egypt. A total mischaracterization of both.

Turning to the help and encouragement given by friendly sister Arab States, he saluted **Saudi Arabia, the United Arab Emirates, Kuwait, Bahrain, the Hashenite Kingdom of Jordan and the State of Palestine.**

As to those States which used the stressful period of transitional Egypt to denigrate it or to interfere into its internal affairs, **Adly Mansour,** in an

409

even tone that shed light not heat said: **"To the other camp, I say: Egypt is as old as history. With God's help, it shall stand forever tall with you or without you. Like it or not, be advised that Egypt is making a historic come back. Your persistence in moving along your wrong path shall only make corrections more costly."**

Addressing his successor, **Abdel-Fattah El-Sisi,** he said: **"Today, I turn Egypt's rulership, which has been entrusted to me for a year, to the next president who has been chosen by the voice of the people. I turn to him a State which has a Constitution, a democratically-elected President, and very soon with an elected Parliament. It is a State destined to regain its place and role internationally, both economic and political."**

Harking back tot he past 3 years when international aid was offered at the price of Egypt's dignity and its sovereign right to decision-making, he affirmed: **"Never again shall anyone bargain with this nation on it dignity for a loaf of bread or on its security for the price of freedom. This is now a country whose wealth shall be dedicated to its citizens. It security shall be ensured by its responsible practice of freedom within the framework of loyalty to the homeland. In this regard we must beware of special interest groups whose greed obfuscates facts and produces an atmosphere of opportunism."**

As a former **President of the Supreme Constitutional Court**(which the Islamists regime was bent on its destruction), **Adly Mansour** addressed **El-Sisi** saying: **"Mr. President, I state before you and before all of Egypt that the judiciary is the impenetrable citadel of justice, which it administers without fear or regard to material benefits. Our new Constitution has provided for its independence. Justice is the pillar on which governance rests. And human rights, in its broadest meaning, also covers economic development which should, in time, extend to southern Egypt, Sinai, the western desert, the triangle** of Halayeb **and Shalatin**(adjoining the borders of the Sudan).**"**

Faith, **Adly Mansour** declared in his farewell address, must be rediscovered as a comprehensive movement for enlightenment. It should not affect morals and values only. It should uplift the level of popular culture and style. In this enlightenment movement, our writers, poets, journalists, artists and innovations should warn against the pitfalls of prejudice and the aversion towards **"the other."**

Ending up his historic farewell speech, **Judge Adly Mansour**addressed the Coptic community. He said, **"Coptic Egypt is an integral part of this blessed country. To the Copts I say that your contributions to the strength of the texture of the Egyptian nation have been limitless. Your blood in Sinai was mixed with the blood of your Muslim brethren in the defense of the common homeland."**

Then he continued: Your great sons and daughters continue to enrich Egypt. No one can forget the late great **Pope Shenouda III,** the late **Makram Obeid, Fouad Aziz Ghali, Boutros Boutros Ghali, Kamal El-Mallakh, Dr. Louis Awad; Dr. Younan Rizk, Dr. Magdy Yacoub** - all luminous Egyptians in whose contributions we shall forever revel. This is especially so during the 1919 uprising against British occupation whose symbol shall forever be the**Crescent and the Cross in an eternal embrace.**

Devoting this blog posting to that farewell speech has behind it a historic reason: No such speech symbolizing the peaceful transfer of power has ever been delivered to the Egyptians. It is an iconic occasion not to be lost in the avalanche of daily news. By that speech of June 3, 2014, Judge Adly Mansour has redefined his homeland and its mission.

El-Sisi Begins His Presidential Reign By a Bicycle Ride in Egypt - How Appropriately Symbolic!!

Friday, June 20, 2014

By leading a bicycle marathon in Cairo, President El-Sisi was sending multiple appropriate signals: the importance of the safety of the Egyptian street; the need to conserve energy in order to reduce subsidies; and the willingness to make governmental pragmatism a national cause.

There is another added symbolism in that bicycle marathon. Nowhere have we ever seen in the Arab world a head of state on a bicycle. For generations, we have been accustomed to watch from a distance a long caravan of black limos with tinted glass windows, surrounded by sirens and a host of motorcycles signaling the ultra-speedy movement of the Head of State on his country's streets. So you had to take a double look at that youthful Egyptian President on his bicycle, surrounded by sportsmen as if you were watching a scene from a Scandinavian country, not an Arab State.

Am I here romanticising the significance of that El-Sisi presidential parade? You bet I am. And why not if I were to link that symbol of pragmatism to this new era of Egypt's struggle to regain its composure and sanity after 3 very long troublesome years.

So here is more welcome symbolisms:

Egypt is in sore need for housing. So who is now its Prime Minister? **Dr. Ibrahim Mehlib,** a former Minister of Housing.

Egypt's Ministry of Information has existed in the midst of multiple codes of professional conduct for the media, and numerous official spokesman for nearly all the other ministries. **Redundancy, and no appreciable impact on the flow, style or analysis of public information in or about Egypt. Result:** Disbanding that ministry from the line-up of 31 Cabinet portfolios.

Prior to El-Sisi presidency, there was a ministry for **"Transitional Justice,"** charged with dealing with integrating personnel of prior regimes. It has to do with inclusiveness within a framework of the Rule of Law. **Result:** Because it straddles the portfolios of justice, human rights, and civil liberties, that ministry has also been disbanded. Its replacement is a Board, or a Council on which various shades of opinion shall be represented.

An uptick has occurred in the ugly phenomenon of sexual assault by hordes of young men against females in public places. Prior to the transfer of power to El-Sisi, **Judge Adly Mansour,** the interim president, had toughened the laws applicable to this heinous crime.

Yet on the day of that transfer of power, a massive attack against a young woman took place in **Tahrir Square** generating public revulsion all over Egypt . Consequently, one of the first public acts by President **El-Sisi** was to visit the victim and her family at the hospital. The new president did not only offer the victim roses. He publicly expressed apologies and in a blunt language promised that the newly promulgated laws shall be enforced in full measure.

In regard to Africa, several commentators noted the absence of several Heads of State from the festivities of El-Sisi installation as President earlier this month. They saw in this a sign of a low ebb in Cairo relations with Africa. Even those five African Heads of State who took part, including **Chad, Eritrea and Equatorial Guinea**were impunged by those commentators. Their take on this was that those presidents came to power in coups similar to what they perceived to have been the path of **El-Sisi** to power.

Nonsense. It is the same old story of whether the **Second Egyptian Revolution of June 30, 2013** represented **"a coup"**or a legitimate popular recall of Morsi. What these commentators gloss over is that in the new Egypt, the old Nasserite way of thrusting the nose of Egypt into the internal affairs of its neighbors -Africa and Arab- is over. Those days are gone, thanks to the pragmatic priorities in foreign policy for the new Egypt. The summit level of representation of **Saudi Arabia, the Emirates, and Kuwait** (present sources of funding of the transition in Egypt) and **Jordan,** meant, more in practical terms, to the Egypt of El-Sisi.

In addition, the suspension of Egypt's membership in the **African Union,** a symbolic bow to the faulty **"coup"** argument, played a part in the absence of several African Heads of State and Government. Now this suspension is over, and Egypt, as a Charter member since 1963 of African unity, whatever that means, is back to that African conclave. Its primary goal is mending relations with Ethiopia in regard to her share, together with the Sudan, of Nile water.

The disparaging comments on El-Sisi's installation as president fall in what I call **"the Law of Anticipated Reactions."** That is the law of **"leap to faulty conclusions, then ponder!!"**

Behind all these symbols of the pragmism of the new Egypt are hard realities. Some of these realities are domestic, and some are external as discussed above. A tectonic shift in foreign policy in the **Egypt of El-Sisi** has taken place. It denotes staying clear from armed conflicts either in the backyards or the frontyards of your neighbors. Leaders with military experience like El-Sisi are usually the best assessors of the high price of war in both blood and treasure. Egypt's developmental decline began with Nasser's wars.

With the containment of Islamism in Egypt, and with the daily assertion of national sovereignty and security in Sinai, through, among other measures, keeping **Hamas** at bay, Egypt is now pivoting in one essential and logical direction: **Egypt.**

Let us here look at how the present **Obama doctrine** and the emerging **El-Sisi doctrine** are largely similar. The two leaders seem to be seeing the world through the same prism: **"Unless the homeland is directly threatened, no boots on the ground or bombs from the air shall be employed beyond national borders."**

Endless wars have caused both Cairo and Washington, D.C. retardation at home. For **Obama,** building America's infrastructure has greater priority than building Afghanistan super-structure. For El-Sisi, **Hamas** and the **Brotherhood** are terrorist organizations which should be repulsed in order to develop Egypt and keep the peace with Israel.

Both the U.S. and Egypt are now pivoting toward Asia, with America toward the pacific and Egypt towards Sinai. As Cairo has downgraded the cause of pan-Arabism in favor of Egyptianism, **D.C.** has abandoned the cause of fighting other peoples' wars, whether in **Libya, Syria or Iraq** which is now on the verge of sectarian civil war and dismemberment.

It should not escape our attention that for the foreign affairs portfolio of the new Egypt, an able Minister of Foreign Affairs, **Nabil Fahmy,** has been replaced by an equally able new Cabinet member: **Sameh Shukri.** Shukri has been plucked from his post as Ambassador to the U.S. for managing a different Egyptian foreign policy: warmth towards America with equal openness to other world and regional powers. That is in spite of the recent misguided U.S. benign outlook on the Muslim Brotherhood as a legitimate and peaceful opposition.

In conclusion, this blogger says to President El-Sisi:

We applaud your riding a bicycle in the streets of Cairo as an impetus for the security of the Egyptian street and for the development of Egypt through energy conversation. Better riding a bicycle at home than riding a tank crossing over other national boundaries.

In the presently tumultously and fractured Middle East, peace is a strategic path to prosperity at home.

DEDICATED TO THE VICTIMS OF TERRORISM IN QUEBEC, OTTAWA, AND QUEENS, NEW YORK CITY.

The most important dispute in the Arab and Muslim Worlds is how to contain terrorism. The mixing of Islamic law (Sharia), undigested and ill-informed with governance has created a pan-regional, indeed global, frantic search for answers. Neither the League of Arab States (LAS), nor the Organization of Islamic Cooperation (OIC) has manifested any capability to effectively deal with the catastrophe of misunderstanding Jihad in Islamic jurisprudence. Their anti-terror conventions of the late 1990s stand today as toothless instruments facing wild animals masquerading as true Arabs or true Muslims.

The present process of mitigating criminal jihad is a fake process. It is fake because it relies on mere statements of condemnation which are bereft of any collective enforcement. The reason lies in the fact that these organizations, much like the UN itself, are state-based. The worlds of the Arabs and the Muslims of today have largely sidelined the state. Only the non-State actor stands today powerful, cruel, ignorant and defiant not only regionally but globally.

I am therefore obliged to focus today on the only viable instrument, complementing the use of force for years to come, in mitigating this calamity. It is an instrument which I might call "From Here We Begin." We have to begin by a massive plan for re-educating ourselves and the world in the intricacies of Islamic jurisprudence to deny terrorism any legitimacy.

ISIS is neither Islamic nor a State. It, and similar organizations, are criminal offenses. A criminal offense is a legal creature requiring sanction. In this framework, the present International Coalition of nearly 40 countries represent, under Islamic Law, the authentic meaning of what "jihad" is. Within this framework, the U.S. and its coalition partners are the true face of jihad directed against FASAD, (meaning corruption in Arabic) through terroristic jihadism. So when such criminal gangs like ISIS, horasan, Al-Nusra, Boko Haram, and Islamic Jihad, call themselves "Islamic," they are masquerading under that nomer. Their sole purpose is an illegal power grab. Legally, the most appropriate appellation for them is "jihadism." By this definition I mean an industry which began in the early

1990s in consequence of Al-Qaeda's successful combat against the Soviets in Afghanistan in the late 1980s. But Al-Qaeda franchises have grown, diversified, and multiplied. Yet the UN and the LAS and the OIC are still issuing empty nonsense.

The list of Islamic jurisprudential rules delegitimizing Jihadism is long. Therefore here is a shorter list, based on the Quran, the Sunna (Muhammad's traditions in word and deed), ijtihad, and legislated law in nearly all the 57 State Members of the Organization of Islamic Cooperation (OIC):

-The Quran, though providing only 200 verses with legal input from a total of its 6400 verses, call for Jihad under specific rules. Culled from the Quran, which is the primary source of Islamic Law (sharia), these rules are:
 • Fight only those who fight you;
 • Fight proportionally, otherwise you become a transgressor;
 • If your adversary sues for peace, accept it through a written contract;
 • Let there be no hostility except toward those who are oppressing you;
 • God (in Arabic, Allah) is with those who restrain themselves;
 • Be just by not fighting those who do not fight you;
 • With those non-combatants, deal kindly and justly with them, for God loves those who are just;
 • "Respect your obligations" is the first verse in Qur'anic Chapter Number 5 entitled: "The Table-Al-Maida" it says: "O Ye who believe, fulfill all your contracts;" and
 • The term "Shaheed" (martyr) does not apply to a dead terrorist. It applies to all those who perished on 9/11, and in Quebec, and in Ottawa, and in Queens, New York.

The clear conclusion from this short list of rules, regarding legally-supported jihad, is the exact opposite of Jihadism. Jihadism is a rebellion against humanity, including Islam and the Muslim world. For the rules of war under Islamic Law can be summed up as follows:
 • Muslims should fight only when they have been wronged;
 • Persecution, as in all legal systems, is a casus belli;
 • The aim of combat is self-defense, but within one's own territory;
 • Self-defense includes defense of one's faith;
 • Faith is not the monopoly of Muslims;
 • In Islamic Law, redressing grievances is not for mere revenge. It is for the establishment of peace.

From the above, it can be seen that Islamic jurisprudence is not alien to the text or import of the Geneva

Conventions, or of other universally-accepted conventions. This is Islamic jurisprudence, which does not even call for a minaret or for a Burka. Beyond this enumeration, there is a rich culture. For Islam is not only a faith. It is also culture flowing like the Nile River through 1.6 billion Muslims with women at par with men, as in the time of the Prophet Muhammad.

Examining this culture, it is important to keep in mind that Islam is the now (the State), and the hereafter. Of course, law and practice are two different issues, especially when we find glaring mistakes, and gaping holes in Islamic practice.

While Islamic law calls for the removal of dictators, one finds the prevalence of dictatorships in Muslim countries. Dictatorial regimes look upon conciliation as weakness, on treaties as a non-ending process; on Hamas's non-acceptance of the right of Israel to exist as a legitimate entity; on international conferencing as only photo-ops.

Islam accepts supplementation of Sharia, as based on the Quran and Prophetic tradition, by legislated law. But in practice, one finds such supplementation resisted by sectors of Islamic society. This is a society which covers a huge land mass from the Atlantic to the west, to the Pacific to the east. There is no uniform or coordinated Islamic instruction to ameliorate such resistance. There is not even a voice raised in the OIC that Shii Islam is the other legitimate wing of the Muslim Umma.

In this regard, the LAS and the OIC are mere talk shows in Cairo and in Jedda respectively. By their silence in regard to this dangerous fiction of a sunni/shii religious divide, they are contributing to its translation into a war –a war of possibly a 100 years!! The Quran and the Sunna equate between man and woman in nearly all aspects of life. Yet, we find gender equality woefully lacking. That is revealed in the case of driving a vehicle: Women in certain areas are prevented from driving a car. This is while women in other areas are taught to be civilian pilots in (Egypt), fighter pilots (in the United Arab Emirates), and valiant front-line combatants (within the Kurdish troops fighting ISIS in Kobani -the new

Middle Eastern Stalingrad.) While Islamic Law encourages diversity, namely the acceptance of the other, even if the other has no religion or faith, we find this woefully lacking in application. These are loopholes in the proper understanding of Islamic Law and conforming practices. It is not different from the injunction in the U.S. Constitution against degrading punishment. We find the subversion of this constitutional principle when juxtaposed against the ready acceptance by Cheney and Rumsfeld, the new American warlords, of torture including waterboarding.

It is abundantly clear from Sharia that jihadism is anti-Islamic. Jihadism constitutes crimes against humanity and against the State. The proper word for it is FITNA - "Mayhem." Take ISIS as an example. Under Islamic Law it is abhorrent. It is a prime candidate for jihad against it as defined by Islamic jurisprudence. Why?

1. It persecutes non-Muslims, and Muslims who are not Sunni, and Sunnis who do not wish to submit to its Diktat;

2. It butchers its hostages. Together with ISIS videos, Jim Foley and others, whether Americans, Canadians, British or French, are voices from the grave confirming this horrendous fact. This is while Islamic Law, in its Rules of War, matches the Geneva Conventions of 1949 in regard to the protection of civilians in times of war. In its brutality, ISIS is no more than "Butchers Without Borders."

3. Its fascist propaganda, especially through social media, is a horrendous violation of Islamic injunction against falsehood defined in Sharia as FASAD, corruption;

4. It has eliminated national boundaries by the force of arms and panzer-like shock and awe. The sanctity of the international frontier is an important aspect of the Quranic call for abiding by treaties. The UN Charter is a treaty. Admission to UN membership is an acknowledgment of a fixed boundary. Violation of national boundaries is, in Islamic Law, a clear violation of a contract.

5. It confuses jihad as meaning Qital (the first meaning struggle, the latter meaning combat);

6. It wrongly re-defines the Muslims, not as a community of believers, but as a State. Al-Azhar, the citadel of Islamic learning, established in Cairo since 975 A.D., in its document of August 2011 has delegitimized a State based solely on religion. This historic document has been fully supported by the Egyptian Coptic Church.

7. As supported by the Egyptian Coptic Church, ISIS shreds the Fatwas (non-enforceable legal opinion by an authorized scholar) of moderate Islam.

Moderation is the lifeblood of that faith.

8. It holds civilians, especially in non-Muslim societies as culpable for the acts of their governments. Qur'anic Chapter 6, Verse 164 delegitimized holding an individual to be culpable for the acts of others. Here Governments are to be regarded as "others." It says: "No bearer of burdens can bear that burden of others." This is the essence of modern laws which regard "crime" as personal. It is not transferrable unless there is proven conspiracy. And at the same time, it regards "torture" as an Islamic mode of behavior. Utter nonsense.

9. ISIS aims at the destruction of law and order, unless based on its interpretation of these constructs. It has its head, in Iraq where I served from 2006 to 2008 as a defense attorney, Al-Baghdadi - a thug from Anbar Province. ISIS anointed him as Caliph. Contrary to what Bernard Louis of Princeton claims when he accepts the Caliphate as a pan-Islamic goal, the Caliphate since 1924 has become a mythical form of government, which lures to its black banner ignorant young from across the world. They have now flocked to ISIS by the hundreds, seeking an express entry to paradise. How stupid!! At least the Crusaders in the 11th century were driven by a papal ideology in their quest for reclaiming Jerusalem. Even Saladin, the victor, reconciled with his adversaries. He respected the norms governing the rights of POWS. That was ten centuries ago, before the Geneva Conventions.

10. When it existed, the Caliphate was originally a social contract between the Caliphah and the Umma (the community of believers). It does not exist in Ramadi (Iraq) or Raqqah (Syria), the claimed capitals of the satanic hordes of barbarian ISIS. Contrary to the image of a black-clad executioner with a knife in his hand, Islamic Law, nearly fifteen-hundred years ago, has propounded the principle of "No Crime Without a Decreed Law." In conclusion, there is no way to vanquish this world terror except through determined armed struggle. Together with an educational campaign, a true Marshall Plan for Re-Education, with the translation of Arabic, Farsi, Turkish, and Urdu and Pushtu as one of its tools.

This shall take years. And this should include the reform of the judiciary in Muslim countries. It is contrary to universal judicial cooperation for some States in the US to legislate the denial of any reference or use of Islamic Law (Sharia) in state courts. This is an unintended boon to jihadism. And our efforts to prevail in this Third World War should also be combined with efforts in the West to abate Islamophobia whose aspects are manifest in the US in various forms. These include Guantanamo, and Congressional hearings where Muslims are quizzed on ill-defined matters, such as the degree of their cooperation with the Police and other agencies in profiling their neighbors. This is nothing but a retrograde new McCarthyism of Congressional Representative Peter King of New York, a graduate of a humanistic great college in Brooklyn Heights, St. Francis College!!

Time to strike back. ISIS has abolished all curricula which it regards a contrary to its idiotic interpretation of Sharia. In our global campaign against jihadism, we have to shun deceptive sources of information on Islamic law and practices such as the books by Ayaan Hirsi Ali who authored "The Caged Virgin," and "Infidel." In fact, in Islamic law, the term "infidel" does not mean a non-Muslim or an "apostate." It means a person with no values. The refrain of "Allahu Akbar" legally means "We are equal before God, regardless of our faith or our non-faith." I would rather look up to Malala of Pakistan or Al-Khuthaila of Saudi Arabia than look down on Hirsi of Somalia.

Let us also not forget that the 57 Islamic States, by adopting the UN Charter, have acceded to the legal principle of integrating within national law, both Sharia and legislated, to form a world of peace. That world of peace is underpinned in Islamic Law by two pillars: The first is TAWHEED -meaning God is One for all humanity; the second is the nullification of intercession between a believer and her/his Creator. Between these two (Creator and created), there is a conceptual hotline. A declaration of non-belief by another human being is outside of private jurisdiction. The Creator, not the human, is the final judge. In the Quran, God admonishes Muhammad by saying, "You Are Not Their Master!!"

ABOUT THE AUTHOR

Dr. Yassin El-Ayouty has a Ph.D. from New York University (NYU) in international law and international organization (1966); and a J.D. from Cardozo School of Law (1994). He was a Fulbright Scholar in the U.S. (1952-1954). Dr. El-Ayouty was also the recipient of other honors: The Founders Day Award from NYU for his Ph.D.; the Faculty Award for the best legal writing from Cardozo School of Law, class of 1994; and Distinguished Visiting Professor at the Nova Law Center, Florida, amongst others. Dr. El-Ayouty established SUNSGLOW - Global Training in the Rule of Law in 1998. He practices law in the U.S. and abroad. He was involved in cases for CBS and the Associated Press in Iraq, and represented all Caribbean countries at the U.N. He is emeritus professor at Stony Brook University; adjunct professor at Fordham University School of Law, teaching (Islamic Law & Global Security); Cairo University Faculty of Law; and St. Francis College, Brooklyn. He served the U.N. as Political Director, working in various war zones. He has authored many articles and 10 books in both English and Arabic on international law and politics. He drafted the Statute of UNITAR, and annually conducts "El-Ayouty Seminar" on the Arab Spring. Dr. El-Ayouty currently writes a blog, "Tahrir Forever", on the current struggles in Egypt, which can be found at http://tahrirforever.blogspot.com.

www.ingramcontent.com/pod-product-compliance
Lightning Source LLC
Chambersburg PA
CBHW071326280526
45787CB00001B/3